# Blueprint for the Environment

## A PLAN FOR FEDERAL ACTION

Muir Woods National Monument, 1936. George A. Grant photograph. *National Park Service.*

# Blueprint for the Environment

## A PLAN FOR FEDERAL ACTION

Edited by

**T Allan Comp, Ph.D.**

**HOWE BROTHERS**

Salt Lake City

1989

*published by*
Howe Brothers
P.O. Box 6394
Salt Lake City, Utah 84106
*shipping address: 1127 Wilmington Avenue*

*Manufactured in the United States of America*

Library of Congress Catalog Card Number 89-80293
*Library of Congress Cataloging in Publication information is available*

ISBN 0-935704-50-7

# Foreword

*Blueprint for the Environment* is a cooperative effort by America's environmental community. The participants include the organizations listed below, together with staff members from many other organizations and concerned individuals.

More than 750 detailed recommendations, assembled by cabinet department or agency, have already been delivered to representatives of the new administration. Most of the organizations which assembled the Blueprint do not deal with all the issues discussed in this report, and cannot endorse every recommendation. However, they all agree with its overall thrust and the urgent need for additional federal actions to address environmental problems.

The participants wish to acknowledge the following people and organizations for their contributions to the development of the Blueprint:

## STEERING COMMITTEE

Thomas B. Stoel, Jr., Chair, *Natural Resources Defense Council*; Jan Hartke, Vice Chair, *Global Tomorrow Coalition*; William Howard, Vice Chair, *National Wildlife Federation*; Tina Hobson, Personnel Chair, *Renew America*; Elizabeth Raisbeck, Development Chair, *National Audubon Society*; Mike Clark, *Environmental Policy Institute*; Cynthia Wilson, *Friends of the Earth*; Richard Ayres, *Natural Resources Defense Council*; Ruth Caplan, *Environmental Action*; Peter Coppelman, *The Wilderness Society*; Clifton E. Curtis, *The Oceanic Society*; M. Rupert Cutler, *Defenders of Wildlife*; Christopher Flavin, *Worldwatch Institute*; Robert L. Herbst, *Trout Unlimited*; Jack Lorenz, *Izaak Walton League*; Michael McCloskey, *Sierra Club*; Bob Pollard, *Union of Concerned Scientists*; Paul Pritchard, *National Parks and Conservation Association*; Susan Weber, *Zero Population Growth*; Andrea Yank, *Natural Resources Council of America*.

## TASK FORCE CHAIRPERSONS

INTERNATIONAL: Thomas B. Stoel Jr., *Natural Resources Defense Council*; AGRICULTURAL CONSERVATION: Justin Ward, *Natural Resources Defense Council*; FOREST SERVICE: Barry Flamm, *The Wilderness Society*; GENETIC ENGINEERING: Jane Rissler, PhD, *National Wildlife Federation*; OCEANS AND COASTAL: Clifton E. Curtis, *The Oceanic Society*; DISARMAMENT: Shira Flax, *Sierra Club*; ENVIRONMENTAL EDUCATION: S. Douglas Miller, PhD, *National Wildlife Federation*; ENERGY: Ruth Caplan, *Environmental Action*, Christopher Flavin, *Worldwatch Institute*;

POPULATION: Patricia Baldi, *National Audubon Society*, Susan Weber, *Zero Population Growth*; BUREAU OF LAND MANAGEMENT: Johanna Wald, *Natural Resources Defense Council*; LAND LAW: Durwood Zaelke, *Sierra Club Legal Defense Fund*; CRITICAL ECOSYSTEMS: William Lienesch, *National Parks and Conservation Association*; FISH AND WILDLIFE : William C. Reffalt, *The Wilderness Society*, J. Scott Feierabend, *National Wildlife Federation*; MINERALS POLICY: Philip M. Hocker, *Minerals Policy Center*; NATIONAL PARK SERVICE: T. Destry Jarvis, *National Parks and Conservation Association*; WATER RESOURCES POLICY: David R. Conrad, *Friends of the Earth*, Edward Osann, *National Wildlife Federation*; WILD AND SCENIC RIVERS: Kevin Coyle, *American Rivers*; GRAZING POLICY: Maitland Sharpe, *Izaak Walton League*; TRANSPORTATION: David G. Burwell, *Rails-To-Trails Conservancy*; DEBT FOR CONSERVATION: Barbara J. Bramble, *National Wildlife Federation*; MULTILATERAL DEVELOPMENT BANKS: Stewart Hudson, *National Wildlife Federation*; CLEAN AIR: Richard Ayres, *Natural Resources Defense Council*; CLEAN WATER: Robert Adler, *Natural Resources Defense Council*; GROUNDWATER: Erik Olson, *National Wildlife Federation*; PESTICIDES: Maureen K. Hinkle, *National Audubon Society*, Janet S. Hathaway, *Natural Resources Defense Council*; SOLID WASTE: Ruth Lampi, *Environmental Action*, Cynthia Pollock-Shea, *Worldwatch Institute*, Jeanne Wirka, *Environmental Action*; TOXICS: Jacqueline M. Warren, *Natural Resources Defense Council*; COUNCIL ON ENVIRONMENTAL QUALITY: Michael McCloskey, *Sierra Club*; BUDGET: Brent Blackwelder, *Environmental Policy Institute*; FORESIGHT: Donald R. Lesh, *Global Tomorrow Coalition*; CONSERVATION ADMINISTRATIVE MATTERS: Joel Thomas, *National Wildlife Federation*.

### *STAFF*

Clay E. Peters, *Executive Director*; Terry Kilpatrick, *Assistant Director*; T Allan Comp, PhD, *Managing Editor*; Ric Barrick, *Talent Bank Coordinator*; Edward J. Barks, *Director of Communications*; Kevin D. Kilpatrick, *Project Assistant*; Catherine I. Connor, *Project Assistant*.

Finally, the participants wish to express their deep appreciation for the encouragement and generous financial support of the following donors:

Beldon Fund; Janelia Foundation; Jesse Smith Noyes Foundation; Mr. John R. Harris IV; Ottinger Foundation; The Educational Foundation of America; The Schumann Foundation; The W. Alton Jones Foundation, Inc.; Wallace Genetic Foundation, Inc.

Of course, these donors are in no way responsible for the content of this report.

*This book is dedicated to the small army*
*of student interns on whom the Blueprint project — and much of*
*America's environmental effort — so heavily depends.*

# Contents

**Introduction** *ix*

## I. Department of Agriculture *1*

Agriculture Initiatives *5*

International Actions *9*

Subsidies *11*

Forest Service Planning *15*

Cooperation *19*

Farmlands and Wetlands *23*

Range Management *27*

Forests and Timber *31*

Rivers and Fisheries *35*

Pesticide Prevention *39*

Recreation, Archaeology, Minerals *41*

## II. Department of Commerce *43*

Treaties *45*

Fisheries *47*

Coasts *51*

Initiatives *53*

## III. Department of Defense *55*

Waterways *57*

Wetlands *59*

Planning *61*

Pollution *63*

## IV. Department of Education *65*

Environmental Education *67*

## V. Department of Energy *71*

Policy *77*

Global Warming *79*

Conservation *83*

Renewable Resources *87*

Efficiency *91*

Vehicle Emissions *95*

Nuclear Energy *99*

Nuclear Regulartory Commission *103*

Federal Energy
Regulatory Commission *109*

Tennessee Valley Authority *115*

## VI.  Department of Health and Human Serivices  *121*

Food Safety  *123*                 Health Sciences  *127*
Family Planning  *125*

## VII.  Department of the Interior  *129*

Initiatives  *135*                Coastal Protection and Leasing  *161*
Solicitor  *141*                      Mining  *163*
Public Lands  *143*                    Parks  *167*
Grazing  *147*                      Research  *171*
Watersheds and Minerals  *149*        Education  *173*
Mining  *153*                    Preservation  *175*
Refuges  *155*                      Greenways  *177*
Coastal Barriers  *159*                Rivers  *179*

## VIII.  Department of Justice  *181*

Protection  *183*                    Policy  *187*
Litigation  *185*

## IX.  Department of State *and* Agency for International Development  *189*

State: Global Warming  *193*      AID: Developmental Assistance  *217*
State: Cooperation and Continuity  *199*        AID: Agriculture  *219*
State: Biological Diversity  *201*              AID: Energy  *221*
State: International Negotiations  *203*         AID: Population  *223*
State: Ocean Protection  *207*      AID: Conservation Lending  *227*
AID: Sustainable Development  *213*

## X.  Department of Transportation  *229*

National Policy  *233*                Highways  *243*
Mass Transportation  *239*         Ocean Protection  *245*
Trucks  *241*

## XI.  Department of the Treasury  *247*

Debt  *249*

Tax Policy  *257*

Multilateral Lending  *253*

Public Participation  *259*

## XII.  Environmental Protection Agency  *261*

International Leadership  *263*

Drinking Water  *291*

External Affairs  *267*

Water Quality  *295*

Enforcement  *269*

Pesticide Prevention  *299*

Research  *271*

Toxic Substances  *303*

Air Quality  *273*

Waste Reduction  *305*

Water  *279*

Hazardous Waste Reduction  *309*

Wetlands  *283*

Hazardous Sites  *313*

Groundwater  *287*

## XIII.  Executive Office of the President  *317*

Presidential Actions  *317*

Council on Environmental Quality  *323*

Office of Management and Budget  *327*

## Appendix  *335*

The Blueprint Steering Committee

# Introduction

A little more than one year ago—before the floods and fires and droughts and pollution of the summer of 1988—America's environmental leaders met to develop a new approach to their environmental concerns. Fearful that Americans were already becoming immune to the cries of impending environmental disaster and acknowledging the need for positive federal government involvement, these leaders decided to develop a specific new agenda for domestic and international action by the next presidential administration. It was to be non-partisan in its development and focused on the President and the offices that make up the Executive branch of our government. It was to cover every aspect of environmental concern—it was to be a Blueprint for the Environment.

One year later the world had witnessed the devastation of massive floods in some regions and droughts in others, while the United States suffered from forest fires, beach pollution, and a 100 billion dollar price tag for clean-up at its nuclear weapons facilities. In that same year, Blueprint for the Environment became perhaps the most comprehensive approach to our environmental concerns ever assembled. When finally presented to President-elect Bush at a breakfast meeting on November 30, 1988, the Blueprint was over 1500 pages in length, containing nearly 730 individual recommendations for needed federal action within the environment. The symbolism for the breakfast meeting was not lost: it was literally a break in the fast, the first significant meeting between environmentalists and a President since the 1970s.

The movement of Blueprint from idea to final document was a remarkable demonstration of America's environmental capacity. While twenty major groups served on the Blueprint Steering Committee, more than one hundred actually participated in the process of developing recommendations. Thirty-two different task forces organized the work on their respective topics and coordinated the volunteer efforts of hundreds of individuals. Blueprint for the Environment became the umbrella under which groups with differing approaches to specific problems could come together and work for the national welfare. It was that umbrella—and the seven million voters represented by the groups under that umbrella—that united the Blueprint Executive Committee in its meeting at the White House with the President-elect. It is that same umbrella, now in book form, that will continue to unite the Blueprint groups and all Americans in their ongoing efforts to encourage responsible federal environmental action at home and abroad.

Each of the original Blueprint recommendations, contained on a single sheet of paper, is directed to a specific assistant secretary or administrator within a specific cabinet office. The front side contains the particular office to which the recommendation is directed, a brief recommendation statement and several paragraphs of explanatory text. The back side contains the budget saving or expenditure that results from this specific recommendation, both the House and Senate committees and subcommittees involved with the particular issue and relevant studies on the topic. It also lists other related federal programs, some of the best sources of expertise from among the Blueprint participants, and, on occasion, specific implementation steps and a budget history of the office or program involved.

Each federal department, from Agriculture to Treasury, is preceded by a short summary text to acquaint the reader with the largest issues facing that particular department and some of its history as well. A few of the smaller independent agencies of the government are included where they seem to fit best. For example, the Nuclear Regulatory Commission, the Federal Energy Regulatory Commission, and the Tennessee Valley Authority will all be found at the end of the Department of Energy chapter. The Department of State and the Agency for International Development also share a single chapter. Recommendations for direct Presidential action, those for the President's Council on Environmental Quality, and the overall budget recommendations derived from the Blueprint and directed to the Office of Management and Budget will all be found in the Executive Office of the President chapter, the last (in alphabetical order) in the book.

Most of the original Blueprint recommendations are reproduced here. To make the entire document more accessible, recommendations are now organized by topic within each cabinet office or administration. In many cases, complementary recommendations were either grouped on a single front page or reworked as lists of recommendations on a single topic. The result retains the complete substance of the original Blueprint for the

Environment without subjecting the reader to the several pounds of paper required by its original design and organization.

The reader will find here a total of 511 approaches to national environmental problems, each one a reasoned solution for a specific concern best addressed by the federal government. Demonstrating that the sum can be greater than the parts, there is little that is new within any specific topic in the Blueprint, but nowhere else will the reader find so much. Outlined in ninety "topic chapters" is the massive effect of federal action on our environment, the remarkable range of those effects, and the myriad ways in which the federal establishment can cooperate—or not cooperate—in the effort to bring good stewardship to all aspects of federal administration. Equally significant, Blueprint casts the federal government as neither enemy nor savior, but as a partner with us all in seeking remedies to past mistakes and better approaches to the future. More than non-partisan, Blueprint clearly demonstrates that our environment is more important than politics and that its problems are more enduring than any single administration at any level of government. Only a team effort as comprehensive and reasoned as that contained in these pages will assure the greater sum, a clear step forward for the whole nation.

Blueprint for the Environment thus becomes a checklist for responsible federal action, a guide to the complex workings of our government and a clear indication of the astounding impact of federal environmental action—or inaction. It is also clear that each of these issues will remain, even worsen, until they are addressed effectively by a government willing to act in the largest public interest. Yielding to the smaller concerns of polluters, politics, or simple procrastination will only allow the problems addressed here to multiply. It is a simple truth that each of these issues would have been easier to avoid and cheaper to fix before now. Each will also be easier and cheaper to fix now than in the future, and none of them will go away just because we as a government choose not to look at them. The era of avoidable governmental responsibility within the environment is over, whether or not we choose to admit so. We must move quickly and responsibly toward a sustainable future or suffer the long-lived consequences of an irresponsible past.

While the Blueprint for the Environment project accumulated its list of acknowledgements, this book has its own special debts. Clay Peters, executive director for Blueprint, encouraged my original idea for this book and the Blueprint Executive Committee, particularly Tina Hobson, supported the commitment to the public access this book provides. My friend from the Environmental Protection Agency provided perspective, depth, and humor, while Catherine Conner and Karen Fedor assisted and Terry Kilpatrick kept the Blueprint office at bay. Lynne Hughes transformed the original sixteen million "bytes" of Blueprint data into book form in record time, and Paul Cirac flowed camera copy at a similar pace. Richard Howe remained an editor's ideal—a patient and supportive publisher—throughout. Special acknowledgement must go to Waste Management, Inc., for its willingness to fund purchase of enough copies of this book to distribute to the new Administration and to the Congress. As in all editorial efforts, the decisions that produced this book are my own.

T Allan Comp, Ph.D.
February 1989
Washington, D.C.

# DEPARTMENT OF AGRICULTURE

Established in 1862, the Department of Agriculture has more employees than there are full-time farmers. The reason is not because the Department maintains a one-on-one relationship with every farmer, but because its responsibilities extend far beyond providing educational and financial help to individuals actively engaged in commercial food and fiber production. Examples: It provides "food stamps" and nutrition education programs for the inner-city poor. It finances the construction of electric power-generation plants. It helps suburban real estate developers address their soil and water management problems. It administers millions of far-flung acres of forest lands and wilderness. It sends teams of experts abroad to teach our natural resources management-related technologies to Third World counterparts.

The environmental impacts of all Department of Agriculture agencies are of concern to the conservation community. The land use-related decisions of the loanmakers of the Farmers Home Administration and the Rural Electrification Administration, which influence the locations of housing subdivisions and power plants, exemplify the scope of this concern. But two of the Department of Agriculture's agencies, the Forest Service and the Soil Conservation Service, bear the brunt of environmentalists' scrutiny because they are the lead federal agencies in their fields and directly or indirectly influence the management of hundreds of millions of acres of land and water.

More professional natural resources scientists, managers and technicians are employed by the Department of Agriculture than by the Department of the Interior or the Environmental Protection Agency. Agencies which report to the Secretary of Agriculture not only administer directly some 200 million acres of federal forests and farm research areas, but strongly influence land use practices of the two-thirds of the Nation's land which is privately owned, through Extension education, Soil Conservation Service technical assistance and Agricultural Stabilization and Conservation Service financial assistance programs.

Because it provides coordination and financial support to state land grant university-based research and extension programs, loans and loan guarantees to rural housing and energy developers, pest and predator management assistance to farmers and ranchers, and enforcement of the endangered plant provisions of the Endangered Species Act, the Department of Agriculture influences in a major way how the nation's environment is impacted by mankind. The Department could well be called the Department of Agriculture and Natural Resources.

## Office of the Secretary

Because of this extensive and all-pervasive influence of the Department of Agriculture's activities on the nation's environment, the Office of the Secretary of Agriculture should include in its table of organization an environmental oversight entity — an Office of Environmental Quality — to assist and monitor the performance of all Department of Agriculture agencies vis-a-vis the National Environmental Policy Act, the Clean Air and Clean Water Acts, the Endangered Species Act and other environmental statutes of executive branch-wide application.

The Office of Environmental Quality should issue an annual report — Agriculture and the Environment — the publication of which was initiated in 1980 by Secretary Bergland but suspended in 1981 by Secretary Block. This report helps the Department as well as the public at large understand the totality of the Department's influence on the environment.

The incoming Department of Agriculture leadership will want to name a new chief of the Soil Conservation Service immediately. This person should be an experienced administrator from the ranks of the soil and water conservation profession with a strong track record of concern for the quality of the environment (land treatment rather than structural emphasis). A respected professional environmentalist should be appointed to head the Office of Environmental Quality. The Office may be staffed with detailees from agencies and experts from state agencies and universities on loan to the federal government through the Intergovernmental Personnel Act program. Among the criteria used to select the new heads of the Rural Electrification Administration, the Farmers Home Administration, the Animal and Plant Health Inspection Service and the Cooperative Extension Service should be their proven interest in environmental quality-protection.

As vacancies occur in Senior Executive Service-level positions in the Forest Service and the Soil Conservation Service, the Assistant Secretary for Natural Resources and Environment should consult with the environmental community regarding the qualifications of a set of alternative candidates for these positions and not leave these key staffing decisions entirely to the agency administrators.

As early as possible in 1989, the Secretary of Agriculture should announce his plan to personally host and chair a series of town meeting-type forums across the nation to hear the views of the American public on the value of most appropriate uses of the National Forest System. To the extent that the public's current vision of the highest and best use of their forests is at odds with Forest Service tradition or even current statutory authority, steps should be taken to bring that policy direction into line with today's needs and expectations.

## U.S. Forest Service

The Forest Service was created by Congress at the turn of the century in response to an outpouring of public concern over flooding and watershed instability caused by deforestation. Forest reserves segregated from the public domain by presidential order for "preservation" purposes beginning in 1891 and administered by the Department of the Interior General Land Office were transferred to the Department of Agriculture and became the nuclei of the National Forest System. Enlarged since that time by both additional withdrawals and purchases, that public land system is now 191 million acres in size.

The Forest Service has the primary federal responsibility for national leadership in forestry. It carries out its mission through programs in three major areas: the 191-million-acre National Forest System, forestry and range research, and state and private forestry assistance. In 1988 the Congress appropriated some $2.5 billion for the Forest Service for the administration of these programs. The bulk of these funds went to the administration of the National Forests and Grasslands. Thirty-seven thousand employees (full-time equivalents) carry out a diverse program of research, assistance to states and private forestlands and multiple use management of the national forests.

The small band of trained foresters in the Department of Agriculture who became managers of this priceless national resource inherited their utilitarian forest management approach from the German "forestmeister" tradition. Their view of forestry was described by their own leaders as "tree-farming." It remains the dominant view of the forestry profession: trees are grown to supply the forest products industry with raw material. Other forest uses and users are regarded as constraints on wood production; those which appear to pay their way through fees and royalties, such as resort development, domestic livestock grazing and oil and gas production, may be accepted more readily than those which don't, such as the protection of water quality, biological diversity or the beauty of the landscape.

This utilitarian view of the role of the forest runs contrary to that of the environmental conservation community. Environmentalists place more value on the unique ecological, recreational and aesthetic contributions which the public's forests could be making to American society. They regard the current rate and manner of timber harvest in the National Forest System as unsustainable.

In addition to seeking a modification of the dominant view of the National Forest System as a network of tree farms, the environmental conservation community advocates the creation of a "level playing field" for private commercial woodland owners via an end to tax disincentives and subsidized sales of the public's timber. Privately owned woodlands often can provide wood products at less environmental cost than the typically steep, high-altitude back country of our national forests and are thus a preferable source of this essential commercial raw material.

The National Forest System, by virtue of its size and geographical breadth, may be the United States' most important reservoir of biological diversity. The national forests provide the most diverse recreation opportunities and host more people enjoying their opportunities than any other federal land system. They include 84 percent of the National Wilderness Preservation System in the contiguous 48 states, providing outstanding opportunities for primitive recreation and protection of biological and geological diversity.

Approximately 75 percent of the Forest Service's appropriated funds, however, are used in connection with its timber-sale program. This continues to occur despite laws such as the Multiple Use-Sustained Yield Act and the National Forest Management Act which call for a more balanced program. The environmental conservation community believes that the Forest Service is ignoring congressional mandates to provide responsible stewardship of the national forests and is pursuing resource exploitation that is environmentally damaging and economically unsound instead.

The Forest Service motto, "The greatest good for the greatest number," exists today only on paper. To deal with today's and tomorrow's needs, the Forest Service must make major changes in the administration of its programs. The Forest Service task force of Project Blueprint for the Environment recommended

26 specific actions that must be taken if the Forest Service is to fulfill our nation's needs in the next century. These actions fall into the following categories:

1) The critically important task of protecting the nation's biological diversity.
2) Sustainable forestry.
3) Mining and mineral leasing reform.
4) Improved recreation programs.
5) Greater emphasis on environmentally sound private-land forestry.
6) Increased research to provide sound basis for resource management in the United States and internationally.
7) Resource Planning Act programs and annual budgets that provide for sound land stewardship and protection of biological diversity.
8) Full opportunity for public participation in planning and decision-making.

## Soil and Water Conservation

Title XII of the 1985 Farm Act contains the most significant soil conservation measures in history. The law's Conservation Reserve Program seeks establishment of perennial, soil-saving grass and tree cover on severely eroding croplands. Companion "sodbuster" and "conservation compliance" provisions withhold commodity price supports and related federal farm assistance for destructive annual crop production on highly erodible fields. All merit strong support.

The new Administration should work toward meeting the existing 40—45 million-acre Conservation Reserve Program target and, ultimately, promote legislation to enlarge the program. An expanded reserve could build upon the erosion control accomplishments of the 1985 Farm Act, enable a transition to more sustainable commercial uses of excessively eroding croplands, and help solve the chronic problem of commodity surplus. With proper "targeting" of problem croplands, expansion could work also to abate nonpoint source pollution of streams, lakes and aquifers.

The Department of Agriculture's Farmers Home Administration, the agricultural "lender of last resort," should promptly implement authority in the Farm Act

to accept conservation easements in partial fulfillment of delinquent farm debts. To further promote good stewardship, the Secretary of Agriculture should recommend that soil and wetland conservation conditions be attached to the lending policies of the Farm Credit System.

The Department should also initiate multi-year cropland set-asides, to substitute for current annual acreage adjustment programs. Annual set-asides often leave idled farmlands vulnerable to soil erosion, provide insufficient wildlife habitat and discourage beneficial crop rotations. Equally significant, perennial plant cover under the multi-year approach could provide valuable livestock forage during drought periods.

Sustainable tree farming on private forest lands can also prevent or abate excessive soil erosions. The new Administration should greatly expand the Forestry Incentives Program, a popular direct assistance program administered by the Agricultural Stabilization and Conservation Service. To prevent "cut and run" logging, the Department of Agriculture should impose reforestation standards as a condition of Forestry Incentives Program assistance.

## Wetland Conservation

The 1985 Farm Act's "swampbuster" provision withholds federal farm program benefits for crop production on agriculturally converted wetlands, an

important check against further liquidation of scarce natural wetlands. So far, regulatory loopholes and lax enforcement have diminished the

## Blueprint for the Environment

Farm Act's effectiveness in deterring destructive wetland drainage and cultivation, but this could be remedied through changes to Department of Agriculture policies.

The Secretary of Agriculture should also request full funding for the Water Bank program. Administered by the Agricultural Stabilization and Conservation Service, the Water Bank compensates farmers for protecting wetlands under long-term conservation contracts. The need is to add to the historic program emphasis of protecting natural wetlands from conversion, an equal emphasis on restoring wetlands that have been drained for crop production.

In addition, the Water Bank should contain an option for conservation easements that protect wetland values in perpetuity.

The Department of Agriculture's latest conservation program names water quality protection as a top national priority. The Secretary of Agriculture should issue specific direction on how this priority will find expression in the Department's various functions. Once the states have identified "priority watersheds," the Department of Agriculture should give priority to enrolling croplands that are both "highly erodible" and shown to present a site-specific pollution problem.

## Low-Input Research and Education

The Agricultural Productivity Act authorizes the Department of Agriculture-sponsored research in farming practices involving reduced reliance on synthetic pesticides and fertilizers. The Blueprint for the Environment recommends increased appropriations for this important initiative, which is helping facilitate a transition to more sustainable agricultural systems.

Complementing the Agricultural Productivity Act, the Appropriate Technology Transfer for Rural Areas Program is a recently-formed clearinghouse for alternative agriculture. Among other services, farmers may use the Program's toll-free "hotline" for practical advice on how to conserve natural resources, lower consumption of energy and agricultural chemicals, and save on production costs. This program has been highly successful in its first two years of operation. The new Administration should seek additional budget for Appropriate Technology Transfer for Rural Areas expansion, continue private-sector program management by the National Center for Appropriate Technology, and formally designate Appropriate Technology Transfer for Rural Areas as the principal program for transfer of low-input farming techniques.

## Biotechnology

Biotechnology is a new field of scientific endeavor and industrial activity that will impact the environment in numerous ways. The genetic alteration of plants, animals and microorganisms, through recombinant DNA and other genetic-engineering techniques, offers potential benefits and potential risks for society.

Of considerable concern to the ecological and environmental communities has been the planned introduction and use of genetically altered organisms into the environment on a large and continuing commercial scale in the absence of an adequate data base and regulatory protocols needed to insure sound ecological and environmental risk assessment.

In terms of federal regulation of the various environmental and agricultural applications of biotechnology, a status quo, "do-not-interfere-with-high-technology" approach has generally prevailed, permeating most federal agencies. Using a purely administrative rule-making approach with the White House Science Office in the lead, the Administration created a "Coordinated Framework for Regulation of Biotechnology" (June 1986), which is a five-agency system of review and regulation that relies on some 14 different existing statutes for its legal authority. This framework, if allowed to operate in its current mode, will become a legal and administrative nightmare, slowing progress in the industry while leaving the environment and public safety inadequately protected.

**Blueprint for the Environment**

## INITIATIVES

# DEPARTMENT OF AGRICULTURE
### ASSISTANT SECRETARY for Natural Resources and Environment
### Forest Service

**RECOMMENDATION**

**The Secretary of Agriculture should immediately announce his intention to sponsor and attend a series of "town meetings" throughout the nation during 1989. These meetings will provide the Secretary the opportunity to listen to interested Americans' views of the importance and appropriate future management direction of the national forest system. After these meetings, the President should announce approval of a new mission statement for the national forest system and propose whatever legislative changes are necessary to implement this new mission.**

• These public forums should be moderated by the Secretary and attended by the Assistant Secretary and the Chief. Experienced facilitators and small-group discussion should be utilized. University-based staff or other outside-of-government persons should be employed to monitor and record the meetings and digest and summarize the public's recommendations.

• Discussion should cover sound long-term management of the nation's public forest lands to protect their long-term productivity, beauty, and utility for non-commodity services as well as commodity-production uses. Objectives include watershed stability to protect downstream water quality and quantity, protection of wilderness, roadless, natural and scenic areas for their scientific, educational and recreational values, and maintenance of biological diversity and ecological stability through conscious protection of the habitats of all rare native plant and animal species.

• On the basis of these town meetings and the subsequent President's statement and accompanying Executive Order, with the support of the Office of Management and Budget, and within the framework of the Forest and Rangeland Renewable Resources Planning Act, the Secretary should propose reallocations of Forest Service budget and manpower to reflect and implement new priorities reflecting the current values and demands of today's National Forest-use constituencies.

## BUDGET RECOMMENDATION
F.Y. 90: **Increase** of $ 1 million          F.Y. 91: no funding —one-year project

## PRINCIPAL AUTHORIZING LEGISLATION
Multiple Use-Sustained Yield Act
Wilderness Act
National Environmental Policy Act
Forest and Rangeland Renewable Resources Planning Act
National Forest Management Act

## CONGRESSIONAL JURISDICTION
**House Authorizing Committee/Subcommittee**
    Committee on Agriculture
        Subcommittee on Forests, Family Farms and Energy
**Senate Authorizing Committee/Subcommittee**
    Committee on Agriculture, Nutrition and Forestry
        Subcommittee on Conservation and Forestry
**House Appropriations Subcommittee**
    Subcommittee on Interior
**Senate Appropriations Subcommittee**
    Subcommittee on Interior and Related Agencies

## RELEVANT STUDIES
**"Position Paper on Saving Our National Forest,"** by Edward C. Fritz, Dallas, Texas
**"Forest Action Report,"** The Wilderness Society, in press

## RELATED FEDERAL PROGRAMS
Resources Planning Act five-year plans
National Forest Management Act-based national forest 10-year plans
RARE II implementation
The Chief's "National Recreation Strategy"

## PRINCIPAL SOURCES OF EXPERTISE
Defenders of Wildlife — 202-659-9510
The Wilderness Society — 202-842-3400
National Wildlife Federation — 202-797-6800
National Audubon Society — 202-547-9009
Natural Resources Defense Council — 202-783-7800

## NOTES:

## Blueprint for the Environment

# Blueprint for the Environment

## INITIATIVES

# DEPARTMENT OF AGRICULTURE

**RECOMMENDATION**

**The Secretary of Agriculture should direct the Forest Service to include an examination of a conservation scenario in the Resource Planning Act assessment and to develop a new program that gives emphasis to protection of biological diversity, watersheds, wildlands, and recreation opportunities on the national forests. The new program should also emphasize the important role of private timberlands in meeting future supply needs.**

• The Forest Service should develop a Resource Planning Act (RPA) program which would reflect and implement a new mission of the Forest Service oriented towards stewardship and environmental values. This should be done working closely with the conservation community. The assessment and program are required by RPA to be prepared periodically to assess the nation's resource situation and to develop a program to meet the identified needs. The 1985 RPA program document expanded the dominant use of the national forests for timber, mining, and grazing at the expense of biological diversity, fish and wildlife, recreation, wilderness and watershed protection.
• The 1989 RPA assessment has been re-cently released and is presently undergoing review. The assessment assumes the demand for most products is likely to continue to rise in the decade ahead and add various pressures on supplies that will cause increased prices and other effects generally considered undesirable. "Timber Famine" has been used in the past by the Forest Service to justify large timber budgets and programs. The assessment will be used to aid in development of the RPA program.
• The new Administration will have the opportunity to develop a RPA program which provides a new and brighter future for our nation's national forests and better management, stewardship and profits for private timberland.

**RECOMMENDATION**

**The Secretary of Agriculture should link the Forest Service technical expertise and Extension Service delivery capability to develop and implement a major urban forestation grants program. This should be done with cooperation from the Department of the Interior greenways and trails programs and Department of Energy programs for energy conservation and clean air incentives to cities.**

• Trees remove harmful air pollutants and reduce urban temperatures, thereby improving public health and conserving energy. In most cities only one tree is planted for every four trees that disappear. When we build cities and towns we replace trees with brick, concrete and as-phalt, materials that store heat and increase urban temperatures. The tree loss not only exacerbates our urban temperature problems, but we lose a principal absorber of excess carbon dioxide ($CO_2$) and various airborne pollutants as well.

## RECOMMENDATION
**The Secretary of Agriculture should request and advocate funding at the full authorization level of $15,000,000 for the Agricultural Productivity Act.**

• Funding for the program should be increased to $15 million for FY 1989 and $15 million for FY 1990. This would provide a level adequate to: 1) employ a director and assistant to provide a full-time federal presence for the APA program; 2) contribute a significant percentage of financial support for regional research programs; and 3) contribute a significant percentage of financial support for cooperative federal/state programs for information dissemination. These three steps would significantly further the knowledge and use of agricultural systems that enhance productivity without excessive soil erosion, contamination of surface and groundwater resources, or harm to adjacent ecosystems.

## RECOMMENDATION
**The Secretary of Agriculture should promote and support funding for the Renewable Resources Extension Act at the full authorization level of $15 million per year.**

• The Renewable Resources Extension Act of 1978 authorized the Secretary of Agriculture to establish natural resource education programs in the Cooperative Extension System. Since its inception, the program has provided funds for state natural resource specialists such as forestry and range experts.
• The program has been enhanced by attracting complementary funding from state and local sources. For every federal dollar spent on the program, three dollars of state and local funds are generated for natural resource programs.
• There is a desperate need for a professional natural resource expert in each state extension service to develop programs that encourage wise stewardship of the resource base. Since the enactment of this legislation, the Administration has neglected this important policy initiative. Minimal appropriations have been provided by Congress, but more vigorous support is needed to expand the program to its authorized level.

## RECOMMENDATION
**The Secretaries of the Interior, Agriculture and Commerce should improve the efficiency and effectiveness of federal fisheries management by consolidating and strengthening integration and coordination of now-fragmented staff and functions of those various agencies.**

## RECOMMENDATION
**The Secretary of Agriculture should cut the funding request for the Soil Conservation Service's small watershed project by $50 million per year to eliminate dam building and stream channelization. The focus of the Soil Conservation Service should be on conserving the soil rather than on behaving like a construction company.**

• The Soil Conservation Service was set up to conserve soil and prevent erosion, but the small watershed program established under the Small Watershed Act (P.L. 566) has been transformed into a mini-engineering program of dam building and channelization, with relatively little emphasis on land treatment and soil conservation measures.
• The engineering and bulldozing of streams destroys fish and wildlife habitats. All major national conservation groups vigorously fought and largely succeeded in eliminating this destructive activity in the 1970s. Now it is reappearing.
• By reducing the funding for the Small Watershed Program, a clear message will be sent that scarce dollars should go into soil conservation, not into expensive construction.

## Blueprint for the Environment

# Blueprint for the Environment

## INTERNATIONAL ACTIONS

## DEPARTMENT OF AGRICULTURE
### OFFICE OF THE SECRETARY

**RECOMMENDATION**

**The Secretary of the Interior should take the lead in establishing an inter-agency task force with the Department of Agriculture and the Department of the Treasury to evaluate how well the United States government is implementing the Convention on International Trade in Endangered Species of Wild Fauna and Flora and to make recommendations to improve performance for the agencies.**

• The United States is a leader in international trade in wild plants and animals. Yet the budget and trained personnel to handle wildlife trade do not reflect the importance of this issue to the U.S.

• Given overall constraints on the federal budget, priorities must be set in building a better cooperative program among the agencies for control of international wildlife trade. The proposed task force should seek to establish these priorities.

• The impacts of large-scale harvest of U.S. species exported in large quantities, particularly plant species, have not been studied: subsequently exports are being approved without

proper scientific basis.

• U.S. actions have considerable affects on rare species outside our borders. The most direct affect is usually trade. Many species in trade are either not yet on Convention on International Trade in Endangered Species of Wild Fauna and Flora (CITES) appendices, or are nevertheless being traded in numbers which appear to threaten their survival. The only procedure the U.S. has for curbing the import of such species is listing them under the Endangered Species Act. Other U.S. activities which affect rare species abroad include financing of development assistance projects and training and basing of military forces.

**RECOMMENDATION**

**The Secretary of Agriculture should work to halt MOSCAMED and CAPMED — the programs to eliminate the Mediterranean fruitfly —pending the development of environmentally benign control methods.**

• MOSCAMED is a plan to eliminate the Mediterranean fruitfly (medfly) from Guatemala with extensive reliance on the pesticides malathion and methyl bromide. The program consists of widespread and indiscriminate aerial spraying of a malathion-laced bait. The fumigant methyl bromide is used to treat produce moving from a fly-infested area to a "free-fly" zone. CAPMED would extend the program currently operating in Guatemala, south to the Darien Gap in Panama.

• The Medfly can be contained indefinitely with no loss to U.S. agriculture until acceptable alter-

natives to malathion and methyl bromide become available.

• There is no urgency to proceeding with MOSCAMED now or in the foreseeable future. The Department of Agriculture and Animal Health Inspection Service (APHIS) 1985 "Technical Report" submitted to the Senate Subcommittee on Agriculture, Rural Development and Related Agencies of the Senate Committee on Appropriations recognized that the risk of a U.S. infestation from all of Central America is less than one-tenth that posed by produce shipped to the mainland from Hawaii.

## BUDGET RECOMMENDATION
F.Y. 90: **Increase** of $ 10,000          F.Y. 91: **no change**

## PRINCIPAL AUTHORIZING LEGISLATION
Endangered Species Act of 1973, as amended.

## CONGRESSIONAL JURISDICTION
**House Authorizing Committee/Subcommittee**
   Committee on Merchant Marine and Fisheries
      Subcommittee on Fisheries and Wildlife Conservation and the Environment
   Committee on Foreign Affairs
**Senate Authorizing Committee/Subcommittee**
   Committee on Environment and Public Works
      Subcommittee on Environmental Protection
   Committee on Foreign Relations
**House Appropriations Subcommittee**
   Subcommittee on Interior
   Subcommittee on Rural Development, Agriculture and Related Agencies
**Senate Appropriations Subcommittee**
   Subcommittee on Interior and Related Agencies
   Subcommittee on Agriculture, Rural Development and Related Agencies

## RELEVANT STUDIES
World Wildlife Fund/TRAFFIC is analyzing U.S. CITES implementation now
World Wildlife Fund, Natural Resources Defense Council, and others submitted detailed testimony to Congress in July 1988
AID Environmental Assessment due out Summer, 1988

## RELATED FEDERAL PROGRAMS

## PRINCIPAL SOURCES OF EXPERTISE
World Wildlife Fund — 202-293-4800
National Audubon Society — 202-547-9009
Natural Resources Defense Council — 202-783-7800

### IMPLEMENTATION STEPS
(1)  Hire three additional biologists at cost of $150,000 per year. One would carry out analyses required for approval of permits for exports of U.S. species protected by CITES and for re-exports of foreign species and imports of such species protected by Appendix I of the treaty.
(2)  The other two would develop proposals for listing of foreign species under the U.S. Endangered Species Act (a responsibility transferred to this Office only in FY 1988).
(3)  Provide an additional $30,000 per year to fund status surveys on foreign species under consideration for listing.

## NOTES:

## Blueprint for the Environment

# Blueprint for the Environment

## SUBSIDIES

## FARM CREDIT ADMINISTRATION

**RECOMMENDATION**

**The Secretary of Agriculture should promote legislation that applies soil and wetland conservation conditions to the beneficiaries of federal assistance to agricultural lenders. This would reduce subsidies inherent in federal farm credit assistance that promote degradation of highly erodible lands and wetlands.**

• In 1987 the Farm Credit System (FCS) received a multi-billion-dollar federal bailout intended to rescue that network of agricultural lenders from massive financial losses. In the bailout law, the Agricultural Credit Act of 1987, Congress unfortunately rejected a proposal to make soil and wetland stewardship a condition of farm loans. This leaves FCS credit policy at cross-purposes with national conservation policies administered by USDA.

• The "sodbuster" and "swampbuster" provisions of the Food Security Act of 1985 require borrowers from USDA's Farmers Home Administration (FmHA) to practice soil and wetland conservation as a condition of loan eligibility. Similar conditions should govern borrowers from FCS institutions as well as borrowers from institutions participating in the federally guaranteed secondary market for agricultural loans. This will put FmHA borrowers on equal footing with other farmers and will prevent future sodbusting and swampbusting, including the plowout of fragile land now under conservation reserve contracts.

**RECOMMENDATION**

**The Secretary of Agriculture should direct the Agricultural Stabilization and Conservation Service to prepare an Environmental Impact Statement for the Department's commodity support programs.**

• For more than half a century, the U.S. government has supported farm product prices and farmers' incomes. At a current annual cost exceeding $20 billion, commodity programs administered by the Department of Agriculture (USDA) have become one of the largest and fastest growing sets of federal entitlements. The programs affect management of hundreds of millions of acres of land nationwide.

• Despite their enormous effects on land and natural resources, the USDA programs have never been subjected to the Environmental Impact Statement (EIS) process. This is unfortunate, given mounting evidence that the programs impede farming practices — notably "low-input" alternatives relying on reduced fertilizer and pesticide applications — that could abate groundwater contamination, improve stream quality and protect wildlife habitat throughout rural America.

• A draft EIS issued by The Agricultural Stabilization and Conservation Service (ASCS) in 1986 falls far short of the in-depth analysis that is needed. That document mistakenly assessed USDA's acreage reduction programs designed to limit commodity production in isolation from farm subsidy payments that in many respects send opposite signals to the nation's farmers.

• A more comprehensive EIS would provide the first focused examination of how the federal farm programs affect public health and environmental quality. The process also would enable evaluation of a full range of alternatives (such as beneficial multi-year crop rotations) to the status quo.

11

## BUDGET RECOMMENDATION
F.Y. 90: **no change**          F.Y. 91: **no change**

## PRINCIPAL AUTHORIZING LEGISLATION
The National Environmental Policy Act (42 U.S.C. 4321 et seq); amended by P.L. 94-52, July 3, 1975; P.L. 94-83, August 9, 1975

## CONGRESSIONAL JURISDICTION
**House Authorizing Committee/Subcommittee**
Committee on Agriculture
Subcommittee on Conservation, Credit and Rural Development
**Senate Authorizing Committee/Subcommittee**
Committee on Agriculture, Nutrition and Forestry
Subcommittee on Agricultural Credit
**House Appropriations Subcommittee**
Subcommittee on Rural Development, Agriculture and Related Agencies
**Senate Appropriations Subcommittee**
Subcommittee on Agriculture, Rural Development and Related Agencies

## RELEVANT STUDIES
USDA Draft Acreage Adjustment Programs (1986)

## RELATED FEDERAL PROGRAMS
Conservation provisions of the Farmers Home Administration
Natural resources assessments and programs pursuant to the Soil and Water Resources Conservation Act (RCA)

## PRINCIPAL SOURCES OF EXPERTISE
Natural Resources Defense Council — 202-783-7800
National Audubon Society — 202-547-9009

## IMPLEMENTATION STEPS
(1) Amend the Agricultural Credit Act of 1987 to extend soil and wetland conservation conditions currently governing FmHA to the FCS.
(2) Prepare, and issue for public review and comment, a comprehensive EIS for the USDA commodity programs.

## NOTES:

## Blueprint for the Environment

## SUBSIDIES

# DEPARTMENT OF AGRICULTURE

### RECOMMENDATION
**The Secretary of the Interior should work with the Secretary of Agriculture to end or reduce the "double subsidies" going to western irrigators growing surplus crops.**

• The Bureau of Reclamation provides subsidized water to thousands of farmers, encouraging and enabling them to grow more crops, while the Department of Agriculture is paying farmers nationwide to set aside acres used to grow the same crops. Over 40 percent of the acreage that is supplied with Reclamation water grows surplus crops. The Department of the Interior has estimated the value of the subsidy for the water to be over $500 million per year.

• The Secretary of the Interior and the Secretary of Agriculture should support proposed legislation to end the availability of subsidized irrigation water for the production of surplus crops. Also, the Secretary of the Interior should support legislation to require full cost to be charged for any Reclamation water used to grow crops that are designated as surplus by the Department of Agriculture.

### RECOMMENDATION
**The Secretary of Agriculture should require that, with limited exceptions to prevent economic hardship, soil loss tolerance (T) values be attained on erodible cropland as a condition of federal farm subsidies.**

• The 1985 Food Security Act's "sodbuster" and "conservation compliance" provisions deny federal farm program benefits for destructive annual tillage of highly erodible cropland. The statute provides an exemption for producers who apply locally-approved conservation systems to mitigate soil erosion.
• In 1987, the Department replaced uniform erosion control standards based on T values with substantially looser conservation objectives. In addition, the SCS Chief in 1988 mandated blanket geographic application of "alternative" conservation systems that fail to achieve tolerable erosion rates. The result of these policies is uneven and lax implementation of sodbuster and conservation compliance.

### RECOMMENDATION
**The Secretary of Agriculture should develop and promote legislation making groundwater protection a condition of federal farm program benefits.**

• Agricultural groundwater pollution seriously threatens public health and welfare. Recent data from USDA indicate that 36 states have documented instances of well contamination with pesticides. Contamination with fertilizer nitrates has been detected in 30 states. These are troubling findings, as most residents of rural America obtain their drinking water from underground sources.

13

## RECOMMENDATION

**The Secretary of Agriculture should promote legislation to expand the acreage authority of the Conservation Reserve Program (CRP) once the existing CRP attains or approaches the 40-45 million acre target specified by the 1985 Food Security Act.**

• The conservation reserve program has demonstrated tremendous effectiveness in combating cropland soil erosion and is proving a thrifty alternative to conventional USDA programs that compensate farmers for keeping farmland out of crop production on a year-by-year basis. An expanded reserve would build upon the success of the existing program, and could also help address groundwater contamination, agricultural water pollution, commodity surpluses and other problems arising from unsustainable cropping of erosion-prone fields.

• Legislation similar to the bills introduced by Senators Nunn (S. 1521) and Dole (S. 2045) during the 100th Congress to expand the CRP authority merits strong support from the new administration.

## RECOMMENDATION

**The Secretary of Agriculture should seek cooperative arrangements whereby states provide supplemental funding to induce conservation reserve program participation.**

## RECOMMENDATION

**The Administrator of the Agricultural Stabilization and Conservation Service should, for purposes of "targeting" lands for the Conservation Reserve Program, retain the basic technical criterion based on soil erosion potential and seek the enrollment of highly erodible croplands found in "priority watersheds" identified by the states pursuant to the Clean Water Act's new non-point source control provisions.**

## RECOMMENDATION

**The Administrator of Farmers Home Administration should implement existing authority so conservation easements can be used as a tool for loan restructuring during all phases of the agency's Primary Loan Servicing Program and the Preservation Loan Service Program.**

## RECOMMENDATION

**The Secretary of Agriculture should create multi-year (3+ years) cropland set-aside requirements within commodity support programs for wheat, feed grains, upland cotton, and rice to improve soil and water conservation and enhance wildlife habitat on agricultural lands.**

• U.S. Department of Agriculture (USDA) annual farm commodity programs (Acreage Reduction Program, Paid Land Diversion, 50/92, 0/92) require participants to set-aside a portion of their productive lands each year. However, because program requirements are subject to annual change, farmers lack necessary planning horizons for practicing conservation on set-aside acreage. In particular, producers are reluctant to invest in long-term vegetative cover. As a result, as much as 60 percent of lands idled under annual set-asides are inadequately protected against excessive erosion and are frequently the source of serious surface and groundwater contamination.

## Blueprint for the Environment

# Blueprint for the Environment

## FOREST SERVICE PLANNING

# DEPARTMENT OF AGRICULTURE
## ASSISTANT SECRETARY for Natural Resources and Environment
### Forest Service

### RECOMMENDATION

**The Chief of the Forest Service should request funding to implement a forest resources planning program so that 25 million acres of private non-industrial forestland have forest resource and conservation plans by 1993.**

• Individual plans should include reforesting following timber harvest and requirements that will protect and enhance unique features found on the land such as: wildlife and fish habitat, wetlands, soils, biological diversity, aesthetics and recreation.

• Only landowners with approved, environmentally sound plans would qualify for benefits which might include federal cost-share programs to reforest, technical assistance and tax benefits from timber harvesting.

• The Forest Service working with other concerned federal agencies, State Foresters and interested publics will develop national guidelines for forest resource and conservation plans.

• State Foresters will head state-level committees that would oversee this process and spell out specific guidelines. Others on the committee could include the Soil Conservation Service, the Extension Service, The Fish and Wildlife Service, State Wildlife and Fisheries Agencies, and Conservation Districts and other interested parties. Local committees will approve specific plans that follow state and national guidelines.

### RECOMMENDATION

**The Chief of the Forest Service should promote legislation that will grant a limited income tax benefit to private, long-term forest production and will secure full annual deductions for ordinary and necessary business expenses associated with long-term forest management to stimulate long-term, environmentally sound stewardship on private forestlands.**

• Nearly three-fourths of the productive timberland in the United States, some 348 million acres, lies in private hands. Over 260 million acres of this land is held by a diverse assembly of almost 8 million non-industrial private foresters (NIPF). Government projections indicate that better management of lands owned by NIPFs could increase the country's annual net timber growth by some nine billion cubic feet, more than enough to meet foreseeable increases in demand for wood products. Such a course could bring significant environmental benefits, including reduced development pressure on public forests.

## BUDGET RECOMMENDATION
F.Y. 90: **Increase** of $ 25 million      F.Y. 91: **Increase** of $ 25 million

## PRINCIPAL AUTHORIZING LEGISLATION
Cooperative Forestry Assistance Act of 1978 (P.L. 95-313)

## CONGRESSIONAL JURISDICTION
**House Authorizing Committee/Subcommittee**
Committee on Agriculture
Subcommittee on Forests, Family Farms and Energy
**Senate Authorizing Committee/Subcommittee**
Committee on Agriculture, Nutrition and Forestry
Subcommittee on Conservation and Forestry
**House Appropriations Subcommittee**
Subcommittee on Interior
**Senate Appropriations Subcommittee**
Subcommittee on Interior and Related Agencies

## RELEVANT STUDIES
Benfield, Kinsinger and Ward, **"Taxing the Tree Farm — Sensible Policies for Sensible Private Forestry,"** Natural Resources Defense Council, May 1988, Washington D.C.
Force and Lee, **"NIPF Landowner Survey for Northern Idaho — A Survey of Landowner Objectives,"** University of Idaho, Moscow, Idaho, September 1987
Jack P. Royer, **"Use and Effects of the Reforestation Tax Incentives and Cost Sharing in the South,"** Duke University, June 1987
Fesco, Kaiser, Royer, and Wiedenhamer, **"Management Practices and Reforestation Decisions for Harvested Southern Pinelands,"** Statistical Reporting Service, No. AGE5821230, Washington, D.C., December 1982
Cubbage, Skinner, Risbrudt, **"An Economic Evaluation of the Georgia Rural Forestry Assistance Program,"** University of Georgia, January 1985, Bull. No. 322

## RELATED FEDERAL PROGRAMS
Department of Agriculture Conservation Reserve Program
Conservation Compliance
Forestry Incentives Program

## PRINCIPAL SOURCES OF EXPERTISE
The Wilderness Society — 202-842-3400    Natural Resources Defense Council — 202-783-7800
National Assoc. of State Foresters — 202-624-5415    American Forestry — 202-667-3300
Forest Farms — 404-325-2954    National Woodland Owners Association — 703-255-2300

## IMPLEMENTATION STEPS
(1)   Increase the budget request to $25 million for five years to be matched with state and local funds to improve forestland productivity and environmental quality. Withdraw funding from uneconomic sales of national forest timber to accomplish this at no increased cost.
(2)   Implement strategies to reach nonindustrial forest landowners before they harvest their timber.
(3)   Establish a mechanism that develops and implements locally approved forest resources management plans. This should be similar to Conservation Compliance (administered through SCS for farmers with soil erosion problems) but should include a broader range of resource specialists.
(4)   Change Department regulations to allow only landowners with adequate forest resource plans to qualify for cost-share programs and technical assistance.
(5)   Limit preferential tax rates to those gains on timber sales that accrue over 20 years or longer.
(6)   Full annual deductions for ordinary and necessary forest management expenses.
(7)   Require landowners utilizing these tax provisions to follow an approved forest resource management plan.

## Blueprint for the Environment

# Blueprint for the Environment

## FOREST SERVICE PLANNING

# DEPARTMENT OF AGRICULTURE

**RECOMMENDATION**
**The Forest Service should form diversity planning teams to coordinate the management of contiguous national forests and adjacent public lands to assess the cumulative impact of fragmentation and to ensure the long-term viability of species requiring large areas of relatively undisturbed habitat.**

• Habitat fragmentation is one of the most serious problems facing wildlife in our national forests. A generation of research has revealed that when natural areas are fragmented by development, ecological processes go awry and species become extinct.

• National Forest plans have failed to coordinate habitat management between adjacent national forests or across agency boundaries when national forests abut national parks or national wildlife refuges. Instead, the current plan-ning process emphasizes finely divided man-agement areas within individual forests. Wide ranging predators and other animals that re-quire large areas of relatively undisturbed or unfragmented habitat are especially vulnerable to extinction under such circumstances. The Forest Service should take a regional perspec-tive with respect to conservation to prevent the loss of biological diversity from the national forests and adjacent federal lands.

**RECOMMENDATION**
**The Forest Service should amend forest planning regulations to require special attention be given to the preservation of native species whose habitats and populations are diminishing in the state and commonwealth or Forest Service administrative regions to prevent the loss of biological diversity from the national forests.**

• Populations of native vertebrates should be maintained at a 99 percent probability of persis-tence for 100 years or longer. More attention should be devoted to the protection of plants and invertebrate animals by including more of them as sensitive species.

• Four categories of species should be given special protection on the national forests:

1) Any globally imperiled species, as de-termined by the federal government or The Nature Conservancy.

2) Regionally imperiled species — those species whose long-term viability in a particular state or region is imperiled. They may be common in other states or regions, however.

3) Wilderness species — those species that require large expanses of wildlands. These tend to be large predators or ungulates, and include such animals as the gray wolf, grizzly bear, black bear, and great gray owl. Also included here are aquatic species particularly sensitive to the deteriora-tion of water quality, such as the arctic grayling or any one of a number of darters. Many wilderness species now occupy only small fractions of their original ranges, due to the impact of humans.

4) Area-sensitive, forest-dependent spe-cies — those species that cannot sur-vive in open country or edge habitats.

## RECOMMENDATION

**The Chief of the Forest Service should seek additional full-time staff for the Wildlife and Fisheries Division to help manage and thereby ensure viable populations of federally listed endangered and threatened species and candidates for such listing, on the national forests and grasslands.**

• To accomplish the backlog of work on the National Forest System, there is a need to hire by FY 90 enough additional wildlife biologists, and particularly botanists, to:

    1) Ensure that threatened and endangered species' needs are included in land-use plans and environmental impact analyses;

    2) Determine protective actions necessary to bring about species recovery and carry them out.

• At present, there are 153 listed species on lands under Forest Service jurisdiction and over 600 candidate species.

• The Forest System includes 191 million acres of lands and waters which provide basic habitat needs for thousands of wildlife species. The present staff capability (70 full-time) to properly meet responsibilities under the Endangered Species Act is simply inadequate.

## RECOMMENDATION

**The Chief of the U.S. Forest Service should protect representative examples of all natural communities occurring on each of the national forests by greatly expanding the Research Natural Area program and the National Wilderness Preservation System.**

• At least three to five examples of each of the ecosystem types in the Bailey-Kuchler classification scheme should be included within the National Wilderness Preservation System. Redundancy in representation is essential to guard against catastrophic loss of individual ecosystems and to protect species or genetic resources that may not be uniformly distributed within an ecosystem type. In some cases, it may be necessary to close roads or restore lands in order to achieve the desired coverage.

• The Forest Service should take the lead in filling ecosystem types missing within the National Wilderness Preservation System. Although the Forest Service cannot fill all of the gaps by itself, it should do whatever it can to ensure that three to five representatives of each of the 261 Bailey-Kuchler ecosystem types are protected as wilderness, and managed to minimize adverse impacts on the biological community.

• An immediate goal of the Forest Service should be to protect representative examples of all of the natural communities occurring on each of the national forests. To accomplish this goal, the Forest Service should expand greatly its Research Natural Area (RNA) program. The current RNA program focuses on rare communities or unusually fine examples of more wide-spread ones. An expanded program would ensure that examples of even the most common communities are protected on each national forest. Roads, regenerating clearcuts, and other signs of human activity would not necessarily eliminate an area designation, provided a less-disturbed example of the community in question does not occur elsewhere in the national forest. Logging, mining, grazing and other manipulative activities would not be allowed in RNAs, unless necessary to maintain the communities.

## Blueprint for the Environment

# Blueprint for the Environment

## COOPERATION

# DEPARTMENT OF AGRICULTURE
## ASSISTANT SECRETARY for Natural Resources and Environment
## United States Forest Service

### RECOMMENDATION

**The Secretary of Agriculture and the Administration should support the thrust of and encourage the enactment of legislation to advance the operation of the Land and Water Conservation Fund as embodied in the "American Heritage Trust Act of 1988" (H.R.4127 and S.2199 of the 100th Congress).**

• The Land and Water Conservation Fund (LWCF) has since 1965 constituted the major source of federal funds for the acquisition of federal lands for outdoor recreation purposes, as well as for 50/50 matching grants to state and local governments for both land acquisition and facilities development. The Fund has been immensely popular and has resulted in the acquisition of 5.5 million acres of land and the development of almost 20,000 state and local park facility projects.

• The Reagan administration generally proposed termination of funding support for the last eight years and Congress has appropriated an annual average of only about 25 percent of earlier high year funding.

• Congress has authorized the acquisition of approximately $200 million worth of federal park, forest and refuge lands which must yet be paid for from this Fund. As money remains unavailable for such purchase, land prices continue to rise and some lands are converted to other uses and thereby lost for all time.

• There is a desperate need for greatly increased funding levels. Legislation introduced in the House (H.R.4127) and Senate (S.2199) (the "American Heritage Trust Act of 1988") majorly rectifies problems with the current operation of the Fund and is geared to assuring higher annual levels of funding, providing a more stable annual level of funding, creating a source for a flow of funds in perpetuity, and increasing long term constituency support. It is critically important that the thrust of this legislation be supported by the new administration.

## BUDGET RECOMMENDATION
F.Y. 90: **Increase** of $345,000,000    F.Y. 91: **Increase** of $ 160,000,000

## PRINCIPAL AUTHORIZING LEGISLATION
Land and Water Conservation Fund Act of 1965 (P.L. 88-578, as amended) (expiration date September 30, 2015)
National Historic Preservation Act (P.L. 89-665, as amended) (expiration date September 30, 1993)

## CONGRESSIONAL JURISDICTION
**House Authorizing Committee/Subcommittee**
   Committee on Interior and Insular Affairs
      Subcommittee on National Parks and Public Lands
**Senate Authorizing Committee/Subcommittee**
   Committee on Energy and Natural Resources
      Subcommittee on Public Lands, National Parks and Forests
**House Appropriations Subcommittee**
   Subcommittee on Interior
**Senate Appropriations Subcommittee**
   Subcommittee on Interior and Related Agencies

## RELEVANT STUDIES
**"Report and Recommendations to the President of the United States,"** President's Commission on Americans Outdoors, December, 1986
**"Report to Congress—LWCF Grants In Aid,"** U.S.D.I., N.P.S. (for each fiscal year)

## RELATED FEDERAL PROGRAMS
Historic Preservation Fund, National Park Service
Urban Parks and Recreation Recovery Program, National Park Service

## PRINCIPAL SOURCES OF EXPERTISE
National Recreation and Parks Association — 703-820-4940
National Conference of State Historic Preservation Officers — 202-624-5465
National Parks and Conservation Association — 202-944-8530
The Nature Conservancy — 703-841-5300
The Wilderness Society — 202-842-3400
American Rivers — 202-842-6900
Land Trust Exchange — 703-683-7778
The Conservation Foundation —   202-293-4800

## IMPLEMENTATION STEPS
(1)   Support the enactment of legislation to improve the operation of the LWCF (such as H.R.4127/S.2199, 100th Congress).
(2)   Recommend greatly higher budget figures for annual appropriation (at least $1 billion/year).

## BUDGET HISTORY (IN MILLIONS OF DOLLARS BY FISCAL YEAR)

|              | 79  | 81  | 83  | 85  | 87  | 88  | 89  |
|--------------|-----|-----|-----|-----|-----|-----|-----|
| Authorized   | 900 | 900 | 900 | 900 | 900 | 900 | 900 |
| Requested    | 725 | 275 | 38  | 167 | 17  | 18  | 18  |
| Appropriated | 737 | 288 | 335 | 286 | 193 | 170 | 206 |

## NOTES:

# Blueprint for the Environment

## COOPERATION

# DEPARTMENT OF AGRICULTURE

### RECOMMENDATION
**The Forest Service, through its urban forestry programs and Wildlife and Fisheries Office, should provide technical assistance to state and local governments and non-profit groups for the purpose of encouraging the planning and creation of greenway systems.**

• Linking a region's natural corridors and open spaces into a lineal network of forests, parks, trails, historical sites, stream valleys, etc., is the concept behind the nation's booming greenways movement. Because the Forest Service is concerned with the protection, design and management of forest lands, trails, rivers and historical sites, possesses valuable expertise in all of these subject areas, and has qualified people in regional offices throughout the nation, it could provide a wide variety of services to communities for creating greenway networks.

• Greenways are the most effective means to provide safe, easily accessible recreation op-portunities close to where we live and work. They are used by people of all ages and physical abilities; build partnerships among private enterprise landowners, local governments and citizen groups; enhance civic awareness and community pride; and can increase property values. Greenways also preserve parts of our historical and cultural heritage and are becoming recognized as one of the most exciting planning and land use concepts to appear in this century. The idea of creating greenways was a major recommendation of the President's Commission on Americans Outdoors in 1986.

### RECOMMENDATION
**The Department of Agriculture should require that its agencies or bureaus develop and distribute environmental education programs and materials dealing with all appropriate natural resource related activities of the Department of Agriculture.**

• Implicit within the authority of the Federal government with respect to its natural resource programs is the responsibility to consider the wishes of the public relative to the environmental impacts of the recommendations or actions of government agencies. Citizen involvement can be obtained in a variety of ways including the provision of programs, materials, and technical assistance which give citizens a fundamental understanding of the operation of natural human-altered ecosystems.

• Specific responsibilities for environmental education should be assigned to an office within each agency, a mission statement and objectives developed, and appropriate staff and fund-ing provided. Among the programs that could be developed are in-service training of agency staff who should be trained in the practices and programs of environmental education.

• Agencies should develop environmental education materials for distribution, through formal and nonformal education programs to the general public, and provide technical assistance to state and local governments, schools and private organizations which share the federal government's concern over the environment. All materials should present balanced and objective information on natural resource topics.

• These environmental education programs

should be coordinated through the proposed Office of Environmental Education within the Department of Education and through the activities of the existing Federal Interagency Committee on Education (FICE). The Deputy Under Secretary for Intergovernmental and Interagency Affairs (within the Department of Education) has been asked to develop suggested guidelines and standards for all federal agencies to consider in developing their own programs.

## RECOMMENDATION
**The Chief of the Forest Service should expand existing programs to provide opportunities for private sector/nonfederal participation in federal fisheries management, hereafter called "partnerships," and review agency operations to formulate recommendations for creation of new opportunities.**

• In the U.S., fish are common property resources and are often highly migratory. Thus, governments are charged with fish stewardship responsibilities, and these duties are often performed, of necessity, in cooperation (partnerships) with other governments. Historically, private users of fisheries resources have supplied several user fees devoted to conducting government fisheries management. State fisheries activities are funded largely by fishing licenses and taxes collected on fishing equipment and motorboat fuels taxes.

• The Challenge Cost-Share program was started in Fiscal Year (FY) 1985 through the federal appropriations process. The purpose of the program is to involve public and private agencies and organizations in improving wildlife and fish habitat on federal lands. The program involves matching federal funding with nonfederal resources (money, in-kind services) to conduct projects benefiting fish and wildlife on federal lands. The program currently is in effect for three agencies: the Bureau of Land Management, Forest Service, and the Fish and Wildlife Service. The program has no authorizing legislation.

• Due to projected severe budget shortfalls in the near future it appears likely that sufficient funding and manpower to manage an increasingly scarce fisheries resource will not be available. The future of federal fisheries management will rely increasingly on private sector/nonfederal partnerships. Federal agencies with fisheries responsibilities already have in place some mechanisms to facilitate these partnerships. This proposal calls for expansion of existing, successful mechanisms, and investigation of potential new opportunities for private sector/nonfederal participation in fisheries management.

• The Secretary of Agriculture, in consultation with other agencies proposed for participation, should develop and submit to Congress legislation to authorize the Challenge Cost-Share program. This legislative package should include authorized levels of appropriations for each of the four agencies, criteria for fundable projects, criteria for organizations with which a partnership project may be conducted, and reporting requirements of the agency for the program. A legislative package should be developed in close association with constituent groups and representatives of state and local governments. Three components are essential to the Fisheries Partnership:

1) Develop and submit to Congress authorizing legislation for the Challenge Cost-Share program.

2) Direct the participating agencies to conduct a review of agency operations for the purpose of identifying other means of enhancing partnerships with private sector/nonfederal organizations that would improve the agency's capabilities.

(3) Direct the Federal Aid Division of the FWS to encourage states to use a portion of their federal Sport Fish Restoration fund allocation on projects to be matched by private sector/nonfederal contributions.

# Blueprint for the Environment

## FARMLANDS AND WETLANDS

# DEPARTMENT OF AGRICULTURE
ASSISTANT SECRETARY for Natural Resources and Environment
Soil Conservation Service
Conservation Planning and Application Division

## RECOMMENDATION

**The Secretary of Agriculture should implement statutory authority to withhold federal support for the avoidable loss of prime farmland in order to minimize the contribution of federal activities to the unnecessary and irreversible conversion of prime farmland to non-agricultural uses.**

• Congress enacted the Farmland Protection Policy Act (FPPA) in 1981 to protect agricultural lands considered "prime," "unique," or "of state-wide or local importance." The law responded to the 1980 National Agricultural Lands Study (NALS), showing federally-sponsored activities (e.g. highways, airports, subsidized housing) responsible for substantial agricultural land conversion across the country, often in conflict with state and local programs designed to keep good farmland in production.

• Following years of administrative recalcitrance by USDA, Congress strengthened FPPA within the 1985 Food Security Act. In February 1987, the Soil Conservation Service proposed a rule implementing these amendments (52 Fed. Reg. 1465). The proposal affirmed that federal assistance may be withheld in situations where alternatives to prime farmland conversion have not been appropriately considered and adopted, and that states may seek judicial relief under FPPA when their farmland protection programs are compromised by federally-assisted, non-agricultural development.

• Unfortunately, chronic regulatory delay continues to impede fulfillment of FPPA's purposes. This could be cured by prompt promulgation of the USDA rule implementing the statute.

## RECOMMENDATION

**The Administrator of the Agricultural Stabilization and Conservation Service should modify agency management of the Water Bank program to emphasize restoration of agriculturally converted wetlands.**

• Agriculture has been by far the leading cause of wetland destruction in this country; in some midwestern states only a tiny fraction of the pre-settlement natural wetland base remains. USDA's Water Bank Program has provided a modest, but important, check against wetland extinction, particularly in the North Central United States. Under the program, the federal government compensates farmers for forgoing agricultural wetland drainage under 10-year contracts. Although helpful in "holding the line" against wetland extinction, the program has done little to reverse the trend of inexorable wetland loss.

• Agricultural Stabilization and Conservation Service (ASCS) has statutory and regulatory authority to use the Water Bank for purposes of restoring converted wetlands. The agency administrator should issue guidance to ASCS field offices affirming a preference for wetland restoration.

## BUDGET RECOMMENDATION

F.Y. 90: **no change**     F.Y. 91: **no change**

## PRINCIPAL AUTHORIZING LEGISLATION

Farmland Protection Policy Act, as amended, 7 U.S.C. § 4201 et. seq.
Water Bank Act, P.L. 91-559, 16 U.S.C. §§ 1301-1311, amended by P.L. 96-182, §§ 1-4, 93 Stat. 1317-1318

## CONGRESSIONAL JURISDICTION

**House Authorizing Committee/Subcommittee**
  Committee on Agriculture
    Subcommittee on Conservation, Credit and Rural Development
**Senate Authorizing Committee/Subcommittee**
  Committee on Agriculture, Nutrition and Forestry
    Subcommittee on Agricultural Research, Conservation, Forestry and General Legislation
**House Appropriations Subcommittee**
  Subcommittee on Rural Development, Agriculture and Related Agencies
**Senate Appropriations Subcommittee**
  Subcommittee on Agriculture, Rural Development and Related Agencies

## RELEVANT STUDIES

USDA, **"National Agricultural Lands Study,"** January 1981
USDA, **"Water Bank Program: From Inception of Program through September 30, 1986."** 1987

## RELATED FEDERAL PROGRAMS

Subtitle C, Wetland Conservation, Food Security Act of 1985

## PRINCIPAL SOURCES OF EXPERTISE

Natural Resources Defense Council — 202-783-7800
American Farmland Trust — 202-659-5170
National Audubon Society — 202-547-9009
Izaak Walton League — 612-941-6654
National Wildlife Federation — 202-797-6880
Soil and Water Conservation Society — 202-659-5668

## IMPLEMENTATION STEPS

(1) Promulgate proposed 7 CFR part 658 (52 Fed. Reg. 1465), "Revision of FPPA."
(2) Issue policy guidelines to ASCS field office personnel favoring wetland restoration under the Water Bank Program.

## NOTES:

## Blueprint for the Environment

# Blueprint for the Environment

## FARMLANDS AND WETLANDS

# DEPARTMENT OF AGRICULTURE

**RECOMMENDATION**
**The Secretary of Agriculture should request and advocate funding at the full authorization level of $30 million for the Water Bank Program to restore natural wetland areas on agricultural lands.**

• The Water Bank Program compensates farmers for protecting wetlands on their property through long term rental contracts with the Secretary of Agriculture. Recognizing the imperative for conserving these vanishing natural resources, Congress amended the Water Bank Act in 1980 and authorized $30 million in program spending per year (up from $10 million under previous authority). In recent years, the administration has proposed to "zero out" the program, and annual appropriations have dropped to $8.3 million.

**RECOMMENDATION**
**The Secretary of Agriculture should develop and promote legislation enabling permanent wetland conservation under the Water Bank Program.**

**RECOMMENDATION**
**The Secretary of Agriculture should develop and promote strengthening amendments to the 1985 Food Security Act's wetland conservation provision ("swampbuster") to withhold farm subsidies from producers who drain natural wetlands, regardless of whether annual crops are planted on the damaged land.**

• Under the current swampbuster provision, federal farm program benefits may flow to producers who drain wetlands, provided they do not drain and plant the land to an "agricultural commodity" during the same crop year. This makes the swampbuster provision much less effective in conserving wetlands and harder for USDA officials to monitor in the field than if wetland drainage per se triggered a loss of subsidies. For example, farmers can retain agricultural program eligibility by converting a wetland and planting an alternative crop not treated by the statute and USDA regulations as "agricultural commodity." Alternatively, the swampbuster may simply wait for the next cropping year, vacate the farm programs, and plant without restrictions.
• A strengthening amendment to the farm act would cure this dangerous loophole.

**RECOMMENDATION**
**The Secretary of Agriculture should amend U.S. Department of Agriculture regulations to enable citizen appeals of adverse swampbuster determinations.**

• The 1985 Food Security Act contains an appeal provision whereby aggrieved persons may seek administrative relief from adverse local swampbuster determinations. Developing

25

rules to implement swampbuster in 1987, the Department of Agriculture (USDA) rejected a conservationist recommendation for third-party citizen appeals; the rules restrict the right of appeal to producers faced with the loss of farm program subsidies from wetland cultivation.

• This narrow formulation ignores that injury from arbitrary USDA enforcement of swampbuster may manifest itself not just in lost subsidies, but in reduced duck populations, lower water tables, stream pollution, and other "off-farm" impacts of agricultural wetland loss. The right of appeal under swampbuster should not be limited to the immediately affected producers, but rather, should extend to all local citizens with a stake in the process.

## RECOMMENDATION
**The Secretary of Agriculture should amend U.S. Department of Agriculture regulations to require U.S. Fish and Wildlife Service concurrence on swampbuster exemptions.**

• The 1985 Food Security Act specified limited exemptions that enable subsidized crop production on wetlands. U.S. Department of Agriculture (USDA) implementation of those exceptions has unfortunately been lax and uneven. In particular, destructive swampbusting has occurred under an overly-liberal interpretation of the law's "commenced" exemption, which waives swampbuster sanctions wherever wetland conversion was initiated before enactment of the farm act. Similar problems have arisen with the "minimal effect" exemption, which allows farm subsidies provided planting crops does not harm natural wetland characteristics.

• This loose enforcement could be partly cured by requiring U.S. Fish and Wildlife Service (FWS) concurrence on swampbuster exemptions. At present, the regulation mandates only USDA consultation with the FWS. Such a requirement would ensure that needed wildlife expertise is brought to bear on determinations affecting the fate of important wetland habitat. This role for the FWS also would lend outside objectivity to swampbuster compliance decisions which now rest entirely with Agricultural Stabilization and Conservation Service county and state committees composed of the "regulated" community.

## RECOMMENDATION
**The Soil Conservation Service should work to maintain or restore flood-damaged fish habitats on a priority, emergency basis to a productive condition as flood restoration is accomplished.**

• The Soil Conservation Service (SCS) working with the Fish and Wildlife Service (FWS) should develop a National Response team of specialists trained in all applicable regulations, procedures, and skilled in coordination and communication, to lead flood response efforts and to aid local colleagues for the first few weeks after a flood event. Emergency actions should be, to the extent practical, insulated form local political pressures beyond lives and property. The resource base must be protected as a public trust, and insured through an orderly and publicly-reviewed permit process. Field review teams should be balanced, small, and without a preponderance of parochial concerns. "Resource first" is the motto applicable to these situations nationwide.

## RECOMMENDATION
**The Soil Conservation Service should adopt rules stating that before any project will be constructed or permitted on a river on the Nationwide Rivers Inventory, this agency or another appropriate federal agency will study the affected river segment for possible inclusion in the National Wild and Scenic Rivers system. If the agency recommends that the river be designated, the Congress should have the opportunity to consider the designation.**

# Blueprint for the Environment

## RANGE MANAGEMENT

# DEPARTMENT OF AGRICULTURE
## ASSISTANT SECRETARY for Natural Resources and Environment
## Forest Service

**RECOMMENDATION**

**The Assistant Secretary for Natural Resources and Environment should actively support and encourage current efforts to expand the scope of Forest Service range management beyond its traditional emphasis on livestock and forage production to a broader perspective that emphasizes a full range of values and uses, including watersheds, wildlife and fish, riparian areas, soils and recreation.**

• Historically, public rangelands have been managed primarily as grazing lands for livestock, with other non-commodity uses subordinate to livestock's needs. Today, a number of factors are converging to change the demands for range outputs and the focus of range management. The West is urbanizing. Outdoor recreation is becoming more popular. Public awareness of National Forest rangelands is increasing rapidly, bringing new demands for recreation, water, wildlife and riparian values. As water is becoming a scarcer and more valuable commodity, water yields and silt retention are becoming more important components of range management. Livestock is becoming a less important component of Western states' economics.

• In response to these changes, range profes-

sionals are focusing on vegetation management, rather than livestock. Range management is evolving into the integrated management of soils, water and vegetation to achieve the balanced array of multiple uses that the public and the economy now demand. The Forest Service is leading this evolution.

• Shifting the focus of National Forest range management to accommodate this new emphasis on non-commodity uses will require:

Policy leadership from the Secretary down;

Increased funding and staffing;

Expanded interdisciplinary recruitment;

Revising Forest Service range management policies and procedures to reflect a broader, non-commodity focus; and

An emphasis on a full spectrum of rangeland values throughout the planning process.

## BUDGET RECOMMENDATION
F.Y. 90: **Increase** of $ 8.0 million     F.Y. 91: **Increase** of $ 10.0 million

## PRINCIPAL AUTHORIZING LEGISLATION
National Forest Management Act
Multiple Use Sustained Yield Act
Taylor Grazing Act
Federal Land Policy and Management Act, 1976
Public Rangelands Improvement Act, 1978

## CONGRESSIONAL JURISDICTION
**House Authorizing Committee/Subcommittee**
   Committee on Interior and Insular Affairs
      Subcommittee on National Parks and Public Lands
**Senate Authorizing Committee/Subcommittee**
   Committee on Energy and Natural Resources
      Subcommittee on Public Lands, National Parks and Forests
**House Appropriations Subcommittee**
   Subcommittee on Interior
**Senate Appropriations Subcommittee**
   Subcommittee on Interior and Related Agencies

## RELEVANT STUDIES
Report of the National Range Workshop, USDA-FS, May 1987
**Grazing Fee Review and Evaluation — A Report From The Secretary of Agriculture and the Secretary of the Interior,** 1988
GAO, **Public Rangeland Improvement,** 1982
GAO, **Rangeland Management,** 1986
GAO **Riparian Management,** 1988
House Committee on Government Operations, **Federal Grazing Program: All Is Not Well On The Range,** 1986 (House Report No. 593, 99th Congress)

## RELATED FEDERAL PROGRAMS
Bureau of Land Management, Department of the Interior — Range
Department of Defense — grazing leases on D.O.D. reservation
Fish and Wildlife Service — refuge grazing leases

## PRINCIPAL SOURCES OF EXPERTISE
Natural Resources Defense Council — 415-777-0220    National Wildlife Federation — 202-797-6800
Izaak Walton League — 703-528-1818    American Fisheries Society — 301-897-8616
Sierra Club — 202-547-1141

## IMPLEMENTATION STEPS
(1)   The Secretary of Agriculture should direct the Forest Service to budget for and implement Forest Land Management Plans.
(2)   Direct the Chief of the Forest Service to implement range resource programs that are integrated with non-commodity programs.
(3)   Recruit hydrology, wildlife, fisheries, recreation and soil sciences.
(4)   The Chief should direct the regions to emphasize the non-grazing uses and values of National Forest rangelands in the formulation of all amendments to Forest Plans and throughout the next cycle of forest planning.
(5)   The Assistant Secretary should actively support and encourage the Forest Service range management initiative currently underway as "Change on the Range," revising manual sections, guidelines and procedures to accommodate a view of range management that looks beyond forage and livestock benefits.

—————————— **Blueprint for the Environment** ——————————

# Blueprint for the Environment

## RANGE MANAGEMENT

# DEPARTMENT OF AGRICULTURE

### RECOMMENDATION

**The Secretary of Agriculture should raise livestock grazing fees on the National Forests to reflect the fair market value of the forage. At least 25 percent of the fee receipts should be earmarked for fish and wildlife habitat enhancement and watershed improvement work, emphasizing riparian area rehabilitation.**

• Subsidized federal grazing fees stimulate artificial demand for federal forage and make it difficult to control overgrazing. Moreover, the current, less-than-market grazing fees fail to generate the funds needed to repair the damage to the public rangelands caused by historic overuse by livestock.

• The grazing fee formula now in use on the public lands administered by the Forest Service and the Bureau of Land Management (BLM) under-values federal forage — returning only about one fourth the fair market value of the forage consumed by livestock. In 1985, the fee was only $1.35 per month for each mature cow. The 1985 Grazing Fee Review and Evaluation Report by the Secretaries of Agriculture and the Interior found that comparable private land grazing fees ranged from $5.50 to $10.00 in 1983.

• Grazing fees fail to cover even the direct costs of administering federal grazing management programs. In 1986, the total cost of administering the Forest Service Grazing Program in the 16 western state was $24,016,000 while total grazing fee receipts were only $7,288,000.

• The practice of subleasing grazing privileges granted by Bureau of Land Management and Forest Service permits demonstrates that the federal land grazing fees are far below market value. In 1982-83 nearly 1,000 BLM and Forest Service permittees subleased their grazing permits to other ranchers at an average of over $7.00 per cow-calf unit per month; at the time, federal grazing fees averaged $1.63.

• Other federal agencies charge far higher grazing fees on their lands. In 1984, the Army charged between $7.36 and $12.45, the Bureau of Indian Affairs $8.64, the Fish and Wildlife Service $4.50, and the Bureau of Reclamation $5 to $16. Grazing fees charges by 12 federal agencies varied from a low of $1.37, for the BLM and the Forest Service, to a high of $18 for the Air Force.

• Federal grazing fees represent a subsidy to only two percent of American livestock operators and only seven percent of western livestock producers — those who hold permits to graze federal lands.

### RECOMMENDATION

**The Secretary of Agriculture and the Chief of the Forest Service should secure increased funding for range inventories. Expanded range inventory work should focus initially on allotments where the current management is not meeting the standards, guidelines and management requirements of the Forest Plans.**

• Up-to-date inventory and monitoring data is the key to Forest Service range planning and management. Baseline inventories are needed to establish the condition and trend of the resource, to prepare for the next round of forest plans, and to bring allotment management

29

plans into compliance with current standards and guidelines.

• The GAO determined that at least nine percent of Forest Service rangeland is declining in condition. They found this fact "particularly important because once damaged, rangeland recovery to its prior condition is slow, and in some cases never occurs, resulting in a permanent loss of the resource." GAO stated that "…the Forest Service should focus priority on completing new livestock carrying capacity assessments for grazing allotments that their range managers believe are overstocked and therefore have the greatest potential for range deterioration."

## RECOMMENDATION
**The Secretary of Agriculture should seek increased funding and personnel for range management and related skills necessary for the Forest Service to meet its statutory commitment to implement Forest Plans.**

• The Forest Service administers over 9,000 grazing allotments, spread over 103 million acres of forest and rangeland. Between 1980 and January of 1988, the number of Range Conservationists in the Forest Service declined from 554 to 440, or about 21 percent. That means that, on the average, each Range Conservationist has the task of overseeing 20 grazing allotments covering 234,000 acres. Similar declines occurred in other skills needed to support the range program, such as soil scientists and hydrologists. The job of implementing Forest Plan provisions on grazed rangelands will not be accomplished without substantial increases in funding and personnel.

## RECOMMENDATION
**The Assistant Secretary should seek funding and support for (1) rangeland and forested range ecological research which will enhance management efforts to correct the unsatisfactory condition of an estimated 20 percent of National Forest System range and for (2) balanced implementation of Forest Land Management Plans.**

• The following actions need to be implemented immediately:

Develop ecological relationships that are important to predicting probable effects of management actions and provide a basis for monitoring of range vegetation management actions.

Examine riparian areas with emphasis on effects of different management strategies and treatments on riparian areas and their dependent resources.

Design monitoring techniques which are cost effective, understood by the public and provide defensible support for management actions.

Improve understanding of the roles wild and domestic animals can play in regeneration and growth of timber stands and for protection of wildlife and fish habitat.

Determine critical biotic and physical requirements for threatened and endangered plants to ensure species conservation and recovery.

Improve integrated measures for managing unwanted range plants.

## RECOMMENDATION
**The Forest Service and the Department of Agriculture should secure increased funding for on-the-ground administration of grazing permits and recruit additional range conservationists to carry out this function.**

• Careful monitoring of range condition and levels of use is essential to management and resource protection. Forest Service personnel should monitor each allotment annually to determine whether permit conditions have been met, and inspect for overgrazing and damage to the resource base. This information is essential to making the basic management decisions that are needed to protect the vegetation resource itself, wildlife, watersheds, and other rangeland values.

—————————— **Blueprint for the Environment** ——————————

# Blueprint for the Environment

## FORESTS AND TIMBER

# DEPARTMENT OF AGRICULTURE
ASSISTANT SECRETARY for Natural Resources and Environment
Forest Service
Timber Management

**RECOMMENDATION**
**The Secretary of Agriculture should direct that harvest levels and silvicultural practices of the Forest Service not adversely affect the natural, scenic or recreational values of the National Forests.**

• The timber cut in national forests reached an all time record of 12.7 billion board feet (bbf) in 1987 and a near-record cut in 1988 is predicted. These high logging levels have and will cause significant degradation of watersheds, biological diversity, fish and wildlife habitat, scenic beauty, outdoor recreation opportunities and other forest resources. The proposed timber program exceeds the sustainable capacity of some forests, particularly in the Pacific Northwest.

• A contributing factor to the adverse effects from the timber program is the Forest Service choice of clearcutting as the dominant silviculture practice, even though concerns for clearcutting were a major factor behind passage of the National Forest Management Act in 1976. The Act allows the use of clearcutting only where it is determined to be the "optimum method" of harvest. Congress clearly intended for other methods to predominate. Alternative silvicultural systems are available which would better meet overall land management objectives.

• These important changes in the timber program must be done gradually to ensure a smooth economic transition. Therefore, it is recommended that for Fiscal Year 1989, the sale level should not exceed 10 bbf, declining to as little as 5.0 to 6.9 bbf/yr by 1997. This level provides for the elimination of below-cost sales, estimated by the Forest Service at 40 percent of the current harvest (a 3.0-to-4.0 bbf reduction), and threats to water, wildlife, and recreation resources (a 1.0-to-1.5 bbf reduction). Reaching long-term sustainable levels will entail a further 0.6-to-1.0 bbf reduction.

## BUDGET RECOMMENDATION
F.Y. 90: **decrease** of $ 20 million   F.Y. 91:   additional **decrease** of $ 20 million

## PRINCIPAL AUTHORIZING LEGISLATION
Multiple Use Sustain Yield Act (MUSYA)
National Forest Management Act (NFMA)

## CONGRESSIONAL JURISDICTION
**House Authorizing Committee/Subcommittee**
Committee on Agriculture
Subcommittee on Forests, Family Farms and Energy
**Senate Authorizing Committee/Subcommittee**
Committee on Agriculture, Nutrition and Forestry
Subcommittee on Conservation and Forestry
**House Appropriations Subcommittee**
Subcommittee on Interior
**Senate Appropriations Subcommittee**
Subcommittee on Interior and Related Agencies

## RELEVANT STUDIES
**Sustain Yield, Proceedings of a Symposium,** Washington State Univ., 1982
**The Redesigned Forest,** Chris Maser, in press
**Area Ecology Workshop on Longterm Productivity, Region 6,** U.S. Forest Service, 1988

## RELATED FEDERAL PROGRAMS
Bureau of Land Management Timber Program

## PRINCIPAL SOURCES OF EXPERTISE
The Wilderness Society — 202-842-3400
National Wildlife Federation — 202-797-6800
National Audubon Society — 202-547-9009
Defenders of Wildlife — 202-659-9510
Natural Resources Defense Council — 202-783-7800

## IMPLEMENTATION STEPS
(1)   For Fiscal Year 1990 the sale level should not exceed 10 bbf declining to as little as 5.0 to 6.9 bbf/yr by 1997.
(2)   Practice ecological forestry and limit use of clearcutting to exceptional situations.

## NOTES:

## Blueprint for the Environment

# Blueprint for the Environment

## FORESTS AND TIMBER

# DEPARTMENT OF AGRICULTURE

**RECOMMENDATION**
**The Secretary of Agriculture should declare that the national forest major road system is complete, thus eliminating additional, unnecessary road construction.**

• The Forest Service costs the Treasury about $300 million per year for its roads. The size of the permanent road network within the National Forests is over 343,000 miles. End to end, this road system would reach 14 times around the world. Moreover the Forest Service plans significant increases in the road system. In the next ten years alone the agency expects to build new permanent roads about equal to the entire interstate highway system.

• Forest road construction and maintenance is very costly and claims a major portion of the Forest Service budget. Besides the cost to the Treasury, these roads are a major source of environmental damage causing erosion, stream sedimentation, and destruction of fish and wildlife habitat. In each of the past five fiscal years, the Forest Service has built or rebuilt more miles of roads than it requested in its annual budget message as necessary to carry out its timber sales program. Cumulatively, this overbuilding totals 3,789 miles. Based on this fact alone, enough excess capacity exists to accommodate the next three years of timber sales without any further road construction or reconstruction.

**RECOMMENDATION**
**The Secretary of Agriculture should direct the Forest Service to phase-out below-cost timber sales by eliminating the most costly sales first and curtailing all such sales by January 20, 1993.**

• On the majority of national forests, the Forest Service spends more money on sale preparation and administration, mitigation, road construction and reforestation than it receives for the timber. Documented reports indicate that the Forest Service timber program will result in expenditures that exceed receipts by $265 million or more each year.

• The practice of selling national forest timber for less than the cost to the federal government of growing and selling the timber is not in the nation's best interest.

• For purposes of determining costs of making timber available for sale and cutting, "costs" means all capital, annual operating, planning, and overhead costs incurred by the federal government due to the sale of timber. Such costs shall include — but are not limited to — road construction, reconstruction, and maintenance; sale preparation and administration; timber stand improvement; mitigation; reforestation; payments to state and local governments; and a prorated share of general administration. Alleged benefits to other forest uses must not be included in the benefit-cost calculations.

**RECOMMENDATION**
**The Secretary of Agriculture should direct that timber not be cut from lands that are biologically and economically unsuitable for timber harvesting.**

## RECOMMENDATION
The Secretary of Agriculture should direct the Forest Service to comply with the requirements of the National Forest Management Act which prohibits logging in national forests except where reforestation is assured within five years.

## RECOMMENDATION
The Secretary of Agriculture should direct an end to all type conversions in the national forests except to restore the original vegetation of an area or protect threatened or endangered species.

• From an ecological perspective, type conversions are among the most damaging practices that occur in national forests. A conversion promotes the regeneration of cut-over stands using tree species that would not occur naturally on the site. An example would be the conversion of a hardwood stand into a softwood stand.

• Forests managed in this way typically support neither the quality nor quantity of wildlife associated with natural forest communities. Not surprisingly then, conversions were the subject of considerable debate during drafting of the National Forest Management Act (NFMA). Note, for example, that the diversity provision of the NFMA requires that steps be taken "to preserve the diversity of tree species similar to that existing in the region controlled by the plan," yet type conversions continue to be a part of the forest plans.

## RECOMMENDATION
The Secretary of should ask the President to issue an executive order placing a moratorium on cutting Pacific Northwest old growth forests until an inventory is completed and a management decision made.

• At one time, the Pacific Northwest was covered by approximately 19 million acres of old growth forests. Today, the majority of the old growth remains on national forests and Bureau of Land Management lands. Currently, there is much debate over the amount of Pacific Northwest old growth forests remaining. The Forest Service claims there are five to six million acres primarily on public lands, while scientists say only one-half that amount meets the ecological definition of old growth forest.

• The confusion over the amount of old growth remaining affects the management decisions made. If the Forest Service numbers are correct, then perhaps additional old growth can be harvested. If the scientists and environmentalists are correct, then we may need to cease cutting immediately because the amount of old growth forests will be at or below the critical amount needed to maintain old growth dependent species.

## RECOMMENDATION
The Secretary of Agriculture should strive to secure increased funding for scientific research and equipment in order to maintain and foster adequate research capability and allow Forest Service the flexibility to respond to new research initiatives when the need arises.

## RECOMMENDATION
The Secretary of Agriculture should create a national research unit devoted to finding natural control agents for forest pests.

## RECOMMENDATION
The Forest Service should expand tropical forest research and forestry assistance to tropical countries.

## Blueprint for the Environment

# Blueprint for the Environment

## RIVERS AND FISHERIES

# DEPARTMENT OF AGRICULTURE
## ASSISTANT SECRETARY for Natural Resources and Environment
### Forest Service

### RECOMMENDATION
**The Secretary of Agriculture should seek to increase program funding and staffing level to protect, restore and enhance commercial and recreational fisheries resources management within the National Forest System.**

• The National Forest System manages 191 million acres of lands and waters, including thousands of miles of streams and rivers. Current emphasis in timber production and other direct economic activities within the national forests (even when such timber cutting and activities such as grazing are a net loss to the government) have often degraded water areas through erosion, temperature increases, increased salinities, sedimentation and nutrient loading.

• A major deficiency exists within the Forest Service to provide adequate numbers of trained biologists and related expertise during the planning and management of economic operations.
• This proposal would enable better fisheries resource input to management and planning decisions, while allowing needed, proper economic development to occur. It would also result in greatly improved capabilities of the forests to provide high-quality fisheries protection and recreation.

### RECOMMENDATION
**The Chief of the Forest Service should act promptly to ensure that riparian area and watershed management be given a high priority by the Forest Service's wildlife range programs.**

• Riparian areas occupy only about one percent of the 250 million acres of federal rangelands managed by the Forest Service and the Bureau of Land Management, but they have ecological importance far beyond this relatively small acreage in the arid and semi-arid West. Unfortunately, the majority of riparian areas administered by the Forest Service have been degraded, primarily as a consequence of livestock grazing. According to the General Accounting Office there are two primary reasons for the lack of progress in restoring and properly managing these areas: a) lack of skilled field staff to plan, implement and monitor riparian areas; and b) to a lesser degree in the Forest Service, lack of support for riparian management efforts at high agency management levels.

• Actions needed to restore and properly manage riparian areas occurring on public rangelands administered by the Forest Service include:

Increase funding for riparian area management by $10 million per year.
Provide increased staff to develop, implement and monitor (enforce) riparian area programs on Forest Service lands.
Inventory the condition of riparian areas where acceptable data is lacking.
Implement currently identified projects to enhance the condition of riparian areas.
Implement a riparian area demonstration and education program, on all Districts, targeted to all employees and public lands users, to demonstrate the importance of proper management of riparian areas.

## BUDGET RECOMMENDATION
F.Y. 90: **Increase** of $ 12 million     F.Y. 91: **no change**

## PRINCIPAL AUTHORIZING LEGISLATION
National Forest Management Act of 1976
Multiple Use Sustained Yield Act of 1980
Federal Land Policy and Management Act of 1976
Public Rangelands Improvement Act (1978)

## CONGRESSIONAL JURISDICTION
**House Authorizing Committee/Subcommittee**
  Committee on Interior and Insular Affairs
    Subcommittee on National Parks and Public Lands
**Senate Authorizing Committee/Subcommittee**
  Committee on Energy and Natural Resources
    Subcommittee on Public Lands, National Parks and Forests
**House Appropriations Subcommittee**
  Subcommittee on Interior
**Senate Appropriations Subcommittee**
  Subcommittee on Interior and Related Agencies

## RELEVANT STUDIES
National Fisheries Task Force Report — USDA Forest Service
GAO: **Public Rangelands: Some Riparian Areas Restored, But Widespread Improvement Will Be Slow,** 1988

## RELATED FEDERAL PROGRAMS
Riparian Management, Bureau of Land Management, Dept. of the Interior
Soil Conservation Services, USDA

## PRINCIPAL SOURCES OF EXPERTISE
American Fisheries Society — 301-897-8616
Trout Unlimited — 703-281-1100
National Wildlife Federation — 202-797-6800

## IMPLEMENTATION STEPS
(1)  Support increases in manpower and funding in annual budget documents
(2)  The Secretary, with the Chief of the Forest Service, should secure increased funding and personnel for rangeland riparian management in fiscal 1990.
(3)  The Secretary should seek a supplemental appropriation of $4 million for riparian management for FY 90.
(4)  Review staffing levels and report to Congress on extent of riparian improvement that can be expected at current and projected staffing levels.
(5)  Annually document specific progress being made in riparian area improvement.
(6)  Document instances where restoration programs have been thwarted or rejected.

BUDGET HISTORY (millions of dollars by fiscal year)

|  | . | 81 | 83 | 85 | 87 | 88 | 89 |
|---|---|---|---|---|---|---|---|
| Authorized (Agency Request) | n/a | n/a | n/a | 4.48 | 7.64 | 6.57 | 14.51 |
| Requested (President's Budget) | n/a | 8.45 | 6.09 | 3.69 | 4.21 | 3.74 | 5.58 |
| Appropriated | 3.18 | 6.08 | 6.25 | 5.59 | 6.39 | 7.97 | 10.58 |
| Actual | n/a | n/a | 131 | 130 | 122 | 129 | n/a |

## Blueprint for the Environment

# Blueprint for the Environment

## RIVERS AND FISHERIES

## DEPARTMENT OF AGRICULTURE

### RECOMMENDATION
**The Forest Service should file with the Federal Energy Regulatory Commission all comprehensive plans prepared by this agency relating to river conservation and development.**

• The Electric Consumers Protection Act (ECPA) of 1986 directs the Federal Energy Regulatory Commission (FERC) , to consider the extent to which proposed hydroelectric projects are consistent with comprehensive plans prepared by states and federal agencies.

This provision provides an important opportunity for federal agencies to influence FERC decision — making and to make sure that hydroelectric development is consistent with existing plans for balanced conservation and use of river resources.

### RECOMMENDATION
**The Forest Service should assert their existing authority to direct hydro development to appropriate sites and away from inappropriate sites on federal public lands.**

• Several hundred applications to construct private hydroelectric projects on federal public lands are now pending before the Federal Energy Regulatory Commission (FERC). To ensure that these proposed projects are consistent with Forest Service resource plans, the agencies must play a strong role in the regulation of these projects.
• Under section 501(a) (4) of the Federal Land Policy and Management Act, the Forest Service

has the authority to issue rights of way for hydroelectric and other types of energy development on federal public lands. The FERC has taken the position, however, that hydro developers subject to Commission jurisdiction need not obtain rights from the Agency. While the Agencies apparently maintain that their right of way authority extends to hydro projects, they have so far failed to vigorously assert that authority.

### RECOMMENDATION
**The Forest Service should adopt procedures that would direct public land managers to improve watershed conditions. Such improvements would increase or extend stream flows of all rivers and streams on public domain lands and would enable land managers to better identify and manage aquifer recharge areas in the public domain.**

• The largest land planning efforts in history — that of the Forest Service and the Bureau of Land Management — have largely ignored their respective duties to provide more dependable and cleaner water to the water-starved West. Rivers on public domain lands including poten-

tial Wild and Scenic Rivers are not being managed for optimum stream-flow despite the fact that the National Forests are often originally established as watersheds. The advantages of a bold new program to restore watershed condition would be to reduce peak flows of a river, extend base flows and raise water tables. In addition, there would be more interaction with aquifer recharge areas. Eighty-five percent of all the rivers in the West originate in National Forests and many of the most important aquifer recharge areas are on public domain land.

## RECOMMENDATION

**The National Park Service, Fish and Wildlife Service, Bureau of Land Management and Forest Service should enter into a joint memorandum of understanding that they will evaluate all potential wild and scenic rivers on their respective lands in a coordinated fashion.**

- Section 5(d) of the Wild and Scenic Rivers Act calls upon all federal agencies to consider potential Wild and Scenic Rivers in the preparation of their land and related water resource planning. Nearly 800 rivers are being evaluated by these agencies. When these agencies conduct such studies, they confine their evaluations to the area inside their respective boundaries and seldom coordinate with an agency having contiguous or nearby lands.

- Rivers do not respect the boundaries of federal land managing agencies and as a result lengthy river reaches can be artificially divided into shorter segments that make little or no sense. Different segments of the same river may be studied at different times or one segment may studied while another is not.

## RECOMMENDATION

**The Secretaries of Agriculture and the Interior should, by joint secretarial order, establish a new Joint Interagency Office of River Protection to coordinate and implement a wide range of river planning, technical assistance and management programs for river protection.**

- This new office is necessary to:
  1) Assist with planning coordination and river management coordination issues that affect the respective federal land managing agencies.
  2) Provide technical assistance to state and local groups concerned with river protection.
  3) Have oversight responsibility for the review of federal projects on rivers included in the national rivers system, rivers being studied under Section 5 of the Act, or rivers that are included in state river systems.

## RECOMMENDATION

**The Forest Service should administratively initiate, and seek appropriations for, a state and local rivers technical assistance program as it is directed to do under Section 11 of the Wild and Scenic Rivers Act.**

- Although the Forest Service, through the Secretary of Agriculture, is directed to provide technical assistance to state and local organizations for the protection of rivers, the program has never been implemented. The National Park Service has operated a technical assistance program of this nature for several years and it has been instrumental in the development of statewide rivers assessment, local river corridor protection programs and the adoption of new river protection programs by state and localities at no cost to the federal government. Forest Service land contains the headwaters of the majority of rivers in the West and hundreds of critical rivers in the East. Just as there is a need for the Forest Service to coordinate its studies of these rivers with adjacent or nearby federal land management agencies, assistance should be provided to the state to protect downstream segments of rivers well.

# Blueprint for the Environment

## Pesticide Prevention and Reduction

# DEPARTMENT OF AGRICULTURE
## ASSISTANT SECRETARY For Food and Consumer Services

### RECOMMENDATION
**The Department of Agriculture, the Food and Drug Administration and the Environmental Protection Agency should eliminate the environmental and public health threats associated with livestock production by regulating pesticides found in animal foods and groundwater and prohibiting the use of antibiotics in animal foods.**

• The environmental and health consequences of the misuse of pesticides and drugs are well documented. Their excessive application of pesticides is harmful to public health and adversely affects fish and wildlife. One great threat comes from animals raised in factory farms where the routine application of chemicals to crops and feed is intense. For example, the Environmental Protection Agency has reported that 50 or more pesticides, many of them carcinogenic, are found in the groundwater of 30 or more states. And relative to antibiotics the General Accounting Office reported that over 140 pesticides and drugs remain in meat products after slaughter. Over half of these are known or suspected carcinogens or likely to cause birth defects.

### RECOMMENDATION
**The Secretary of Agriculture should urge the President to issue an Executive Order to restructure the Animal Damage Control Program that would emphasize an ecological approach in reducing wildlife damage by developing non-lethal techniques.**

• The Animal Damage Control (ADC) Program, with authority for reducing conflict between humans and wildlife, was transferred to the Department of Agriculture in 1986. The program has traditionally focused on controlling coyotes as predators of domestic livestock and secondarily on rodent control for the protection of agricultural crops. In recent years, the Program has received increasing requests for assistance with avian problems, such as blackbird roosts, depredation on croplands and hatcheries and interference with aircraft.
• The effectiveness of the lethal control work has been questioned for decades. Non-lethal techniques have been developed, largely outside the Program, and are proving effective in reducing predation and conflicts in many situations. Yet the ADC Program continues its reliance, in both operations and research, on lethal methods.

### RECOMMENDATION
**The Assistant Secretary for Marketing and Inspection Services should amend the market order cosmetic standards to reduce excessive pesticide application for cosmetic purposes.**

## BUDGET RECOMMENDATION
F.Y. 90: **no change** *               F.Y. 91: **no change** *

## PRINCIPAL AUTHORIZING LEGISLATION
Animal Damage Control Act of 1931
7 U.S.C. 601 et seq.

## CONGRESSIONAL JURISDICTION
**House Authorizing Committee/Subcommittee**
  Committee on Agriculture
    Subcommittee on Department Operations, Research , and Foreign Agriculture
**Senate Authorizing Committee/Subcommittee**
  Committee on Agriculture, Nutrition and Forestry
    Subcommittee on Agricultural Research
**House Appropriations Subcommittee**
  Subcommittee on Rural Development, Agriculture and Related Agencies
**Senate Appropriations Subcommittee**
  Subcommittee on Agriculture, Rural Development and Related Agencies

## RELEVANT STUDIES
Environmental Impact Statement of 1979, prepared by the Fish and Wildlife Service when the Animal Damage Control Program was in the Department of the Interior
John Robbins, **Diet For A New America**, Stillpoint Publishers, 1987
Dr. M.W. Fox, **Agricide: The Hidden Crisis That Affects Us All**, Schocken Books, 1988
National Academy of Sciences, **"The Effects on Human Health of Sub-Therapeutic Use of Anti-Microbials In Animal Feed,"** 1980
1981 Presidential Task Force on Regulatory Relief

## RELATED FEDERAL PROGRAMS
Animal control work by Fish and Wildlife Service to protect nesting waterfowl and endangered species reintroductions, etc.

## PRINCIPAL SOURCES OF EXPERTISE
Defenders of Wildlife — 202-659-9519
Humane Society of the United States — 202-452-1100
Friends of the Earth — 202-543-4312
U.S. Public Interest Research Group — 202-546-9707
Natural Resources Defense Council — 212-949-0049
National Audubon Society — 202-547-9009
Institute for Alternative Agriculture — 202-979-8777
Natural Resources Defense Council — 202-783-7800
American Farmland Trust — 202-659-5170
National Coalition Against the Misuse of Pesticides — 202-543-5450

## Blueprint for the Environment

# Blueprint for the Environment

## RECREATION, ARCHAEOLOGY, MINERALS

# DEPARTMENT OF AGRICULTURE

**RECOMMENDATION**
**The U.S. Forest Service should work to assure the provision of recreation opportunities and the protection of recreation resources be given increased funding and priority to provide recreation experiences not available elsewhere.**

• More people recreate on national forest lands than anywhere else. Recognizing this, the Chief of the Forest Service introduced a new recreation initiative in 1988. The increased visibility to recreation was a move in the right direction. However, the new initiative calls for an increased reliance on partnerships with the private sector which would, in essence, privatize recreation management. Those opportunities which will provide the greatest monetary return will be those implemented.

**RECOMMENDATION**
**The Forest Service should immediately close all Off-Road Vehicle Open Areas (areas in which there are no management constraints on where vehicles are driven) in accordance with Executive Order 11989.**

• Open areas for off-road vehicular recreation violate the principles of Multiple Use and Sustained Yield, the Executive Orders (11644 and 11989) issued to protect resources and the regulations derived from the Executive Orders and virtually all other sound management practices.
• A scientifically credible monitoring system of the condition of natural resources in off-road vehicular recreation areas must be established to prevent or reduce long-term or permanent losses of those resources. Such a system is also necessary to determine the need for reclamation. The system should include comprehensive inventory of soils, vegetation, and wildlife in areas designated for off-road vehicle use, annual quantitative monitoring and public reporting of the condition of those resources, and specific standards for cutoff of use — either temporarily or permanently — for protection and rehabilitation of resources.

**RECOMMENDATION**
**The Secretary of Agriculture should propose the adoption of a recreation users pass similar to the Golden Eagle Passport used by the National Park Service.**

• All the money collected would be returned to the Forest Service to be specifically spent on recreational programs such as trail construction and maintenance, development of picnic areas, boat ramps and similar facilities, and on the protection and management of nongame species. Since the pass would allow the user to enter all national forests, the money would be returned to each forest according to a formula based on recreation visitor use and forest need.

# RECOMMENDATION

**The Secretary of Agriculture should support increased funding for the enforcement of historic and archaeological resource protection laws, and for the creation of a central office for coordinating the enforcement efforts to promote and increase the protection of historic and archaeological resources from vandalism and looting on federal lands.**

• Under law, archaeological and historic sites located on lands owned or managed by the federal government are protected from vandalism and looting. However, the looting of archaeological sites for artifacts is a growing problem, particularly as the commercial value of "antiquities" increases. Hundreds, if not thousands, of sites on federal lands have been ravaged by commercial "pothunters," destroying significant portions of the American heritage. Although some prosecutions have been successful under the Archaeological Resources Protection Act (ARPA, P.L. 96-95, 1979), adequate protection is limited by agency funding, staffing and inter-agency coordination problems.

# RECOMMENDATION

**The Secretary of Agriculture should pursue legislation to replace the 1872 Mining Law with a complete reform to protect environmental quality from damage due to unmanaged mining activity on the public lands.**

• The 1872 Mining Law permits a variety of abuses of the public domain, ranging from patenting surface ownership for as little as $2.50 per acre to location of vast mining complexes in unsuitable areas. The location of a metals mine is generally the greatest determinant of its long-term reclaimability. Location of mines in wild areas is a serious threat to the protection of wildlife habitat and wilderness lands. Mining activity is spreading into new location, due to the economic revival of the industry and the lower international value of the dollar. Reform of this 116-year-old legal eyesore is urgently required for sound land management on Bureau of Land Management and National Forest lands.

# RECOMMENDATION

**The Forest Service should base petroleum exploration and development decisions on comprehensive analysis of full field development and on rigorous site-specific stipulations to protect the environment against damaging oil and gas activities in the National Forests.**

• The Forest Service says 45 million of its 191 million acres have oil and gas potential. Currently, about 18 million acres are under valid 10-year oil and gas leases. Interest in leasing and development depends largely on the petroleum market. Most interest centers on the Rocky Mountain region, where exploration and development require roadbuilding and facility construction that has been particularly harmful to streams and to fish and wildlife habitat.

# RECOMMENDATION

**The Secretary of Agriculture should support the intent of the Master Agreement between the Department of Agriculture and the Department of Defense and encourage the creation of a military activity monitoring system.**

• The goal is to strike a proper balance between the public and military activity on the National Forest System. In pursuing that goal it is necessary to prevent and/or discontinue military activity which involves the use of live munitions and pyrotechnics on national forest lands. These materials have the potential to cause harm to national forest visitors and Forest Service employees as well as damage to the environment.

## Blueprint for the Environment

# Blueprint for the Environment

## DEPARTMENT OF COMMERCE

Within the Department of Commerce, the National Oceanic and Atmospheric Administration plays an important role as our lead civilian oceans and atmospheric agency. Based on recent fiscal year appropriations figures, the National Oceanic and Atmospheric Administration comprises about one-half of the Department's total budget, and over one-third of its personnel. Within the Blueprint for the Environment Project, the Oceans and Coastal Task Force developed a number of recommendations directed to the National Oceanic and Atmospheric Administration's ocean and coastal mandate. These recommendations, if implemented, would contribute significantly to the protection and wise use of our oceans and coastal environment. While most of the Department of Commerce recommendations are directed to the National Oceanic and Atmospheric Administration, those recommendations addressing other departmental activities also merit attention.

Over 70 percent of the earth's surface is covered by water. The immense oceans that separate land masses have been a source of wonderment and incalculable value through the ages. They are the planet's primary life-support system, providing most of our oxygen, moisture and weather patterns. Without healthy oceans, life as we know it would end.

Widespread pollution and critical habitat loss jeopardize the future of our nation's oceans and coastal waters. There are serious consequences for the public health and our national economy.

• According to U.S. government data, over one-third of our shellfish-producing areas are either closed or have restrictions on harvesting due to chemical or bacterial pollution;

• Over 16 trillion gallons of sewage and industrial waste, much of it laden with toxic contaminants, are dumped into rivers and coastal waters each year;

• Every major harbor, bay and estuary in the continental United States has been damaged or degraded, some perhaps irreparably;

• Pollution threatens fisheries and tourism — vital economic activities which generate tens of thousands of jobs and billions of dollars of income;

• Contaminated fish and shellfish pose dangers to the health of consumers;

• Human waste, plastic debris, and medical wastes foul beaches around the country;

• Pollution kills countless marine mammals and other vital aquatic organisms annually, including endangered species;

• Coastal barrier islands and other sensitive coastal areas are being strained to the limit by overdevelopment; and

• Offshore oil and gas activities degrade air quality and, as they move into frontier areas, they threaten marine and coastal life from oil spills.

The facts are ominous: ocean pollution poses a clear and present danger to our priceless coastal waters and direct threats to human health. Some of those waters are dying while many others are gravely threatened. Most alarmingly, the situation is deteriorating at an ever-increasing speed, especially in nearer coastal waters where marine life is most plentiful. Much less is known about the deeper ocean, but there are strong signs of damage there, too.

Just this past summer, our nation's shores were inundated with garbage, dead marine life and medical waste. While these manifestations of carelessness and disregard for the ocean are offensive and disgusting, they are merely the "tip of the iceberg," reminders of the vast quantities of unseen pollutants and wastes that are continually dumped or find their way into the ocean.

To some extent, stress on the ocean and coastal environment is not unexpected. This is where many of our people live and work. Nearly 60 percent of Americans live within an afternoon's drive from the ocean, with this percentage expected to increase significantly in coming years. Most of our largest metropolitan areas are located near the coast, and many of the fastest growing communities are concentrated in the nation's coastal states.

We can, and must, deal with this stress. We can, and must, develop ways to halt and reduce pollution of our marine and coastal environment. It is imperative that the country launch a major initiative to insure the restoration and preservation of America's oceans, coasts, Great Lakes and estuaries. At the same time, this nation must take advantage of any and all opportunities to develop regional and global strategies that help meet that same challenge.

Of all the federal agencies, the Department's National Oceanic and Atmospheric Administration is by far the best suited to take the lead in launching such a major initiative. It has a dedicated staff of skilled scientists, resource managers and policy makers who can make invaluable contributions to that effort. Moreover, its links with the oceans and coastal community, broadly defined, are unmatched elsewhere.

It is in this context that numerous National Oce-anic and Atmospheric Administration-directed ocean and coastal recommendations were put forward for inclusion in the Blueprint for the Environment. Those recommendations, summarily stated, call for substantially strengthened efforts to:

• use all existing authorities to prohibit release of toxic wastes into the marine environment;

• increase special protective measures to protect marine resources; and

• support and promote domestic and international oceans policies that give greater attention to protection and wise use of the marine environment.

For each recommendation, there is a listing of "Principal Sources of Expertise" which includes one or more of the participants in Project Blueprint's Ocean and Coastal Task Force. Those organizations, and others involved in Project Blueprint, look forward to working with Department of Commerce and National Oceanic and Atmospheric Administration officials in the coming months.

**Blueprint for the Environment**

# Blueprint for the Environment

## TREATIES

## DEPARTMENT OF COMMERCE
National Oceanic and Atmospheric Administration
International and Intergovernmental Affairs

### RECOMMENDATION
**The Administrator of the National Oceanic and Atmospheric Administration should give full support to the dominant view of treaty parties within the London Dumping Convention to the effect that seabed burial of high-level radioactive wastes is "dumping" under that Convention, and therefore covered by the London Dumping Convention and prohibited.**

• They should require that any efforts to amend the London Dumping Convention (LDC) to permit such activities be grounded in clear and convincing evidence that such High Level Radioactive Wastes (HLW) burial is technically feasible and environmentally acceptable, including a determination that such waste can be effectively isolated from the marine environment.

• In 1984, the treaty parties to the LDC debated the "legality" of seabed burial of HLW. A strong majority of the parties concluded that it was dumping under the LDC, and therefore prohib-ited since HLW is on the Annex I "black list." The U.S. opposed this view, contending that HLW is not covered by the LDC, and therefore not prohibited.

• The U.S. delegation to future meetings of the LDC should reverse its position and support the majority view on this important issue, and should lend its full support to the application of rigorous criteria along the lines noted in the recommended action before any consideration is given to the possibility of amending the LDC to allow such practices.

### RECOMMENDATION
**The Administrator of the National Oceanic and Atmospheric Administration should support the United States delegation to London Dumping Convention meetings to resist any efforts to abandon or diminish the use of "black list" and "grey list" emissions control annexes, and examine other criteria for regulating ocean dumping, such as water quality standards, as complementary measures to such annexes.**

• At recent meetings of the London Dumping Convention (LDC) treaty parties, intersessional gatherings, some individuals, including one or more U.S. officials, have expressed a desire for the LDC parties to consider abandoning, diminishing or relaxing the use of black list/grey list annexes. Those annexes are a foundation of the LDC, and are critical to its success in ensuring effective protection of the marine environment.

Under U.S. law, the Ocean Dumping Act and the Clean Water Act appropriately require both emissions control-type lists and other environmental quality criteria. Both are needed, and U.S. delegations to LDC meetings should make clear their strong support for continuation and strengthening of both approaches, and others that will ensure protection of the marine environment.

45

## BUDGET RECOMMENDATION
F.Y. 90: **no change**     F.Y. 91: **no change**

## PRINCIPAL AUTHORIZING LEGISLATION
Ocean Dumping Act, P.L. 96-572, 33 U.S.C. 1401 et seq. (1972)
London Dumping Convention 26 U.S.T. 2403, TIAS 8165 (1972)

## CONGRESSIONAL JURISDICTION
**House Authorizing Committee/Subcommittee**
Committee on Merchant Marine and Fisheries
Subcommittee on Oceanography
**Senate Authorizing Committee/Subcommittee**
Committee on Environment and Public Works
Subcommittee on Environmental Protection
**House Appropriations Subcommittee**
Subcommittee on Commerce, State and Judiciary
**Senate Appropriations Subcommittee**
Subcommittee on Commerce, State and Judiciary

## RELEVANT STUDIES
**Sea Changes? Ocean Dumping and International Regulation**, Georgetown Int. Env. Law Review, Vol. 1: issue 1 (Spring 1988)
**Emplacement of High Level Radioactive Waste: Comparison of LOS, LDC and Domestic Law**, by C. Curtis, The Oceanic Society (June 1988)

## RELATED FEDERAL PROGRAMS
EPA's Office of International Activities
DOS Bureau of OES/Law of the Sea

## PRINCIPAL SOURCES OF EXPERTISE
The Oceanic Society — 202-328-0098

## IMPLEMENTATION STEPS
(1)   Address this issue in the Ocean Dumping Advisory Committee, after internal and interagency governmental input/preliminary actions consistent with recommendation.
(2)   National Oceanic and Atmospheric Administration officials should take immediate steps to meet with key representatives of other nations in order to achieve widespread acceptance and ratification, by the United States and all other nations, for the 1982 Law of the Sea Convention, either as-is or amended, to address reasonable United States concerns regarding provisions dealing with seabed mining.
(3)   The Administrator of the National Oceanic and Atmospheric Administration should suspend efforts to finalize regulations for commercial recovery of manganese nodules and support an increase in appropriations for research.

## NOTES:

## Blueprint for the Environment

# Blueprint for the Environment

## FISHERIES

# DEPARTMENT OF COMMERCE
National Oceanic and Atmospheric Administration
National Marine Fisheries Service
Office of Protected Resources and Habitat Protection

**RECOMMENDATION**

**The Administrator of the National Oceanic and Atmospheric Administration should standardize management of protected species to facilitate the identification and recovery of vulnerable stocks and species covered under the Endangered Species Act and Marine Mammal Protection Act.**

- Steps to accomplish this are:
  1) Developing a candidate species list of marine species including fish, invertebrates and grasses for listing under the Endangered Species Act;
  2) Determining the status of marine mammal stocks which are subject to interactions with fisheries;
  3) Developing and implementing recovery and/or conservation plans for species listed under the Endangered Species Act and species and stocks listed as depleted under the Marine Mammal Protection Act;
  4) Revising regulations covering permits for scientific research and display of protected species.

**RECOMMENDATION**

**The Administrator of the National Oceanic and Atmospheric Administration should shift the federal living marine resource research and management program from a single species focus to a multi-species/ecosystem approach as outlined in the Ecosystem Monitoring and Fisheries Management Program Development Plan.**

- Fisheries Management as currently practiced in the United States relies on the concept of maximum sustainable yield and catch. Effort data for each stock of fish for the most part has a single-species focus. This method of management only takes into account the interactions between the fish and the fishermen and does not sufficiently address environmental parameters in the management equation. In many respects this form of management has proven ineffective.

- A shift in the emphasis of fisheries management is needed to account for the regional variations in the total marine ecosystem. Such an approach is necessary to understand the many climatic, interspecies, and human-induced factors that affect the size of fish stocks. An increased level of coordination and communication between and among the various National Oceanic and Atmospheric Administration agencies is imperative for the shift to be effective.

47

## BUDGET RECOMMENDATION
F.Y. 90: **Increase** of $ 2.5 million    F.Y. 91: **Increase** of $ 5.0 million

## PRINCIPAL AUTHORIZING LEGISLATION
Endangered Species Act, September 30, 1985
Marine Mammal Protection Act — September 30, 1988

## CONGRESSIONAL JURISDICTION
**House Authorizing Committee/Subcommittee**
  Committee on Merchant Marine and Fisheries
    Subcommittee on Fisheries and Wildlife Conservation and the Environment
**Senate Authorizing Committee/Subcommittee**
  Committee on Environment and Public Works
    Subcommittee on Environmental Protection (ESA)
  Committee on Commerce, Science and Transportation
    Subcommittee on National Ocean Policy Study (MMPA)
**House Appropriations Subcommittee**
  Subcommittee on Commerce, Justice, State and Judiciary
**Senate Appropriations Subcommittee**
  Subcommittee on Commerce, Justice, State, the Judiciary and Related Agencies

## RELEVANT STUDIES
Annual Reports of National Marine Fisheries Service and Marine Mammal Commission on MMPA
Selected Marine Mammals of Alaska — Species Accounts with Research and Management Recommendations — Marine Mammal Commission
General Accounting Office Report on Protected Species Programs — in preparation

## RELATED FEDERAL PROGRAMS
Marine Mammal Commission, Fish and Wildlife Service
Office of Endangered Species

## PRINCIPAL SOURCES OF EXPERTISE
Center for Environmental Education — 202-829-5609
Greenpeace — 202-462-1177        American Cetacean Society — 703-920-0076
Humane Society of the United States — 202-452-1100
Environmental Defense Fund — 202-387-3500
Defenders of Wildlife — 202-659-9510

## IMPLEMENTATION STEPS
(1)  Develop plan to regularize the listing process under the ESA.
(2)  Develop a candidate species list — solicit suggestions from interested parties.
(3)  Establish priorities for research to determine OSP levels.
(4)  Revise regulations governing scientific and display permitting.

**BUDGET HISTORY** (in millions of dollars by fiscal year)

|  | 79 | 81 | 83 | 85* | 87* | 88* | |
|---|---|---|---|---|---|---|---|
| Authorized | 2.5 | 3.0 | 3.5 | 3.5 | | | ESA |
| | 8.5 | 9.5 | 8.0 | 8.8 | 8.8 | 8.8 | MMPA |
| Appropriated | 2.095 | 2.543 | 2.939 | 3.652 | 3.114 | 3.364 | ESA |
| | 7.042 | 7.080 | 7.475 | 9.225 | 7.177 | 8.307 | MMPA |

* Under the MMPA an additional $4.0 million is authorized for period October 1, 1984 — September 30, 1988 for a trends in abundance study of dolphin stocks in the eastern tropical Pacific

## Blueprint for the Environment

# Blueprint for the Environment

## FISHERIES

# DEPARTMENT OF COMMERCE

**RECOMMENDATION**

**The Administrator fo the National Oceanic and Atmospheric Administration should request additional funding for the enforcement activities of the National Marine Fisheries Service.**

• An increase in resources is needed if the laws governing such things as protecting endangered species and marine mammals or fishing methods and quotas are to be enforced. Over the last year, enforcement agents have averaged between 90 and 95 officers for the entire United States. Such a situation has required shifting officers from area to area to meet crisis situations.

• Programs currently underfunded include fisheries enforcement and marine mammal operations off Alaska, salmon enforcement in the Pacific Northwest (where only one or two agents are able to do marine mammal work), fisheries enforcement on Georges Bank, Threatened and Endangered enforcement in the Gulf of Mexico and regulation of whale watching activities. This situation is complicated by increased responsibilities, such as enforcing new Threatened and Endangered regulations.

**RECOMMENDATION**

**The Administrator of the National Oceanic and Atmospheric Administration should determine allowable biological catch for fisheries based upon the best scientific evidence. Regional fishery management councils should then allocate this catch among user groups.**

**RECOMMENDATION**

**The Administrator of the National Oceanic and Atmospheric Administration should conduct an evaluation and assessment of incidental catch in marine fisheries and recommend policy and technological changes.**

• The dramatic innovations in fishing technology that followed World War II have aggravated the problem of incidental catch. Each year, billions of pounds of marine life are incidentally captured in the larger synthetic nets used today. This catch is made up of species that may or may not have any direct commercial worth and of species that have a special status, such as marine mammals and endangered and threatened species.

**RECOMMENDATION**

**The Secretaries of the Interior, Agriculture and Commerce should improve the efficiency and effectiveness of federal fisheries management by consolidating and strengthening integration and coordination of now-fragmented staff and functions of those various agencies.**

• The Secretaries should direct an immediate, comprehensive, joint assessment of all federal fisheries research and management activities as now conducted by the Fish and Wildlife

49

Service (FWS) in the Department of the Interior, National Marine Fisheries Service (NMFS) and the National Oceanic and Atmospheric Administration (NOAA) in the Department of Commerce, and the Cooperative State Research Service (CSRS) in the Department of Agriculture, and other federal enti-ties, to achieve the goal stated in the recommendation above to achieve an effective federal fisheries research and management program capable of addressing the many urgent problems facing our saltwater, anadromous and freshwater fisheries resources.

## RECOMMENDATION
**The Administrator of the National Oceanic and Atmospheric Administration should expand existing programs to provide opportunities for private sector/nonfederal participation in federal fisheries management, hereafter called "partnerships," and review agency operations to formulate recommendations for creation of new opportunities.**

• Due to projected severe budget shortfalls in the near future it appears likely that sufficient funding and manpower to manage an increasingly scarce fisheries resource will not be available. The future of federal fisheries management will rely increasingly on private sector/nonfederal partnerships. Federal agencies with fisheries responsibilities already have in place some mechanisms to facilitate these partnerships. This proposal calls for expansion of existing, successful mechanisms, and investigation of potential new opportunities for private sector/nonfederal participation in fisheries management.

## RECOMMENDATION
**The Administrator of the National Oceanic and Atmospheric Administration should request a comprehensive study of the funding needs of the National Marine Fisheries Service's fish and wildlife resource programs and recommend alternatives for providing the proper funding level, with special attention given to developing sound user fee proposals.**

## RECOMMENDATION
**The Administrator of the National Oceanic and Atmospheric Administration and the Commerce Secretary should actively pursue full funding for the United States Antarctic Marine Living Resources Program of directed research.**

# Blueprint for the Environment

## COASTS

## DEPARTMENT OF COMMERCE
### National Oceanic and Atmospheric Administration

**RECOMMENDATION**

**The Administrator of the National Oceanic and Atmospheric Administration of the Department of Commerce should carry out diverse activities in support of COASTWEEKS '89 as the initial event of the YEAR OF THE COAST 1990.**

• Raising the public awareness of the beauty and value of the coastline, both salt and fresh water, is an ongoing responsibility of the federal natural resource agencies. The President as the chief administrative officer of the nation should call the agencies to their task.

• Building upon the experience of the last seven years, COASTWEEKS has become a national celebration. The last YEAR OF THE COAST was in 1980. Both projects were the ac-

complishments of a network of national organizations, state and local governments, citizen groups and marine industrial organizations. Both help to focus public attention on the value of the coast and the dangers of further degradation of its vitality and to educate people about the importance of protecting, conserving and restoring our salt water and fresh water coastlines.

**RECOMMENDATION**

**The Administrator of the National Oceanic and Atmospheric Administration should provide stable funding for the Coastal Zone Management Program through at least 1995 to enhance the protection and wise management of our nation's coastal resources.**

**RECOMMENDATION**

**The Administrator of the National Oceanic and Atmospheric Administration should support a strong federal consistency requirement to enhance the protection and wise management of our nation's coastal resources.**

**RECOMMENDATION**

**The Administrator of the National Oceanic and Atmospheric Administration should make the Coastal Zone Management Program more active and effective in addressing emerging issues of public concern such as coastal pollution, sea level rise, coastal hazards and estuarine protection.**

**RECOMMENDATION**

**The Administrator of the National Oceanic and Atmospheric Administration should work to foster a cooperative relationship between Ocean and Coastal Resource Management, the coastal states and the Management Act's environmental community.**

## BUDGET RECOMMENDATION
F.Y. 90: **no change**          F.Y. 91: **no change**

## PRINCIPAL AUTHORIZING LEGISLATION
None

## CONGRESSIONAL JURISDICTION
**House Authorizing Committee/Subcommittee**
Committee on Merchant Marine and Fisheries
Subcommittee on Fisheries and Wildlife and Conservation
Committee on Interior and Insular Affairs
Subcommittee on Energy and the Environment
**Senate Authorizing Committee/Subcommittee**
Committee on Commerce, Science and Transportation
Subcommittee on National Ocean Policy Study
Committee on Environment and Public Works
Subcommittee on Environmental Protection
**House Appropriations Subcommittee**
Subcommittee on Commerce, State and Judiciary
**Senate Appropriations Subcommittee**
Subcommittee on Commerce, State and Judiciary

## RELEVANT STUDIES
**And Two If By Sea: Fighting the Attack on America's Coasts**, by Beth Millemann, Coast Alliance (1986)

## RELATED FEDERAL PROGRAMS
National SeaShore Parks
Minerals Management Systems
Dept. Commerce
National Fish and Wildlife Service
Dept. Interior
Coastal Zone Management
Sea Grant Programs
EPA

## PRINCIPAL SOURCES OF EXPERTISE
Sierra Club — 202-547-1141
League of Women Voters — 617-349-2834
Coast Alliance — 202-265-5518
Coastal States Organization — 202-628-9636
The Oceanic Society — 202-328-0098

## IMPLEMENTATION STEPS
(1) Executive Order/Proclamation by President of the United States.
(2) Designation of Steering Committee of Departments of Commerce, the Interior, Agriculture, and the Environmental Protection Agency to design and oversee the federal role in COASTWEEKS '89 and YEAR OF THE COAST 1990

## NOTES:

## Blueprint for the Environment

# Blueprint for the Environment

## INITIATIVES

## DEPARTMENT OF COMMERCE

**RECOMMENDATION**
**The Secretary of Commerce should develop and support legislation to designate national water efficiency standards for plumbing fixtures and products in order to provide for the conservation and protection of the nation's water resources, and to maintain an orderly national market for such products.**

• New technology to improve the performance of plumbing fixtures is available commercially but the installation of these water-conserving fixtures represents a small share of the market. The potential savings are huge and could both substitute for supplies from new reservoirs to meet growing populations, and reduce the overload on existing waste water treatment plants and septic systems. Households could reduce their indoor water consumption by up to 25 percent simply by installing currently-available water closets that use 1.6 gallons per flush, instead of a 5 gallon flush toilet, in new construction and renovations. Efficient washers and showers save energy as well as water.
• Some local jurisdictions have exercised

regulatory authority to improve water use efficiency standards for plumbing fixtures, but these varying standards can create manufacturing, marketing, and inventory problems for manufacturers serving national markets. Uniform national standards would facilitate the manufacture and installation of state-of-the-art water conservation fixtures.
• Substantial federal and local investment has been made in water supply and waste water treatment facilities. Water conservation achieved through the installation of conserving fixtures will reduce the operating costs of existing facilities and lessen the requirements for expensive new facilities.

**RECOMMENDATION**
**The Commerce Department should establish a moratorium on the issuance of animal patents to allow full consideration of the environmental consequences of producing genetically engineered animals.**

• Animal patenting is at a legal and political turning point that will have long-term implications for the future of the nation's wildlife. Availability of patents for animal inventions will encourage rapid development of animal engineering techniques that may pose risks and/or undesirable changes to the environment and wild species of animals. Genetically engineered animals — animals containing a mix of characteristics unlike any existing in nature — will either intentionally or inadvertently be released to the environment. Scientists cannot predict how genetically engineered animals will affect

other wildlife — whether they will replace existing animals, destroy food needed by other organisms or shift natural balances the way the gypsy moth, the Japanese beetle and the kudzu vine have done.
• A moratorium will allow the time needed to put in place necessary regulations before providing the powerful commercial incentive of patenting for the development of genetically engineered animals. A moratorium will also provide opportunity for Congressional and public debate on the impacts of patenting animal life.

## RECOMMENDATION
**The Environmental Protection Agency should develop a methodology for lifecycle costing that incorporates the social, environmental and economic costs of producing and disposing products and packaging materials. The Department of Commerce should then require that the methodology be adopted by all vendors of wholesale and retail products.**

- The three goals of lifecycle costing should be to:
  1) make product prices to manufacturers and consumers reflect the true costs to society of using those items;
  2) educate consumers about the environmental and social impacts of the products they buy so they can make informed choices; and
  3) encourage durability as a major form of waste reduction. The goal is to preserve natural resources, minimize litter and minimize the creation of pollution caused by unnecessary virgin-material production and use.

## RECOMMENDATION
**The Administrator of the National Oceanic and Atmospheric Administration should develop proposals for new sanctuary sites, particularly in Alaska and the Northwest Atlantic; should prepare a plan for designating at least one new site each year to the year 2000; should designate and finalize management plans for Flower Garden Banks, Outer Coast of Washington, Monterey Bay, and Northern Puget Sound; and should increase support for research and education activities at all sanctuaries.**

- The national marine sanctuary program provides a unique means of providing special protection to outstanding marine areas of national significance due to their ecological, scientific, biological, recreational, or historical values. Since 1972 only seven sites have been established; only one site was established in the last eight years. At the same time, several sites have been rejected for little reason and research and education at existing sanctuaries has withered.

## RECOMMENDATION
**The Department of Commerce should require that its agencies or bureaus develop and distribute environmental education programs and materials dealing with all appropriate natural resource related activities of the Department of Commerce.**

- Specific responsibilities for environmental education should be assigned to an office within each agency, a mission statement and objectives developed, and appropriate staff and funding provided. Among the programs that could be developed are in-service training of agency staff who should be trained in the practices and programs of environmental education.
- Agencies should develop environmental education materials for distribution through formal and nonformal education programs to the general public. Agencies should also provide technical assistance to state and local governments, schools, and private organizations which share the Federal government's concern over the environment. All materials should present balanced and objective information on natural resource topics.

Blueprint for the Environment

# Blueprint for the Environment

# DEPARTMENT OF DEFENSE

Twenty years ago, Congress authorized the formation of a National Water Commission to review water resources problems and policies. The Commission's final report in 1973 was a major landmark in American natural resources management, containing far-reaching recommendations for greater non-federal financial responsibility for water resources development, more innovative non-structural approaches to water related problems, and greater attention to environmental values in the management of water resources.

Since that time, the implementation of these reforms has been fitful and uneven. The use of water is so closely bound up with economic activity and patterns of human settlement that water resources policy has been and will continue to be a highly political issue. The federal government spends well over $4 billion per year on water resources development, along with additional billions for such related programs as navigation aids, flood insurance, disaster assistance, wetlands and water quality protection, and wastewater treatment. State prerogatives over the allocation and use of water are jealously guarded, and the bureaucratic inertia behind development plans that are decades in the making has been notoriously formidable.

The Water Resources Development Act of 1986 reflects a belated but enormously significant political consensus regarding the need for fiscal and environmental reform of the Corps of Engineers civil works construction program. After a decade of increasing budgetary strictures, sharp environmental controversies, and a lack of new construction projects, the Corps program has been redirected toward greater state and local participation in project planning and financing, and more meaningful accommodation of environmental concerns. Greater non-federal cost-sharing and stronger environmental accountability are leading the Corps program to structural and non-structural measures that are more in tune with contemporary problems, opportunities and values, rather than grandiose feats of civil engineering or politically contrived make-work projects.

Reduced federal funds for new water resources development and wastewater treatment, along with rising costs for municipal borrowing as a result of tax law changes, will require improved management of public water supplies and innovative approaches toward meeting future needs. Water conservation is taking on new importance, and has major potential under current and foreseeable economic conditions to compete favorably with traditional structural water supply measures. Currently, technology is available to greatly improve the efficiency of water use. In recognition of these benefits, the Corps of Engineers should take steps to facilitate water conservation.

Existing laws, institutions, and practices, largely at the state level, often impede the sale or exchange of water. In some states, those who conserve water may actually be penalized, through a loss of water rights. Nevertheless, the sale, lease and banking of water and water rights is stimulating new interest in water marketing. With appropriate regulation to account for potential environmental effects and protection of basins of origin, such markets may be able to supply new users without the adverse consequences of the construction of major new facilities. As the states adopt policies that encourage water marketing while protecting environmental resources, federal statutes and regulations conflicting with this approach should be modified.

The Corps should seek to improve the management of existing surface and ground water supplies, including re-regulating discharges from existing reservoirs to meet contemporary needs. In particular, many older projects that pre-date environmental planning procedures need significant operational, and in some cases, facility changes, to provide added public benefits such as habitat restoration and public recreation, or different levels of benefits in functions such as water supply, flood protection, power generation, or navigation than the projects were originally designed to provide.

Global warming and sea-level rise also pose far-reaching challenges for shore protection and municipal and agricultural water supplies nationwide. With the rate of climate change uncertain, and the pattern of weather conditions becoming increasingly variable, federal water resources agencies need flexible management strategies that allow them to respond to changing conditions in a cost effective way.

The National Dam Inventory of the Corps of Engineers has identified some 68,000 major dams already constructed on the nation's waterways. In recent years, it has been repeated in many circles and in the halls of Congress that the dam building era in the United States is largely over, due in part to the fact that most potential water development sites are already in use. Clearly, the future in water resources is in management, not development, and this represents a fundamental change for the Corps of Engineers.

# Blueprint for the Environment

## WATERWAYS

## DEPARTMENT OF DEFENSE
### DEPARTMENT OF THE ARMY
### ASSISTANT SECRETARY for Civil Works
### Army Corps of Engineers
### Office of the Chief of Engineers

### RECOMMENDATION
**The Assistant Secretary of the Army should support legislation that would require that fifty percent of the costs of operating and maintaining the Inland Waterway Navigation System of the U.S. Army Corps of Engineers be provided from the Inland Waterways Trust Fund and through additional user fees for use of Corps facilities.**

• The 1986 Water Resources Development Act imposed a gradually increasing tax on diesel fuel used in commercial waterway transportation, dedicating the funds to new construction activities on the inland waterway system. The Act requires all new construction to be at least 50 percent cost-shared from the Trust Fund. However, none of these funds may be used for operation and maintenance and most rehabilitation activities.

• All operation and maintenance costs are currently borne at 100 percent U.S. taxpayer expense, creating no incentive for the barge industry to share in the planning efforts to cut costs and identify operation and maintenance priorities. This situation further encourages the Corps to carry out channel straightening and dredging projects under the Operation and Maintenance budget category that may not represent the priorities of the commercial users and may not be necessary. Because no market test is applied, the maintenance projects go forward at full federal expense, often with significant and unnecessary environmental harm.

• Barge operators are currently allowed to help identify priorities for construction projects. By requiring that the costs of inland waterway operation and maintenance will also be cost-shared, the barge industry could be joined with the Corps in identifying those efficiency improvements and operation and maintenance projects that are of most importance to commercial navigation.

• The Secretary should develop and support legislation to establish a schedule of user fees for Corps navigation facilities to supplement the non-federal contribution of operating and maintaining the inland waterway system.

### RECOMMENDATION
**The Administration should support legislation that would require marine diesel fuel taxes or other user fees to pay for the construction and maintenance of the waterway system.**

• No more than 20 percent of the costs of the construction of locks and dams for barge navigation and the maintenance of barge channels are paid for by the commercial users of the waterway system. Yet maintenance of this system is a continuing source of environmental problems, from alteration of critical riverine habitats to toxic pollution of water resources, as a result of dredging and dredge-spoil disposal.

## BUDGET RECOMMENDATION
F.Y. 90: **anticipate** $ 180 million in revenues F.Y. 91: **no change**

## PRINCIPAL AUTHORIZING LEGISLATION
Water Resources Development Act of 1986

## CONGRESSIONAL JURISDICTION
**House Authorizing Committee/Subcommittee**
    Committee on Public Works and Transportation
        Subcommittee on Water Resources
    Committee on Ways and Means
**Senate Authorizing Committee/Subcommittee**
    Committee on Environment and Public Works
        Subcommittee on Water Resources, Transportation, and Infrastructure
    Committee on Finance
**House Appropriations Subcommittee**
    Subcommittee on Energy and Water Development
**Senate Appropriations Subcommittee**
    Subcommittee on Energy and Water Development

## RELEVANT STUDIES
**Fragile Foundations: A Report on America's Public Works**, National Council on Public Works Improvement (February 1988)

## RELATED FEDERAL PROGRAMS

## PRINCIPAL SOURCES OF EXPERTISE
Friends of the Earth — 202-543-4312    National Wildlife Federation — 202-797-6800

## IMPLEMENTATION STEPS
(1) Secretary of the Army should develop legislation for submittal to Congress which requires 50 percent of Operations and Maintenance costs of Inland Waterways to be cost-shared from the Inland Waterways Trust Fund and user fees for Corps facilities.
(2) Hearings and opportunity for Administration testimony should be sought in the House and Senate Public Works Committees.
(3) Draft legislation increasing waterway fuel tax from 10 cents per gallon or 20 percent of operation and maintenance costs for locks, dams and maintenance dredging to 50 cents per gallon in 1990.
(4) The Assistant Secretary of the Army for Civil Works should review all remaining elements of the Mississippi River and Tributaries Project that are authorized but unbuilt.
    First authorized in 1928, the Mississippi River and Tributaries project is actually a collection of projects in seven states of the Lower Mississippi Valley. The authorized project consists of main stem levee and channel work, most of which is complete, and tributary drainage work, much of which remains to be built. Most of this remaining backlog is exempt from the local cost-sharing requirements enacted in 1986, and nearly all the remaining work involves substantial environmental impact.
    Within the full extent of existing authority, the Assistant Secretary should modify the project to: place greater emphasis on predominantly non-structural measures; protect and restore wetlands; remove incentives for clearing and draining lands for the production of surplus agricultural commodities; deauthorize obsolete features; and reduce federal outlays. Where necessary, the Assistant Secretary should develop and support legislation needed to accomplish these modifications.

## NOTES:

——————— **Blueprint for the Environment** ———————

## WETLANDS

# DEPARTMENT OF DEFENSE
## DEPARTMENT OF THE ARMY
## ASSISTANT SECRETARY for Civil Works
## Army Corps of Engineers

### RECOMMENDATION
**The Assistant Administrator for Water should establish clear wetlands mitigation policy requiring sequencing (avoidance first, compensation last) for all Clean Water Act Section 404 permits, and require full compensation in instances of unavoidable impacts to wetlands.**

• There are currently several different mitigation policies for wetlands now used by the various federal agencies. These inconsistencies should be eliminated and clear guidance given to the agencies charged with mitigation. Their policies need to be strengthened and must do more to protect wetlands as well as to offset fully those losses to wetlands that must occur.

### RECOMMENDATION
**The Assistant Administrator for Water should promulgate biological water quality standards for the protection of wetlands functions.**

• The Environmental Protection Agency (EPA) should use its authority under sections 303 and 304 of the Clean Water Act (CWA) to encourage states to promulgate water quality standards protecting wetlands. State water quality standards play an important role in protecting waters from pollutants that degrade water quality. A state can block the issuance of a federal permit or license that does not comply with its water quality standards (§401 of the CWA).

### RECOMMENDATION
**The Army Corps of Engineers should strengthen and clarify the Government's wetlands mitigation policy.**

• Considerable confusion exists over the government's policy on mitigating wetland losses. The Army Corps of Engineers (Corps) has implemented a policy which applied mitigation as a means of avoiding regulatory prohibitions against filling of wetlands. In some Corps Districts, abuses in mitigation banking, unwarranted off-site compensation of wetland losses or compensation of losses with different types of wetlands from those converted have resulted in significant loss of certain types of wetlands (e.g. , seasonal wetlands). A clear, consistent statement of regulatory policies on this topic would add uniformity to the program and prevent future wetland losses through application of an unfavorable wetland mitigation policy.

# RECOMMENDATION

## The Army Corps of Engineers should address cumulative wetlands losses in individual and general permit applications.

• The tragedy of wetland losses is that although they are occurring in small increments around the country, entire watersheds may be lost through these fills. Small, incremental losses can profoundly affect wetland hydrology or an ecosystem's biological productivity. The 404 program, as it focuses on issuances of individual permits, has no present mechanism for examining cumulative losses, let alone wetland losses that are not generated by issuance of a 404 permit.

• Implementation of §404 (issuance of dredge and fill permits) should assess the cumulative losses from individual dredge and fill permit applications, and from the reliance on general or nationwide permits.

## BUDGET RECOMMENDATION

F.Y. 90: **no change**     F.Y. 91: **no change**

## PRINCIPAL AUTHORIZING LEGISLATION

National Environmental Policy Act
Water Resources Act of 1986
Fish and Wildlife Coordination Act
Clean Water Act

## CONGRESSIONAL JURISDICTION

**House Authorizing Committee/Subcommittee**
Committee on Merchant Marine and Fisheries
Subcommittee on Fish and Wildlife Conservation and the Environment
Committee on Public Works and Transportation
Subcommittee on Water Resources
**Senate Authorizing Committee/Subcommittee**
Committee on Environment and Public Works
Subcommittee on Environmental Protection
Committee on Energy and Natural Resources
Subcommittee on Water and Power
**House Appropriations Subcommittee**
Subcommittee on Interior
**Senate Appropriations Subcommittee**
Subcommittee on Interior and Related Agencies

## RELEVANT STUDIES

**Wetlands: Their Use and Regulation** (1984)
**Wetlands of the United States: Current Status and Recent Trends**
GAO Report on the Corps-EPA Implementation of Section 404 of the Clean Water Act (1988)

## RELATED FEDERAL PROGRAMS

Similar alignments need to be made in a number of other federal agencies charged with implementing and enforcing mitigation for wetlands alterations. The most important of these include:
Army Corps of Engineers     Federal Highway Administration
U.S. Department of the Interior     Department of Commerce
Council on Environmental Quality     Federal Energy Regulatory Commission

## PRINCIPAL SOURCES OF EXPERTISE

National Wildlife Federation — 202-797-6876     National Audubon Society — 202-547-9009
Environmental Defense Fund — 202-387-3500

## Blueprint for the Environment

# Blueprint for the Environment

## PLANNING

## DEPARTMENT OF DEFENSE
### DEPARTMENT OF THE ARMY
### ASSISTANT SECRETARY for Civil Works
### Army Corps of Engineers
### Office of the Chief of Engineers

**RECOMMENDATION**

**The Assistant Secretary of the Army should initiate the study, authorized by Congress in 1986, of the potential costs and impacts of rising sea-level and its implications for the shoreline protection and beach erosion control policies of the Corps of Engineers and coastal communities.**

• Authority for this study, called the Study of Rising Oceans, was provided in Section 731 of the Water Resources Development Act of 1986 (P.L. 99-662, 100 Stat. 4165). However, funding has neither been requested nor appropriated to begin the study since the authorization.

• It is obvious that a significant rise in ocean levels caused by climate change would have extremely far-reaching effects on the coastal zone, among them losses of wetlands and wildlife habitat, increases in flooding and flood damages, permanent inundation of low-lying areas, implications for location of new public facilities and other development, water quality and water supply effects and many others. While the Corps study would address only a limited range of these concerns, potential for sea-level rise has critically important implications for Corps water development which should be immediately considered. Most Corps projects have expected lives of 50 or more years, well within the time horizons raised by climate scientists.

• In addition, the Assistant Secretary should consider development and support for further legislation to authorize studies of other aspects of sea-level rise and climate change which affect water resources.

**RECOMMENDATION**

**The Assistant Secretary of the Army should review the operation of all reservoirs and water resource developments under the Corps of Engineers' jurisdiction and make recommendations for adding fish and wildlife management and recreation as project purposes, both within project boundaries and downstream of Corps reservoirs.**

• The inclusion of recreational boating and fishing will improve environmental and recreation management of existing Corps of Engineers reservoirs and water resource developments. The Secretary should develop and support legislation, where necessary, to provide these additional benefits.

• In recent years it has become apparent that many older Corps projects were authorized before modern planning requirements caused fish and wildlife and recreation needs to be addressed in project designs. Many projects can be better managed for great public benefit if operations, and, in some cases, facilities, are modified to provide these benefits. Often management or operations can be instituted or have already been instituted without impact on original project purposes.

61

## BUDGET RECOMMENDATION
F.Y. 90: $ 1 million (start-up funds)    F.Y. 91: $ 2 million
For Reservoir and Water Resource Review:
F.Y. 90: **Increase** of $ 500,000          F.Y. 91: **no change**

## PRINCIPAL AUTHORIZING LEGISLATION
Water Resources Development Act of 1986 (P.L. 99-662)

## CONGRESSIONAL JURISDICTION
**House Authorizing Committee/Subcommittee**
  Committee on Public Works and Transportation
    Subcommittee on Water Resources
**Senate Authorizing Committee/Subcommittee**
  Committee on Environment and Public Works
    Subcommittee on Water Resources, Transportation, and Infrastructure
**House Appropriations Subcommittee**
  Subcommittee on Energy and Water Development
**Senate Appropriations Subcommittee**
  Subcommittee on Energy and Water Development

### RELEVANT STUDIES
**Greenhouse Effect and Sea Level Rise,** Michael Barth and James Titus eds., Van Nostrand Reinhold, 1984

U.S. Environmental Protection Agency, **"Impact of Sea Level Rise on Coastal Wetlands,"** Report, 1988

President's Commission on Americans Outdoors (Island Press) Mark Hunt of Sunburst Adventures

**Opportunities for the Future,** Address by Dave Brown (March 1985) Proceedings of the Outdoor Recreation Trends Conference

## RELATED FEDERAL PROGRAMS
Strategic Studies Program, Environmental Protection Agency
Federal Emergency Management Agency
U.S. Fish and Wildlife Service
National Park Service — Wild and Scenic Rivers Program
National Marine Fisheries Service — Anadromous Fish Restoration

## PRINCIPAL SOURCES OF EXPERTISE
Friends of the Earth — 202-543-4312
National Wildlife Federation — 202-797-6829

## IMPLEMENTATION STEPS
The Army Corps of Engineers should adopt rules stating that before any project will be constructed or permitted on a river on the Nationwide Rivers Inventory, this agency or another appropriate federal agency will study the affected river segment for possible inclusion in the National Wild and Scenic Rivers system. If the agency recommends that the river be designated, the Congress should have the opportunity to consider the designation.

## NOTES:

## Blueprint for the Environment

# Blueprint for the Environment

## POLLUTION

# DEPARTMENT OF DEFENSE

### RECOMMENDATION
**The Department of the Navy should implement P.L. 100-220 by implementing recommendations of the Ad Hoc Advisory Committee on Plastics in "Reducing Navy Marine Plastic Pollution," A Report by the Ad Hoc Advisory Committee on Plastics to the Assistant Secretary for the Navy for Shipbuilding and Logistics.**

• Each year, hundreds of thousands of marine mammals, birds, and sea turtles fall victim to plastic pollution in the ocean. The animals become entangled in plastic debris or ingest the plastic, leading to injury and often times death. One source of plastic garbage in the ocean is ships. In 1987, the United States ratified Annex V of the International Convention for the Prevention of Pollution from Ships, known as MARPOL. Annex V bans the discharge of plastics from all ships, except public vessels, and further restricts discharges of other garbage from ships. The Marine Plastic Pollution Research and Control Act of 1987 (P.L. 100-220, Title II) was enacted to implement Annex V. This new law requires public vessels of the U.S. to comply with the requirements of the Annex within five years. The U.S. Coast Guard has the responsibility to enforce the new law, and is currently developing regulations for its implementation. Navy personnel participated in an Ad Hoc Advisory Committee on Plastics, sponsored by the Keystone Center, which also included representatives from the environmental community and Congressional staff. The Committee prepared a report and recommendations to assist the Navy in complying with the new law. Implementation of those recommendations is expected to enable the Navy to meet its obligations under the new law.

### RECOMMENDATION
**The Assistant Secretary of the Army should request authority from Congress to impose a fee of two dollars per cubic yard of dredge spoil materials dumped into the ocean. The fee should be charged to the non-Federal sponsor of any navigation project.**

• The ocean is a cost-free and convenient place to dump many materials which are difficult or controversial to dispose of on land. Control over the ocean dumping of harmful materials was established by law in 1972, with deadlines set to phase out the dumping of harmful sewage sludge. Approximately 80 million tons (60 million cubic yards) of material (sewage sludge, industrial waste, and dredge spoil) are dumped into the ocean annually under regulations and permits issued by the Corps of Engineers and the Environmental Protection Agency (EPA). Over 85 percent of the material dumped into the ocean is dredge-spoil from Corps of Engineers harbor deepening or maintenance.

• A dumping fee would supplement regulatory control, rather than be a substitute for such controls. A significant user fee would deter unnecessary ocean dumping and spur the search for economic, environmentally sound alternatives. Under current law, EPA collects very limited fees for ocean dumping and dump site designation, but Federal and local agencies, most notably including the Corps and local port operators, are exempt. These new fees would recover at least a part of the environmental and administrative costs associated with ocean dumping.

# RECOMMENDATION

**The Secretary of Defense should support the intent of the Master Agreement between the Department of Agriculture and the Department of Defense and encourage the creation of a military activity monitoring system.**

• The lands of the National Forest System have been used by the U.S. military to train forces since World War I. These lands are used for a number of reasons:

1) their unique terrain;
2) the lack of land on military bases; and
3) the maintenance of properly trained military forces for the national defense.

These reasons aside, the Forest Service and the Department of Defense (DOD) have no nationwide or regional record of the amount and the types of military activity on National Forest System lands. In 1987, the Forest Service verified the lack of a record of the military activity with the estimate "... in excess of 80 national forests receive some type of military use ..."

• Ironically, the military's need for land is in competition with the recreational demands on a number national forests. On a few national forests the public uses have collided with the military activity in the press and on the ground.

• The goal is to strike a proper balance between the public and military activity on the National Forest System. In pursuing that goal it is necessary to prevent and or discontinue military activity which involves the use of live munitions and pyrotechnics on national forest lands. These materials have the potential to cause harm to national forest visitors and Forest Service employees as well as damage to the environment.

• The liabilities associated with military ordnance do not justify their use on the National Forest System lands. Military activities that use ordnance should remain on Department of Defense managed lands.

**Blueprint for the Environment**

# Blueprint for the Environment

## DEPARTMENT OF EDUCATION

The first graduating class of the 21st century started school this Fall. Secretary of Education William J. Bennett recently estimated that almost 50 million children will attend elementary schools in the United States in the next decade. How are we preparing them to analyze and solve the complex array of environmental problems they will encounter? Blueprint for the Environment's recommendations are intended to put support for environmental education back on the federal government's agenda. They all underline the global nature and magnitude of environmental problems.

Responding to the building momentum and the broad public support for environmental initiatives following Earth Day in April of 1970, the United States Congress passed the Environmental Education Act (Public Law 91-516) in 1970. This legislation had broad bipartisan support and received unanimous approval by the Senate (64-0) and overwhelming support by the House (289-28). With passage of this Act in 1970, America was poised for international leadership in this important endeavor. The Act clearly identified what needed to be accomplished and how to do it.

Unfortunately, from the very beginning, administration and congressional support for the Act and its programs were largely rhetorical. Not once in the Act's 12 years of existence did appropriations even attain 50 percent of authorized funding levels. State Departments of Natural Resources and Education throughout the country had great expectations for the promised state/federal partnerships in the areas of teacher training, model curriculum development and community education programs.

When Congress decided not to extend the Act beyond 1982, total responsibility for these programs fell to the states. It is true that education, particularly content and implementation, is the prerogative of state and local governments. However, because of the interstate and international importance of environmental initiatives, the federal government should provide leadership, coordination, technical assistance and funds for model programs and materials.

Our recommendations are really quite simple. Though individually targeted throughout the Executive Branch of Government, they are unified by a single theme. Each recommendation is intended to better prepare citizens of today and tomorrow to participate in the development of informed and environmentally sound resource management decisions. We ask that the federal government once again assume an important leadership and coordinating role in the development of an environmentally literate citizenry.

The top three recommendations of the Environmental Education Task Force:

• The Secretary of Education should re-establish an Office of Environmental Education within the Department of Education.

• The Deputy Under Secretary for Intergovernmental and Interagency Affairs should develop guidelines and standards on the global nature of environmental problems for all federal agencies to follow in their environmental education programs.

• The President of the United States should issue an Executive Order requiring each federal agency to develop goals and objectives for environmental education. This statement should be developed from the recommendations of the proposed Office of Environmental Education and the National Advisory Council on Environmental Education.

# Blueprint for the Environment

## EDUCATION

# DEPARTMENT OF EDUCATION
ASSISTANT SECRETARY for Elementary and Secondary Education
Office of Environmental Education

### RECOMMENDATION
**The Secretary of Education should re-establish an Office of Environmental Education to provide leadership and coordination of environmental education activities throughout all federal agencies.**

• Little of the promise of the 1970 Environmental Education Act has been attained. The Act expired in 1982 and in its 12 year history all of its many worthwhile programs and activities were severely hampered by a lack of appropriations and direction. The environmental concerns that led to passage of the 1970 Act have worsened. There have been almost no funds for the past decade to assist states in implementing their own programs.

• Re-establishing an Office for Environmental Education would allow the following functions:

1) Act as the clearinghouse agent in the federal government for environmental education-related activities carried out by other agencies of the federal government.

2) Provide technical assistance to state and local governments developing environmental education components.

3) Assess the development of environmental education as well as conduct rigorous evaluations of environmental education programs.

4) Perform as a link between the formal educational community and environmental groups.

• The proposed Office of Environmental Education is not envisioned to be responsible for developing materials in-house. Because expertise in environmental education is diffused throughout the United States, what is needed to efficiently use this talent is a source of funding for material development, production, evaluation, implementation, and teacher training.

### RECOMMENDATION
**The Secretary of Education should appoint a National Advisory Council on Environmental Education to advise the Department on the establishment of programs and materials dealing with environmental education.**

• A broad-based council would be the most effective means to bring the best available expertise at the national level to assist in setting environmental education priorities and designing programs, and to infuse state and regional needs into the planning of national programs. Further, such a council would facilitate state and regional acceptance of national programs, thus improving efficiency of implementation. Finally, this council should work in coordination with the proposed Office of Environmental Education.

• This recommendation would encourage cooperation among the federal, state, and non-governmental organizations with interests in environmental education. The National Advisory Council on Environmental Education could also work with the secretary to encourage all these groups to develop and use national networks for the dissemination of materials and programs.

## BUDGET RECOMMENDATION
F.Y. 90: **Increase** of $20 million          F.Y. 91: **no change**

## PRINCIPAL AUTHORIZING LEGISLATION
Environmental Education Act of 1970 (P.L. 91-516)

## CONGRESSIONAL JURISDICTION
**House Authorizing Committee/Subcommittee**
Committee on Education and Labor
Subcommittee on Elementary, Secondary and Vocational Education
**Senate Authorizing Committee/Subcommittee**
Committee on Labor and Human Resources
Subcommittee on Education, Arts and Humanities
**House Appropriations Subcommittee**
Subcommittee on Labor, Health and Human Services and Education
**Senate Appropriations Subcommittee**
Subcommittee on Labor, Health and Human Services, Education and Related Agencies

## RELEVANT STUDIES
**Our Common Future.** 1987. The World Commission on Environment and Development — Chairman: Gro Harlem, Bruntland (Norway)
**First Lesson** — A Report on Elementary Education in America 1986. William J. Bennett, Secretary of Education.
**The Global 2000 Report to the President** — 1980 Council on Environmental Quality.
**Environmental Education Activities of Federal Agencies** 1978. Subcommittee on Environmental Education of Federal Interagency Committee on Education.
**Final Report** — Intergovernmental Conference on Environmental Education organized by UNESCO in cooperation with UNEP — Tibilisi (USSR) 1977.

## RELATED FEDERAL PROGRAMS

## PRINCIPAL SOURCES OF EXPERTISE
National Wildlife Federation — 703-790-4495
North American Association of Environmental Education — 513-698-6493
Alliance for Environmental Education — 202-797-4530
Western Regional Environmental Education Council — 916-971-1953
Edison Electric Institute — 202-778-6591
American Gas Association — 703-841-8670
Zero Population Growth — 202-332-2200
National Audubon Society — 212-832-3200

## NOTES:

## Blueprint for the Environment

# Blueprint for the Environment

## EDUCATION

## DEPARTMENT OF EDUCATION

**RECOMMENDATION**
**The Director of a proposed Office of Environmental Education should develop systems for nationwide dissemination of model or prototype environmental education programs.**

• Of primary importance in assuring the successful dissemination of materials and implementation of programs is the development of extensive training programs. The programs must include either preservice or inservice training of teachers as well as training of federal agency personnel, community and business leaders. Development of materials for mass media distribution is also an essential component of dissemination.

**RECOMMENDATION**
**The Assistant Secretaries for Elementary and Secondary Education, Vocational and Adult Education, and Postsecondary Education should develop environmental curriculum prototypes at every level of education from preschool through continuing education.**

• Although implementation of this action will be within the purview of state and local jurisdictions, the federal government should provide leadership and promote existing state environmental education initiatives. In most cases exemplary curricula exist within states. The responsibility for the federal government will be to evaluate and promote materials.
• This program could best be coordinated by a newly established Office of Environmental Education which would work with formal and nonformal education organizations, state and local Education Departments and others to develop a coordinated environmental education program for all ages so that all citizens are informed and empowered to act in an environmentally sensitive manner.

**RECOMMENDATION**
**The Director of State and Local Programs should develop and administer a challenge grant program that will match state monies to be used for hiring state coordinators of environmental education programs.**

**RECOMMENDATION**
**The Deputy Under Secretary for Intergovernmental and Interagency Affairs should develop guidelines and standards on global environmental problems for all federal agencies to follow in their environmental education programs.**

• Environmental problems such as acid precipitation, depletion of the ozone layer and ocean dumping of wastes are a few examples of issues that do not respect political boundaries. The loss of endangered species and the gene pools they represent is a concern of all nations. Nations, including the United States, cannot afford to be parochial in addressing environmental concerns.

• An emphasis on a global perspective in environmental education programs at the federal level is needed in the educational programs offered by all federal agencies and in agency decision making processes. Clearly, more effort is needed in developing our national guidelines and standards for environmental education, but this work should be done in the context of global environmental problems.

## RECOMMENDATION
**The Director of Federal Interagency Education and Interagency Programs should expand, oversee and, as necessary, develop prototype environmental education programs within all federal agencies dealing with natural resources and the environment.**

• Federal agencies have an opportunity through environmental education programs to assume a proactive posture toward resource management and environmental protection. Leadership and assistance in strengthening environmental education programs within federal agencies such as the Tennessee Valley Authority (TVA), National Park Service, United States (U.S.) Fish and Wildlife Service, U.S. Forest Service, Soil Conservation Service and Environmental Protection Agency are important aspects of an environmental education program.

• The Director should also seek to encourage establishment of cooperative partnerships among federal agencies, their state counterparts, and nongovernmental organizations. Such cooperation should include the development and support of national networks for distribution of programs and materials.

# DEPARTMENT OF ENERGY

The energy future of the United States is a critical determinant of our environmental future. The heavy dependence on fossil fuels is responsible for air pollution in our cities, acid rain that is damaging our forests, and a portion of the nitrogen pollution that is threatening our estuaries. Furthermore, fossil fuels are the major contributors to the increasing concentrations of carbon dioxide that are now irrevocably warming the earth's climate.

Unless the Department of Energy redirects energy trends in the next decade, a host of significant environmental problems will become increasingly unmanageable. Fossil fuels, directly and indirectly, are responsible for about 80 percent of the global warming problem. Only by redirecting U.S. energy policy and by encouraging other countries to do the same, can we prevent catastrophic climate change.

Increased investment in energy efficiency and a continuing gradual shift to renewable energy are the essential cornerstones of a sustainable energy policy. Not only are these two "alternatives" capable of protecting the environment, they can also be used to spur the economy. There are a host of energy efficiency improvements available today that are far more cost-effective than additional investments in fossil fuels. The cost of renewable energy sources continues to fall steadily, and many are ready to make an immediate contribution to the U.S. economy.

If the Department of Energy were to adopt a truly "least cost" national energy policy that allows all energy investments to compete on a fair economic basis, the nation could abandon its failed quest for a short-term energy self-sufficiency through large-supply projects, regardless of the economic and environmental costs. We must remove the unfair and costly tax subsidies now enjoyed by the fossil fuel and nuclear industries. We must begin to implement a policy that allows energy efficiency and renewable energy resources to compete with conventional resources on an equal basis — a "level playing field." Choosing these least-cost resources before more expensive ones will enhance U.S. economic competitiveness, while reducing fossil fuel and nuclear use and their associated environmental problems.

## Energy Efficiency

U.S. energy efficiency has improved by 25 percent since the early seventies, but this impressive U.S. performance was exceeded by Japan and many industrialized European countries. Today, improvement in U.S. energy efficiency again appears to be leveling off. Unfortunately, this progress slowed at a point at which the U.S. still must spend $200 billion more each year on energy supplies than it would have to at energy-efficiency levels already achieved in Japan.

Numerous studies in recent years show that there are extensive investments in improved energy efficiency that are far more cost-effective than investments in offshore oil or electricity from new power plants. Market barriers to improved energy efficiency forestall many of these investments. National policy must be directed to overcome these barriers through new energy pricing programs, utility and government loan programs, and mandatory federal efficiency standards for some technologies.

Sustained improvement in energy efficiency should be the central goal of U.S. energy policy. A national goal of investing in energy efficiency whenever it is less expensive than traditional sources of energy supply should be adopted. Improving energy efficiency by two to four percent annually, would allow a leveling off of fossil fuel use and create a key benchmark against which national energy policies can be measured. Market barriers to improved energy efficiency forestall many of these investments. National policy must be directed to overcoming these barriers via new energy pricing programs, utility and government loan programs, and mandatory federal efficiency standards for some technologies.

The feasibility of such a goal is demonstrated by the fact that the State of California, with some of the most effective energy efficiency programs in the country, achieved a 3.3 percent annual rate of improvement in its efficiency since the mid-seventies, while the nation achieved a rate of only two percent. Unfortunately, since the oil price collapse of 1986, our national energy efficiency has not improved at all.

## Renewable Energy

A sustainable energy future must one day be based on the use of renewable resources that are not depletable, that do not pollute, and that do not lead to global warming.

It has been a goal of U.S. energy policy since 1975 to hasten the development of renewable energy sources. Substantial investments have been made in biofuels, wind energy, geothermal energy, solar energy, and other sources. This combination of public and private investment led to numerous technological advances as well as substantial commercialization of wind power, alcohol fuels, and solar energy. If there were a "level playing field" in which renewable energy sources could compete fairly with conventional energy sources, the use of renewables would grow steadily. Unfortunately, market barriers, the lack of private investment, and resistance by established utilities have all kept growth in renewables to a snail's pace in the mid-eighties.

The boom and bust approach to renewable energy during the past decade must be replaced by a true national commitment and a program of gradual and steady progress. These new renewable energy

## Fossil Fuels

Fossil fuels currently supply the great majority of the energy consumed in the U.S. Since the early seventies, there has been an encouraging decrease in the use of oil and natural gas, partially offset by an increase in the use of more abundant but more environmentally damaging coal. After leveling off in the early eighties, fossil fuel use in the United States is again on the rise. These increases could overwhelm efforts to limit air pollution by requiring the use of abatement devices.

In the past, national energy policy assumed that the government should encourage increased use of fossil fuels. Today, information on global warming

Programs to improve the fuel efficiency of automobiles and the entire transportation system also need special emphasis. Fuel economy of new cars in the United States leveled off at 26 miles per gallon. New technologies are already available, however, that make far higher levels possible. A more-efficient fleet of cars would lower the country's oil-import bill, reduce urban air pollution, and slow global warming. A new national program of fuel economy standards and incentives to encourage their achievement should be seriously pursued, perhaps aiming at a fleet average of 50 miles per gallon by 2010.

programs must be carefully chosen, and funds must be spent in a rigorous and cost-effective manner. Renewable energy research and development programs should be increased at an average rate of 25 percent per year, tripling the size of the programs in five years and bringing them close to the level of support that existed in the early eighties. Special government-university-private councils should be set up to develop five-year renewable energy plans that include commercialization as well as basic research.

The Department of Energy has a responsibility to capitalize on improvements being made in the private sector that were originally encouraged by tax credits and other incentives. New programs should now be developed to cost-effectively support the commercialization of renewable energy sources. Such programs need broad national debate, but the essential focus should be on direct performance-based subsidies that reward only successful projects and that require that private capital be put at risk.

forces the rejection of this notion and urges instead a policy discouraging any increases in the total carbon output of the U.S. energy system. Specifically, federal efforts to develop new oil resources should be stopped and substantial effort must go to cleaning up existing use of coal via the use of abatement technologies and new clean coal technologies. Switching to synthetic fuels, including methanol from coal or natural gas, should not be considered a positive step. Tax policies, comprehensive air emissions policies, and an overall least-cost energy plan must all be part of such a strategy for the Department of Energy.

## Blueprint for the Environment

## Nuclear Power

Increased use of nuclear power may no longer be a viable energy strategy for the United States. Once considered an energy solution, nuclear power has become an environmental and economic problem.

The United States now has over 100 operating nuclear power plants. In recent years, serious questions have been raised about the technical soundness of those plants, the capability of utility company management to operate them safely, and the willingness of the Nuclear Regulatory Commission to serve as an honest watchdog. In the future, the Commission and the Department of Energy must be rededicated to ensuring safe operation of those plants and safely storing the radioactive waste that they create. Both problems are becoming increasingly unmanageable even without the building of additional nuclear plants.

Nuclear proponents are now arguing for the creation of a new generation of supposedly safe fission reactors, 1,000 of which would be required to supply one-fifth of U.S. electricity in 2020. The Department of Energy should not object to some limited research in this area. Such technologies should be put to the same kind of strict cost tests that are applied to efficiency and renewable energy technologies. Any proposed demonstration plants should be funded by private companies.

## Defense-Related Facilities

A major challenge facing the Secretary of Energy will be restoring public confidence in the Department of Energy's management of its nuclear warhead production facilities. These facilities are a vast national complex of warhead production facilities located in 13 states. They occupy a land area twice the size of Delaware and employ approximately 100,000 people.

Revelations of serious safety and environmental problems have provoked public scrutiny of the Department's management of its warhead production complex. Contractor memos indicate that the Department of Energy, over a period of 30 years, failed to disclose serious nuclear reactor accidents. In court documents, the Department admitted it encouraged a contractor not to comply with environmental standards and regulations even if noncompliance placed the public health at risk. These events, in turn, have eroded public confidence in Department of Energy management of the nuclear warhead production complex.

As a consequence, the new Secretary of Energy begins his/her tenure leading a Department lacking public credibility. We believe that the erosion of public confidence can be reversed. It can be restored by the Secretary of Energy swiftly adopting policies that would ensure that nuclear weapons are produced in ways that halt further environmental contamination, and end adverse public health and worker safety conditions.

## Conclusion: Re-Directing U.S. Energy Policy

The effectiveness both of defense and energy policies would be enhanced if the two were clearly separated. We propose that a new Nuclear Weapons Agency be created, removing these programs from the Department of Energy. This would be relatively easy for Congress to do, would retain civilian control of nuclear weapons, and would not alter the structure of the Department of Energy. For Congress, it would be much easier to evaluate the real trends both in energy research and development support and in nuclear weapons research and development.

The Department of Energy should be directed to implement a least-cost national energy strategy similar to the approach now taken by several states. All programs should be evaluated on a level playing field, and efforts should be made to support states, cities, and utilities that are pursuing a least-cost approach.

One of the cornerstones of a sustainable energy policy is the enactment of higher energy taxes, chiefly on gasoline. The next Administration and Congress should carefully consider using higher gasoline taxes to encourage efficiency, offset income taxes, and reduce the federal deficit. These new taxes should be introduced slowly, at a rate of about 10 cents per gallon per year, so as to prevent a resurgence in inflation. The long-term goal should be a national gasoline tax at the levels now found throughout Europe.

Everything from nuclear power to U.S. intervention in the Persian Gulf is now argued on energy

## Blueprint for the Environment

security grounds. However, real energy security is promoted by an energy future that is economically competitive and ecologically sustainable. For example, if we continue to spend $200 billion more than the Japanese on energy each year, our national economic strength will continue to dissipate. If we continue to foster global warming, we will eventually be in the same position as the Netherlands — spending as much on protecting our land from encroaching seawater as on national defense.

Energy policy changes must be urgently addressed. The country's energy policy must simultaneously become a climate-protection strategy and a national-competitiveness strategy. Security must be based on improved energy efficiency and a gradual transition to renewables. It must also be based on a cooperative international effort to create a sustainable energy system. Fortunately, the same approach can lead to achievement of both goals. The time for action is now.

PROJECT BLUEPRINT

PROPOSED DEPARTMENT OF ENERGY BUDGET

| | 1981 | 1989[1] | 1990 | 1993[2] |
|---|---|---|---|---|
| Nuclear Weapons | $3,700 | $7,100 | xx[3] | xx |
| Energy R&D | --- | $3,777 | $3,700 | $3,800[4] |
| Efficiency | $709 | $150 | $200 | $500 |
| Renewables | $711 | $125 | $200 | $500 |
| Fossils[5] | $994 | $692 | $600 | $500 |
| Nuclear[6] | $1,443 | $714 | $650 | $500 |
| Basic Science[7] | --- | $1,713 | $1,700 | $1,700 |
| Support Research[8] | --- | $383 | $350 | $100 |
| Energy Efficiency Grants[9] | --- | $250 | $350 | $750 |
| Nuclear Waste | --- | $1,800 | $900[10] | $1,000 |
| Uranium Enrichment[11] | $31 | $1,184 | $1,200 | $500 |
| Oil Purchases[12] | --- | $781 | $500 | 000 |
| Power administrations[13] & Other | --- | $1,135 | $1,000 | 000 |
| Energy Information Administration | --- | $63 | $63 | $65 |
| Federal Energy Regulatory Commission | --- | $107 | $110 | $110 |
| Miscellaneous | --- | $206 | $200 | $200 |
| ENERGY TOTAL | --- | $9303 | $8,023 | $6,425 |
| GRAND TOTAL | | $16,403 | $8,023 | $6,425 |

# Blueprint for the Environment

1. Figures for fiscal year 1989 are in most cases the Reagan administration's requested budget though in cases where congressional decisions had been made, the figures reflect actual appropriations.

2. Proposed budgets for 1990 and 1993 are expressed in constant 1988 dollars.

3. We propose that by 1990, all nuclear weapons activities be moved into a new specialized civilian agency.

4. The goal of this budget is to keep total federal expenditures on energy R&D approximately level while shifting funds to create a balanced program that gives equal sums of $500 million to nuclear power, fossil fuels, efficiency, and renewable energy.

5. These figures reflect the total nuclear R&D budget, including safety research, advanced reactors, and fusion. We suggest a scaling back of spending on fusion and advanced reactors, and an increase in safety related research.

6. These figures reflect all federal R&D on fossil energy, including the recently completed "clean coal" program. We recommend that these funds be cut somewhat, focusing on the most promising ways of reducing pollution at existing coal-fired facilities. Expanded use of coal should not be encouraged for environmental reasons.

7. These figures reflect mainly research into fundamental areas of physics, and should be continued.

8. Much of this budget reflects support of expensive facilities needed to conduct nuclear research. These facilities can be scaled back or closed as the programs are trimmed.

9. These programs to assist states in promoting energy efficiency were drastically cut back under the Reagan administration. They can have a catalytic and important role, and should be rapidly increased.

10. About half of existing funds go to cleanup of nuclear weapons related wastes. These funds should be transferred to the new nuclear weapons agency that we recommend establishing, allowing for a lowering of this budget. This budget should be funded largely by the "nuclear waste fund" established by congress and funded by mandatory utility contributions. That fund received about $450 million in FY 1989.

11. Uranium enrichment for nuclear power plants is currently heavily subsidized by the federal government, and current budget figures reflect this. The Department of Energy is sitting on about $9 billion of unrecovered costs, forcing a steady increase in the annual enrichment cost to the government. This subsidy can be reduced by raising enrichment fees charged to the utilities and by closing uneconomical facilities. The long-range goal should be to eliminate this subsidy entirely.

12. These figures largely reflect the cost of purchasing oil for the strategic petroleum reserve in Louisiana. We believe that this cost should be paid for by an excise fee on oil imports, taking the burden off taxpayers. In the next few years, while oil prices are low, the government should finish filling the reserve.

13. These figures reflect federal subsidies to electricity users and should be eliminated.

## Blueprint for the Environment

# Blueprint for the Environment

## POLICY

## DEPARTMENT OF ENERGY
### Office of Policy, Planning and Analysis

### RECOMMENDATION

**In order to establish a national commitment to building a far more efficient energy economy, the Secretary of Energy should deliver a speech laying out a sustainable energy strategy for the nation, that will maintain economic growth of 2—2.5 percent per year to 2000 while using less energy per year than is used today.**

• Energy efficiency is generally not given the attention it warrants because it permeates the whole economy and many different agencies in the federal government.

• It is critical that the Secretary establish a concerted federal effort for increased energy efficiency early in his term. Energy efficiency must be the keystone of a new natural resource policy which addresses energy and environmental issues simultaneously. Energy efficiency frees us from energy/environmental/economic "tradeoffs," because it provides simultaneous "wins" in each area. If the President does not establish a government-wide push for increased energy efficiency, we will stumble from one conflicting, expensive and unworkable "solution" to another.

• The program of near-term policies and research and development will be critical to meeting the following major national objectives:

Reduce oil imports and increase energy security.

Reduce or eliminate our trade deficit.

Minimize warming of the earth's atmosphere.

Eliminate the need to drill for oil in environmentally sensitive areas like the Arctic Refuge and the Outer Continental Shelf.

Improve air quality and reduce the threat of urban smog and acid rain.

Increase our international competitiveness.

Provide more affordable housing and minimize energy vulnerability of low-income citizens.

### RECOMMENDATION

**The Secretary of Energy should require that least-cost energy analysis be the basis for determining priorities in the bi-annual National Energy Policy Plan.**

### RECOMMENDATION

**The Secretary of Energy should announce a Department of Energy policy of full compliance with all environmental laws within the first month following his/her confirmation.**

**BUDGET RECOMMENDATION** for full compliance with environmental laws

F.Y. 89: **Increase** of $6 billion        F.Y. 90: **Increase** of $7 billion

Figures were suggested by General Accounting Office in oral testimony before the Senate Committee on Governmental Affairs, July 10, 1988.

## PRINCIPAL AUTHORIZING LEGISLATION

None

## CONGRESSIONAL JURISDICTION

**House Authorizing Committee/Subcommittee**

Committee on Energy and Commerce

Subcommittee on Transportation, Tourism and Hazardous Materials

Subcommittee on Energy and Power

Subcommittee on Health and the Environment

Committee on Armed Services

Subcommittee on Procurement and Military Nuclear Systems

**Senate Authorizing Committee/Subcommittee**

Committee on Environment and Public Works

Subcommittee on Environmental Protection

Subcommittee on Hazardous Wastes and Toxic Substances

Subcommittee on Superfund and Environmental Oversight

Committee on Armed Forces

Subcommittee on Strategic Forces and Nuclear Deterrence

**House Appropriations Subcommittee**

Subcommittee on Energy and Water Development

**Senate Appropriations Subcommittee**

Subcommittee on Defense

Subcommittee on Energy and Water Development

## RELEVANT STUDIES

Roger W. Sant, **The Least-Cost Energy Strategy,** The Energy Productivity Center, Arlington, Virginia, 1979

Solar Energy Research Institute, **Building a Sustainable Future,** Report to the House Committee on Energy and Commerce, 1981

**Energy Efficiency: A New Agenda,** American Council for an Energy Efficient Economy, Washington, D.C., 1988

**Least-Cost Electrical Strategies,** Energy Conservation Coalition, Washington, D.C., 1987

H.S. Geller, E.L. Miller, M.R. Ledbetter, Peter M. Miller, **Acid Rain and Energy Conservation,** American Council for an Energy Efficient Economy and Energy Conservation Coalition, Washington, D.C., June 1987

**Alternative Budget for Energy Conservation, Fiscal Year 1989,** Energy Conservation Coalition, 1988

The General Accounting Office investigative reports on the atomic defense production complex:
**Dealing with Problems in the Nuclear Defense Complex Expected to Cost Over $100 Billion** (July 1988)
**Summary of Problem Areas Within The DOE Nuclear Complex** (March 1988)
**Unresolved Issues Concerning Hanford's Waste Management Practices** (November 1986)
**Environmental Issues at DOE's Nuclear Defense Facilities** (September 1986)

## PRINCIPAL SOURCES OF EXPERTISE

Energy Conservation Coalition — 202-745-4874    Natural Resources Defense Council — 202-783-7800
Sierra Club — 202-547-1144    American Council for an Energy Efficient Economy — 202-429-8873
Environmental Defense Fund — 202-387-3500    World Resources Institute — 202-638-6300
Alliance to Save Energy — 202-857-0666    Renew America — 202-466-6880

---

## Blueprint for the Environment

# Blueprint for the Environment

## GLOBAL WARMING

# DEPARTMENT OF ENERGY
## OFFICE OF THE SECRETARY

### RECOMMENDATION

**The Secretary of Energy should establish a Global Warming Program under the direction of the Deputy Secretary to coordinate a high-priority, agency-wide effort to minimize global warming of the atmosphere.**

• Global warming presents major threats to the world and the United States, including possible loss of the U.S. Midwestern grain belt, 80 percent of U.S. global wetlands, and most U.S. forests. The biggest cause of the problem is carbon dioxide emissions from burning of fossil fuels. Actions to reduce these emissions are essential if we are to minimize global warming.

• The Department of Energy must be a major force if the United States is to do its part in reducing $CO_2$ emissions. All elements of the Department must take appropriate actions. A Global Warming Program overseen by the Deputy Secretary would be an effective way of ensuring supervision and coordination.

• This Program should include:
1) Development of an action plan aimed at reducing U.S. $CO_2$ emissions at least 20 percent by the year 2000.
2) Expanded research efforts.
3) Efforts to stimulate actions by other nations and international institutions, and coordination with them.
4) Mechanisms for coordination with related efforts by other U.S. agencies.

### RECOMMENDATION

**The Secretary of Energy should encourage the Organization for Economic Cooperation and Development and International Energy Agency to establish programs and take vigorous actions to minimize global warming of the atmosphere.**

• Global warming presents major threats to the world and the United States, including possible loss of the U.S. Midwestern grain belt, 80 percent of U.S. global wetlands, and most U.S. forests. The members of the Organization for Economic Cooperation and Development (OECD) and the International Energy Agency (IEA) emit most of the "greenhouse gases" that cause global warming, so these organizations are excellent fora for fostering cooperation on actions to address the problem.

• The Secretary should take initiatives, in cooperation with the State Department, to make prevention of global warming a high-priority issue for the OECD and IEA. The United States should encourage OECD and IEA to carry out a study, to be completed within a year, of carbon dioxide ($CO_2$) emissions and trends in member nations and actions that could be taken by member countries to reduce $CO_2$ emissions 20 percent below present levels by the year 2000. The Department of Energy should cooperate with the State Department in placing "energy attachés" in key OECD nations to promote energy efficiency and other actions to minimize global warming.

• The IEA has always been charged with evaluating progress on energy efficiency in its member countries. In recent years, however, the IEA has reduced its efforts to chart progress and to analyze what is working and what is not. These efforts need to be resumed and stepped up, with wide dissemination of the resulting information to governments and the public.

## BUDGET RECOMMENDATION
F.Y. 90: **Increase** of $ 300,000          F.Y. 91: **Increase** of $ 300,000

## PRINCIPAL AUTHORIZING LEGISLATION
Department of Energy Organization Act of 1977 (P.L. 95-91)

## CONGRESSIONAL JURISDICTION
**House Authorizing Committee/Subcommittee**
Committee on Energy and Commerce
Subcommittee
**Senate Authorizing Committee/Subcommittee**
Committee on Energy and Natural Resources
Subcommittee
**House Appropriations Subcommittee**
Subcommittee on Energy and Water Development
**Senate Appropriations Subcommittee**
Subcommittee on Energy and Water Development

## RELEVANT STUDIES
The best overview of the global warming problem is **"The Changing Atmosphere: Implications for World Security,"** (report of conference sponsored by the Government of Canada at Toronto) June 1988

## RELATED FEDERAL PROGRAMS
The Interagency Committee on Earth Sciences, chaired by the Geological Survey, is coordinating the work of various federal agencies on research concerning the global warming issue.

## PRINCIPAL SOURCES OF EXPERTISE
Environmental Policy Institute — 202-544-2600
Natural Resources Defense Council (T.B. Stoel Jr.) — 202-783-7800
Energy Conservation Coalition — 202-745-4874
Renew America — 202-466-6880

## BUDGET AND STAFFING LEVELS FOR THE OFFICE OF INTERNATIONAL AFFAIRS:

|  | FY 87 | | FY 88 | | FY 89 Request | |
|---|---|---|---|---|---|---|
|  | $ | FTE | $ | FTE | $ | FTE |
| Int. R & D Policy | 1207 | 17 | 1317 | 17 | 1313 | 17 |
| Nonproliferation | 1031 | 12 | 1169 | 12 | 1247 | 12 |
| Intl. Energy Assess. | 1019 | 13.2 | 1167 | 13.2 | 1257 | 13.2 |
| IOs & Policy Dev. | 861 | 8.8 | 929 | 8.8 | 796 | 8.8 |

# Blueprint for the Environment

## GLOBAL WARMING

## DEPARTMENT OF ENERGY

**RECOMMENDATION**
**The Department of Energy should expand and increase its current research effort concerning carbon dioxide emissions, and should include the impacts of other gases generated by human activity such as chlorofluorocarbons, methane, nitrous oxide and tropospheric ozone, in its research on global warming.**

• The Carbon Dioxide Research Program was organized in 1978. It is made up for four study areas: 1) Energy Systems and Carbon Cycle Research, 2) Climate Systems, 3) Ecological and Agricultural Systems, and 4) Resource Analysis. Its goal is to gain scientific and technological understanding of the impacts and effects of emissions of carbon dioxide ($CO_2$) and other gases released by energy production, agriculture and industrial processes, and their contribution to global warming. The Department of Energy's (DOE) research currently involves the study of increasing atmospheric carbon dioxide concentrations, and the detection of $CO_2$-induced climate changes.
• DOE is the lead Agency in $CO_2$ research, and provides a little over half of federal funding. Between FY 1978 and FY 1987, Federal Agencies spent $147 million on research directed toward understanding the carbon cycle, climate modeling, response of vegetation to elevated atmospheric $CO_2$ and related areas. DOE has spent 51 percent of this research investment, or $74.97 million; the National Science Foundation, National Oceanic and Atmospheric Administration — 46 percent , or $67.62 million; and the U.S. Geological Survey, National Aeronautic and Space Administration and the Environmental Protection Agency — 3 percent, or $4.41 million.
• All of the work of DOE is contracted out. A little less than 50 percent of the budget goes to National Laboratories, a little less than 50 percent goes to Universities, and the rest goes to the private sector.

**RECOMMENDATION**
**The Secretary of Energy should direct the Industrial Co-Generation Subprogram to promote and expand research and development projects into practical and innovative fossil fuel energy producing technologies (both industrial and domestic) that are highly efficient and pose minimal climatic impacts.**

• The objective of the Industrial Cogeneration Subprogram is to conduct research on new improved energy conversion systems which offer energy conservation benefits not available in present-day technology. Benefits include higher electrical to thermal output and choice of alternative fuel systems to provide greater fuel flexibility to the industrial sector.
• Specific recommendations to expand research projects into highly efficient fossil fuel energy producing technologies include:
1) Increasing and expanding the current Department of Energy program on energy cogeneration for the industrial sector as well as domestic technologies;
2) Create a research and development program on gas turbine technology. Of particular interest are advanced technologies such as steam-injected gas

81

turbines and the combined cycle system. This project should also work with the Defense Department on jet aircraft turbine research (currently funded at $500 million per year) to develop domestic spin-offs.

• Developing and fostering commercialization of efficient cogeneration and gas turbine technologies will help to expand natural gas use (as an alternative to coal) and will minimize fossil fuel consumption for electricity production. This project should be closely coordinated and co-sponsored with related programs under the Department of Energy's Assistant Secretary for Fossil Fuels, as well as with related projects sponsored by the utility industry.

## RECOMMENDATION
**The Secretary of Energy should take steps to develop and implement a program of cooperation with newly industrialized nations, middle-income developing nations and low-income developing nations aimed at meeting human needs while minimizing global warming.**

• The Secretary should:
1) Announce that the Office of International Affairs will develop and implement, in cooperation with the State Department and the Agency for International Development (AID), a program of cooperation with newly industrialized nations, middle-income developing nations, and low-income developing nations aimed at meeting human needs while minimizing global warming;

2) Immediately hire or assign three full-time staff persons to begin the Program, and provide them $100,000 in contractual authority;

3) In FY 90, hire or assign a full-time staff of 10 to carry out this program, and provide them with contractual authority of $500,000.

• The Program should include active personnel exchanges with developing nations on relevant energy efficiency policies and technologies. These exchanges should be coordinated with AID but not limited to AID countries (i.e., nations like Brazil and China should be included). Such exchanges are badly needed because most developing countries have little access to information about workable energy efficiency technologies and policies.

## RECOMMENDATION
**The Department of Energy should cooperate with the Department of State and the Environmental Protection Agency in efforts to increase cooperation with the Soviet Union in the area of energy efficiency.**

• The two superpowers should by formal agreement exchange scientists, industrial leaders, workers and students to promote the creation and use of energy-efficiency techniques in their own and other countries. The nations would sponsor both short- and longer-term visits by qualified personnel to research institutes, universities and factories. The focus of these exchanges would be technologies for saving energy, means of fostering energy-efficient behavior, and the application of energy conservation to ameliorate environmental problems, particularly the greenhouse effect.

**Blueprint for the Environment**

# Blueprint for the Environment

## CONSERVATION

# DEPARTMENT OF ENERGY
ASSISTANT SECRETARY for Conservation and Renewable Energy
Office of Buildings and Community Systems

### RECOMMENDATION
**The Department of Energy should expand its effort to help utilities, states and localities improve the effectiveness and understanding of conservation programs.**

• Utilities, states and localities are spending at least $1 billion per year on conservation and load management programs. Only limited research, however, has been conducted on alternative forms of program design and delivery. Considerable uncertainty remains about the significance of different program elements, response rates, and the net effects these programs have on energy demand and peak loads.

• The Department of Energy needs a stronger effort to reduce fossil fuel and nuclear energy use for power generation through research, evaluation and information dissemination to improve utility, state and local energy conservation programs. The program should:

1) Develop guidelines for conservation program experiments and evaluations;

2) Provide technical assistance to utilities, states and local agencies. For example, a team of conservation experts funded by the federal government could be available to help with conservation program design and evaluation.

3) Conduct research and demonstrate new techniques for evaluating the impacts of conservation programs.

### RECOMMENDATION

**The Secretary of Energy should increase the effectiveness of the Weatherization Assistance Program for low-income residences by evaluating the effectiveness of existing state programs, removing technical and cost restrictions on the program, and establishing "partnerships" with utilities and community businesses.**

• The Weatherization Assistance Program (WAP) increases the energy efficiency of residences occupied by low-income citizens across the nation, particularly the homes of the elderly and the handicapped. Approximately 17.6 million households are eligible to receive assistance under this program. By Fiscal Year 1988, only 3 million of these homes had been weatherized and program funding has been decreasing both from federal appropriations and from oil overcharge monies. The billions of oil overcharge monies have created raised expectations among the most vulnerable members of our population. Oil overcharge funds are dwindling rapidly. We cannot make up all the difference in funding levels given federal budgetary pressures, but we should at least take steps to return to funding levels of Fiscal Year 1980, $199 million, from the present level of $161 million. In addition, we need to increase the impact of the funds we use.

• With this federal effort, it will be possible for state weatherization programs to gain increased assistance from state legislatures, utilities and other members of the private sector. Taken all together, these efforts will enable us to take steps to protect low-income citizens from trade-offs between energy or food and clothing.

## BUDGET RECOMMENDATION
F.Y. 90: **Increase** of $ 2 million      F.Y. 91: **Increase** of $ 3 million

For Weatherization Assistance Program:
F.Y. 90: **Increase** of $ 10 million      F.Y. 91: **Increase** of $ 30 million

## PRINCIPAL AUTHORIZING LEGISLATION

## CONGRESSIONAL JURISDICTION
**House Authorizing Committee/Subcommittee**
Committee on Science, Space and Technology
Subcommittee on Energy Research and Development
**Senate Authorizing Committee/Subcommittee**
Committee on Energy and Natural Resources
**House Appropriations Subcommittee**
Subcommittee on Interior
**Senate Appropriations Subcommittee**
Subcommittee on Interior and Related Agencies

## RELEVANT STUDIES
Eric Heist, et al., **Energy Efficiency in Buildings: Progress and Promise**, American Council for an Energy-Efficient Economy, Washington, D.C., 1986
Department of Energy, **DOE State and Local Assistance Programs,** October 1986

## RELATED FEDERAL PROGRAMS
State and Local Assistance Programs, Department of Energy
Energy Assistance Program

## PRINCIPAL SOURCES OF EXPERTISE
American Council for an Energy-Efficient Economy — 202-429-8873
Energy Conservation Coalition — 202-745-4874
Alliance to Save Energy — 202-857-0666
National Association of State Energy Officials — 202-639-8749

## IMPLEMENTATION STEPS
(1)  The Department of Energy (DOE) should request funding and Congress should appropriate funds to enable DOE to expand its research, evaluation and information dissemination activities related to utility, state and local conservation programs.
(2)  Evaluate the energy efficiency impact and cost effectiveness of existing programs in order to generalize best practices to other states.
(3)  Revise pertinent regulations to remove the technical and cost restrictions on WAP and to allow the establishment of partnerships.
(4)  Establish "partnerships" with utilities and other community businesses to weatherize whole neighborhoods of low-income housing.

## Blueprint for the Environment

# Blueprint for the Environment

## CONSERVATION

# DEPARTMENT OF ENERGY

**RECOMMENDATION**
**The Secretary of Energy should increase the flexibility and impact of the State Energy Conservation Program both by permitting use of program funds for energy efficiency demonstrations and revolving low-income loan funds, and by encouraging development of non-profit energy service companies to assist low-income residential consumers, particularly multi-family housing.**

• The State Energy Conservation Program (SECP) helps states implement energy conservation programs that meet localized energy needs. Under this program states are developing and maintaining an energy emergency response network, helping the industrial sector become more efficient and developing more efficient transportation programs.
• SECP goals include the following:
1) Expanding the state role in transferring energy efficient technologies into the market place;

2) Enhancing the state energy emergency planning capabilities, especially by increasing regional cooperation and developing uniform set-aside programs; and
3) Encouraging new state initiatives that include innovative energy financing, integrated (least-cost) energy planning, new programs in transportation and industrial energy efficiency, and promotion of alternative transportation fuels and renewable resources.

**RECOMMENDATION**
**The Secretary of Energy should increase the energy conservation servicing of schools and hospitals under the Institutional Conservation Program 1) by permitting states to use half of their Institutional Conservation Program funds as seed money for partnerships with private firms; 2) by funding an institutional energy manager for individual schools and hospitals; and 3) by using existing grant sites to demonstrate new efficiency technologies.**

• The Institutional Conservation Program (ICP) was established to encourage energy efficiency initiatives in the institutional buildings sector. Such public and private non-profit institutions use significant amounts of energy, the cost of which represents a large proportion of their operating budgets. As a result, energy conservation measures result in significant energy and economic savings. Through Fiscal Year 1987, the program awarded over 21,000 grants for energy conservation projects in over 59,000 school and hospital buildings.
• In 1986, a new initiative was developed in

ICP, which provided seed monies to state energy offices to conduct innovative projects such as new energy efficiency financing concepts, building expertise, and sharing information. This new initiative was designed to complement the basic ICP program. We recommend expanding the seed money program to further leverage ICP funds. We also recommend loosening regulations to permit funding of on-site energy managers on a trial basis. Experience has shown that these managers more than pay their own way with energy savings and assure the effectiveness of ICP capital grants.

## RECOMMENDATION
**The Secretary of Energy should increase the effectiveness of the Energy Extension Service program by implementing specific measures to increase the flexibility and impact of the program, including intra-state regional councils, professionally trained extension agents, use of national labs and state universities and partial funding by service users.**

• The Energy Extension Service (EES) provides information and technical assistance tailored to the smaller scale energy users to help determine their most cost effective and productive energy conservation and renewable options. Energy technologies and techniques are demonstrated through such methods as on-site technical assistance, hands-on training workshops, and development of how-to workbooks. This unbiased information is generally not available to this audience through any other source. EES also provides a method that the latest technical advice developed in the nation's laboratories and universities can be disseminated quickly to the public. These programs, although each are small scale, cumulatively enable this sector to save millions of dollars each year.

## RECOMMENDATION
**The Secretary of Energy should expand energy conservation Research and Development to improve the energy efficiency of products, processes and buildings.**

## RECOMMENDATION
**The Secretary of Energy should take the lead in developing new incentives and guidelines to reduce energy use by the federal government.**

• Federal buildings, excluding public housing, annually consume about $4 billion worth of energy. Largely because of limited resources and lack of government-wide support, the 12-year-old Federal Energy Management Program has had little effect on federal government energy consumption. We propose a vigorous and comprehensive commitment to improve the energy efficiency of federal buildings.
• The effort should establish new incentives and guidelines for federal officials. Agency managers, for example, could be allowed to retain part of their energy savings to meet other budgetary needs of their agency. Guidelines for investment in conservation measures should unambiguously require minimum life-cycle costs. New aggressive energy conservation goals for federal buildings should be set, such as 25 percent savings per square foot of floor space within ten years. And model federal facilities can be used as showcases to bolster the overall effort.
• The effort should also include technical and institutional research and information programs, taking advantage of the expertise residing in the national laboratories and other research centers. The program should also seek improvements for indoor air quality and thermal comfort.

# Blueprint for the Environment

## RENEWABLE RESOURCES

# DEPARTMENT OF ENERGY

**RECOMMENDATION**

**The Secretary of Agriculture should link the Forest Service technical expertise and Extension Service delivery capability to develop and implement a major urban forestation grants program. This should be done with cooperation from the Department of the Interior greenways and trails programs and Department of Energy programs for energy conservation and clean air incentives to cities.**

• Trees remove harmful air pollutants and reduce urban temperatures, thereby improving public health and conserving energy. In most cities only one tree is planted for every four trees that disappear. When we build cities and towns we replace trees with brick, concrete and asphalt, materials that store heat and increase urban temperatures. The tree loss not only exacerbates our urban temperature problems, but we lose a principal absorber of excess carbon dioxide ($CO_2$) and various airborne pollutants as well.

• Researchers propose three ways to reduce carbon dioxide and other air pollutants: 1) improving auto emissions; 2) reforming energy sources; and 3) increasing the number of trees in city areas. If implemented, improving auto emissions would cost $.10 per pound of $CO_2$. Trees would cost only $.01 per pound of $CO_2$.

• One tree assimilates about 13 pounds of $CO_2$ per year — enough to offset the $CO_2$ produced by driving one car 26,000 miles. Planting trees in urban areas is doubly effective because they provide shade, cooling urban areas, which in turn reduces energy consumption.

**RECOMMENDATION**

**The Secretary of Energy and the Assistant Secretary for Conservation and Renewable Energy should immediately initiate a program of increased federal support of biomass energy technology development and commercialization. The main target should be to develop economical, efficient means of deriving transportation fuels from biological sources, including waste materials, trees and crops.**

• Priority areas for collaborative research involving government and private industry include improved production of low-cost biological feedstocks such as wood and aquatic plants. Thermochemical and biochemical production of liquid and gaseous fuels are also important. Alcohol fuels must be produced more efficiently, relying on wastes and energy crops that do not compete for prime agricultural land, thus promoting increased use of biological energy sources, which can be used in buildings, power generation, and most importantly in transportation to replace oil and other fossil fuels. Biofuels have the potential to be cost-effective and non-polluting if the right technologies can be developed.

## RECOMMENDATION

**The Secretary of Energy should work to protect the stratospheric ozone layer, slow greenhouse warming and avoid other environmental problems by developing technologies that simultaneously save energy and cut reliance on ozone-depleting chlorofluorocarbons.**

• Currently available substitutes for chlorofluorocarbons (CFCs) CFC-11 and CFC-12, the compounds which most seriously deplete ozone, are less energy efficient. For example, replacing CFC-12 in refrigerators or mobile air conditioners could result in a 10—20 percent increase in unit energy consumption. Replacing all uses of CFC-11 and CFC-12 with presently available substitutes could increase U.S. energy use by 4 percent.

• To avoid these energy penalties, we propose that the Department of Energy, working with the Environmental Protection Agency, undertake an urgent research, development and demonstration program on promising technologies which could both reduce or eliminate CFC use and increase efficiency in energy-related application. Possibilities include:

Evacuated panel insulation — highly insulating panels that could replace foam insulation.

Alternative refrigeration systems and less damaging CFCs such as R-22 and R-134a.

Advanced automotive glazing — improved windows and other techniques for reducing automotive air conditioner requirements.

• The effort would integrate and expand smaller, separate research projects on CFC substitutes and energy efficiency now being conducted. For example, DOE has provided limited funds for research and development on evacuated panel insulation and EPA did the same for a novel refrigerator concept employing R-22.

## RECOMMENDATION

**The Secretary of Energy should encourage continued development of geothermal energy. The goal should be to make lower grade geothermal resources commercially viable where appropriate — throughout the nation.**

• The federal government has supported geothermal energy since the seventies, helping spur development of 2,200 megawatts of geothermal capacity. However, support has fallen over 80 percent in this decade, and technological development is now lagging. For geothermal energy to achieve its potential to displace environmentally damaging fossil fuels, steady increases in federal support are needed, up to a steady level of about $50 million annually in the mid-nineties. A carefully designed Five Year Plan should be developed to guide this program and to promote a steady increase in national reliance on geothermal energy.

## RECOMMENDATION

**The Secretary of Energy and the Assistant Secretary for Conservation and Renewable Energy should initiate a program of gradual but substantial increases in federal support for research, development and commercialization of wind energy. The goal should be to make wind power fully cost-competitive with coal-fired electricity by 1995.**

• Emphasis should be placed on working with U.S. companies currently in the field. The Wind Energy Systems Program must have a more-ambitious Five-Year Plan prepared, with a small technically competent research committee formed to oversee it. Appropriations should be $24 million in 1989, $40 million in 1990, and $80 million annually for 1993—95.

• Wind electricity generation is already a commercial energy source in the United States, providing 1,400 megawatts of power. Further cost reductions are needed, and new technologies and manufacturing techniques have already been identified that will make this possible. This will require a long-term commitment by the new Administration.

• Particular emphasis should be placed on developing a third generation of more economical turbines that is suitable for use on small grids in the developing world. Utility involvement in integrating windpower in grid systems should be encouraged.

## Blueprint for the Environment

# RECOMMENDATION

**The Secretary of Energy and the Assistant Secretary for Conservation and Renewable Energy should immediately implement a program of increased federal support for ocean energy technologies. The goal should be to make these economically competitive with fossil-fuel-based power generation by the late nineties and to encourage the transfer of these technologies to developing nations.**

• Ocean thermal energy conversion is a technology that is particularly applicable in warm tropical seas, including the coast of Hawaii in the United States. Steady federal support could make this an economically efficient, non-polluting and decentralized form of power generation in many nations. It deserves more federal support than it has received in recent years.

# RECOMMENDATION

**The Secretary of Energy and the Assistant Secretary for Conservation and Renewable Energy should initiate a program of accelerated development of solar photovoltaics. The goal should be to make photovoltaics fully competitive with new coal-fired power plants by 1998.**

• United States (U.S.) government support of photovoltaics has fallen from $160 million in 1981 to $35 million in 1988. Photovoltaics costs have continued to fall and efficiencies have continued to increase, but not as rapidly as they would have with steadier government support.

• Stepped up support of Research and Development should be combined with effective new commercialization programs to ensure continued development of a private market for photovoltaics. Special emphasis should be given to thin-film technologies and others with high potential to lower costs dramatically.

• Photovoltaic cells have the capability to one day supply at least 30 percent of U.S. electricity clearly and cost-effectively. They are also an important strategic industry, the future of which is an important element of U.S. economic competitiveness. The new administration confronts an historic opportunity to accelerate the development of this critical energy source.

# RECOMMENDATION

**The Secretary of Energy and the Assistant Secretary for Conservation and Renewable Energy should initiate a program of increased support for the research, development and commercialization of solar thermal technologies, making them fully competitive with coal-fired power by 1998.**

• Solar thermal power technologies have become substantially more economical during the past decade, due to a combination of federal and private support. They have the potential to begin displacing coal by the early nineties. However, commercialization of these technologies has lagged as oil prices have; sustained government support is essential to continuing their technological evolution. Support should be raised to a level of $35 million in 1990 and $50 million annually from 1993—95.

• This support will promote increased national reliance on solar thermal energy systems, which have the potential to economically provide electricity and industrial heat, displacing coal and other fossil fuels used for electricity generation. These systems also have potential to be used to neutralize chlorofluorocarbons and dangerous toxic wastes.

## Blueprint for the Environment

# RECOMMENDATION

**The Secretary of Energy and the Assistant Secretary for Conservation and Renewable Energy should step up federal programs for the development of solar technologies to be incorporated by the private sector in existing and new buildings. These have a large potential to further reduce the use of oil, natural gas and electricity in buildings.**

• Active solar hot water systems and passive solar designs are already incorporated in hundreds of thousands of U.S. buildings, thanks in part to federal support in the late seventies and early eighties. However, in recent years federal Research and Development programs have been cut so much as to seriously impede progress. The Department of Energy should immediately begin a study on how to best utilize increased federal support for solar in private buildings of all types.

# RECOMMENDATION

**The Secretary of Energy and the Assistant Secretary for Conservation and Renewable Energy should give the Solar Energy Research Institute in Golden, Colorado, a more central role in directing and carrying out the government's renewable energy Research and Development programs.**

• The Solar Energy Research Institute (SERI), founded in the late seventies, continues to be an important element of the U.S. renewable energy program. After surviving drastic budget cuts in the early eighties, federal support of SERI has been increasing again in the past few years. Photovoltaic, biomass and wind power programs are now directed to a large degree by SERI researchers.

• However, many renewable energy programs are still divided among various national laboratories, causing redundancy and confusions. Consolidating most of these efforts at SERI will bring more coherence to the programs. A federal center of excellence in renewable energy would also be a good public showcase for new technologies, and would assist in technical cooperation with other nations.

# Blueprint for the Environment

EFFICIENCY

## DEPARTMENT OF ENERGY
### ASSISTANT SECRETARY for Conservation and Renewable Energy
### Office of Industrial Programs

**RECOMMENDATION**
**The Secretary of Energy should establish research centers for energy-intensive industries. The proposed centers would conduct basic and applied research on common industrial processes in order to develop multiple improvements, one of which would be energy efficiency.**

• American industry must improve its efficiency, as well as the value and quality of its products, to compete more effectively in the international market.

• Energy consumption costs American manufacturers over $100 billion per year. Despite impressive gains in the last decade, U.S. industry is far less energy efficient than most of its major trading partners. Improving the energy efficiency of American industry, especially energy intensive industries, can make U.S. industry more competitive by reducing the final cost of products.

• Several studies suggest that successful technological innovations tend to offer benefits not just in energy use, but in labor, materials, capital and product quality. Thus, energy efficiency will be advanced by industrial process innovation aimed at solving many problems simultaneously.

• Unfortunately, U.S. industry significantly under-invests in technology development. The federal government could help correct for this deficiency by establishing research centers for energy intensive industries. The research centers would be co-funded and co-managed by the industries they serve, and would serve as the catalyst and core of a larger industry research effort.

## BUDGET RECOMMENDATION
F.Y. 90: **Increase** of $ 5 million        F.Y. 91: **no change**

## PRINCIPAL AUTHORIZING LEGISLATION
None

## CONGRESSIONAL JURISDICTION
**House Authorizing Committee/Subcommittee**
  Committee on Science, Space and Technology
    Subcommittee on Energy Research and Development
**Senate Authorizing Committee/Subcommittee**
  Committee on Energy and Natural Resources
    Subcommittee on Energy Research and Development
**House Appropriations Subcommittee**
  Subcommittee on Interior
**Senate Appropriations Subcommittee**
  Subcommittee on Interior and Related Agencies

## RELEVANT STUDIES
J.A. Young, **"Global Competition — The New Reality: Results of the President's Commission on Industrial Competitiveness,"** U.S. Government Printing Office, 1985
C.A. Berg, **"Energy Conservation in Industry: The Present Approach, the Future Opportunities,"** Report to the President's Council on Environmental Quality, Washington, D.C. 1979

## RELATED FEDERAL PROGRAMS
The National Science Foundation's Centers of Excellence

## PRINCIPAL SOURCES OF EXPERTISE
American Council for an Energy-Efficient Economy — 202-429-8873
Renew America — 202-466-6880

## IMPLEMENTATION STEPS
The Assistant Secretary for Conservation and Renewables should first seek authorization and appropriations from Congress to establish at least 10 centers within the next three years. Once authorization is received, a study should be conducted on which industries would be appropriate for such centers, where the centers would be located, what kind of research should be conducted, and what responsibilities private industry would take in the centers. When the studies are completed and commitments from industries are obtained, the centers should be established. If after several years the centers appear to be successful, the program should be expanded to other industries.

## NOTES:

# Blueprint for the Environment

## EFFICIENCY

# DEPARTMENT OF ENERGY

**RECOMMENDATION**

**The Secretary of Energy should redirect limited federal Research and Development funds from clean coal to other needed projects, and focus existing appropriated funds toward short-term pragmatic clean coal projects.**

• The overall goal of the Federal Clean Coal Technology Demonstration Program is to conduct, in conjunction with the private sector, cost shared demonstration projects that will demonstrate the feasibility of future commercial applications of these technologies.

• Clean coal funding should favor or emphasize high energy efficiency and thus should favor steam injected gas turbines using gasified coal rather than subsidizing weaker technology such as fluidized beds, coal liquification or underground conversions. Criteria for research grants should be: 1) emission reduction retrofit technology projects, and 2) projects whose technology can be quickly deployed.

• After the current Appropriated Program expires, it is recommended that this funding be redirected to other research and development projects such as Global Warming Research, energy conservation and fuel efficiency programs and the development of renewable energy sources. The coal industry should be encouraged to continue clean coal technology projects under private sector funding.

**RECOMMENDATION**

**The Secretary of Energy should assure the Unconventional Gas Recovery program will continue to develop new technologies (secondary and tertiary recovery methods) for the extraction of natural gas from currently unrecoverable gas resources.**

• Maximizing natural gas recovery through unconventional recovery technology in active gas fields is beneficial as long as the recovery technology causes minimal impact to the environment. Use of this technology is desirable because maximizing gas recovery in currently disturbed areas lessens the need to explore or begin new drilling operations in virgin or fragile areas.

• The Department of Energy (DOE) current Unconventional Gas Recovery program should be continued at $11 million per year.

**RECOMMENDATION**

**The Secretary of Energy should assure the Enhanced Oil Recovery Program will continued to develop new technologies (secondary and tertiary recovery methods) to increase the recovery of oil from a reservoir and ultimately allow for the recovery of a significant amount of oil that remains in the ground after "conventional" techniques have been applied.**

• Maximizing oil recovery through enhancement technology in active oil fields is beneficial as long as the enhancement technology causes minimal impart to the environment. Use of this technology is desirable because maximizing oil recovery in currently disturbed areas lessens the need to explore or begin new drilling operations in virgin or fragile areas such as off-shore, or in the Arctic Wildlife Refuge.

• The Department of Energy (DOE) current Enhanced Oil Recovery program should be continued at $11 million per year.

## RECOMMENDATION
**The Secretary of Energy should develop standards to reduce the amount of electric energy consumed by fluorescent and incandescent lamps.**

• Similar to recently passed minimum efficiency standards for consumer appliances and fluorescent lamp ballasts, minimum efficiency standards for fluorescent and incandescent lamps can cost effectively save a substantial amount of energy. The American Council for an Energy- Efficient Economy estimates that lamp efficiency standards could reduce peak electricity demand by 5000 milliwatts and save consumers about $ 2 billion per year by 2000.
• The standards for fluorescent lamps should be strong enough to ensure that only lamps as efficient as those that use improved phosphors could be produced. Standards for incandescent lamps should be set so that only those as efficient as "watt-miser" lamps could be produced. Such standards would be highly cost-effective for consumers and could be met by many products already commercially available. The standards should be periodically reviewed by the Department of Energy and strengthened if justified.

## RECOMMENDATION
**The Secretary of Energy should establish a uniform national window performance rating system. Once the rating system has been developed, the Federal Trade Commission should require that labels containing the ratings be affixed to all new windows sold in the United States.**

• The energy efficiency of windows has improved dramatically in recent years, primarily because of new glass coating technologies developed with the help of the Department of Energy's (DOE) Conservation Research and Development program. New technologies being researched, such as windows filled with special gases, promise to improve window efficiency even more. Many new window designs promise to make windows so efficient that they gain more energy for buildings than they lose.
• Almost all manufacturers claim their products are "energy-efficient" despite the high variability of energy performance among different products. Consumers have difficulty determining which windows are truly efficient. A uniform national window rating and labeling system is thus needed. These ratings and labels would be akin to the efficiency labels required on new appliances and cars.
• Energy loss through windows in the United States amounts to the equivalent of 1.4 million barrels per day. If given reliable information on window performance, window buyers can make more informed decisions and reduce energy lost through windows.
• Before such ratings and labels can be established, some unresolved questions on window performance rating need to be researched. The rating and labeling program should therefore be preceded by a one year window rating research program.

# Blueprint for the Environment

## VEHICLE EMISSIONS

## DEPARTMENT OF THE TREASURY
### ASSISTANT SECRETARY for Tax Policy
### ASSISTANT SECRETARY for Domestic Finance

**RECOMMENDATION**
**The Secretary of Energy and the Secretary of the Treasury should work together to develop and support legislation to enact a $.10 cent per gallon tax increase on gasoline and diesel fuel in each year of a 10-year period. Ten percent of this revenue should be designated for low-income needs.**

• This tax is intended to reduce the consumption of motor fuels in order to reduce the emission of carbon dioxide and local and regional air pollutants.

• Vehicle fuel economy ranks first in priority for reducing imported oil. Cars and light trucks require one-third of all U.S. oil, a volume equal to imports. It also ranks as a top environmental priority — cars and light trucks produce one-fifth of all U.S. carbon emissions. And though the fuel economy of cars has improved since the 1973 oil crisis, fuel economy can be cost-effectively doubled with existing technology. Unfortunately, fuel economy standards, proposed elsewhere by Project Blueprint, cannot work alone. Price incentives must be used to complement regulatory policy, or else consumers will not be interested in buying fuel-efficient cars.

• The market price for imported oil does not reflect its true cost to the U.S. economy. Some studies estimate that national security costs roughly amount to $10 per barrel. The costs of air pollution and the risks of climate change from using oil make the true cost even higher. Logically, one would assume that these costs should be internalized through a tax on oil regardless of where it is used in the economy. Practically, however, a tax on transportation fuels would be more workable. The potential for increasing the efficiency of oil use in the transportation sector is large. Taxes on transportation fuels would cause fewer problems for competitiveness and employment than taxes in other sectors. Moreover, the collection mechanism is already in place for a road fuels tax.

## BUDGET RECOMMENDATION
Policy will generate revenues.
F.Y. 90: revenue **Increase** of $ 6.1 billion    F.Y. 91: revenue **Increase** of $ 18.4 billion

## PRINCIPAL AUTHORIZING LEGISLATION
New legislation required

## CONGRESSIONAL JURISDICTION
**House Authorizing Committee/Subcommittee**
Committee on Ways and Means
**Senate Authorizing Committee/Subcommittee**
Committee on Finance
**House Appropriations Subcommittee**
Subcommittee
**Senate Appropriations Subcommittee**
Subcommittee

## RELEVANT STUDIES
**"Energy Security,"** Department of Energy, 1986

## RELATED FEDERAL PROGRAMS

## PRINCIPAL SOURCES OF EXPERTISE
Energy Conservation Coalition — 202-745-4874
American Council for an Energy-Efficient Economy — 202-429-8873
Renew America — 202-466-6880

## IMPLEMENTATION STEPS
(1)   The House of Representatives Committee on Ways and Means must consider and approve legislation to enact a gasoline tax which would increase by $0.10 in each of three to five years, beginning in 1990. The committee must also create a means of recycling approximately ten percent of the revenues to low income persons. This mechanism should be described in a study to be conducted by the Joint Economic Committee or Department of Energy, with assistance form the Department of the Treasury.
(2)   We propose a tax on vehicle fuels sufficient to capture the long-run costs of high oil use. Specifically, we urge the application of a tax on gasoline and diesel equal to $.10 per gallon beginning in 1990 and rising by $.10 per gallon each year through the year 1999. The intent of such a tax structure is to make the tax responsive to market changes so that whatever happens, consumers are given a price signal that will encourage efficiency.
(3)   A fuels tax will have the major drawback of disproportionately affecting poor people. This problem can be mitigated by rebating a portion of tax collected form persons with incomes under a specified level. For the working poor or retired persons, the income tax and social security systems could directly convey income transfers. For those not paying taxes or receiving social security benefits, other mechanisms such as aid to families with dependent children and public housing subsidies could be used to convey benefits that offset the tax increase.

## NOTES:

---

**Blueprint for the Environment**

# Blueprint for the Environment

## VEHICLE EMISSIONS

# DEPARTMENT OF ENERGY

### RECOMMENDATION

**The Department of the Treasury should both encourage the production and sale of very highly efficient new cars and light trucks by providing rebates, and discourage inefficient vehicles by imposing an excise tax in order to reduce greenhouse gas and air pollutant emissions.**

• Fuels taxes and fuel economy standards would effectively raise average fuel efficiency, but would not address two important problems. The first is the continued large-scale production of very inefficient cars — gas guzzlers — and the second is the need to encourage the production of highly efficient cars. A gas-guzzler tax would address the first problem; a rebate mechanism would address the second.

• Since high fuel economy levels do not greatly reduce the costs of driving, U.S. manufacturers face a high barrier to fuel economy innovations. Manufacturers thus would run considerable risks if they produced vehicles innovative in fuel efficiency and would have little prospect for rewards in the marketplace.

• A rebate on the order offered by dealers in promotional campaigns — say $1,000 — would be offered by this federal program to consumers purchasing the initial production runs of high-efficiency vehicles. Manufacturers could qualify a limited number of vehicle models for the rebate by producing cars that meet a specified level of fuel economy, such as 50 percent higher than best models now available, and other important criteria, such as safety and low emissions. Different fuel-economy criteria could be set for different size classes of cars, and eligibility would be limited to models produced in significant quantities. Eligibility would also be restricted to cars manufactured primarily in North America, but it would not be restricted only to U.S.-owned firms. This incentive would help assure a market for high-efficiency cars.

### RECOMMENDATION

**The Secretary of Energy should take steps to bring increased focus and effectiveness to the light vehicle research program in the Department of Energy and in the nation.**

• The Secretary of Energy should ask the National Academy of Sciences to conduct a comprehensive assessment on the nature of international research being conducted on light vehicles that could be introduced in or around the turn of the century.

• Based upon the results of the assessment, the Secretary of Energy should direct the Assistant Secretary for Conservation and Renewable Energy to establish a research program with the goal of improving the energy efficiency of the transportation sector so as to reduce environmental degradation, particularly with regard to global warming. Technologies to be supported by such a program would be selected based upon the following criteria:

Technology promises to be both efficient and cost effective;

American companies have not made a commitment to Research and Development on the technology; and

Failure to develop technology could lead to competitive advantage by companies in other countries.

• A steering committee to oversee the Research and Development program would be set up with representatives from American auto companies, parts suppliers and researchers in the field. Funding would be shared, with private-to-public ratio determined by how well developed the technology is: the more it is developed, the smaller the percentage of government funding.

## RECOMMENDATION
**The Secretaries of Energy and Transportation should work together to establish new fuel economy standards for both automobiles and light trucks such that the overall new fleet will be achieving 45 miles per gallon for automobiles and 35 miles per gallon for light trucks by 2000.**

• Instead of using the CAFE approach of setting a single fleetwide fuel economy requirement for all manufacturers regardless of the mix of their vehicles, a percentage improvement requirement will be applied uniformly to all manufacturers. The base year would be 1990; percentage improvements would be calculated based on the fleetwide fuel economy of each manufacturer in that year. Milestone percentage improvements would be set every three to four years, culminating in a final requirement for 2000. Failure to meet the required improvements would result in fines based upon the size of the fleet and the amount of the shortfall. Manufacturers that met the original 1985 CAFE requirements would be granted more time to meet the new requirements.
• These new requirements should be accompanied by both a directive to the National Highway Traffic Safety Administration to improve its fuel economy test and ensure compliance by vehicle manufacturers, and expanded semi-annual Gas Mileage Guides that are widely distributed throughout the country, not only through dealerships but through state and local offices and private organizations.

## Blueprint for the Environment

## NUCLEAR ENERGY

# DEPARTMENT OF ENERGY
## ASSISTANT SECRETARY for Environment, Safety and Health

### RECOMMENDATION
**The Secretary of Energy should transfer administrative and budget control of its environmental programs from the Office of the Assistant Secretary for Defense Programs to the Office of the Assistant Secretary for Environment, Safety and Health. This will help insure that the Department of Energy acts expeditiously to cleanup serious environmental contamination resulting from over 40 years of nuclear weapons production.**

• The Department of Energy (DOE) funds for environmental cleanup and compliance are currently administered by DOE's Defense Program officials, whose primary responsibility is to manage the Department's nuclear weapons production program. The DOE Assistant Secretary for Environment, Safety, and Health is responsible for environmental protection programs and therefore should be able to exercise final control over DOE funding for environmental clean-up and compliance. The same DOE officials who administer DOE's weapons production program should not be in charge of the Department's environmental programs, especially in light of the significant environmental contamination that has resulted from nuclear weapons production and the magnitude of the cleanup effort required. In July 1988, DOE estimated that environmental compliance and cleanup at DOE weapons facilities could cost a staggering $66 to $110 billion.

• By transferring the responsibility for administering DOE environmental funds to DOE's Environment, Safety and Health office, the Secretary of Energy would not only establish a more effective administrative structure for dealing with DOE waste problems, but could also help solve the complex accounting problems that plague the Department and facilitate proper prioritization of DOE waste cleanup projects.

• In addition, this transfer would shift oversight to Congressional authorizing committees with greater environmental expertise. Currently, DOE requests for environmental funds are appropriated by committees with expertise on issues relating to nuclear weapons production.

### RECOMMENDATION
**The Secretary of Energy should urge the President to create a Nuclear Waste Advisory Group to assure that major attention is devoted to public health and environmental safety in the development and implementation of national nuclear waste management programs.**

## BUDGET RECOMMENDATION

## PRINCIPAL AUTHORIZING LEGISLATION

## CONGRESSIONAL JURISDICTION
**House Authorizing Committee/Subcommittee**
Committee on Armed Services
Subcommittee on Procurement and Military Systems
**Senate Authorizing Committee/Subcommittee**
Committee on Armed Services
Subcommittee on Strategic and Theater Nuclear Forces
**House Appropriations Subcommittee**
Subcommittee on Energy and Water Development
**Senate Appropriations Subcommittee**
Subcommittee on Energy and Water Development

## RELEVANT STUDIES
Department of Energy, **"Environment, Safety and Health Report for the Department of Energy Defense Complex,"** July 1, 1988
General Accounting Office, **"Dealing With Problems in the Nuclear Weapons Production Complex Expected to Cost Over $100 Billion,"** GAO/RCED-88-197BR, July 1988
Also see GAO reports, GAO/RCED-88-62 and GAO/RCED-86-192

## RELATED FEDERAL PROGRAMS

## PRINCIPAL SOURCES OF EXPERTISE
Natural Resources Defense Council — 202-783-7800
Energy Conservation Coalition — 202-745-4874
Renew America — 202-466-6880

## IMPLEMENTATION STEPS
The Secretary of Energy should transfer administrative and budget control of DOE environmental programs from the Office of the Assistant Secretary for Defense Programs to the Office of the Assistant Secretary for Environment, Safety and Health.

## NOTES:

**Blueprint for the Environment**

# Blueprint for the Environment

## NUCLEAR ENERGY

## DEPARTMENT OF ENERGY

**RECOMMENDATION**

**The Secretary of Energy should mandate that until such time as nuclear power can be demonstrated to present the "least cost" option to meeting the nation's future energy needs, funding for new reactor designs, including fusion, should be limited to basic research. Funding for fusion research should be drastically reduced. Other Department of Energy funding should be directed towards nuclear safety: decommissioning, nuclear waste transportation and disposal of nuclear waste.**

• The current generation of nuclear reactors has been plagued with extensive and significant environmental and health hazards, which have driven up the cost of construction and maintenance of commercial reactors.

• The Department of Energy (DOE) has not directed sufficient attention to safety issues relating to the "back end" of the fuel cycle: plant decommissioning; nuclear waste transportation; on-site storage of spent fuel; final geologic waste disposal.

• Given that light water reactors (LWRs) have been built in the United States for over 30 years, private enterprise should be capable of handling the development and demonstration of this technology. At the very least, private enter-

prise should share a major share of this cost.

• There should be no federal funding for development and demonstration of any new reactor technology until the safety of decommissioning, waste transportation and final geologic disposal can be assured.

• The magnetic fusion program offers no hope as a near-term energy option. The most optimistic projections suggest that a demonstration facility will not be available for at least another 35 years. Nor is the cost of fusion-produced electricity projected to be competitive with other energy options. Even to achieve a sustained fusion reaction would require a major infusion of federal (and international) funds above and beyond the levels already being allocated.

**RECOMMENDATION**

**The President and the Secretary of Energy should declare a two-year moratorium on plutonium production and challenge the Soviet Union to negotiate a bilateral, verifiable halt to the manufacture of plutonium — and highly enriched uranium — for nuclear weapons.**

**RECOMMENDATION**

**The Department of Energy should demonstrate Waste Isolation Pilot Plant compliance with the Environmental Protection Agency Standards for the Management and Disposal of Spent Nuclear Fuel, High Level and Transuranic Radioactive Wastes (40 C.F.R. 191 Subparts A and B) before receipt of waste at Waste Isolation Pilot Plant.**

• When it opens, the Waste Isolation Pilot Plant (WIPP) in New Mexico will be the nation's first underground repository for defense nuclear

wastes. Before the Department of Energy (DOE) begins accepting wastes at the facility for disposal or any other purpose, the public must be assured of the facility's ability to contain and isolate these dangerous radioactive materials from the biosphere.

• Radioactive waste disposal is subject to regulations currently being developed by the Environmental Protection Agency (EPA) that set standards for disposal system performance (40 C.F.R. 191). These standards set numerical limits on human exposure to radiation and long-term releases of radioactive materials to the environment from repositories. Before DOE begins accepting wastes at WIPP, the Department should ascertain that the WIPP disposal system can contain wastes within the bounds of these standards. Compliance with EPA standards is the only independent means of assessing whether or not WIPP is a safe and environmentally sound facility.

## RECOMMENDATION
**The Secretary of Energy should assure that a New Production Reactor for producing nuclear weapons materials is built only if absolutely necessary and that, if built, it meets all relevant environmental and safety standards.**

## RECOMMENDATION
**The Department of Energy should make environmental cleanup and compliance at its weapons facilities a higher priority by immediately and significantly increasing the Production Assurance and Environment, Safety, and Health budgets.**

• In July 1988, the Department of Energy (DOE) estimated that environmental cleanup of its weapons facilities could cost between $66 and $110 billion. At the current rate of DOE spending on environmental activities, it could take well over a century to cleanup the DOE weapons complex. The Secretary of Energy should double the Department's budget for Production Assurance activities over two years and, as needed, increase the budget of DOE's Office of Environment, Safety and Health (ES&H), which is the internal oversight body for environment and safety at DOE weapons facilities.

## RECOMMENDATION
**The Department of Energy should separately account for all funds dedicated to environmental compliance and cleanup at the Department's weapons production facilities. The Department should also submit an annual report to Congress demonstrating that the Department's environmental funding is adequate to comply with the requirements of the Resource Conservation and Recovery Act and Superfund.**

## RECOMMENDATION
**The Department of Energy should immediately halt all plans for development of the Special Isotope Separation plutonium facility proposed for construction at the Idaho National Engineering Laboratory.**

• The Department of Energy (DOE) has estimated that waste cleanup at its weapons facilities will cost $66 to $100 billion. In an era of fiscal constraint and in the face of DOE's staggering environmental bill, unnecessary nuclear weapons production initiatives, such as the Special Isotope Separation (SIS) facility, should be scrapped in order to meet critical environmental cleanup needs.

## RECOMMENDATION
**The Secretary of Energy should give full support to the dominant view of treaty parties within the London Dumping Convention to the effect that seabed burial of high-level radioactive wastes is "dumping" under that Convention, and therefore covered by the London Dumping Convention and prohibited.**

Blueprint for the Environment

# Blueprint for the Environment

## NUCLEAR REGULATORY COMMISSION

In 1954 Congress enacted the Atomic Energy Act, which created the Atomic Energy Commission. The Atomic Energy Commission was charged with both promotion and regulation of commercial nuclear power, as well as with maintaining the national nuclear weapons materials production complex. The Commission moved aggressively to encourage the commercial use of nuclear technology. The regulatory function, however, received less attention.

Eventually Congress came to see that the dual role of the Atomic Energy Commission was inappropriate. An agency charged with promotion of an industry cannot serve as an independent regulator.

In the Energy Reorganization Act of 1974, the promotional and defense functions of the Atomic Energy Commission were separated from the regulatory function by creating two new agencies, the Energy Research and Development Administration (later to become part of the Department of Energy) and the Nuclear Regulatory Commission.

The Nuclear Regulatory Commission was given the mandate to license and regulate commercial use of nuclear technologies, as well as waste storage and transportation of materials arising from such use. Research necessary to promulgate regulations and licensing criteria would be conducted by the Commission.

Initially the Nuclear Regulatory Commission focused primarily on licensing new reactors. Their focus shifted to nuclear safety after the Three Mile Island nuclear accident, and regulations were tightened. Unfortunately, budget cuts and efforts to lessen nuclear regulation resulted in less attention to safety issues. Staff recommendations for safety improvements have been ignored by commissioners. Moves to "stream-line" the licensing process have been initiated. Budget cuts have also taken a toll on existing safety research and review programs.

The Blueprint recommendations for the Nuclear Regulatory Commission have one primary thrust: The Commission should carry out its mandate to regulate nuclear safety.

The specific recommendations to implement this mandate are these:

1) Assure that stringent criteria are established for "inherently safe" reactor designs — do not allow standardized licensing for present reactor designs;
2) Withdraw the "back-fit rule" which discourages safety improvements at existing plants by requiring justification on a cost-benefit basis;
3) Aggressively address known safety problems at existing plants;
4) Require significant up-grading of containment capability, particularly in the case of General Electric plants;
5) Require that states be involved in emergency planning for power plant licensing;
6) Review past safety research which has suffered from budget cuts, and initiate research to identify further safety problems at existing plants.

# Blueprint for the Environment

## NUCLEAR REGULATORY COMMISSION

## NUCLEAR REGULATORY COMMISSION
### Office of Nuclear Materials Safety and Safeguards
### Division of Low-Level Waste Management

### RECOMMENDATION
**The Nuclear Regulatory Commission should rescind its Below Regulatory Concern policy and halt all activities that would generically redefine radioactive materials as ordinary garbage or hazardous waste.**

• Under a new Below Regulatory Concern policy (BRC) it is estimated that up to 40 to 50 percent of what is currently considered "low-level" radioactive waste could be deregulated and treated like solid, liquid or hazardous waste. Consumer products using radioactive materials could be exempted from regulation and put on the market. Both of these practices will be generically approved by the Nuclear Regulatory Commission under its Below Regulatory Concern (BRC) policy, adopted in 1986 (8/29/86 Federal Register). Nuclear waste would go to landfills, incinerators, sewers — anywhere ordinary garbage goes, completely unregulated or monitored for radioactivity.
• Such deregulation will lead to environmental

contamination and involuntary, uninformed public and worker exposure to ionizing radiation. The health risks from exposure to low-levels of radiation have been shown in several recent studies to be much greater than previously assumed by some national and international agencies. Any increase in radiation exposure increases the risk of health and genetic effects.
• The Nuclear Regulatory Commission should rescind its BRC policy and stop all activities (development of implementing regulations, discussions of "acceptable" doses, acceptance and processing of applications, etc.) in support of this policy.

### RECOMMENDATION
**The Nuclear Regulatory Commission should redefine "low-level" radioactive waste to exclude all waste which remains hazardous longer than the 100-year institutional control period required by the Nuclear Regulatory Commission for "low-level" radioactive waste disposal sites. Wastes longer-lived than 100 years should be dealt with as high-level waste, with the intent to isolate them from the environment for their entire hazardous lives.**

• The Nuclear Regulatory Commission definition of "low-level" radioactive waste includes components which will remain hazardous for hundreds, thousands, in some cases, millions of years. Despite a lack of certainty that the federal government will be capable of isolating such long-lived waste from the environment, states are now required to dispose of long-lived radioactive waste.
• A relatively small volume of the "low-level"

radioactive waste stream contains the majority of the radioactivity. This small percentage of the volume, but large percentage of the radioactivity, should be redefined out of the "low-level" waste stream and included with high level waste. All waste containing elements hazardous for longer than 100 years should be redefined as high-level waste, thus a federal, rather than a state, responsibility.

# BUDGET RECOMMENDATION

## PRINCIPAL AUTHORIZING LEGISLATION

Low-Level Radioactive Waste Policy Amendments Act of 1985, Title I, Section 10 (P.L. 99-240) (99 Stat. 1859)
Low-Level Radioactive Waste Policy Act of 1980, (P.L. 96-573) (94 Stat. 3347)
Atomic Energy Act of 1954 (68 Stat. 921)

## CONGRESSIONAL JURISDICTION

**House Authorizing Committee/Subcommittee**
Committee on Interior and Insular Affairs
Subcommittee on Energy and the Environment
Committee on Energy and Commerce
Subcommittee on Energy and Power
**Senate Authorizing Committee/Subcommittee**
Committee on Environment and Public Works
Subcommittee on Nuclear Regulation
Committee on Energy and Natural Resources
Subcommittee on Energy Research and Development
**House Appropriations Subcommittee**
Subcommittee on Energy and Water Development
**Senate Appropriations Subcommittee**
Subcommittee on Energy and Water Development

## RELEVANT STUDIES

Nuclear Regulatory Commission (NRC) Draft Advance Notice of the Development of a Commission Policy on Exemptions from Regulatory Control for Practices Whose Public Health and Safety Impacts are Below Regulatory Concern, advance copy 10-14-88, available from NRC Public Document Room, Washington, D.C.
Nuclear Information and Resource Service Comments on NRC Advance Notice of Proposed Rulemaking on Radioactive Waste Below Regulatory Concern, 10 Code of Federal Regulations parts 2 and 20. March 2, 1987 (available from NIRS or NRC public document room)
**"Federal Ruling Permits Unregulated Disposal of Wastes,"** The Waste Paper, Winter 1987, Radioactive Waste Campaign, 625 Broadway, NY, NY 10012
**"Childhood Cancers in the U.K. and Their Relation to Background Radiation,"** G.W. Kneale and A.M. Stewart. Proceedings of the International Conference on Biological Effects of Ionizing Radiation, Hammersmith Hospital, London. November 24-25, 1986
**Living Without Landfills,** A Special Report by the Radioactive Waste Campaign, New York, 1987

## RELATED FEDERAL PROGRAMS

Superfund
Clean Air Act
Clean Water Act

## PRINCIPAL SOURCES OF EXPERTISE

Natural Resource Defense Council — 202-783-7800
Nuclear Information and Resource Service — 202-328-0002
Food and Water — 814-237-3900
Renew America — 202-466-6880

## Blueprint for the Environment

# Blueprint for the Environment

## NUCLEAR REGULATORY COMMISSION

# NUCLEAR REGULATORY COMMISSION
### Nuclear Reactor Regulation

**RECOMMENDATION**
**The Nuclear Regulatory Commission should establish a regulatory framework that will establish the criteria for inherently safe reactors and standardize only inherently safe designs.**

• The current generation of large, complex nuclear plants is a failure: their cost is prohibitive, the risk of accident is too high and their complexity is such that the potential for human error throughout design, construction and operation is too great. The Nuclear Regulatory Commission (NRC) itself estimates that the chance of a meltdown in a U.S. plant in the next 15—20 years is almost one in two.

**RECOMMENDATION**
**The Nuclear Regulatory Commission should move aggressively toward reducing the probability of catastrophic accidents at the approximately 115 licensed nuclear power plants by withdrawing the so-called "backfit" rule which has operated to eliminate consideration of safety improvements at nuclear plants.**

• The 1985, the Nuclear Regulatory Commission (NRC) adopted a rule which requires a skewed cost-benefit justification as a pre-condition for ordering safety improvements at existing plants. While all conceivable "costs" are included, a great many benefits are arbitrarily excluded.
• This rule was struck down by the U.S. Court of Appeals in Union of Concerned Scientists v. NRC 824 U.S. 108 (D.C. Cir. 1984) as contrary to the Atomic Energy Act's mandate that only safety issues, not cost, may be considered in setting basic safety standards. However, NRC has re-promulgated the rule in a slightly changed form in an effort to get around the court's ruling.

**RECOMMENDATION**
**The Nuclear Regulatory Commission should move aggressively toward reducing the probability of catastrophic accidents at the approximately 115 licensed nuclear power plants by ensuring that known design and operational problems with the current generation of nuclear plants are addressed expeditiously.**

**RECOMMENDATION**
**The Nuclear Regulatory Commission should require that an effective emergency response plan endorsed by the state government must be a prerequisite to operation of a nuclear plant.**

**BUDGET RECOMMENDATION**

**PRINCIPAL AUTHORIZING LEGISLATION**

**CONGRESSIONAL JURISDICTION**
**House Authorizing Committee/Subcommittee**
Committee on Interior and Insular Affairs
Subcommittee on Energy and the Environment
Committee on Energy and Commerce
Subcommittee on Oversight and Investigations
Subcommittee on Energy and Power
**Senate Authorizing Committee/Subcommittee**
Committee on Environment and Public Works
Subcommittee on Nuclear Regulation
**House Appropriations Subcommittee**
Subcommittee on Energy and Water Development
**Senate Appropriations Subcommittee**
Subcommittee on Energy and Water Development

**RELEVANT STUDIES**
NUREG-1150
Kemeny Commsision **"The Report of the President's Commission on the Accident of Three Mile Island: The Need for Change, the Legacy of TMI,"** 1979
**Three Mile Island, A Report to the Commissioners and the Public,** NRCSpecial Inquiry Group, 1979

**RELATED FEDERAL PROGRAMS**

**PRINCIPAL SOURCES OF EXPERTISE**
Union of Concerned Scientists — 202-332-0900
Energy Conservation Coalition — 202-745-4874
Renew America — 202-466-6880

**NOTES:**

## Blueprint for the Environment

# THE FEDERAL ENERGY REGULATORY COMMISSION

In the wake of worldwide energy upheavals in the 1970s that led to the formation of the Department of Energy, the Congress also established the Federal Energy Regulatory Commission, under the Department of Energy umbrella. The Federal Energy Regulatory Commission retains most of the functions of the previous Federal Power Commission, including interstate regulation of certain electric utility activities, natural gas pipelines and rates, and hydroelectric power siting and operation. The Commission also retains "independent" regulatory agency status, maintaining considerable institutional, policy and budget distance from the Department of Energy.

It is the Commission's hydroelectric licensing program and especially its environmental review and decisionmaking, which received the greatest criticism in recent years from federal and state resource agencies, tribes, conservation organizations, Congress and the courts. During this decade, the Commission's hydroelectric workload skyrocketed in both numbers and complexity of reviews, driven by hydropower tax and marketing incentives adopted in the late 70s and early 80s and by a quirk of history that now brings some 200 of the nation's oldest hydroelectric developments before the Commission for "relicensing" in 1993.

Environmentalists and resource agencies have expressed serious concern that major potential exists for environmental damage from construction and operation of dams and water diversions from thousands of proposed "small hydro" projects that have flooded the Federal Energy Regulatory Commission's dockets. Often the energy benefits of such projects are negligible, when compared with their accompanying irreversible losses of fisheries, wildlife, other water uses and public recreational opportunities, yet the Commission's processing of applications all too often fails to give adequate weight to environmental factors. Despite the huge growth in its workload, the Commission consistently failed to adequately staff and budget its environmental review functions and has been criticized widely for failure to provide appropriate opportunity for public involvement. Even after its December 1987 adoption of the Council on Environmental Quality's National Environmental Policy Act guidelines, a decade after most other agencies, the Commission continues in many cases to shirk its responsibilities to prepare environmental impact statements and cumulative impact studies.

Congressional passage of the 1986 Electric Consumers Protection Act with new environmental provisions requiring "equal consideration" for environmental values in licensing and greater deference to the recommendations of federal and state natural resource agencies and their comprehensive plans provides a foundation for change at the Commission. However, the Commission has taken only the most preliminary of steps toward updating its licensing policies and procedures to conform with the environmental concerns and values of the 1980s.

The Blueprint recommendations made are intended to facilitate a licensing program modernization that is long overdue. Many are relevant to the other Commission programs as well. Hundreds of critically important hydroelectric licensing decisions by the Commission are on the immediate horizon. These will affect water rights and beneficial uses, fishery and wildlife restoration efforts and other key natural resource plans in most states of the Union. The Commission and the Congress must act quickly and decisively to adopt proposed program changes to avoid major environmental damages on river systems throughout the nation.

## FEDERAL ENERGY
## REGULATORY COMMISSION

# DEPARTMENT OF ENERGY
### Federal Energy Regulatory Commission

**RECOMMENDATION**
**The Chairman of the Federal Energy Regulatory Commission should establish an expanded Public Outreach and Involvement program and seek public suggestions through Federal Register notice to improve public participation in its hydropower licensing, environmental reviews and other Commission programs.**

• Among the public participation improvements which the Commission should implement immediately are:

1) Re-establishment of standing computerized Commission mailing lists on request of interested members of the public for distribution of Notice of Proposed Rulemakings (NOPRs), National Environmental Policy Act (NEPA) Documents, Final Orders, notices of applications and other Commission documents;

2) A policy of printing in the Federal Register the full text of preambles as well as proposed rules in NOPRs and providing for telecommunications availability during full comments period, not just the current 10 days;

3) To improve NEPA decision-making, adopt a regulation to require at least a 30-day public comment period for both environmental assessments with "mitigated finding of no significant impacts (FONSI's)", and draft license terms and conditions underlying the FONSI;

4) Establish a staff position in the Office of Congressional and Public Affairs to develop needed informational materials and to assist members of the public in understanding and participating in Commission procedures;

5) Re-establish bi-weekly publication of the FERC Monitor or its equivalent and make available to the public at reasonable cost;

6) Because evaluation of whitewater recreation is an area of limited Federal Energy Regulatory Commission (FERC) experience, acquire a full national set of whitewater guides for each river basin for staff and public use;

7) Additional public participation procedures should be committed to regulation, including: a) procedures for implementing the new Federal Powers Act (FPA) subsection 10(j) regarding FERC establishment of license conditions for protection of fish and wildlife, b) numerous procedures described in draft Memorandum of Understanding (MOUs) with federal agencies Army Corps of Engineers, Bureau of Reclamation, Fish and Wildlife Service, National Marine Fisheries Service, and Forest Service (Corps, BOR, FWS, NMFS, USFS), and c) modification of FERC regulations to allow automatic intervenor party status on filing timely rehearing motions.

## BUDGET RECOMMENDATION
F.Y. 90: **Increase** of $100,000          F.Y. 91: **no change**

## PRINCIPAL AUTHORIZING LEGISLATION
Federal Power Act (16 U.S.C. 701, et. seq.)
National Environmental Policy Act (42 U.S.C. 4321)

## CONGRESSIONAL JURISDICTION
**House Authorizing Committee/Subcommittee**
   Committee on Energy and Commerce
      Subcommittee on Energy and Power
**Senate Authorizing Committee/Subcommittee**
   Committee on Energy and Natural Resources
      Subcommittee on Energy Regulation and Conservation
**House Appropriations Subcommittee**
   Subcommittee on Energy and Water Development
**Senate Appropriations Subcommittee**
   Subcommittee on Energy and Water Development

## RELEVANT STUDIES

## RELATED FEDERAL PROGRAMS
President's Council on Environmental Quality
Army Corps of Engineers
Bureau of Reclamation
Fish and Wildlife Service
Forest Service
National Marine Fisheries Service

## PRINCIPAL SOURCES OF EXPERTISE
Friends of the Earth — 202-543-4312   National Wildlife Federation — 202-797-6800
American Rivers — 202-547-6900   American Whitewater Affiliation 518-674-5519
National Audubon Society — 202-547-9009

## IMPLEMENTATION STEPS
In the first quarter of 1989 the Commission should:
(1)   Establish a staff position within the Office of Congressional and Public Affairs specifically to develop and make publicly available explanatory materials and assistance in understanding and participating in Commission proceedings.
(2)   In the Federal Register, issue a request for public comments on methods and actions the Commission should institute to improve public participation and commit to instituting within six months the necessary changes and proposed rulemaking proceedings to implement the program.
(3)   Begin rulemaking proceeding to establish procedures for implementation of FPA Section 10(j) under the Electric Consumers Protection Act.

## NOTES:
Public Outreach and Involvement Program for hydropower can be accomplished and funded through additional annual charges under Federal Power Act (16 U.S.C. 803 (e)) with revenue offset

---

## Blueprint for the Environment

# Blueprint for the Environment

## FEDERAL ENERGY REGULATORY COMMISSION
## DEPARTMENT OF ENERGY

### RECOMMENDATION
**The Commission should, at a minimum, triple its environmental review budget and its personnel levels in FY 1990 (over FY 1989) to assure compliance with the requirements of the National Environmental Policy Act.**

• In the coming three fiscal years, the Commission will experience a major increase in numbers and complexity of hydroelectric licensing cases requiring NEPA reviews. Without at least a tripling of the environmental review budget, environmental reviews will become the single greatest cause of delay in Commission licensing. The Commission has never before faced such a large increase in its environmental workload, which anticipates an unprecedented 200 relicensings in FY 1993, with many of the most difficult original licensing cases currently pending, and a projected six-fold increase in the licensing of unlicensed projects.

### RECOMMENDATION
**The Commission should assure that each licensed hydroelectric power project fully complies with state certification requirements of the Clean Water Act.**

• The Commission should support legislation in the 101st Congress to restore the applicability of the Section 401 state certification requirements of the Clean Water Act. This will affect approximately 227 hydropower projects proposed for license that were affected by the retroactive application of the Commission's Order 464, issued in February, 1987. The Commission should also adopt the policy of assuring that the conditions of all its licenses will be fully consistent with issued state certifications or the recommendations of the state or interstate agency charged with the implementation of state Clean Water Act responsibilities. The Commission should indicate to license applicants that licenses will not be issued for those projects that are inconsistent with either the certifications or written recommendations.

• The highly unusual decision by the Commission to apply Order 464 retroactively represents an unprecedented waiver of the Clean Water Act requirements for more than half of the Commission's pending licensing dockets, and has met with strong disapproval from Congress, state resource agencies and environmental organizations. Without enactment of this legislation and adoption of the interim policy, a large number of hydroelectric licenses may be issued which do not meet state water quality standards, even though at the time of the Commission's waiver order, states maintained full and good faith intention to either issue certifications with conditions that bring projects into compliance or to deny certification where projects cannot meet the state water quality standards.

• This unnecessary problem was caused by a poor Commission decision. By now supporting legislation to finally resolve the problem and by establishing an interim policy, the Commission should have a role in its proper resolution.

113

# RECOMMENDATION

**The Federal Energy Regulatory Commission should adopt, in the form of an official rule, a policy prohibiting the construction of hydroelectric projects on rivers designated for preservation under state law.**

• At present, the Commission continues to accept hydroelectric applications on rivers that states have identified as being worthy of preservation. The result is a substantial perceived threat to state river protection efforts. In addition, hydro developers are ill-served by the Commission's present policy because they seldom are able to overcome local public and governmental opposition to the construction of these projects. An Agency policy against hydroelectric development of state-protected rivers would provide important federal support for state river protection efforts and establish a more predictable,

and less costly, regulatory environment for hydroelectric development.

• Thirty-one states now have river programs that comprise more than 11,000 miles of designated river. These programs are expanding in several states and state officials are concerned that there is no current policy of consistent action by the Federal Energy Regulatory Commission (FERC). A stated purpose of virtually all state river programs is to maintain rivers in a free-flowing condition and yet FERC now ignores such state policies.

# RECOMMENDATION

**The Chairman of the Federal Energy Regulatory Commission should instruct its Director of Office of Hydropower Licensing to evaluate state comprehensive waterway plans and to work in consultation with the state and federal resource agencies to establish model guidelines for state plans that will encourage state comprehensive river planning and assist the Commission in achieving consistency with state plans in hydroelectric licensing.**

# RECOMMENDATION

**The Federal Energy Regulatory Commission should adopt a rule stating that, before a hydro project will be approved on a river included in the Nationwide Rivers Inventory, the Commission or another appropriate federal agency will study the affected river segment for possible inclusion in the Federal Wild and Scenic Rivers System and, if the agency recommends in favor of designation, Congress will have an opportunity to decide whether or not to add the segment to the System.**

• The Nationwide Rivers Inventory, published by the National Park Service in 1982, is the appropriate starting place for identifying "potential" wild and scenic rivers within the meaning of Section 5(d). The Nationwide Rivers Inventory lists about 1500 river

segments — about 2 percent of the river mileage in the United States — that the Park Service has determined possess characteristics that would make them potentially worthy additions to the Federal System.

# RECOMMENDATION

**The Commission should assure that hydropower licensing is conducted consistently with the Protected Areas plans of the Northwest Power Planning Council and encourage other states and regions to develop similar comprehensive river protection plans.**

• A clear Commission policy of seeking to license consistently with state and regional river conservation plans would serve to encourage other states and regions to develop comprehensive river protec-

tion plans. It would greatly assist the Commission in carrying out its mandates in the Federal Power Act and the 1986 Electric Consumers Protection Act.

## Blueprint for the Environment

# TENNESSEE VALLEY AUTHORITY

The Tennessee Valley Authority is in crisis — worse than any in its 55-year history. The Authority, the nation's largest electric utility, is approaching financial insolvency. It owes over $16 billion on nuclear power plants that contribute — and will continue to contribute — little or no power. The Tennessee Valley Authority's conservation and resource management responsibilities have become very low priorities during this crisis. Only Presidential leadership — and major changes in the Tennessee Valley Authority's charter — can end the continuing crisis at the Authority.

The Tennessee Valley Authority was created in 1933 to provide navigation, flood control, power generation, economic development and basin-wide conservation in a region touching seven states. It provides electric power to over six million people, principally in Tennessee, Mississippi, Alabama and Kentucky. While the Authority became the nation's largest utility, its regional development and resource conservation efforts largely atrophied. Over 97 percent of the Tennessee Valley Authority's budget now goes for power generation.

The Tennessee Valley Authority's importance for the next President comes both in its potential for crisis and for opportunity. Tennessee Valley Authority's power system offers great opportunities for national leadership — it could be a test-bed for innovative energy solutions for the greenhouse problem. Although it once had in place an innovative energy-efficiency program, the Tennessee Valley Authority recently dismantled it, concentrating instead on completing power plants.

The Tennessee Valley Authority could cause major problems for the next Administration. If the Authority defaults on the more than $20 billion in loans it has obtained through the Federal Financing Bank, the President will face a financial crisis of his own. At the same time, the Authority could create a dangerous public safety problem as it rushes to place on-line power plants that currently are unsafe to operate. Nine Tennessee Valley Authority nuclear units have been completed or are near completion, but only one has recently been permitted to re-start operation.

A three-member board of directors runs the Tennessee Valley Authority. Each member is appointed by the U.S. President for a term of nine years. The board authorizes all projects, sets all rates, directs programs totalling $100 million in appropriations, makes all power investment decisions, and thus has responsibilities more akin to those of a management committee than a conventional board of directors. No state or federal regulatory body oversees the Tennessee Valley Authority's activities. Congressional oversight is sporadic and nominal.

It is clear that the Tennessee Valley Authority now is accountable to almost no one. It does not have to answer to competition in the marketplace. The board does not have to answer to an electorate. It is not subject to state or federal regulation. This lack of accountability directly contributed to the current debt crisis.

For these reasons, Blueprint recommends that the President take four major actions with regard to the Tennessee Valley Authority:

1) Amend the Tennessee Valley Authority Act to elect directly the Board of Directors on a basis of proportional representation. The purpose of this policy is to facilitate citizens' control of regional environmental quality, electric rates, and utility decision-making.

2) Create a planning process to require delivery of least-cost utility services. The purpose of this plan would be to resolve a pending, severe Tennessee Valley Authority debt crisis, protect environmental quality, and provide least-cost energy services.

3) Freeze additions to the Tennessee Valley Authority's debt due to capital additions until a least-cost utility services planning process is established. The President would direct the Office of Management and Budget to analyze the full implications of the Tennessee Valley

Authority debt situation and make recommendations to resolve it.

4) Direct the Tennessee Valley Authority not only to observe existing environmental standards but to serve as a model to the nation in improving environmental quality. The Tennessee Valley Authority's original mandate called for the Authority to be the steward of the Tennessee River and its tributaries. Activities should include, for example, controlling both point and non-point sources of water pollution. The agency should also be directed to correct the Tennessee River water quality problems caused by the Authority's multi-purpose dams. This action could be accomplished by presidential directive, and would require the Tennessee Valley Authority to retrofit hydroelectric facilities to increase dissolved oxygen levels in waters downstream of the dams. Many such areas fall below minimum dissolved oxygen requirements to support fish life for two-month periods each year.

These programs would solve both specific problems that could present serious crises of debt and public safety for the President, and they would address fundamental structural flaws in the Tennessee Valley Authority which have contributed to the current crisis in the Tennessee Valley.

# TENNESSEE VALLEY AUTHORITY
## BOARD OF DIRECTORS

### RECOMMENDATION
**The Board of Directors should freeze additions to the Tennessee Valley Authority's debt due to capital additions until a least-cost utility services planning process is established. The Board should also direct the Office of Management and Budget to analyze the full implications of the debt situation and make recommendations to solve it.**

• The Tennessee Valley Authority's (TVA) FY 1987 financial statements show over $16 billion in debt attributable to its nuclear power plant construction program. TVA's nuclear debt grew by about $1.2 billion between FY 1986 and FY 1987; its overall debt grew by $1.4 billion between FY 1986 and FY 1987.

• TVA owes almost $7.9 billion on two units at Watts Bar and two at Bellefonte, and over half a billion dollars on additions and modifications to Sequoyah and Browns Ferry. These sums have not yet been added to TVA's rate base.

• Coopers and Lybrand, TVA's independent accountant, has become so uncomfortable with TVA's debt that the firm has qualified its opinion letters on TVA's FY 1986 and FY 1987 financial statements, writing: "the Board of Directors may elect not to recover from the ratepayers all costs associated with the nuclear power program.

The ultimate outcome of these matters cannot be determined at this time." (Included in Financial Statements for the Fiscal Year Ended September 30, 1987, TVA)

• One implication of this statement is that the Federal Government might have to cover billions of dollars in TVA bonds sold through the Federal Financing Bank (despite the fact that the TVA Act requires rates to cover all TVA power costs). Another is that the TVA could become technically insolvent in the near future. Yet, TVA continues to spend billions of dollars to complete the nuclear power construction program, despite the fact that demand for power is not adequate to justify their completion.

• Only immediate and dramatic action can extricate TVA from an impending debt crisis — with both regional and national implications.

## BUDGET RECOMMENDATION
F.Y. 90: **no change**          F.Y. 91: **no change**

## PRINCIPAL AUTHORIZING LEGISLATION
Tennessee Valley Authority Act of 1933

## CONGRESSIONAL JURISDICTION
**House Authorizing Committee/Subcommittee**
Committee on Public Works and Transportation
Subcommittee on Water Resources
**Senate Authorizing Committee/Subcommittee**
Committee on Environment and Public Works
Subcommittee on Nuclear Regulation
**House Appropriations Subcommittee**
Subcommittee on Energy and Water Development
**Senate Appropriations Subcommittee**
Subcommittee on Energy and Water Development

## RELEVANT STUDIES
**TVA: A Path to Recovery, Report of the Advisory Committee on the Tennessee Valley Authority,** Southern States Energy Board, Gov. Gerald L. Boliles, Chairman, Atlanta, September 1, 1987

## RELATED FEDERAL PROGRAMS

## PRINCIPAL SOURCES OF EXPERTISE
TVA Board Appointment Coalition — 615-637-6055
Tennessee Valley Energy Coalition — 615-637-6055
Sierra Club, Southeast Regional Office — 615-588-1892
Renew America — 202-466-6880

## IMPLEMENTATION STEPS
The President should instruct the Department of the Treasury to sell no more TVA bonds for new capital development until the TVA has drafted its least-cost plan. (See other proposal.)

## NOTES:

# Blueprint for the Environment

# TENNESSEE VALLEY AUTHORITY
## BOARD OF DIRECTORS

### RECOMMENDATION

**The Board of Directors should provide for citizens' participation in the use and protection of Tennessee Valley natural resources by amending the Tennessee Valley Authority Act to elect directly the Tennessee Valley Authority Board of Directors on a basis of proportional representation.**

• The purpose of this policy is to facilitate citizens' control of regional environmental quality, electric rates and utility decision-making. The directors are currently appointed by the President for nine year, overlapping terms.

• The citizens of the Tennessee Valley, who bought and paid for the modern Tennessee Valley Authority (TVA) system, have accepted all risk for the solvency of the TVA corporation and logically should own it. Transfer of ownership, or at least control, would not only be fair, but it would help control many of the growing problems at TVA.

• TVA's growing problems include possible insolvency. The Authority now owes over $16 billion for nine nuclear power units. Drastic and arbitrary cost-cutting measures have been implemented recently, including termination of several thousand employees, dismantling of the TVA energy conservation program, and downgrading of the natural resources program to caretaker status.

• TVA is the only unregulated electric utility in the United States. The federally-owned Bonneville Power Administration (BPA) is regulated by the Federal Energy Regulatory Commission (FERC). Private utilities must obtain approval for rate increases or power plant construction from their state utility commissions, while BPA and all U.S. power administrations must obtain approvals from FERC.

• TVA is accountable only to the President. Directors run the agency like an executive committee. They ask no one's permission to build power plants or raise rates. This lack of accountability directly contributed to the current debt crisis and nuclear power safety crisis.

### RECOMMENDATION

**The President should instruct the Tennessee Valley Authority Board of Directors to draft a plan of action to 1) improve the dissolved oxygen content of the Tennessee River, particularly in areas where the problem is created and exacerbated by Tennessee Valley Authority reservoirs; and 2) reduce the flow of non-point sources of pollution — including agricultural and mining wastes — into the Tennessee River and its tributaries.**

• The Tennessee Valley Authority's (TVA) original mandate called for TVA to be the steward of the Tennessee River and its Tributaries. TVA should be directed not only to observe existing environmental standards but to serve as a model to the nation in improving environmental quality. Activities should include, for example, controlling both point and non-point sources of water pollution.

• Water quality throughout the system has been diminished by oxygen depletion, toxic chemicals and waste. Recent rediscovery that tons of mercury have been lost to "Industrial Ditch," a creek which flows through the Oak Ridge, Tennessee federal weapons laboratory and empties into the Clinch River, has quickened the debate.

Water has always been nominally TVA's raison

119

d'etre. TVA has long regarded water as the means for development, but has recently shown increased concern for water conservation and water quality. This concern has been reflected in scientific surveys and in efforts to ameliorate water quality problems. A central water quality problem in the Tennessee River, however, is the reservoirs themselves. The conflicts between development and environmental values will only grow unless TVA — and the federal government — commits the resources required to fulfill its responsibilities in ameliorating the problems it has caused in regional water quality.

• Unfortunately, TVA's potential for contributing to water quality protection in the Tennessee Valley is constrained by the severe institutional crisis at TVA. Only the President can, by direct order, make regional environmental quality an important priority for TVA.

## RECOMMENDATION
**The Board of Directors of the Tennessee Valley Authority should avoid the unnecessary and environmentally destructive consumption of additional electric power in the Tennessee Valley region by creating a planning process to require delivery of least-cost utility services.**

• The Tennessee Valley Authority's (TVA) power program has caused both very serious environmental and economic problems. TVA was once the largest violator of the Clean Air Act emissions controls on sulfur dioxide, but now is in compliance. TVA has also violated Nuclear Regulatory Commission (NRC) regulations more than any power company.

And despite some efforts in energy efficiency, the TVA region continues to use far more electricity per capita than the rest of the nation. Yet, TVA recently dismantled its energy conservation program. This action will mean unnecessary waste of consumer money as well as unnecessary air pollution, coal strip mining and water impacts.

## RECOMMENDATION
**The Tennessee Valley Authority should expand existing programs to provide opportunities for private sector/nonfederal participation in federal fisheries management, hereafter called "partnerships," and review agency operations to formulate recommendations for creation of new opportunities.**

• In the U.S., fish are common property resources and are often highly migratory. Thus, governments are charged with fish stewardship responsibilities, and these duties are often performed, of necessity, in cooperation (partnerships) with other governments. Historically, private users of fisheries resources have supplied several user fees devoted to conducting government fisheries management. State fisheries activities are funded largely by fishing licenses and taxes collected on fishing equipment and motorboat fuels taxes.

• Due to projected severe budget shortfalls in the near future it appears likely that sufficient funding and manpower to manage an increasingly scarce fisheries resource will not be available. The future of federal fisheries management will rely increasingly on private sector/nonfederal partnerships. Federal agencies with fisheries responsibilities already have in place some mechanisms to facilitate these partnerships. This proposal calls for expansion of existing, successful mechanisms, and investigation of potential new opportunities for private sector/nonfederal participation in fisheries management.

## Blueprint for the Environment

# Blueprint for the Environment

## DEPARTMENT OF HEALTH AND HUMAN SERVICES

The Department of Health and Human Services is the central agency in the federal government for research into the public health effects of environmental hazards and for family planning efforts. Both of these programs insure a better future and a healthier environment and both are addressed in the Blueprint recommendations.

The National Institute of Environmental Health Sciences plays several roles which should be strengthened.

The Division of Toxicological Research and Testing should have its capacity expanded to ensure adequate testing of environmental chemicals. Expanded testing and the development of more effective test methods are vital to support the protection of public health and to support the development of effective environmental regulations.

The Institute's Superfund Basic Research and Research-Training Program met with enthusiasm when established, but has realized only part of its potential. The support of research under this program should be expanded, and a reauthorization of the program, which expires in 1991, should be supported.

Finally, the Institute's Environmental Health Sciences Program should be expanded in two other areas. Basic and applied research, which is essential to scientific progress in this area, should be enhanced. The various fields of research should be integrated in developing methods for the safe and permanent disposal of hazardous substances. A new clinical research program should also be instituted to address the prevention, diagnosis and treatment of environmentally related illnesses and disabilities.

One specific thrust for the Surgeon General is recommended in the Blueprint for the Environment, a study on Diet Choices and the Environment. What is needed is a close look at the environmental consequences of American eating habits and positive directions to change the negative environmental effects while recommending a healthier diet.

The Office of Population is responsible for the primary federal family planning program, the Title X Program. This program is key to reducing unwanted pregnancies through voluntary family planning. While Title X should continue to provide quality maternal and child health care services, it can also, by reaching those who wish to avoid or delay pregnancies, reduce the pressures which population growth places upon the environment.

The Title X Program, however, has not been reaching all of those who are eligible for the program or those who need the program. It has been estimated that current efforts leave one-third of those needing family planning services without help, and this must be remedied. In addition, the program should increase its educational efforts targeted at adolescent pregnancy and sexually-transmitted diseases. Unwanted teen pregnancies are a dual tragedy. They not only add to population pressures, but to the personal problems and the future possibilities available to the persons involved.

Finally, many women do not use contraceptives because they fear the side effects of those now available. Only one manufacturer is currently researching new contraceptives, in part due to liability questions. Contraceptive research efforts need to be expanded and supported by the Office of Population. In addition, the office should work with the Food and Drug Administration to ensure that safe and effective contraceptives do not face unnecessary problems in reaching the marketplace.

# Blueprint for the Environment

## FOOD SAFETY

# DEPARTMENT OF HEALTH AND HUMAN SERVICES
## ASSISTANT SECRETARY for Health
### Surgeon General

**RECOMMENDATION**
**The Department of Health and Human Services, in cooperation with the Department of Agriculture, the Department of the Interior and the Environmental Protection Agency, should develop a comprehensive study on Diet Choices and the Environment, like the Surgeon General's report on Diet and Health, examining the impact of various diets on the environment.**

• While over 85 percent of agricultural land and water use in the U.S. is devoted to the production of animal foods, there is no federal effort to assess the impact of this industry on major environmental concerns including global warming, deforestation, destruction of wildlife habitat, extinction of species, water pollution, loss of soil productivity and desertification.

• A growing body of scientific evidence suggests that the emphasis on meat in the typical U.S. diet, coupled with the intensive animal husbandry techniques that have evolved to meet growing demands, is harmful to the delicate natural systems upon which the agricultural industry depends. For example:

1) Internationally, to accommodate the burgeoning demand for beef, more than 5 million acres of Central and South American rainforests are cut down each year to create more grazing land for cattle, much of which is imported by U.S. companies because of its "cheap price."

2) In June 1988, the General Accounting Office (GAO) reported that at least 50 percent of the public range lands (Bureau of Land Management and Forest Service) remain in poor or fair condition due to livestock ranching (the lowest categories describing range conditions).

3) The typical American meat diet requires up to 10 times as much land and eight times the amount of water to produce the same number of calories as a non-meat diet (most of it from indirect consumption by livestock).

• By eating lower on the food chain, many of the ills described above could be overcome. There are few things that the individual could do that could have a greater positive impact on the environment. Therefore, a comprehensive study that would elucidate the links between diet and the environment should be undertaken by the Administration to educate consumers so that they may make better informed choices.

## BUDGET RECOMMENDATION
F.Y. 90: **no change**          F.Y. 91: **no change**

## PRINCIPAL AUTHORIZING LEGISLATION

## CONGRESSIONAL JURISDICTION
**House Authorizing Committee/Subcommittee**
Committee on Energy and Commerce
Subcommittee on Health and the Environment
**Senate Authorizing Committee/Subcommittee**
Committee on Environment and Public Works
Subcommittee on Environmental Protection
**House Appropriations Subcommittee**
Subcommittee on Labor, Health and Human Services and Education
**Senate Appropriations Subcommittee**
Subcommittee on Labor, Health and Human Services and Education and Related Agencies

## RELEVANT STUDIES
John Robbins, **Diet For A New America**, Stillpoint Publishers, 1988
Dr. M.W. Fox, **Agricide: The Hidden Crisis That Affects Us All**, Schocken Books, 1988
GAO, **Rangeland Management: More Emphasis Needed on Declining and Overstocked Grazing Allotments**, Washington, D.C., June, 1988
GAO, **Pesticides: Better Sampling and Enforcement Needed on Imported Foods**, GAO/RCED-86-219 (September 1986)
GAO, **Pesticides: Need to Enhance FDA's Ability to Protect the Public from Illegal Residues**, GAO/RCED-87-7(October 1986)
National Academy of Sciences, Board on Agriculture, **Regulating Pesticides in Food: The Delaney Paradox**, 1987
Natural Resources Defense Council: Pesticide Alert: A Guide to Pesticides in Fruits and Vegetables, 1988

## RELATED FEDERAL PROGRAMS
Forest Service
Bureau of Land Management
Environmental Protection Agency

## PRINCIPAL SOURCES OF EXPERTISE
Humane Society of the U.S. — 202-452-1100
Friends of the Earth — 202-543-4312

## IMPLEMENTATION STEPS
(1) The Commissioner of the Food and Drug Administration should ensure that pesticide residues in the food supply do not exceed tolerance levels set by the Environmental Protection Agency by improving its capacity to monitor for pesticide residues and to ensure that foods which bear illegal pesticide residues are removed from the market.
(2) The Department of Agriculture, the Food and Drug Administration and the Environmental Protection Agency should eliminate the environmental and public health threats associated with livestock production by regulating pesticides found in animal foods and groundwater and prohibiting the use of antibiotics in animal foods.

## Blueprint for the Environment

# Blueprint for the Environment

## FAMILY PLANNING

## DEPARTMENT OF HEALTH AND HUMAN SERVICES
### ASSISTANT SECRETARY for Health
### Office of Population Affairs

### RECOMMENDATION
**The Assistant Secretary for Health should work to assure that the Title X Family Planning program is funded adequately to reach all currently eligible women is expanded to reach marginal-income women, increases its information and education efforts, and fosters research into new and improved contraceptive devices.**

• The Title X program within the Public Health Services Act was created to improve maternal and child health by enabling women and families to better decide the timing and spacing of childbearing. The Title X family planning program of the Department of Health and Human Services is the primary source of such services for low-income women. The program is currently being funded at $30 million less than in 1980, is not reaching one-third of the women who are eligible, and many marginal-income women need to be brought into the program.

• Although there is an information and education section of Title X, it is not being utilized to its fullest potential. The high incidence of teen pregnancies and sexually transmitted diseases makes it essential that the public receive information to prevent them. The Title X program should be expanded to encourage community-based programs to assist individuals to make responsible and informed decisions concerning human sexuality, pregnancy and parenthood. Such information should include materials on a broad range of acceptable and effective family planning methods, basic sexuality education and information on AIDS.

• New and improved contraceptive devices, drugs and methods are needed to ensure optimum safety and choice for each individual desiring to use contraception. There are many new methods which are well along in the research pipeline, but have encountered serious obstacles to their completion. The Title X program should be expanded to foster applied research leading to the development, evaluation and marketing of new contraceptives.

## BUDGET RECOMMENDATION
F.Y. 90: **Increase** of $ 31 million     F.Y. 91: **Increase** of $ 39 million

## PRINCIPAL AUTHORIZING LEGISLATION
Title X, Public Health Service Act.

## CONGRESSIONAL JURISDICTION
**House Authorizing Committee/Subcommittee**
Committee on Energy and Commerce
Subcommittee on Health and the Environment
**Senate Authorizing Committee/Subcommittee**
Committee on Labor and Human Resources
Subcommittee
**House Appropriations Subcommittee**
Subcommittee on Labor, Health and Human Services and Education
**Senate Appropriations Subcommittee**
Subcommittee on Labor, Health and Human Services and Education and Related Agencies

## RELEVANT STUDIES
Committee Report, Senate Labor and Human Resources Committee, February 18, 1988 (to accompany S. 1366) Report 100-286
GAO/HRD-82-106; September 24, 1982, regarding restrictions on family planning programs
**Risking the Future,** National Academy of Sciences, 1987
CRS Report; 87-840 — Title X Regulations

## RELATED FEDERAL PROGRAMS
Medicaid — Health Care Financing Administration
Titles V and XX, Social Security; Maternal and Child Health and Social Services block grants
Appropriations legislation regarding the National Institute of Child Health and Human Development

## PRINCIPAL SOURCES OF EXPERTISE
The Alan Guttmacher Institute — 202-296-4012
Planned Parenthood Federation of America — 202-785-3351
National Family Planning and Reproductive Health Assn. — 202-628-3535
Zero Population Growth — 202-332-2200

### IMPLEMENTATION STEPS
(1) Change leadership personnel at the Office of Population Affairs.
(2) Withdraw March 2, 1988 Title X regulatory changes (42 C.F.R. Part 59) and settle pending litigation by reinstating former regulations.
(3) Support Title X reauthorization with appropriate funding levels and authorization for new initiatives, e.g., S. 1366 in 100th Congress.
(4) Seek revision of FDA regulations and/or special contraceptive injury fund to encourage manufacture of new contraceptive drugs and devices.

## BUDGET HISTORY (in millions of dollars by fiscal year)

|             | 79  | 80    | 83  | 85    | 87  | 88  | 89  |
|-------------|-----|-------|-----|-------|-----|-----|-----|
| Authorized* | 200 | 264.5 | n/a | 158.4 | n/a | n/a | n/a |
| Requested   |     | Admin. req block grant pgm | | | | 140 | |
| Appropriated | 135 | 161  | 124 | 142   | 142 | 139 | ?   |

* program has been reauthorized annually as part of appropriations process. Multi-year reauthorization of program has not been enacted.

## NOTES:

———————— **Blueprint for the Environment** ————————

# Blueprint for the Environment

## HEALTH SCIENCE

# DEPARTMENT OF HEALTH AND HUMAN SERVICES

**RECOMMENDATION**
**The Secretary of Health and Human Services should establish a clinical research program for the diagnosis, prevention and treatment of environmentally caused disease and disabilities.**

**RECOMMENDATION**
**The Secretary of Health and Human Services should pursue the development of methods to improve the scientific basis for developing realistic estimates of the potential human health risks posed by exposure to environmental and occupational chemical toxins.**

• The importance of quantitative risk assessment in the environmental regulatory process is increasingly being recognized in industrialized nations. But recent federal studies found that quantitative risk assessment (the estimation of cancers and other health risks associated with exposures to environmental and occupational hazards), as currently practiced, is a complex blend of scientific fact, assumption, and policy decisions. Because presently-used risk assessment procedures are so crude, the estimated risks may far overstate or understate the actual risk involved with a given exposure. The use of crude risk estimates may have negative health and/or economic impacts.

• The scientific basis of risk assessment must be improved. Federal funding for both basic and applied risk assessment related research at molecular level must be increased. Emphasis must be placed on identifying and understanding the events which take place inside the cell as a result of a chemical exposure.

**RECOMMENDATION**
**The Secretary of Health and Human Services should expand the testing of environmental chemicals for toxicity (health effects) in experimental systems to ensure a sound scientific basis for environmental regulation.**

• The Division of Toxicologic Research and Testing in the National Institute of Environmental Health Sciences is the principal federal program concerned with evaluating the potential human health effects posed by environmental chemicals. It also strengthens and coordinates the Dept. of Health and Human Services (HHS) activities in characterizing the toxicity of chemicals through its management of the HHS National Toxicology Program.

• For at least 25 years there has been increasing concern both within the scientific community and throughout the world, about the extent to which physical and chemical agents in the environment (including air, soil, water, food, drugs, cosmetics, consumer products, the workplace, the home and the neighborhood) may contribute to the occurrence of disease.

• After reviewing 65,725 substances of highest environmental concern, the National Academy of Sciences concluded that there are very few where there is enough toxicity and exposure information to conduct a complete human health-hazard assessment. For the great majority the data is lacking.

• More than half the carcinogenicity studies

deemed adequate by the National Academy of Sciences were conducted by the National Institute of Environmental Health Sciences. Expansion of toxicology testing capacity is urgently needed to provide a sound scientific base for regulatory actions taken by federal, state, and local agencies. In addition, there is an urgent need to develop new, effective test methods which are quicker, less expensive, more predictive of human health effects and which do not rely so heavily on the use of laboratory animals.

## RECOMMENDATION
**The Secretary of Health and Human Services should strengthen and expand basic research and long-term applied research in environmental health sciences.**

• Environmental health problems require research for detection, quantification, treatment and prevention. Recent studies of the state of environmental health sciences research stress the need for basic research of the mechanisms through which environmental hazards damage biologic processes and cause illness. Knowledge of the mechanism of toxicity will lead to interventions including early detection, prevention and treatment.

• Basic research has provided most of the truly innovative and beneficial scientific advances. Basic research must be justified on its own merit, not on the basis that a given study will produce a predictable result. Long-term applied biomedical research is vitally important to the success of environmental programs, but these kinds of studies must be sustained, often for periods up to 5 to 10 years or more.

## RECOMMENDATION
**The Secretary of Health and Human Services should strengthen and expand the integrated program of biomedical, engineering, ecological, and geologic/hydrogeologic research necessary for the safe and permanent disposal of hazardous substances.**

• Safe, permanent disposal of hazardous substances and effective response to environmental emergencies are limited by a lack of knowledge on how to detoxify or store them and how to assess impacts on public health and the environment. The Superfund Amendments and Reauthorization Act contain a unique provision to fill these data gaps by a multi-disciplinary, basic research program managed by the National Institute of Environmental Health Sciences (NIEHS). This program was met with enthusiasm by the NIEHS and the research community. However, it has not reached its potential. Only a fraction of the funds authorized to support this research has been appropriated and less than 20 percent of the research proposals for this program have been supported.

• The long-term solution to the management of hazardous wastes will require efforts of scientists with skills in a number of different but inter-related disciplines. The NIEHS Superfund research program is the only coordinated basic research effort of this kind. Its findings will support not only Superfund cleanup and emergency response efforts, but will have direct application to the Resource Conservation and Recovery Act programs, and the Environmental Protection Agency air and ground water protection programs. The NIEHS Superfund basic research program must be reauthorized upon its expiration in 1991 and funded at the authorized level in future years.

**Blueprint for the Environment**

# Blueprint for the Environment

# DEPARTMENT OF THE INTERIOR

The Department of the Interior was established in 1849 to deal with matters of the "interior" of the United States and has since affected the life of almost every American. It has executed policies regarding the American Indians, it has acquired, exchanged, managed, and disposed of millions of acres of public lands; and has been an instrument of public — and sometimes not so public — policy for the disposition of the mineral, timber and rangeland wealth of the nation.

Much has changed in a century and a half, yet the Department of the Interior still touches the lives of many Americans, almost as much as the U.S. Postal Service and the Environmental Protection Agency.

Interior manages well over 500,000,000 acres of land, oversees the disposition of oil and gas from millions more (including the Outer Continental Shelf), and has a basic responsibility for the conduct of coal mining throughout the country. It manages a world-renowned system of national parks, wildlife refuges and fish hatcheries, manages and operates an array of irrigation and water supply projects, is responsible for vast reaches of public lands, generates electric power, carries out the provisions of treaty agreements, and functions as one of the world's finest geological science and mapping organization — and it remains responsible for American Indians.

Americans prize their natural resources and have developed a sophisticated interest in the protection and in the wise and proper use of those resources. Americans object when public coal is sold at prices so low as to be unconscionable; they find no rationale for wholesale leasing of oil and gas from the Outer Continental Shelf in environmentally sensitive areas; they are offended at efforts to give or sell public rights to private citizens; they object to continued public subsidies of water and power which go to produce crops and commodities also subsidized with public funds; and they expect their resources to be managed on the basis of good science and without political influence.

Changes are in order if the Department of the Interior is to play its proper role as the nation moves into a new and complex century, where natural resources and related values must have a new order of importance if the country is to continue to enjoy a stable economy, rational growth, quality recreation, and to ensure the availability of resources for generations to come.

The kinds of changes which should be made are not shattering, do not represent unrealistic increases in funding, and will not require major organic alterations. They will demand a renewed commitment to the ideals of responsible stewardship without deference to political convenience; they will require a reassessment of current priorities; and they will establish a renewed fealty to the idea of long-term, national-level responsibilities and benefits instead of short-term gratification.

Major changes appropriate to the Department of the Interior are the following, in no particular order of importance:

• A new recognition of the importance of the nation's fish and wildlife resources and the habitats supporting them by revitalizing the U.S. Fish and Wildlife Service, redefining its role as a research and management agency, and strengthening and consolidating the fisheries program.

• Giving the National Park Service new energy and purpose by strengthening its scientific and research capabilities; providing the personnel, the money and the accountability required to protect park resources while enhancing the experiences of the citizens who visit them; and recognizing that National Parks are a system which should continue to grow.

• Affirming the concept that the public lands managed by the Bureau of Land Management are public lands — subject to a variety of appropriate uses — which should not be controlled by traditional interest groups: private use of these public lands should be paid for at unsubsidized rates.

• The Bureau of Reclamation is in transition

and its new role should be focused on utilizing the organization's engineering and construction skills for conserving and managing present water supplies and developing ways to use water more efficiently. Multiple uses must be a priority, giving fisheries and wildlife recreation equity with agricultural uses, and developing minimum stream flow plans providing for protection of fishery stocks in rivers and streams.

• Creation of an American Heritage Trust Fund yielding $1 billion annually for land acquisition and the protection and preservation of historic buildings and other features.

• The Department of the Interior should use its experience as a provider and manager of recreational opportunity to help states and localities establish a system of greenway parks and to exploit opportunities to develop greenline parks and protected scenic highways throughout the United States.

• The Department must commit itself to a rational management of oil, gas, coal and other non-renewable resources, based on a conscious determination of the real need for resource extraction, the environmental consequences of that decision, and a recognition of the need to assure that the Department can and will manage the work to achieve the long-term aims of society.

• Volunteers share a commitment to Department of the Interior goals that enables volunteers to supplement and complement the existing and even expanded professional base, providing an important opportunity for many projects throughout all agencies within the Department.

• Finally, the Department of the Interior must be freed from unwarranted political intervention. Any agency must be directed by qualified officials responsive to the political entity in power, of course, but that should be limited to those positions with fundamental policy-making responsibility. The management and direction of organizational components having basically scientific, technical or operational roles to play should not be subjected to political direction. A high value must be placed on scientific objectivity and non-partisan concern for the natural resources for which the Department has a continuing responsibility; partisan political intervention has no place in the management and use of these resources nor should the Department be unduly influenced by local interests.

The specific recommendations making up this document offer more detailed suggestions for seizing the present opportunity for the Department of the Interior and its professional and dedicated employees to make the agency a national and world leader in the arena of resource management.

## Fish and Wildlife Service

Some have called 1988 "The year the earth spoke back." But for those involved with fish and wildlife conservation issues, the revelations during 1988 of coastal beach pollution, acceleration of the greenhouse syndrome, and magnification of the toxic waste problems were really echoes of earlier warnings provided by our nation's beleaguered fish and wildlife heritage.

The drought of 1987—1988 heightened public interest and concern for fish and wildlife and it will influence those human enterprises dependent upon them for many years. The drought resulted in massive fires throughout the West that affected entire ecosystems. In addition, it brought already-reduced waterfowl populations to record low levels — lows not witnessed since the years known as "the dirty thirties." The drought has been detrimental to most wetland-dependent species and fisheries across the country.

The new Administration in 1989 faces many serious and long-term environmental issues that will truly challenge its leadership, wisdom and fortitude. Some of the most demanding and complex challenges await the Assistant Secretary for Fish and Wildlife and Parks. Problems associated with federal cooperation, leadership and management of thousands of species of native fish, wildlife and plants as well as opportunities arising from this nation's vital role in worldwide endangered species and biological diversity programs and issues are within the purview of the Office of Fish and Wildlife and Parks. While fish and wildlife management responsibilities are fragmented among various federal and state agencies, many of the primary federal laws and the accountability to Congress and the public fall directly in the Fish and Wildlife and Parks Office of the Department of the Interior.

Among the most urgent needs for early actions by a new Administration are the following:

1) Nomination of a Fish and Wildlife Service Director with proper background training and experience, a proven commitment to the conservation of fish and wildlife and demonstrated skills and abilities in leadership, decision-making, and team building to assure the rapid recovery of the Service to its highest level of professionalism,

managerial leadership and resource stewardship.

2) Development and support for a Fiscal Year 90 budget increase that will accelerate the pace of endangered species listings, recovery plan development and implementation, and approval and support for cooperative state programs to recover threatened or endangered fish, wildlife and plants.

3) Development and support for a Fiscal Year 90 Land and Water Conservation Fund budget increase for acquiring high quality and threatened lands and habitats for America's fish and wildlife, particularly endangered and threatened species and vulnerable migratory birds.

4) Development and support for a Fiscal Year 90 budget that is adequate to maintain all other Fish and Wildlife Service programs at or above the 1988 support level considering expected inflation rates.

5) Initiation of expedited reviews of the Fish and Wildlife Service policies, programs and organizational structures (including the interagency mechanisms with the Departments of Agriculture, Commerce, Justice, State and the Environmental Protection Agency along with elements within the Department of the Interior and with the several states) to facilitate sound decision-making and to determine the need for remodeling these or related functions. This is essential to achieve maximum agency effectiveness in fish and wildlife conservation programs and to reinstate the ability of the Fish and Wildlife Service to carry out its mission of protecting and enhancing America's fish, wildlife and habitats for the benefit of all Americans today and into the future.

Project Blueprint recommendations for fish and wildlife conservation present an array of urgent challenges and timely opportunities. Many of them will require a sustained commitment by the Assistant Secretary to improve leadership quality and capability, policy development and implementation, and decision-making processes within the Fish and Wildlife Service. It is essential that the Service organizational structure, leadership selections and professional assignments are energized so as to re-ignite the esprit de corps and commitment of all Fish and Wildlife Service employees to their tasks and the Agency's mission. Demonstrated support and respect for the capabilities of the majority of Fish and Wildlife Service employees can yield enormous results. But without early and substantial improvements in the basic quality of leadership and management within the Fish and Wildlife Service, the vital resource conservation goals of the nation will not be achieved and the new Administration will have failed to accomplish some of the most urgent environmental objectives in America.

## National Park Service

National Parks are truly the "university of the out-of-doors," the best places to reach out and to understand our heritage. Wallace Stegner called the national parks "the best idea we ever had."

Today, no one questions the importance of our national park system, but there is danger in becoming complacent about the protection of park resources or expecting too much from them. The national parks are the most protected category of public lands in the nation, yet they face major threats from conditions both inside and outside park boundaries.

While thorough planning for both resource preservation and visitor use is obviously essential, the process used for park planning has become internally cumbersome, while also limiting the opportunity for public involvement. While the National Park Service is inextricably linked to the preservation and wise use of the national park system, the Service as an institution is strained nearly to the breaking point. The Service is drowning in its own paperwork while both visitors and resources suffer the consequences. It is cringing under increasing political interference and suffering morale problems attributable to immobility, interference and rigidity.

For the national park system to continue to be perceived as, and indeed to become, the model for resource stewardship throughout the world that we wish it to be will require fundamental improvements. These fall into three broad categories, including:

1) Development of a comprehensive, research-based, natural and cultural resource management program for all units of the system, coupled with a public education mission which functions to inform the American people, through an understanding of the system's resources, of the magnitude of ecological and cultural change occurring in our nation and throughout the world;

2) A concerted and sustained effort to fully protect the existing units of the system by

## Blueprint for the Environment

completing authorized land acquisition, and by completing thorough studies of the adequacy of the current boundary of each unit of the system as to whether all primary resources are now under National Park Service administration, and implementation of a systemwide policy of cooperative land planning and management for adjacent lands with both other federal, state and local, and private land owners; and

3) Establishment of a continuing process for evaluation and recommendation for inclusion in the system of qualified, nationally significant sites, combined with a renewed emphasis on utilization of the Service's authorities and responsibilities for leadership, technical assistance and grants to state, local and private interests, for natural, cultural and recreational resources throughout the nation.

## Bureau of Land Management

The Bureau of Land Management is responsible for the management of 334 million acres of federal lands, more than any other federal agency. Most of these lands are located in the western United States. Once considered "the lands nobody wanted," these lands today are recognized for the wide variety of natural resource values they provide for all Americans.

Bureau of Land Management lands provide more wildlife habitat than any other federal land management agency, providing homes for over 3,000 species of terrestrial, avian and aquatic species. These lands are also valuable for their mineral resources, including oil, gas, coal, oil shale, and "hard rock" minerals. Bureau of Land Management lands are increasingly important for the recreation opportunities they provide increasing numbers of Americans. A wealth of archaeological artifacts from pre-Columbian native cultures are found on the lands administered by the Bureau, most of which are unprotected and subject to theft and vandalism. And finally, some of America's most beautiful and awe-inspiring natural landscapes are administered by the Bureau of Land Management.

Despite passage in 1976 of the Federal Land Policy and Management Act, the Bureau of Land Management's "organic statute," attitudes within both the Bureau and among traditional Bureau constituencies still dominate the agency's perspective of its management responsibilities. Formed in 1946 from the old General Land Office and the Grazing Service, the Bureau historically has passively reacted to the demands placed on it by western livestock and mining interests — hence the perjorative title, "Bureau of Livestock and Mining." However, with the passage of the Federal Land Policy and Management Act, Congress recognized that the public lands were an important and severely neglected resource which should be managed in a manner that protected their ecological integrity. Though steps were taken in the late 1970s to bring the Bureau out of the shadow of its previous existence, the most recent policies have been designed to continue the Bureau's subservience to a narrow group whose primary interest is the economic exploitation of the public's mineral, timber and range resources.

Any new Administration must recognize that the Bureau's mandate transcends the pecuniary goals of these narrow economic interests. Instead, the new Administration should implement policies that: recognize the abuses wrought upon our public lands by years of neglect and exploitation; recognize the multitude of values contained on Bureau of Land Management lands for all Americans; and implement initiatives that will ensure that the public lands are managed in a manner that will restore and protect their environmental values.

## Minerals Management

Mineral development and processing in the United States is a major industry, and a major cause of environmental problems. Pollution of streams and groundwater with acid runoff, toxic heavy metals and silt, creation of landslide hazards, and destruction of productive and wild lands have been the legacy of past mining. The mineral needs of the country can be met through properly-controlled mining which does not damage the environment. The new Administration should act promptly through regulatory reform, improved administration of key agencies, and enactment of fresh legislation to address these issues.

This section addresses three areas of mineral development in which the federal government plays a crucial role: coal mining, particularly from surface mines (which account for 60 percent of U.S. coal production); "hard rock" minerals (e.g. copper, gold, iron, uranium); and onshore Federal oil and gas. Some related items are addressed in other sections (e.g. offshore mineral development and radioactive waste disposal).

The mineral industries involve very large quantities of activity and materials. Total United States coal production in recent years has been approximately 900 million tons, from more than 3,300 sites. Over 90 million acres of federal land are leased to oil and gas companies for development — more than the area of Virginia, Maryland, Pennsylvania, and New York combined. Metals mining, at over 350 sites around the country, generates over 800 million tons of potentially hazardous waste per year — more than three times as much hazardous waste as all non-mining industries. (Sources: industry data and Environmental Protection Agency studies).

Some problem areas have been addressed in recent legislation, such as the Surface Mining Control and Reclamation Act of 1977 governing surface coal mines. However, weak enforcement has meant that the reforms intended by Congress for surface coal mining have not been achieved. Mining for federally-owned metals is governed by legislation 116 years old, the 1872 Mining Law, which is long overdue for replacement. The federal onshore oil/gas leasing program has been administered as an isolated management activity on Bureau of Land Management and Forest Service lands, and has not been integrated with the other agency actions such as timber, range and recreation planning. This has led to conflicts between the oil industry and other users which should have been foreseen and prevented prior to lease issuance.

Most of the recommendations in this section have little budget impact, either because they are not intrinsically expensive or because they are proposed to be funded through modest user fees. These actions have the potential to provide a major reduction in damage to the nation's environment, at little cost to the Treasury or to national production. The major conservation organizations have a long history of concern over these issues, and can offer both political and technical support. We look forward to working together with the new Administration to accomplish these important reforms.

## Bureau of Reclamation

Twenty years ago, Congress authorized the formation of a National Water Commission to review water resources problems and policies. The Commission's final report in 1973 was a major landmark in American natural resources management, containing far-reaching recommendations for greater non-federal financial responsibility for water resources development, more innovative non-structural approaches to water related problems, and greater attention to environmental values in the management of water resources.

Since that time, the implementation of these reforms has been fitful and uneven. The use of water is so closely bound up with economic activity and patterns of human settlement that water resources policy has been and will continue to be a highly political issue. The federal government spends well over $4 billion per year on water resources development, along with additional billions for such related programs as navigation aids, flood insurance, disaster assistance, wetlands and water quality protection, and wastewater treatment. State prerogatives over the allocation and use of water are jealously guarded, and the bureaucratic inertia behind development plans that are decades in the making has been notoriously formidable.

The Bureau of Reclamation program in the Department of the Interior has been less than accommodating toward reform, and now faces an uncertain future. The Bureau and its would-be protectors have resisted any uniform tightening of cost-sharing requirements, opting instead for case-by-case negotiations for increasing local contributions for new projects. The Bureau's previous handling of repayment requirements has been widely criticized for underpricing water and undercutting conservation efforts. The new cost-sharing agreements have been criticized as well, for overstating local contributions and shielding controversial project features from serious reappraisal.

While the Bureau has resisted the cost-sharing reforms that have reinvigorated the Corps of Engineers program, changes in the agricultural economy have undermined the rationale for many of its remaining projects. By the early 1980s, periodic crop surpluses had become chronic, and the contradiction of federally subsidized water boosting production of such commodities on about 40 percent of the acreage served by the Bureau became increasingly apparent. Additionally, the enactment of the Reclamation Reform Act of 1982, which sanctioned many of the arrangements whereby large farm operations had received subsidized water originally intended for family farmsteads, essentially repealed the social purpose upon which irrigation subsidies were based.

In late 1987, the Department of the Interior made an unprecedented announcement: The Bureau of Reclamation had largely accomplished its original mission, which was to assist in the settlement of the arid West. The Department acknowledged that public values and economic conditions

## Blueprint for the Environment

133

have changed to the point where the Bureau's traditional offerings of dams and diversions, often on a grand scale, were no longer appropriate. The Reclamation program, according to the Department, will put greater emphasis on improved management of its existing facilities, and openly seek new missions. It remains unclear what, if any, new roles can be found for which the Bureau is uniquely suited.

Future trends, such as reduced federal funds for new water resources development and wastewater treatment along with rising costs for municipal borrowing as a result of tax law changes, will require improved management of public water supplies and innovative approaches toward meeting future needs. Water conservation is taking on new importance, and has major potential under current and foreseeable economic conditions to compete favorably with traditional structural water supply measures. Currently, technology is available to greatly improve the efficiency of water use. In recognition of these benefits, the Bureau of Reclamation should take steps to facilitate water conservation.

Existing laws, institutions, and practices, largely at the state level, often impede the sale or exchange of water. In some states, those who conserve water may actually be penalized, through a loss of water rights. Nevertheless, the sale, lease and banking of water and water rights is stimulating new interest in water marketing. With appropriate regulation to account for potential environmental effects and protection of basins of origin, such markets may be able to supply new users without the adverse consequences of the construction of major new facilities. As the states adopt policies that encourage water marketing while protecting environmental resources, federal statutes and regulations conflicting with this approach should be modified.

The Bureau should seek to improve the management of existing surface and ground water supplies, including re-regulating discharges from existing reservoirs to meet contemporary needs. In particular, many older projects that pre-date environmental planning procedures need significant operational, and in some cases, facility changes, to provide added public benefits such as habitat restoration and public recreation, or different levels of benefits in functions such as water supply, flood protection, power generation or navigation than the projects were originally designed to provide.

Global warming and sea-level rise also pose far-reaching challenges for shore protection and municipal and agricultural water supplies nationwide. With the rate of climate change uncertain, and the pattern of weather conditions becoming increasingly variable, federal water resources agencies need flexible management strategies that allow them to respond to changing conditions in a cost effective way.

The National Dam Inventory of the Corps of Engineers has identified some 68,000 major dams already constructed on the nation's waterways. In recent years, it has been repeated in many circles and in the halls of Congress that the dam building era in the United States is largely over, due in part to the fact that most potential water development sites are already in use. Clearly, the future in water resources is in management, not development, and this represents a fundamental change for the Bureau of Reclamation.

**Blueprint for the Environment**

# Blueprint for the Environment

## INITIATIVES

## DEPARTMENT OF THE INTERIOR

**RECOMMENDATION**
**The Secretary of the Interior should take the lead in establishing an inter-agency task force with the Department of Agriculture and the Department of the Treasury to evaluate how well the United States government is implementing the Convention on International Trade in Endangered Species of Wild Fauna and Flora and to make recommendations to improve performance for the agencies.**

• The United States is a leader in international trade in wild plants and animals. Yet the budget and trained personnel to handle wildlife trade do not reflect the importance of this issue to the U.S.
• Given overall constraints on the federal budget, priorities must be set in building a better cooperative program among the agencies for control of international wildlife trade. The proposed task force should seek to establish these priorities.
• The impacts of large-scale harvest of U.S. species exported in large quantities, particularly plant species, have not been studied: subsequently exports are being approved without proper scientific basis.
• U.S. actions have considerable affects on rare species outside our borders. The most direct affect is usually trade. Many species in trade are either not yet on Convention on International Trade in Endangered Species of Wild Fauna and Flora (CITES) appendices, or are nevertheless being traded in numbers which appear to threaten their survival. The only procedure the U.S. has for curbing the import of such species is listing them under the Endangered Species Act. Other U.S. activities which affect rare species abroad include financing of development assistance projects and training and basing of military forces.

**RECOMMENDATION**
**The Secretary of the Interior should request, as part of the Fiscal Year 90 and Fiscal Year 91 budgets, increased funding to enable the National Park Service to cooperate with other nations in ensuring effective implementation of the World Heritage Convention.**

• The World Heritage Convention, which originated as a U.S. initiative, is now the most widely adhered-to international conservation treaty, with 103 State Parties from all parts of the world. It provides for establishment and maintenance of a worldwide list of cultural and natural sites of outstanding importance. The World Heritage Fund administered under the convention makes grants for developing countries for technical assistance, training and other activities necessary for protection of these sites. (The United States will contribute $220,000 to the Fund in FY 1989 from the State Department's International Organizations and Programs account.)
• The National Park Service has lead responsibility for U.S. implementation of the Convention. However, the Service's budget currently includes no funding for cooperation with other nations to identify and protect natural areas under the Convention. This puts the Service under a severe handicap, as it is unable to provide U.S. leadership or respond to the many requests from developing nations for U.S. collaboration and assistance in developing management plans for key sites and helping to build the necessary technical and management skills.

## RECOMMENDATION

**The Secretaries of the Interior, Agriculture and Commerce should improve the efficiency and effectiveness of federal fisheries management by consolidating and strengthening integration and coordination of now-fragmented staff and functions of those various agencies.**

• Today, as many as 37 federal agencies have some degree of fisheries and habitat responsibilities in the U.S. and its territories. Marine and freshwater fisheries resources are National Heritage assets of enormous social, economic, environmental and recreational values. For instance, the recreational fisheries of the U.S. have an estimated annual economic value of $28.2 billion and support over 590,000 jobs. More than 64 million Americans participate in recreational fishing in U.S. waters. Commercial U.S. fisheries valued in excess of $6.2 billion annually provide over 490,000 jobs. In 1986, over 52 percent of the U.S. supply of edible fisheries products had to be met by imports valued at more than $7.6 billion despite the fact that the U.S. controls about 20 percent of the world's fisheries resources.
• The federal mission for fisheries-related functions should be to achieve effective and efficient management and optimum use of our fisheries resources on a long-term and continuing basis for the benefit of the nation. To accomplish that mission,

efforts are needed to achieve the objective stated in the recommendation to better focus scarce resources, remove competing redundancy and achieve integrated coordination with the state programs.
• The Secretaries should direct an immediate, comprehensive, joint assessment of all federal fisheries research and management activities as now conducted by the Fish and Wildlife Service (FWS) in the Department of the Interior, National Marine Fisheries Service (NMFS) and the National Oceanic and Atmospheric Administration (NOAA) in the Department of Commerce, and the Cooperative State Research Service (CSRS) in the Department of Agriculture, and other federal entities, to achieve the goal stated in the recommendation above to achieve an effective federal fisheries research and management program capable of addressing the many urgent problems facing our saltwater, anadromous and freshwater fisheries resources.

## RECOMMENDATION

**The Secretaries of Agriculture and the Interior should, by joint secretarial order, establish a new Joint Interagency Office of River Protection to coordinate and implement a wide range of river planning, technical assistance and management programs for river protection.**

• This new office is necessary to:
   1) Assist with planning coordination and river management coordination issues that affect the respective federal land managing agencies.
   2) Provide technical assistance to state and local groups concerned with river protection.
   3) Have oversight responsibility for the review of federal projects on rivers included in the national rivers system, rivers being studied under Section 5 of the Act, or rivers that are

included in state river systems.
• This new office will give needed focus to river resource protection nationwide thus increasing recreational use of rivers, helping to retain their outstanding natural and cultural attributes, and implementing more cost-effective policies for improving water quality and groundwater recharge through the improvement of watershed condition on outstanding rivers. Moreover, such an office is needed to fully implement the Wild and Scenic Rivers system.

---

## Blueprint for the Environment

## RECOMMENDATION
**The Assistant Secretary and the Administration should support legislation similar to H.R. 3964 (100th Congress) which would strengthen the professional decision-making of the National Park Service and free it significantly from undue political intervention.**

• The National Park Service (NPS) is one of several agencies within the Department of the Interior, and has by far the most preservation-oriented mandate. More and more, within-Department politicization is hurting the Service's effectiveness, the morale of its employees and, ultimately, the preservation of natural and cultural resources. For example, critical resource decisions are being made by non-professional, political appointees. Reports requested by Congress are delayed or withheld.

• There is an urgent need to improve the ability of the agency to respond to decisions of professional managers, rather than political appointees, and engage in long-term planning and policy-making. One approach in addressing this situation is embodied in H.R. 3964 (100th Congress), which provides a new organizational and reporting structure for the Service, but leaves the agency located within the Department of the Interior. Another approach, supported by the National Parks and Conservation Association, proposes removal of the Service from the Department of the Interior and making it an independent agency.

• As an independent agency, the NPS would continue to be controlled closely by the President and Congress, without having its decisions scrutinized by several layers of bureaucracy within the Department. The Director of the NPS should be a professional in the conservation, park and recreation field, whose selection under this approach should be subject to the advice and consent of the Senate, and whose term of office should span the Presidential election cycle (5—7 years). These changes would give the Director a greater opportunity to make professional decisions, or at least to take professional positions, even if overridden by higher authority.

• The Secretary of the Interior's National Park Advisory Board should be reconstituted, to produce a Board with professional, rather than political credentials, and with a small staff of its own, to give greater assurances that the Board can develop and present its own positions, rather than just "rubber-stamping" those of the Administration.

## RECOMMENDATION
**The Administration should create a high-level independent office, whose sole mission is the national historic preservation program as defined by the National Historic Preservation Act.**

• Administration for the national preservation program now occurs in several places in the National Park Service (NPS) and in the office of the Secretary of the Interior. Program managers have dual responsibilities for resources inside the parks and outside the parks. As a result, the national historic preservation program has not fared well in competition for fiscal and personnel resources with the parks. The national preservation program needs visibility, leadership and, most importantly, accountability at the federal level to function efficiently and to realize its full potential.

• A forum of national preservation organizations (see Principal Sources of Expertise) analyzed the administrative and leadership problems with the current program, and reviewed similar efforts by the larger conservation community. The group recommended creation of an independent national heritage agency with three distinct components: the national park system; recreation, conservation and open space Land and Water Conservation Fund (LWCF) programs; and Historic Preservation Fund (HPF) programs.

• A national heritage agency would remove these important programs from the conflicting mandates of a parent department whose major mission is insufficiently strong on conservation, and provide them with needed visibility and leadership. Such an agency could be created through the realignment of existing resources and responsibilities.

**Blueprint for the Environment**

## RECOMMENDATION

**The Secretary of the Interior should immediately resuscitate the Department's struggling natural resource damage assessment and education efforts. The Secretary should seek full funding for these efforts, and should give the natural resource damage program a charter to conduct detailed assessments of damages at all Superfund and Interior Department waste sites.**

• The Secretary of the Interior has the responsibility, under the Superfund law, to act as a "trustee" for all natural resources under the Department's protective jurisdiction, including National Parks and Wildlife Refuges. As a Superfund trustee, the Department must assess any damage done to these natural resources caused by releases of oil and hazardous substances. The Department can recover from the responsible polluters the funds to restore or replace the injured resources.

• The Interior has made little effort to assess toxic damage to natural resources under its trusteeship. Through the "Preliminary Natural Resource Survey" (PNRS) program, the Department conducts "quick and dirty" site reviews, generally costing less than $3,000 per site. This is hardly enough to analyze a few tissue or environmental samples. Yet, on the basis of these inadequate reviews, claims against polluters have been waived or placed on the back burner; some valid claims may die under Superfund's statute of limitations. Because of sketchy reviews, major Superfund settlements may be killed because the Interior does not know enough about the site to agree to settle the case. Inadequate reviews also may necessitate two separate and redundant cleanups: one to comply with EPA's cleanup standards, the second to actually restore the natural resources. To remedy these problems, the natural resource damage program must be made a higher priority and must get an infusion of resources. The Department should undertake a major effort to educate state and federal trustees and the public about the program.

## RECOMMENDATION

**The Secretary of the Interior should seek an Executive Order and declare, pursuant to the Endangered Species Act, that the conservation and recovery of endangered wildlife is the first priority in wildlife policy and that every federal agency must designate an officer responsible for that agency's compliance with the Endangered Species Act and with the details of the Executive Order.**

• As required in Section 7(a)(1) of the Endangered Species Act (ESA) and explained in the proposed Executive Order, each agency must carry out "programs for the conservation of endangered species and threatened species...." The order should require the 7(a)(1) review of all Interior programs by the end of FY 89 and a concurrent review of other agencies, their activities and potential activities. The proposed budget requests for FY 90 and 91 for full implementation as indicated in relevant recovery plans and in the initial review in FY 89 should be submitted by July 1. Semiannual reports to Interior and White House and annual reports to Congress are expected thereafter.

## RECOMMENDATION

**The Secretary of the Interior should support increased funding for the enforcement of historic and archaeological resource protection laws, and for the creation of a central office for coordinating the enforcement efforts to promote and increase the protection of historic and archaeological resources from vandalism and looting on federal lands.**

• Under law, archaeological and historic sites located on lands owned or managed by the federal government are protected from vandalism and looting. However, the looting of archaeological sites for artifacts is a growing problem, particularly as the commercial value of "antiquities" increases. Hundreds, if not thousands, of sites on federal lands have been ravaged by commercial "pothunters,"

## RECOMMENDATION

**The Department of the Interior should require that its agencies or bureaus develop and distribute environmental education programs and materials dealing with all appropriate natural resource related activities of the Department of the Interior.**

• Implicit within the authority of the Federal government with respect to its natural resource programs is the responsibility to consider the wishes of the public relative to the environmental impacts of the recommendations or actions of government agencies. Citizen involvement can be obtained in a variety of ways including the provision of programs, materials, and technical assistance which give citizens a fundamental understanding of the operation of natural human-altered ecosystems.

• Specific responsibilities for environmental education should be assigned to an office within each agency, a mission statement and objectives developed, and appropriate staff and funding provided. Among the programs that could be developed are in-service training of agency staff who should be trained in the practices and programs of environmental education.

## RECOMMENDATION

**The Secretary of the Interior should seek authority to create a centralized "credible" "non-advocacy" agency, similar to the U.S. Geological Survey, to perform Federal biological and environmental data collection and research for all government agencies.**

• At present the biological services of the U.S. Fish and Wildlife Service is sporadic and cyclic in addressing what should be a continuity of biological and ecological data. The Environmental Protection Agency concentrates now on data collection and research primarily as it affects human health rather than the inclusion of adequate fish and wildlife research.

• In addition to inadequate and fragmented data collection and research in the Federal agencies, another problem is the credibility of information. Currently, data collection is often viewed as "being gathered for advocacy purposes." Therefore, a consolidation of existing efforts and the establishment of a non-advocacy research arm of the federal government for biological and environmental data is needed in the Department of the Interior as a neutral source of up-to-date, thorough information.

• It is also recommended that each federal agency having need for biological, ecological and environmental data have its own small department for the specific and urgent information needed to conduct its program.

## RECOMMENDATION

**The Commissioner of Reclamation should develop a program to encourage investments in water-efficient technologies for irrigation. More efficient application of water to crops will save water for other uses, including fish and wildlife, and will reduce pollution from uncontrolled runoff.**

• Water-saving technologies and practices create multiple benefits, because water saved in irrigation contributes directly to preserving fish and wildlife habitat, reduces contamination from irrigation runoff, lowers political pressures to build new dams and diversions, and develops additional water supplies to lessen the effects of droughts.

• Several irrigated areas have acute drainage and salt management problems, exacerbated by the over-application of water. Chemicals and toxic trace elements, including selenium and salts contained in irrigation runoff, damage fish and wildlife habitat, soils, the water quality of lakes, streams, estuaries, and groundwater and threaten public health.

## Blueprint for the Environment

# Blueprint for the Environment

## SOLICITOR

# DEPARTMENT OF THE INTERIOR

### RECOMMENDATION
**The Solicitor's Office should reestablish the Honors Program to recruit new attorneys directly out of law school. This must be the top priority for the new Solicitor.**

• Experience has demonstrated, both within the Solicitor's Office and at other federal agencies, that a competitive Honors Program is an extremely effective way to fill staff-level attorney positions. It is certain to enhance the ability of the Solicitor's Office to provide effective and well-reasoned legal advice, guarantee a continuous supply of capable staff attorneys, and revive the feeling of cohesiveness that has been missing from Interior's legal staff since the Program was abolished. Because this program will be used to fill existing and anticipated vacancies, no additional funding will be necessary other than the costs associated with recruiting.

### RECOMMENDATION
**The Solicitor should reconsider the interpretation of the Migratory Bird Treaty Act expressed in prior Solicitor's Office opinions in light of applicable domestic and international law so as to enable the extraterritorial application and enforcement of the Act.**

• The Japanese driftnet salmon fishery in the U.S. 200-mile Exclusive Economic Zone (EEZ) is responsible for the mortality of hundreds of thousands of migratory sea birds each year. At least 21 species of migratory seabirds are incidentally taken.
• The Migratory Bird Treaty Act (MBTA) between the U.S. and Japan, and the Migratory Bird Treat Act prohibit the taking of these species, but neither the United States nor Japan enforces the provisions of the Treaty or the Act beyond the three-mile territorial sea. The lack of enforcement by the U.S. Fish and Wildlife Service is based in part on two Department of Interior Assistant Solicitor's opinions written in December 1980 and March 1981.

• Neither the cases cited nor the arguments presented in these opinions address the violation of U.S. law by a foreign national in waters within the U.S. EEZ. Further, in the 1981 opinion, it was concluded that takings of migratory birds beyond the three-mile territorial sea could not be prosecuted under MBTA. A review of this interpretation should conclude that the MBTA is a statute that may be applied and enforced extraterritorially. If, after review and reconsideration of the opinion, it is determined that extraterritorial application of the MBTA remains questionable, then the Solicitor should recommend legislative alternatives that would clearly express a Congressional intent to achieve the goal.

# RECOMMENDATION

The Solicitor should issue a comprehensive legal opinion that:

(1) analyzes existing authorities to determine the extent to which they may be used to protect units of the National Park System from the most prevalent external threats; and

(2) recommends steps that should be taken to strengthen those authorities and provide additional legal tools to deal effectively with this problem.

• For many years, the problem of protecting units of the National Park System (NPS) from external threats has been recognized as a top management priority. Even though the importance of this goal is commonly accepted, the manner in which existing legal authorities can be applied to advance the objective has not been given full analysis.

• If NPS is to protect resources inside the parks from activities occurring beyond unit boundaries, it is necessary to define what legal authorities currently are available and, to the extent those authorities are inadequate, identify what additional legal tools are necessary (e.g., new statutory or regulatory requirements, common law precedents, Executive Orders, Solicitor's opinions, cooperative agreements among agencies, etc.). This information should be provided in a legal opinion issued by the Solicitor.

# RECOMMENDATION

The Solicitor should reconsider Solicitor's Opinion M-36914 (Supp. III) July 26, 1988, on reserved water rights for wilderness areas to ensure that the United States claims and protects federal reserved water rights for wilderness areas.

• On July 26, 1988, the Secretary transmitted Opinion M-36914 (Supp. III) to the Attorney General and requested his concurrence in its conclusion that Congress did not intend to reserve federal water rights for wilderness purposes when it enacted the Wilderness Act (16 U.S.C. §§ 1131 et. seq.). Attorney General Meese concurred on July 28, 1988.

• The Attorney General stated in his July 28 letter of concurrence, the United States "will not assert reserved wilderness water rights under federal law in any further litigation on behalf of the United States." There are pending water rights adjudications in which water rights for wilderness are at issue. Based on the Solicitor/Attorney General position, the government would be barred from future claims to water for the wilderness areas involved once those claims are abandoned.

• The Opinion concludes that Congress did not intend to create federal reserved water rights when it provided for the designation of the wilderness areas. According to the Opinion, Congress instead intended wilderness purposes to be secondary to the purposes for which the reservation on which the wilderness area is designated was originally created.

• Critical review should be given to the legislative history analysis set forth in the Opinion. For example, it departs from standard rules of statutory construction and relies on ambiguous correspondence from committee files to make categorical conclusions about the Wilderness Act. It does so even when stronger, more relevant authority indicates that reserved water rights were intended. In addition, careful attention should be given to the Solicitor's Opinion M-36914 of June 25, 1979, 86 I.D. 553-618, and recent case law on this subject.

## Blueprint for the Environment

# Blueprint for the Environment

## PUBLIC LANDS

# DEPARTMENT OF THE INTERIOR
### ASSISTANT SECRETARY for Land and Minerals Management
### Bureau of Land Management

**RECOMMENDATION**
**The Secretary of the Interior should appoint a "blue ribbon" panel of knowledgeable land management policy experts to review the management structure of the Bureau of Land Management and recommend necessary changes which will enhance professional stewardship of the lands and minerals under the Bureau's jurisdiction.**

• The Bureau of Land Management (BLM), an agency within the Department of the Interior, manages more land than any other federal agency — approximately 334 million acres. These lands, most of which are located in the western United States, support natural resources of extraordinary ecological and economic importance. They provide, for example, habitat for over 3,000 kinds of terrestrial, avian and aquatic species. They also contain large quantities of coal, hard rock minerals and oil and gas resources. BLM-managed lands include some of America's most spectacular scenery and provide recreational opportunities for millions of Americans each year.

• Once considered "the lands nobody wanted," these publicly-owned lands are now subject to escalating conflicts over their uses and increasing public concern over their management. Resolution of these controversies as well as sound management of these lands clearly requires enhanced professional stewardship.

• Historically, the Bureau has been inept, poorly staffed and subject to political manipulation — and the public's lands and their resources have suffered tragic abuse as the consequence. Unlike the Chief of the Forest Service, the Director of the BLM is a political appointee who serves at the discretion of the President: the current Director is a rancher whose family has permits to graze livestock on BLM lands in Colorado. Presently, a number of other top-level officials are also nonprofessional, political appointees. Today, as in the past, policy decisions are repeatedly altered and resource decisions made by professionals in the field are frequently overruled. Publicly-owned resources will continue to suffer until the Bureau's current management structure is altered and professionalism supported at all levels of the agency.

## BUDGET RECOMMENDATION
F.Y. 90: **no change**　　　　F.Y. 91: **no change**

## PRINCIPAL AUTHORIZING LEGISLATION
Federal Land Policy and Management Act, 43 U.S.C. § 1701 et seq.

## CONGRESSIONAL JURISDICTION
**House Authorizing Committee/Subcommittee**
　Committee on Interior and Insular Affairs
　　Subcommittee on National Parks and Public Lands
**Senate Authorizing Committee/Subcommittee**
　Committee on Energy and Natural Resources
　　Subcommittee on Public Lands, National Parks and Forests
**House Appropriations Subcommittee**
　Subcommittee on Interior
**Senate Appropriations Subcommittee**
　Subcommittee on Interior and Related Agencies

## RELEVANT STUDIES
General Accounting Office, **"Personnel Practices — Legality of Political Appointments at the Bureau of Land Management"** (1986)
General Accounting Office, **"Public Rangelands — Some Riparian Areas Restored But Widespread Improvement Will Be Slow"** (1988)
U.S. Department of the Interior, Office of the Inspector General, **"Audit Report — Review of the Bureau of Land Management's Grazing Management and Range Improvement Programs"** (1986)

## RELATED FEDERAL PROGRAMS
All BLM programs, including grazing management, wildlife habitat management, soil, water, air, mining, recreation, and onshore oil and gas leasing.

## PRINCIPAL SOURCES OF EXPERTISE
National Wildlife Federation — 202-797-6800
Natural Resources Defense Council — 415-777-0220
The Wilderness Society — 202-842-3400

## IMPLEMENTATION STEPS
(1) Convene a panel of experts to:
　(a) Study BLM's organizational structure, including its administrative structure;
　(b) Identify needed changes, including statutory changes;
　(c) Develop criteria for selection of Director; and
　(d) Support Congressional legislation to implement recommendations.
(2) Draft and support passage of necessary legislation.
(3) Develop and implement a system of incentives and rewards for field employees who adhere to professional resource management principles.

## NOTES:

**Blueprint for the Environment**

## PUBLIC LANDS

# DEPARTMENT OF THE INTERIOR

**RECOMMENDATION**
**The Director of the Bureau of Land Management should work actively to assure the implementation of the principle that all commodities produced from the public lands for private profit should return fair market value to the public.**

• The Federal Land Policy and Management Act established that "the United States receive fair market value of the use of the public lands and their resources unless otherwise provided by law." Notwithstanding this policy, it is clear that in many cases, the government is not receiving fair market value — even where no law provides otherwise.

• In recent years, the Department of the Interior has become an advocate of the industries which benefit from access to commodities on the public lands. Among the most important benefits to commercial users is the Agency philosophy that fees, rents, royalties, appraised values for lands, minerals and other commodities should be set at low levels in order to encourage "economic development." Often this has meant charging the minimum for a commodity allowed by law.

• In some famous cases, the Bureau's policies have led to the severe undervaluing of commodity values, as in the proposed valuation of oil and gas reserves under the Alaska National Wildlife Refuge for purposes of a proposed land/mineral exchange. In another case, fees charged for livestock grazing on public lands are so severely below fair market value that revenues derived from the program cover neither program costs nor the costs of repairing resource damage from abusive livestock grazing practices.

**RECOMMENDATION**
**The Director of the Bureau of Land Management should implement the declared policy of Congress for management of the public lands in accordance with the Federal Land Policy and Management Act, Section 102(a) (8).**

• During the past eight years, the Bureau of Land Management (BLM) has emphasized programs to encourage the private commercial exploitation of commodity resources available from the public lands, to the detriment of the public, non-commodity values. Specifically, there has been a strong emphasis on the aggressive leasing of oil and gas reserves, coal deposits, the opening of withdrawn lands to mineral entry, and the continuation of subsidized livestock grazing for livestock permittees.

• At the same time, the non-commodity values Congress charged the Bureau with managing have suffered from stingy appropriations, personnel cutbacks, and policy directives favoring commodity over non-commodity values.

• This imbalance favoring commodity exploitation must be redressed. With respect to minerals, this means that mineral resources should not necessarily be considered the dominant use of public lands wherever they occur. With respect to livestock grazing, this means that wildlife, fish, watershed values and recreation must no longer take a back seat to the interests of the livestock operators who use the public lands. The Director of the BLM should direct that all existing instruction memoranda and policy guidance be reviewed and revised to convey the clear policy that henceforth the directive in Sec. 102(a) (8) of the Federal Land Policy and Management Act will be followed at all levels of the Agency and in all programs.

## RECOMMENDATION
**The Director of the Bureau of Land Management should take necessary steps to assure expedited completion of meaningful Resource Management Plans.**

• The Federal Land Policy and Management Act (FLPMA) directed that comprehensive land use plans be developed for all lands under the management of the Bureau of Land Management (BLM). Twelve years after FLPMA's enactment, most of the lands managed by the BLM do not have completed "Resource Management Plans." Moreover, the BLM's planning program is largely irrelevant to the resource management decisions made by the Bureau.

## RECOMMENDATION
**The Director of the Bureau of Land Management should implement the policies and funding requirements to ensure an effective monitoring program that will determine whether Resource Management Plan goals and objectives are being met.**

## RECOMMENDATION
**The Bureau of Land Management should direct their regional, state and area directors and managers to review the Bureau's current policies on the identification, designation and protection of Areas of Critical Environmental Concern to ensure that the designations are utilized in compliance with the mandate of Congress as expressed in the Federal Land Policy Management Act.**

• The Federal Land Policy and Management Act of 1976 (FLMPA) established a significant new program for the federal lands under the jurisdiction of the Bureau of Land Management (BLM) — "Areas of Critical Environmental Concern" (ACECs). The statute defined ACECs as areas "where special management attention is required ... to protect and prevent irreparable damage to important historic, cultural or scenic values, fish and wildlife resources or other natural systems or process." In addition, it directed the BLM to give "priority to the designation and protection" of these imperiled public land areas.
• Unfortunately, the promise of FLPMA's ACEC provisions for developing a system of protecting key environmental resources on BLM-administered lands has remained unfulfilled. In Montana, Arizona and Nevada, no effective designation program exists, and very few ACECs have been designated. Designated ACECs in other states are often not managed in a manner that will effectively protect the values for which they were designated. For example, numerous ACECs designated in Wyoming for the protection of important wildlife habitats have been opened up to oil and gas leasing. In the case of many designated ACECs in all the western states, management actions identified as necessary to protect their resource values have yet to be taken.

# Blueprint for the Environment

## GRAZING

## DEPARTMENT OF THE INTERIOR
### ASSISTANT SECRETARY for Land and Minerals Management
### Bureau of Land Management

### RECOMMENDATION
**The Secretary of the Interior should order the Bureau of Land Management to amend its grazing regulations to require land use plans to contain provisions that will control future livestock grazing, balance livestock use with other multiple uses and improve resources that have been degraded by past grazing. In addition, the regulations should require implementation of plan provisions, including elimination of overgrazing, on the basis of the best available data within five years.**

• Livestock grazing is the most extensive economic use made of the federal lands administered by the Bureau of Land Management (BLM). The BLM's planning documents contain extensive evidence of the damage that authorized grazing is causing to the resources of specific public land areas. These documents also reveal the need to change current grazing practices in order to balance livestock use with the needs of other resources and improve degraded conditions.

• The BLM, however, has not been using its planning process to put an end to abusive grazing practices or to achieve sound multiple use management. Under its current approach, land use plans lack basic inventory information, including estimates of grazing capacity, which are needed to determine appropriate numbers of livestock. Even where available data show the need for changes in current management, management decisions must be postponed: current policy requires that, after plans have been completed, monitoring data must be collected for years before changes can be decided upon. In lieu of meaningful constraints on future grazing decisions, plans contain vague, generalized platitudes. Rather than ensure improvement in degraded conditions, they effectively maintain the status quo for livestock.

### RECOMMENDATION
**The Director of the Bureau of Land Management should increase grazing fees by abandoning the formula currently used to calculate annual fees, and replace it with "modified market-value formula." The Director should also specify that at least 25 percent of fee receipts be used for direct fish, wildlife and plant habitat enhancement including, in particular, riparian improvement.**

According to numerous government studies and other sources, the grazing formula in use since 1978 provides a generous subsidy to the two percent of American livestock operators with permits to graze federal lands. Current fees fail to recover fair market value for the public forage (National Forest and Bureau 'of Land Management's) and they also fail to cover costs of federal range programs.

• In addition, the current fee formula fails to generate sufficient funds to cover the costs of on-the-ground rehabilitation projects. Finally, the below-market fees keep demand for federal grazing high and provide an incentive for overgrazing, with resultant environmental damage.

147

## BUDGET RECOMMENDATION
Increased grazing fees will result in increased revenues to BLM

## PRINCIPAL AUTHORIZING LEGISLATION
Taylor Grazing Act, 43 U.S.C. § 315 (b) (1986)
Federal Land Policy and Management Act of 1976, 43 U.S.C. §§ 1701 et seq.
Public Rangelands Improvement Act of 1978, id. §§ 1901; 1905 (1985)

## CONGRESSIONAL JURISDICTION
**House Authorizing Committee/Subcommittee**
Committee on Interior and Insular Affairs
Subcommittee on National Parks and Public Lands
**Senate Authorizing Committee/Subcommittee**
Committee on Energy and Natural Resources
Subcommittee on Public Lands, National Parks and Forests
**House Appropriations Subcommittee**
Subcommittee on Interior
**Senate Appropriations Subcommittee**
Subcommittee on Interior and Related Agencies

## RELEVANT STUDIES
GAO, **Public Rangelands — Some Riparian Areas Restored But Widespread Improvement Will Be Slow** (1988)
GAO, **Rangeland Management — More Emphasis Needed on Declining and Overstocked Grazing Allotments** (1988)
**All Is Not Well On The Range** (1986) (H.R. Rep. No. 593, 99th Congress, 2nd Session)
**Forest Service and BLM, Grazing Fee Review and Evaluation — A Report From The Secretary of Agriculture and The Secretary of the Interior** (1986)
GAO, **Public Rangeland Improvement — A Slow, Costly Process In Need of Alternate Funding** (1982)

## RELATED FEDERAL PROGRAMS
Forest Service — Range
Department of the Interior — Wildlife, Soil, Air and Water

## PRINCIPAL SOURCES OF EXPERTISE
Natural Resources Defense Council — 415-777-0220
Izaak Walton League — 202-528-1818
American Fisheries Society — 301-897-8616
Defenders of Wildlife — 202-659-9510
National Wildlife Federation — 202-797-6800
The Wilderness Society — 202-842-3400

# Blueprint for the Environment

## WATERSHEDS AND MINERALS

## DEPARTMENT OF THE INTERIOR
### ASSISTANT SECRETARY for Land and Mineral Management
### Bureau of Land Management

### RECOMMENDATION
**The Bureau of Land Management should adopt procedures that would direct public land managers to improve watershed conditions. Such improvements would increase or extend stream flows of all rivers and streams on public domain lands and would enable land managers to better identify and manage aquifer recharge areas in the public domain.**

• The largest land planning efforts in history — that of the Forest Service and the Bureau of Land Management — have largely ignored their respective duties to provide more dependable and cleaner water to the water-starved West. Rivers on public domain lands including potential Wild and Scenic Rivers are not being managed for optimum stream-flow despite the fact that the National Forests are often originally established as watersheds. The advantages of a bold new program to restore watershed condition would be to reduce peak flows of a river, extend base flows and raise water tables. In addition, there would be more interaction with aquifer recharge areas. Eighty-five percent of all the rivers in the West originate in National Forests and many of the most important aquifer recharge areas are on public domain land.

• The next cycle of Forest Service Land and Resource Management Plans and associated environmental impact statements should contain an express direction to assess watershed condition system-wide and identify priority watersheds for water supply and ground water recharge. Specific management prescriptions should be adopted in the plans that would enhance the most significant watersheds.

### RECOMMENDATION
**The Director of the Bureau of Land Management should implement appropriate actions to ensure that riparian area management be given a high priority for the Bureau's wildlife and range programs.**

• Riparian areas occupy less than one percent of the 172 million acres of rangelands managed by the Bureau of Land Management (BLM), but have ecological importance far beyond this relatively small acreage in the arid and semi-arid West. Unfortunately, the vast majority of riparian areas administered by the BLM has been severely degraded, primarily as a consequence of livestock grazing. According to the General Accounting Office, there are two primary reasons for the lack of progress in restoring and properly managing these areas: (1) lack of skilled field staff to plan, implement and monitor riparian areas; and (2) lack of support for riparian management efforts at high agency management levels.

149

## BUDGET RECOMMENDATION
F.Y. 90: **Increase** of $ 2 million　　　　　F.Y. 91: **Increase** of $ 3 million

## PRINCIPAL AUTHORIZING LEGISLATION
Federal Land Policy and Management Act, 43 U.S.C. § 1701 et seq.

## CONGRESSIONAL JURISDICTION
**House Authorizing Committee/Subcommittee**
　Committee on Interior and Insular Affairs
　　Subcommittee on National Parks and Public Lands
**Senate Authorizing Committee/Subcommittee**
　Committee on Energy and Natural Resources
　　Subcommittee on Public Lands, National Parks and Forests
**House Appropriations Subcommittee**
　Subcommittee on Interior
**Senate Appropriations Subcommittee**
　Subcommittee on Interior and Related Agencies

## RELEVANT STUDIES
GAO, **"Public Rangelands: Some Riparian Areas Restored, But Widespread Improvement Will Be Slow."** (1988)

## RELATED FEDERAL PROGRAMS
Range Management, Wildlife, Soil, Water and Air

## PRINCIPAL SOURCES OF EXPERTISE
Natural Resources Defense Council — 415-777-0220
National Wildlife Federation — 202-797-6800
Izaak Walton League — 202-528-1818
American Fisheries Society — 301-897-8616
Trout Unlimited — 703-281-1100
The Wilderness Society — 202-842-3400

## IMPLEMENTATION STEPS
(1) Request that funds for riparian area management be increased to $5 million per year.
(2) Provide increased staff to develop, implement and monitor (enforce) riparian area programs on BLM lands.
(3) Inventory the condition of riparian areas where acceptable data are lacking.
(4) Implement currently identified projects to enhance the condition of riparian areas.
(5) Annually document site-specific progress made in riparian area improvement.
(6) Document all instances in which restoration programs have been thwarted or rejected.
(7) Develop and implement a riparian area education program targeted to all BLM employees and public land users that will demonstrate the importance of proper management of riparian areas.

## BUDGET HISTORY (in millions of dollars by fiscal year)

|              | 81  | 83  | 85  | 87  | 88  |
| ------------ | --- | --- | --- | --- | --- |
| Appropriated | 1.5 | 1.5 | 1.5 | 2.0 | 2.0 |

## NOTES:

—————————— **Blueprint for the Environment** ——————————

# Blueprint for the Environment

## WATERSHEDS AND MINERALS

# DEPARTMENT OF THE INTERIOR

**RECOMMENDATION**
**The Director of the Bureau of Land Management should work actively to provide public access to those lands that will support recreational usage.**

• Recent Bureau of Land Management (BLM) estimates reflect that over 30 percent of BLM-administered lands, excluding Alaska, have limited or no public access. Many of these lands offer significant public recreational use values. The limited access to these lands also restricts state wildlife management agency and federal wildlife agency ability to effectively manage wildlife species that utilize those areas.
• The Secretary of the Interior and the BLM

Director should insist on the complete implementation of Federal Land Policy Management Act authority to acquire by purchase, exchange, donation or eminent domain, access to public lands that have been identified as offering recreational use values that do not adversely affect other uses of those lands. The Secretary of the Interior should also request appropriate funding increases to allow for an aggressive access acquisition program.

**RECOMMENDATION**
**The Assistant Secretary for Land and Minerals Management should order that the existing BLM policy, which directs that leases be issued on all available lands, be replaced by new instructions which call for a burden-of-proof test on leasing to demonstrate that a proposed area can be fully developed for oil or gas without unacceptable impacts.**

• Issuance of oil/gas leases on Federal minerals is discretionary under the Mineral Leasing Act. The Secretary of the Interior is charged with the responsibility for determining that oil/gas development is preferable to other uses for a tract,

prior to approving the issuance of a lease. Issuance of a lease places the power to develop in the hands of the lessee, and subsequent NEPA and other regulation can merely influence the manner of development.

**RECOMMENDATION**
**The Bureau of Land Management should adopt regulations that require adequate public notification of leasing and drilling decisions, including printing maps and notices in local newspapers.**

• The Federal Land Policy and Management Act (FLPMA) and the Federal Onshore Oil and Gas Leasing Reform Act of 1987 clearly provide for public notice and comment on agency decisions to lease or approve development of oil and gas leases. Section 309(e) of FLPMA provides that the Secretary shall provide for public participation in the preparation and execution of plans and programs for, and the management of, the public lands. The Federal Leasing Re-

form Act amends the Mineral Leasing Act of 1920 that provides for notice of all lease sales, terms and stipulations for the leases, and approvals of applications for permits to drill for oil and gas. Those notices must include "the terms or modified lease terms and maps or a narrative description of the affected lands." Section 2(d) of the Leasing Reform Act.
• The new regulations to be adopted should establish that terms and stipulations in the

151

leases must be available for public notice at the time of the lease sale. These public notices should include maps and narratives for the public to determine the location of the likely effects of the lease, the stipulations or waiver of stipulations, or the application for permit to drill. Finally, the notice should be included in a newspaper of local circulation, not just be posted in agency offices, for the local public to receive adequate notice of the proposed action. The regulations adopted in 1988 are not adequate on these points.

## RECOMMENDATION
**The Bureau of Land Management should assert their existing authority to direct hydro development to appropriate sites and away from inappropriate sites on federal public lands.**

• Several hundred applications to construct private hydroelectric projects on federal public lands are now pending before the Federal Energy Regulatory Commission (FERC). To ensure that these proposed projects are consistent with Forest Service resource plans, the agencies must play a strong role in the regulation of these projects.

## RECOMMENDATION
**The Secretary of the Interior should reinterpret the 1926 Public Water Reserve #107 Executive Order to allow the Bureau of Land Management to reserve water rights at springs and water holes in sufficient quantity to sustain fish and wildlife.**

• The Bureau of Land Management (BLM) manages more wildlife habitat than any other federal agency. Much of this habitat is located in the 11 contiguous western states where water is a critical commodity. Water sources are typically widely spaced and very limited.
• Earlier Administrations interpreted BLM's spring and water hole withdrawals to allow for the reservation of water rights for fish and wildlife, as well as human and livestock consumption. Recently, the Department of the Interior substantially revised this option and limited reserved water rights only to the amount of water necessary for human and livestock consumption. The new policy will impair BLM's ability to improve habitat conditions for fish and wildlife on the lands under its jurisdiction.

## Blueprint for the Environment

## MINING

# DEPARTMENT OF THE INTERIOR

**RECOMMENDATION**

**The Assistant Secretary for Land and Minerals Management should maintain all existing land withdrawals from the operation of the Mining Law, and establish a nationwide review process for the purpose of identifying additional sensitive public lands which should be withdrawn. The program should include a strong public participation component and a process for public nomination of proposed withdrawal areas with mandatory agency response.**

• Currently, the only action the federal government can take to preclude mining development on federal lands under the 1872 Mining Law is by formally withdrawing lands from mineral development. The Reagan Administration has not exercised its discretion to withdraw sensitive environmental areas from mining. In fact, under the Administration's land withdrawal review program, the Interior Department has a policy of eliminating the withdrawals on lands.

• The review process for lands that should be withdrawn from leasing could be undertaken in the land use planning process. In those areas where the plans have been completed, the land withdrawal reviews could be undertaken through a plan amendment with an environmental impact statement.

**RECOMMENDATION**

**The Assistant Secretary for Land and Minerals Management should increase efforts to contest the validity of inactive Mining Law claims in Wilderness and National Park areas, including Alaska.**

• The 1872 Mining Law requires the discovery of a "valuable deposit" of mineral. When such a deposit is discovered, the finder is entitled to certain rights on the public land, including the potential to obtain fee title to the land for as little as $2.50 per acre.

• However, many mining claims are not valid, due to the absence of an actual discovery and the failure of the claimant to perform annual assessment work required to keep an old claim alive. In other cases, sham claims are used as an excuse for individuals squatting on the public lands.

• Diligent work is needed by Bureau of Land Management, both for its own lands and in a cooperative effort with other surface-managing agencies, to clear invalid claims from the books and from the land. A specific program with target dates should be developed and implemented.

**RECOMMENDATION**

**The Assistant Secretary for Land and Minerals Management should pursue legislation to replace the 1872 Mining Law with a complete reform.**

• The reform legislation should provide for: (i) No surface patenting of public land, (ii) A permit requirement for all surface-disturbing operations, the permit issuance to be discretionary and based upon a public-interest determination of suitability by the surface-managing agency with mandatory weighting of environmental values and management objectives for the area as established in land management plans under the Federal Land Policy and Management Act, (iii) Mandatory reclamation standards for all metals mining, (iv) A royalty-collection process to provide revenue for an Abandoned Mined Land reclamation administration for hardrock sites.

• The 1872 Mining Law permits a variety of abuses of the public domain, ranging from patenting surface ownership for as little as $2.50 per acre to location of vast mining complexes in unsuitable areas. The location itself of a metals mine is generally the greatest determinant of its long-term reclaimability (EPA RCRA Report). Location of mines in wild areas is a serious threat to the protection of wildlife habitat and wilderness lands. Mining activity is spreading into new locations, due to the economic revival of the industry and the lower international value of the dollar. Reform of this 116-year-old legal eyesore is urgently required for sound land management on Bureau of Land Management and National Forest lands.

## RECOMMENDATION
**The Assistant Secretary for Land and Minerals Management should prepare and press for adoption new legislation amending the Federal Land Policy and Management Act of 1976 to require that a thorough analysis of oil field development impacts on an area, integrated with the management plan for other resources, be performed prior to making the area available for oil and gas leasing.**

• The Interior Department is required under the National Environmental Policy Act to prepare an environmental impact assessment that evaluates the impacts of potential development of oil and gas leases, either separately or as part of the land management planning process. Resource management plans issued by the Department to date have failed to include the consideration of the impacts of oil and gas leasing and development on surface resources during the planning process. As a result, little consideration has been given to effects on other resource uses in areas where oil and gas leasing occurs, or to the effective management of oil and gas development in the contest of other resource values. This consideration should be carried out in a balanced multiple-use context, through the Federal Land Policy and Management Act planning process.

## RECOMMENDATION
**The Assistant Secretary for Land and Minerals Management should adopt regulations requiring posting of a bond whose immediate dollar value will be adequate to cover all costs of reclamation, prior to permitting surface-disturbing activity for hardrock mining purposes.**

• The Bureau of Land Management does not routinely require that a mining-claim prospector or operator post a financial guarantee to ensure that damage to the public lands from his operation will be reclaimed at no cost to the public. As a result, many mining sites are abandoned in a damaged condition. The cost to reclaim these sites varies from a few thousand dollars to several millions (e.g., McLaren Tailings, Montana; Holden Site, Washington).

• Bureau of Land Management's current policy is to require financial guarantees "only when an operator has an established record of regulatory noncompliance." (GAO)

• The Bureau should routinely require a bond prior to permitting surface-disturbing mining operations.

Blueprint for the Environment

# Blueprint for the Environment

## REFUGES

# DEPARTMENT OF THE INTERIOR
## ASSISTANT SECRETARY for Fish and Wildlife and Parks
## Fish and Wildlife Service
## Division of Refuges

### RECOMMENDATION
**The Secretary of the Interior and the Administration should support the enactment of legislation in the 101st Congress to establish a goal for the wildlife refuge system, provide appropriate purposes for every refuge, strengthen the protective compatibility standard that governs commercial and recreational uses on refuges and require ongoing refuge planning.**

• Since the first national wildlife refuge was established in 1903 to prevent the continued destruction of colonial nesting bird populations on Pelican Island, Florida, 444 additional refuges have been created by Executive Orders, Public Land Orders, through ongoing land acquisitions, or by Acts of Congress. The Refuge System is intended to save endangered species from extinction, to provide essential habitats for migratory birds and to accomplish other wildlife conservation purposes.

• In 1966, Congress passed the National Wildlife Refuge System Administration Act establishing the National Wildlife Refuge System. The law provides guidelines for refuge management and use. However, it does not spell out the mission of the refuge system nor provide purposes for the units of the system. Furthermore, the law gives discretion to permit any use of refuge lands whenever the Secretary determines such uses "are compatible with the pur-

poses for which such areas were established..." [emphasis added]. Secretary Watt, in a significantly damaging way, actually exercised his discretion to order an increase in economic uses and public activities without increasing refuge manpower or budgets.

• A 1983 Fish and Wildlife Service report revealed more than 7,700 threats to the refuges, such as water quality degradation and numerous negative land use impacts. Additional reports and studies have demonstrated that refuge uses deemed compatible may actually threaten the resources the refuges are supposed to protect. Thus, it is important and timely to provide the refuge system with much needed legislative guidance that will give direction and purpose to the refuges and establish appropriate guidelines for the compatibility standard. Environmental organizations will likely sponsor such legislation but will need administration support to assure its successful passage.

## BUDGET RECOMMENDATION
F.Y. 90: no change          F.Y. 91: no change

## PRINCIPAL AUTHORIZING LEGISLATION
National Wildlife Refuge System Administration Act (16 U.S.C. Sec 668dd et seq) (no expiration date)

## CONGRESSIONAL JURISDICTION
**House Authorizing Committee/Subcommittee**
Committee on Merchant Marine and Fisheries
Subcommittee on Fisheries and Wildlife Conservation and the Environment
**Senate Authorizing Committee/Subcommittee**
Committee on Environment and Public Works
Subcommittee on Environmental Protection
**House Appropriations Subcommittee**
Subcommittee on Interior
**Senate Appropriations Subcommittee**
Subcommittee on Interior and Related Agencies

## RELEVANT STUDIES
**"Final Recommendations on the Management of the National Wildlife Refuge System,"** April 1979, U.S. Fish and Wildlife Service
**"Field Station Threats and Conflicts: National Wildlife Refuges, National Fish Hatcheries, Research Centers",** August 1982, Internal Report prepared by Division of Refuge Management, et al.
**"Economic Uses of the National Wildlife Refuge System Unlikely to Increase Significantly,"** General Accounting Office, June 15, 1984, GAO/RCED-84-108
Currently ongoing GAO study on refuge compatibility issues, due for report by June, 1989

## RELATED FEDERAL PROGRAMS
The Endangered Species Act, recovery programs

## PRINCIPAL SOURCES OF EXPERTISE
The Wilderness Society — 202-842-3400
Defenders of Wildlife — 202-659-9510
National Audubon Society — 202-547-9009

## IMPLEMENTATION STEPS
(1) Secretary and Assistant Secretary request background and briefing from FWS.
(2) Meet with all concerned environmental organizations to discuss needs.
(3) Meet with Congressional Committee Chairpersons.
(4) Consider developing an Administration bill.

## BUDGET HISTORY (in millions of dollars by fiscal year)

|  | 81 | 83 | 85 | 87 | 89 |
|---|---|---|---|---|---|
| Requested | 62.0 | 70.9 | 93.1 | 96.3 | 112.8 |
| Appropriated | 56.9 | 86.9 | 101.4 | 111.5 | 115.6 |

## MANPOWER HISTORY (in F.T.E.'s by fiscal year)

|  | 79 | 81 | 83 | 85 | 87 | 89 |
|---|---|---|---|---|---|---|
| Actual | uk | uk | 1750 | 2008 | 2164 | 2142 |

## REFUGES

# DEPARTMENT OF THE INTERIOR

**RECOMMENDATION**
**The Secretary of the Interior should seek legislation for the National Wildlife Refuge mandating refuges to be managed for the enhancement of wildlife values and habitat as their prime mission, with pressures for other uses removed.**

• Refuge lands have been acquired because of their importance to wildlife and the habitat they provide for breeding and feeding. Other uses should not be permitted if they in any way interfere with this primary purpose. Uses that should not be permitted if they conflict with the native or migratory wildlife using the area are mining, grazing (by cattle, sheep, horses, etc.) or recreational uses by people. A carrying capacity needs to be determined for human use, particularly for refuges along the coast where there are increasing demands for public use of the beach. Nesting areas on refuge beaches should be closed to public access during the nesting season since so few undisturbed beaches remain for shorebirds, and their numbers have been declining at alarming rates. Use of refuge beaches by over-sand vehicles should not be permitted as they destroy biota and vegetation and prevent new dunes from forming, and they disturb and sometimes destroy the chicks.

**RECOMMENDATION**
**The Director of the Fish and Wildlife Service should require that an updated Threats and Conflicts inventory and report on lands administered by the Fish and Wildlife Service should be compiled with specific recommendations for action to resolve all threats or conflicts within the next five years.**

• In 1982, the Fish and Wildlife Service (FWS) compiled a Threats and Conflicts Report documenting over 7,700 problems on refuges, fish hatcheries and research centers. However, little or no action has been taken to resolve these documented problems, to update or monitor the status of the problems, or to develop and coordinate a national plan for dealing with the problems over time.

**RECOMMENDATION**
**The Secretary of the Interior should use funds available through the Land and Water Conservation Fund to accelerate acquisition of important wildlife habitats for addition to the National Wildlife Refuge System.**

**RECOMMENDATION**
**The Director of the Fish and Wildlife Service should make the protection of both tidal and non-tidal wetlands on refuges a subject of special emphasis.**

## RECOMMENDATION

**The Fish and Wildlife Service should take prompt action to reverse the drastic decline in migratory bird populations, by developing and funding an integrated habitat acquisition program.**

## RECOMMENDATION

**The Director of the Fish and Wildlife Service should reestablish regional planning staffs and resume orderly development of refuge master plans.**

- There are about 450 units in the National Wildlife Refuge System. Only about 100 have master plans that are less than 10 years old to guide their future management. In 1981, the existing refuge field stations reported more than 7,000 threats and conflicts. Few of those threats and conflicts have been resolved or even addressed in the last eight years.
- Comprehensive conservation plans setting forth long-term (ten or more years) objectives for resource management and public uses on the refuge would help individual refuges begin to solve many of these problems. During master planning, issues are defined, an interested public is motivated, and problems are confronted. In addition, future problems can be avoided by clearly defining the objectives of each unit.

## RECOMMENDATION

**The Director of the Fish and Wildlife Service, either under existing authority or with Congressional approval, should establish a new concept — a national system to address national recognition and protection of the nation's one natural resource that still is not recognized: the nation's significant fisheries.**

- This system could be established within existing legislative authority. It would have two goals — one natural and one cultural.
- The natural goal will be to identify and conserve the integrity and the diversity of the nationally significant components of the Nation's fish resources and the environment in which they exist. Example: the Iliamna watershed of Alaska in which 27 percent of that state's spawning for salmon takes place. Many other species are found there in abundance.
- The cultural goal will be to identify and conserve the fisheries of special recreational value for the long-term benefit of society. Examples: the Madison River System in Montana, and the Au Sable in Michigan.
- Using the Fish and Wildlife Act of 1956 as the primary authority, the system can be administratively created by the Secretary or by Presidential Executive Order. It could be very similar to the National Historic Landmarks Program of the National Park Service, and it could consist of the following:

The identification and publication of the national areas;

The listing in a registry;

The demarcation by a plaque;

Certification to the owner; and

Protection mechanisms that will involve restrictions, criteria and guidelines in the use of permits, grants, and other processes which affect projects that, in turn, affect fisheries of national significance.

- The recommendations for designation would be submitted by any governmental agency, by any state, or by any individual. The federal government will not gain possessory interest in the land or the fish resources involved.

## RECOMMENDATION

**The Secretary of the Interior should actively support legislation to designate the 1.5 million acre coastal plain of the Arctic National Wildlife Refuge as Wilderness, and should re-examine the Alaska National Interest Lands Conservation Act Section 1002 report to assure a full examination of environmental consequences.**

## Blueprint for the Environment

## COASTAL BARRIERS

# DEPARTMENT OF THE INTERIOR

**RECOMMENDATION**

**The Interior Department should request appropriations for, and conduct, a study which analyzes the effectiveness of the Coastal Barrier Resources Act in accomplishing its legislated goals to reduce wasteful federal expenditure, loss of human life, and damage to fish and wildlife habitat.**

• In the six years since the passage of the Coastal Barrier Resources Act (CBRA), there has been no thorough examination of how development has been affected by the Act or whether the current methods for enforcing CBRA's prohibition on the use of federal development subsidies within Coastal Barrier Resources System (CBRS) units are adequate.

• Such a study would be useful to determine the types of strengthening changes which need to be made to the Act. It should compare the extent of development of the 186 existing CBRS units in 1982, when CBRA was first passed, to their current level of development and attempt to determine the factors which have either discouraged or encouraged development. The study also should examine trends in the types of residencies being constructed in CBRS units — primary, secondary, or rental — and the value of these structures.

• Other questions which should be answered are whether new development on CBRS units is insured with private flood insurance and whether new development has been funded with state, local or private monies. This analysis should also examine the number of personnel and the procedures responsible for implementing CBRA restrictions on the funding activities of federal agencies and assess whether the current annual General Accounting Office reporting procedure is adequate to ensure compliance with CBRA by federal agencies.

**RECOMMENDATION**

**The Department of the Interior should adopt a policy forbidding the construciton of buildings on barrier islands refuges that are not absolutely essential to refuge operations.**

• Barrier islands are subject to severe coastal storms and the government would save a great deal of money if it prohibited any construction that was not essential to operating the refuge. Complexes for administration, other than small on-site structures necessary for operations and information, should be placed on the mainland, out of the floodplain and away from the effects of a major coastal storm. This would include all visitor centers and related facilities. Public transportaiton should be encouraged rather than allowing more and more refuge lands to be made into parking lots.

## RECOMMENDATION

**The Department of the Interior should reverse its position on several recommendations in its 1988 Coastal Barrier Resources System Report to Congress that either weaken or fail to strengthen the scope of protection of the System.**

• Interior is responsible for recommending additions and deletions to the Coastal Barrier Resource System (CBRS) and ways to conserve natural resources in CBRS units. In its 1988 report, however, the Department made several recommendations which would decrease or limit the geographic scope of the System, and others which failed to regulate damaging federal activities in fragile CBRS units. Interior also neglected to recommend any tax code changes or land acquisition strategies which would have helped to conserve valuable coastal barrier resources.

• The Interior Department should reverse its position on these proposals by recommending to Congress the following:

Inclusion of "otherwise protected" areas within the System;

Continued CBRS designation of military and Coast Guard lands;

A prohibition on federal permits for activities within CBRS units which are inconsistent with the goals of the Act;

Deletion of the "essential links" exemption in Section 6(a)(3) of the Act which allows for expansion of highways in CBRS units;

An amendment to the Act requiring the disposal of dredged materials to be consistent with the purposes of the Act;

Removal of the availability of casualty loss deductions for new development in CBRS units;

Restrictions on the availability of tax exempt bonds for infrastructure within CBRS units; and

Establishment of a program for the acquisition of CBRS units.

• Such recommendations would strengthen and expand the System, thereby preserving valuable resources, reducing federal expenditures for unsound coastal development, and protecting human life and property.

## RECOMMENDATION

**The Department of the Interior should inventory the undeveloped coastal barriers along the Great Lakes and Pacific Coasts and recommend that Congress pass legislation to include them within the Coastal Barrier Resources System.**

• The Coastal Barrier Resources System (CBRS) was created in 1982 to correct the inconsistencies between the federal government's coastal zone management goals and its policy of funding coastal development by removing federal subsidies for new flood insurance and infrastructure, such as roads, sewers, bridges, and housing, on undeveloped, hazard-prone coastal barriers. The System's protection, however, is extended only to fragile spits, beaches, wetlands, and dunes on the Atlantic and Gulf Coasts. Although Interior identified over 150,000 eligible acres on the West and Great Lakes Coasts in its 1985 inventory, it failed to propose that any of these units be included within the System in its final report to Congress on recommended System additions.

# Blueprint for the Environment

## COASTAL PROTECTION AND LEASING

## DEPARTMENT OF THE INTERIOR
### ASSISTANT SECRETARY for Land and Minerals Management
### Minerals Management Service

**RECOMMENDATION**
**The Secretary of the Interior should revise the 5-Year Outer Continental Shelf Leasing Program to exclude sensitive areas and ensure that offshore oil activities do not harm ecologically valuable coastal and marine areas.**

• The current 5-Year Offshore Leasing Program proposes leasing in some of the nation's most sensitive coastal and marine areas. As a result, it is fraught with controversy and is meeting resistance from many coastal states, Congressional representatives and environmental groups. The Secretary of the Interior could achieve a more balanced and environmentally sensitive leasing program if he did the following:

1) The Secretary should act immediately to cancel three lease sales planned for 1989: Sale 91 off the northern California coast; Park II of Sale 116 off the Florida Keys and Everglades in the Eastern Gulf of Mexico; and Sale 96 in the North Atlantic. In addition, if Lease Sale 92 (Bristol Bay) has not taken place, that sale too should be cancelled. (If it has already occurred, any further federal approvals should be put on hold pending review and consultation with the State of Alaska, environmental, fishing and Native groups).

2) The rest of the 5-Year Program should be revised with sales in the following areas dropped: the North Atlantic, Bristol Bay, Northern and Central California and Washington/Oregon.

3) Each sale area remaining in the Program should be reviewed and sensitive areas should be deleted, especially in the Eastern Gulf of Mexico and Southern California.

4) The Secretary should, as part of his revision of the program, adopt the joint industry and environmental recommendations for the Bering Sea.

5) Finally, the Secretary should reconsider the wisdom of lowering the minimum bonus bid to $25/acre.

## BUDGET RECOMMENDATION
F.Y. 90: **no change**        F.Y. 91: **no change**

## PRINCIPAL AUTHORIZING LEGISLATION
Outer Continental Shelf Lands Act (OCSLA), 43 U.S.C. 1331 et seq.

## CONGRESSIONAL JURISDICTION
**House Authorizing Committee/Subcommittee**
Committee on Interior and Insular Affairs
Committee on Merchant Marine and Fisheries
Subcommittee on Oceanography
**Senate Authorizing Committee/Subcommittee**
Committee on Energy and Natural Resources
Subcommittee on Mineral Resources Development and Production
**House Appropriations Subcommittee**
Subcommittee on Interior
**Senate Appropriations Subcommittee**
Subcommittee on Interior and Related Agencies

## RELEVANT STUDIES

## RELATED FEDERAL PROGRAMS
Major related statutes and programs include:
Endangered Species Act
Coastal Zone Management Program
Clean Water Act.
Clean Air Act

## PRINCIPAL SOURCES OF EXPERTISE
Natural Resources Defense Council — 212-949-0049
American Oceans Campaign — 301-270-0317

## IMPLEMENTATION STEPS
(1)  The Secretary of the Interior should support the strengthening of controls over and the transfer of jurisdiction over Outer Continental Shelf air emissions to the Environmental Protection Agency. (While the Department of the Interior, Minerals Management Service is the lead on this issue, the same substantive recommendation is being presented to the Environmental Protection Agency, Office of Water.)
(2)  The Secretary of the Interior should initiate a program to designate Outer Continental Shelf areas for long-term protection.
(3)  The Secretary of the Interior should give coastal states a greater role in Outer Continental Shelf leasing decisions affecting their coasts.
(4)  The Secretary of the Interior should give more weight to recommendations made by the National Marine Fisheries Service, National Oceanic and Atmospheric Administration, the U.S. Fish and Wildlife Service, and the Environmental Protection Agency.
(5)  The Minerals Management Service should cancel its leasing and regulatory program for hard minerals under the Outer Continental Shelf Lands Act and support new stand-alone legislation similar to the National Seabed Hard Mineral Resources Act (H.R. 1260).

## Blueprint for the Environment

# Blueprint for the Environment

## MINING

## DEPARTMENT OF THE INTERIOR
### ASSISTANT SECRETARY for Land and Minerals Management
### Office of Surface Mining

### RECOMMENDATION
**The Secretary of the Interior should direct the Office of Surface Mining to develop standards to ensure meaningful post-mining land uses in coal mine areas The Secretary should prevent the wholesale conversion of mixed land uses to pastureland, promoting options such as reforestation and wildlife habitat.**

• The Surface Mining Control and Reclamation Act requires that lands affected by mining be reclaimed to support the uses which it was capable of supporting prior to mining, or a higher or better use. In many areas of Appalachia and the Western coalfields, the land use prior to mining was forestland, wildlife habitat and grazing land. However, a trend is emerging where the land is not replanted in trees and shrubs after mining, thereby eliminating vegetation patterns that are important components of a productive wildlife habitat. Instead, the land is planted in grasses and a "productive" post-mining land use is not achieved during the operator's period of responsibility.

• The Interior Department must revise its regulations addressing post-mining land use to ensure that operators return the land to a productive use for all uses that occurred on the land prior to mining. Equally important, the Department must enforce this provision in federal and state-program states. The wholesale conversion of forest lands and wildlife habitat to pastureland is contrary to the letter and the intent of the Surface Mining Act.

### RECOMMENDATION
**Congress should amend the Surface Mining Control and Reclamation Act to strengthen the role of the federal Office of Surface Mining in the administration and federal enforcement of the Surface Mining Control and Reclamation Act.**

• The Surface Mining Control and Reclamation Act created an enforcement system which allowed state regulatory authorities to take the lead on enforcement of a surface mining regulatory program. However, Congress clearly intended that the Federal/regulatory authority maintain an oversight or back-up role and take enforcement action when a state agency failed to enforce the Surface Mining Act. The Federal responsibility set forth in Surface Mining Control and Reclamation Act to ensure that mining is consistent with the Federal law has been confused by the role of state government, and should be clarified. Sections 520 and 521 of Surface Mining Control and Reclamation Act should be amended to reaffirm Congressional intent that the Secretary and his authorized representatives have a mandatory duty to take enforcement action whenever a violation of the Surface Mining Act occurs on a mining site.

## BUDGET RECOMMENDATION

## PRINCIPAL AUTHORIZING LEGISLATION
Surface Mining Control and Reclamation Act of 1977 (30 USC 1201 et seq.)

## CONGRESSIONAL JURISDICTION
**House Authorizing Committee/Subcommittee**
Committee on Interior and Insular Affairs
Subcommittee on Energy and the Environment
**Senate Authorizing Committee/Subcommittee**
Committee on Energy and Natural Resources
Subcommittee on Mineral Resources Development and Production
**House Appropriations Subcommittee**
Subcommittee on Interior
**Senate Appropriations Subcommittee**
Subcommittee on Interior and Related Agencies

## RELEVANT STUDIES

## RELATED FEDERAL PROGRAMS

## PRINCIPAL SOURCES OF EXPERTISE
National Wildlife Federation — 202-797-6800
Environmental Policy Institute — 202-544-2600

## NOTES:

**Blueprint for the Environment**

## MINING

# DEPARTMENT OF THE INTERIOR

**RECOMMENDATION**
**The Office of Surface Mining should review and tighten up criteria for exemptions from the reclamation requirements of the Surface Mining Control and Reclamation Act.**

• Exemptions from the Surface Mining Control and Reclamation Act reclamation requirements have provided opportunities for massive abuses. In the case of the exemption for extraction of coal where the surface coal mining operation affects two acres or less (originally included in Section 528(2) of Surface Mining Control and Reclamation Act), documented abuses led to congressional revocation of the exemption in 1987. Abuses under another statutory exemption — for operations where coal removal is incidental to the removal of other minerals for commercial sale and the coal is less that 16-2/3 percent of the total tonnage of mineral removed — can and should be dealt with by promulgation and enforcement of a regulation that includes a value test under which operations that receive more than 50 percent of their revenue from coal during any year must obtain a coal mining permit.

**RECOMMENDATION**
**The Office of Surface Mining should assume Federal regulatory enforcement authority in states that are failing to enforce their regulatory programs under the Surface Mining Act.**

• The Office of Surface Mining has been reluctant to use its powers of federal takeover of state programs in other states where systemic noncompliance is occurring. The federal agency routinely outlines major compliance problems by state regulatory authorities during its annual oversight procedure, but then fails to follow through with any definitive action to correct the problem. In many cases, state non-compliance with the surface mining program results in major environmental damage and restricts the rights of citizens living in the coal fields. The problems documented by the Office of Surface Mining will not be corrected without stronger federal pressure. That pressure should be applied through the "733 process" embodied in the federal regulations.

**RECOMMENDATION**
**The Office of Surface Mining should develop and implement an effective and efficient applicant-violator computer system to block or revoke permits to illegal operators.**

**RECOMMENDATION**
**The Assistant Secretary for Land and Minerals Management should promulgate regulations and develop a regulatory program to address the environmental damage caused by underground mining as part of its national program of performance standards for mining.**

## RECOMMENDATION
**The Assistant Secretary for Land and Minerals Management should impose a ban on steep slope coal mining, coupled with incentives to encourage remining and reclamation of previously-mined unreclaimed areas.**

• For coal mine areas left unreclaimed prior to 1977, the best hope for reclamation will be through the development of incentives for coal companies to mine the site again and then reclaim the land to a sustainable post-mining land use. The specific incentives to encourage remining should be determined through a forum that includes representation from the coal industry, coalfield congressmen, environmental organizations and the Interior Department. The remaining program should be federally administered and be financed (at least in part) by leveraging funds available in the Abandoned Mine Land Fund.

## RECOMMENDATION
**The Secretary of the Interior should direct the Office of Surface Mining to redefine design standards for valley fills, especially "durable rock fills", for reclamation of coal surface mining areas.**

• Recent research by the Office of Surface Mining indicates that the valley fills in steep slope areas in central Appalachia are not "durable" at all. In fact, tests of the rocks used in these fills show that the "rock" will disintegrate after 24 hours immersed in water or, in the field, after a good long rain. These findings bring into serious doubt the stability of these massive fills perched along the ridgelines in water courses and above communities, and provide the impetus for significant change in the regulations governing valley fill construction.

## RECOMMENDATION
**The Assistant Secretary for Land and Minerals Management should develop an effective program, including both regulations and enforcement staff, for prevention and control of acid drainage resulting from coal-mining activity, including a mining prohibition in acid and toxic producing areas.**

• Surface mining in areas where exposure of the overburden to air and water creates acid conditions is allowed currently, despite a multitude of evidence that acid-producing soils require long term treatment by the companies. Once the problem is created by opening an acid-producing coal seam, the acid cannot be eliminated and its effects on aquatic life must be mitigated.

## RECOMMENDATION
**The Assistant Secretary for Land and Minerals Management should implement (or if still necessary, develop and propose) legislation to impose felony sanctions and forfeiture for mining coal without a permit and for the knowing purchase of coal so mined.**

## RECOMMENDATION
**Congress should extend and expand the Abandoned Mine Land Fund for coal to increase the fee, make post-1977 abandoned mine sites eligible for reclamation funds and allow the AML Fund to accrue interest.**

## Blueprint for the Environment

# Blueprint for the Environment

## PARKS

## DEPARTMENT OF THE INTERIOR
### ASSISTANT SECRETARY for Fish and Wildlife and Parks
### National Park Service

### RECOMMENDATION
**The Secretary of the Interior and the Administration should support the thrust of and encourage the enactment of legislation to advance the operation of the Land and Water Conservation Fund as embodied in the "American Heritage Trust Act of 1988" (H.R.4127 and S.2199 of the 100th Congress).**

• The Land and Water Conservation Fund (LWCF) has since 1965 constituted the major source of federal funds for the acquisition of federal lands for outdoor recreation purposes, as well as for 50/50 matching grants to state and local governments for both land acquisition and facilities development. The Fund has been immensely popular and has resulted in the acquisition of 5.5 million acres of land and the development of almost 20,000 state and local park facility projects.

• The Reagan administration generally proposed termination of funding support for the last eight years and Congress has appropriated an annual average of only about 25 percent of earlier high year funding.

• Congress has authorized the acquisition of approximately $200 million worth of federal park, forest and refuge lands which must yet be paid for from this fund. As money remains unavailable for such purchase, land prices continue to rise and some lands are converted to other uses and thereby lost for all time.

• There is a desperate need for greatly increased funding levels. Legislation introduced in the House (H.R.4127) and Senate (S.2199) (the "American Heritage Trust Act of 1988") majorly rectifies problems with the current operation of the Fund and is geared to assuring higher annual levels of funding, providing a more stable annual level of funding, creating a source for a flow of funds in perpetuity, and increasing long term constituency support. It is critically important that the thrust of this legislation be supported by the new administration.

### RECOMMENDATION
**The National Park Service should request an annual appropriation of at least $150 million for land acquisition to complete land acquisition and land protection actions for the established units of the system.**

## BUDGET RECOMMENDATION
F.Y. 90: **Increase** of $345,000,000   F.Y. 91: **Increase** of $ 160,000,000

## PRINCIPAL AUTHORIZING LEGISLATION
Land and Water Conservation Fund Act of 1965 (P.L. 88-578, as amended) (expiration date September 30, 2015)
National Historic Preservation Act (P.L. 89-665, as amended) (expiration date September 30, 1993)

## CONGRESSIONAL JURISDICTION
**House Authorizing Committee/Subcommittee**
Committee on Interior and Insular Affairs
Subcommittee on National Parks and Public Lands
**Senate Authorizing Committee/Subcommittee**
Committee on Energy and Natural Resources
Subcommittee on Public Lands, National Parks and Forests
**House Appropriations Subcommittee**
Subcommittee on Interior
**Senate Appropriations Subcommittee**
Subcommittee on Interior and Related Agencies

## RELEVANT STUDIES
**"Report and Recommendations to the President of the United States,"** President's Commission on Americans Outdoors, December, 1986
**"Report to Congress—LWCF Grants in Aid,"** U.S.D.I., N.P.S. (for each fiscal year)

## RELATED FEDERAL PROGRAMS
Historic Preservation Fund, National Park Service
Urban Parks and Recreation Recovery Program, National Park Service

## PRINCIPAL SOURCES OF EXPERTISE
National Recreation and Parks Association — 703-820-4940
National Conference of State Historic Preservation Officers — 202-624-5465
National Parks and Conservation Association — 202-944-8530
The Nature Conservancy — 703-841-5300
The Wilderness Society — 202-842-3400
American Rivers — 202-842-6900
Land Trust Exchange — 703-683-7778
The Conservation Foundation — 202-293-4800

## IMPLEMENTATION STEPS
(1) Support the enactment of legislation to improve the operation of the LWCF (such as H.R.4127/S.2199, 100th Congress).
(2) Recommend greatly higher budget figures for annual appropriation (at least $1 billion/year).
(3) Re-establish a single primary office to administer the overall operation of the LWCF.
(4) Major overhaul (streamline) the entire executive branch land acquisition (approval) process.

## BUDGET HISTORY (in millions of dollars by fiscal year)

|  | 79 | 81 | 83 | 85 | 87 | 88 | 89 |
|---|---|---|---|---|---|---|---|
| Authorized | 900 | 900 | 900 | 900 | 900 | 900 | 900 |
| Requested | 725 | 275 | 38 | 167 | 17 | 18 | 18 |
| Appropriated | 737 | 288 | 335 | 286 | 193 | 170 | 206 |

## NOTES:

—————— **Blueprint for the Environment** ——————

# Blueprint for the Environment

## PARKS

## DEPARTMENT OF THE INTERIOR

**RECOMMENDATION**
**The Director of the National Park Service should seek increased funding for a vigorous and accountable resource management and protection program.**

• There is a long-standing backlog of resource management and protection projects identified by the National Park Service (NPS) for funding. The total exceeds $500 million, split about two-thirds for natural resource projects, and one-third for cultural resource projects. These projects identify needed work that is directly tied to the mandate of the NPS Organic Act.

**RECOMMENDATION**
**The National Park Service should undertake a comprehensive study of the existing boundary of every unit of the National Park System, and make recommendations to the Congress for needed changes to incorporate primary resources.**

• Current law requires that the National Park Service (NPS) assess the adequacy of each park's boundary during the preparation of its general management plan. This requirement has been ignored for years, with the result that encroachments from land use on adjacent lands has threatened or damaged park resources.

**RECOMMENDATION**
**The Director of the National Park Service should move vigorously to complete wilderness studies and to recommend through the President to the Congress, legislative designation of those areas as Wilderness.**

• The Wilderness Act of 1964 authorized this process but few recommendations or designations have been accomplished this decade. Still not designated: Grand Canyon, Yellowstone, Glacier and many others.

**RECOMMENDATION**
**The Director of the National Park Service should seek passage of a Park Protection Act similar to the one approved by the House in 1982 and 1983 to ensure protection of park resources from external influences and to institutionalize a commitment to interagency park protection.**

• While addressing the external-threat issue primarily on a park-by-park basis may appear desirable, a closer look reveals that these transboundary threats are serious and pervasive across the national park system. They have become a generic problem that will require, at least in part, a generic solution. A Park Protection Act will contribute substantially to that solution.

## RECOMMENDATION
The National Park Service should identify a "zone of influence" around each unit of the National Park System, and work with local, state or Federal land managers to assure the most compatible land use possible adjacent to the parks.

## RECOMMENDATION
The National Park Service should promptly determine and implement appropriate visitor carrying capacities for all units of the national park system, as is required by law.

## RECOMMENDATION
The Director of the National Park Service should improve the regulation of park concessioners to assure that all park visitor uses are compatible with both resource preservation and provision of a high-quality visitor experience in the parks.

## RECOMMENDATION
The National Park Service should review and update the 1972 "National Park System Plan" to reflect recent additions, pinpoint gaps in the system and propose qualified new areas which meet the criteria of National significance.

• The National Park System Plan formerly served as the primary document for identification of areas worthy of addition to the National Park System. No funds have been requested or appropriated for this purpose since 1981.

• The plan should be updated to incorporate refined knowledge of natural systems and their degree of representation, and to expand upon cultural themes not currently represented within park units.

## RECOMMENDATION
The Director of the National Park Service should revise and reissue the former NPS-3 Public Involvement Guideline in order to re-establish public opportunities for involvement in helping to plan parks.

• Public involvement for the National Park Service (NPS) used to be incorporated in a document referred to as the "Public Process Review Guideline," NPS-3, which was issued in 1978. In NPS-3, a chronology of steps listed in detail a process detailing how the planners (and agency) were to deal with the concerned public. Unfortunately, NPS-3 was withdrawn for reasons never explained to the public and portions of it were incorporated into NPS-12, the "Environmental Compliance Guideline."

## RECOMMENDATION
The National Park Service should protect park resources from the effects of mining through increased acquisition and improved regulations.

• Approximately 3,000 mining claims and six million acres of mineral rights are held within units of the National Park System. These mineral rights are either severed from the surface land or are part of tracts owned in fee title by nonfederal entities.
• The presence of such a large unacquired backlog of mineral rights poses serious problems to the integrity of the National Park System. Where private mineral-bearing lands exist, unless the government buys out these mineral rights, the National Park Service (NPS) will increasingly face proposals to develop them. Park resources and visitor experiences will suffer if the rights are developed.

Blueprint for the Environment

170

# Blueprint for the Environment

## RESEARCH

## DEPARTMENT OF THE INTERIOR
### ASSISTANT SECRETARY for Fish and Wildlife and Parks
### National Park Service

### RECOMMENDATION
**The National Park Service should help develop and support a specific legislative mandate for National Park Service research which recognizes the unique scientific value of the national parks, defines the role of research, and directs the Service to conduct natural, cultural and social science research as an essential element of its mission.**

• In the 1930s, the first research programs were initiated to gather information on natural and cultural resources. However, by the start of World War II these programs had fallen into disarray and were no longer active initiatives. Recommendations to improve the natural science program were published in 1963 by the Advisory Board on Wildlife Management and by the Advisory Committee to the National Park Service (NPS) on Research by the National Academy of Sciences. The latter group reported that "research by the National Park Service lacked continuity, coordination and depth" and that "recommendations on this subject ... will remain futile ... until the National Park Service becomes research minded."
• While the Forest Service and Fish and Wildlife Service and other agencies have legislative mandates for research, Congress has not enacted one for the NPS. Only a cultural research mandate was established for the NPS by the Historic Sites Act of 1935.

• In the absence of a specific mandate, research will remain ill-defined, and commitment and funding for program continuity will remain inadequate. An appropriate mandate would recognize National Park System units as scientific properties of national and international significance; define the roles of natural, cultural and social science in protecting and preserving park resources; require long-term ecosystem studies which recognize the importance of national parks as examples of minimally disturbed natural systems in a nation of utilized landscapes; require completion of baseline inventories of natural, cultural and human resources for all NPS units; require research to document the extent and significance of internal and external threats to park resources; and require the NPS to establish communication channels to ensure the free flow and accessibility of scientific information.

### RECOMMENDATION
**The Director of the National Park Service should require as part of performance evaluations that regional directors, superintendents, and park employees dealing with natural resources be rated as to their knowledge of the resources within the park units and the condition of the resources. Each should be held accountable for their actions related to the resources, including their efforts to seek all available means to ensure the perpetuity of the resources.**

## BUDGET RECOMMENDATION
F.Y. 90: **no change**        F.Y. 91: **no change**

## PRINCIPAL AUTHORIZING LEGISLATION
National Park Service Organic Act of August 25, 1916
Historic Sites Act of 1935

## CONGRESSIONAL JURISDICTION
**House Authorizing Committee/Subcommittee**
Committee on Interior and Insular Affairs
Subcommittee on National Parks and Public Lands
**Senate Authorizing Committee/Subcommittee**
Committee on Energy and Natural Resources
Subcommittee on National Parks, Public Lands and Forests
**House Appropriations Subcommittee**
Subcommittee on Interior
**Senate Appropriations Subcommittee**
Subcommittee on Interior and Related Agencies

## RELEVANT STUDIES
**State of the Parks: A Report to Congress**, 1980, U.S. Department of Interior
**Research in the Parks: An Assessment of Needs**, 1988, NPCA

## RELATED FEDERAL PROGRAMS
Forest Service and Fish and Wildlife Service research programs

## PRINCIPAL SOURCES OF EXPERTISE
National Parks and Conservation Association — 202-944-8530
The Conservation Foundation — 202-293-4800
Sierra Club — 202-547-1141
The Wilderness Society — 202-842-3400

## IMPLEMENTATION STEPS
(1)   The National Park Service should work with Congress to draft and pass legislation to add research to the Service's legislative mandate.

(2)   The National Park Service should include in its annual budget request a separate line item for research equivalent to at least 10 percent of the total operating budget of the National Park Service. In 1963, the National Academy of Sciences wrote about the impact of inadequate funding for research on national park units: "unless drastic steps are immediately taken, there is good possibility that within this generation several, if not all, the national parks will be degraded to a state totally different from that for which they were preserved and in which they were to be enjoyed." Although funding for research has increased slightly since 1980, it is still inadequate and barely allows any progress on an expanding project list.

(3)   The Director of the National Park Service should help to establish a Science Advisory Board of demonstrably qualified experts to provide independent, balanced, and expert assessment of National Park Service natural, cultural and social science needs and programs.
A 1963 recommendation by the Advisory Committee to the National Park Service (NPS) on research led to the establishment of a Natural Science Advisory Committee in 1964. By the 1970s, however, this committee had dissolved. Since that time no progress has been made to establish an unbiased, permanent consulting group. Later reports, such as that of the NPS Biological Diversity Task Force also stated that a scientific advisory board could help to improve progress in scientific endeavors including maintaining species diversity.

## NOTES:

—————— **Blueprint for the Environment** ——————

# EDUCATION

# DEPARTMENT OF THE INTERIOR

## RECOMMENDATION
**The Director of the National Park Service should seek legislation to provide a statutory mandate for park-based interpretation and education as fundamental to the mission of the national parks.**

• The 1916 legislation that established the National Park Service (NPS) defined its basic mission to protect resources and provide for visitor enjoyment. The term interpretation was not mentioned in the legislation, yet educational activities have always been vital to the fulfillment of the NPS mission.

• It is difficult to provide for visitor enjoyment without also helping the public understand the meaning of what they see. It is difficult to conserve resources and leave them unimpaired without enlightening the public directly about resource protection. As early as 1929, the general plan of administration for the NPS Education Division stated that its primary function "besides the part which it plays in the protection ... of natural phenomena is the interpretation of distinctive features ..." Congress affirmed interpretation's vital role in post-1916 legislation, such as the 1935 Historic Sites, Building and Antiquities Act and in specific park enabling legislation.

• In spite of this evidence, park managers often ignore or downplay interpretation's importance. Because interpretation is merely implied in the 1916 act, because legislative intent is fragmented, and because the results of interpretive efforts also are difficult to measure, it is easy for managers to view interpretation as a "luxury." When the Service is asked to make budget cuts, interpretation is often hit first. The absence of a comprehensive mandate robs interpretation of the ability to compete equally with statutorily authorized responsibilities.

## RECOMMENDATION
**The National Park Service should designate and train specific park personnel to provide liaison, technical assistance and education to local communities regarding park problems, particularly in park units threatened by encroachments from private lands outside their boundaries.**

• The reality that the parks are subject to transboundary influences is now generally accepted; however, mechanisms to mitigate adverse effects are not well developed. While this is particularly true for management of private land around park borders, full cooperation of adjacent federal land managers is lacking as well.

• There is need for National Park Service (NPS) expertise in local land-use planning, zoning law, and development regulation. Individuals with this expertise should be stationed at key park units and be directed to work with local authorities in their planning and development processes, and to serve as advocates for park protection in those processes.

• The NPS Mid-Atlantic Region has led the way in pursuing innovative strategies in cooperative land use planning, literally writing the book for NPS on the subject. NPS should initiate a senior level training course for utilization throughout the system.

## RECOMMENDATION
**The Director of the National Park Service should routinely utilize the interpretive program to provide information to visitors about the resource management problems facing the parks.**

• Building public awareness of park problems is critical to the future integrity of the parks. The public cannot be expected to care for or defend the parks if it is unaware of their needs. Awareness of critical resource issues can lead to strong, active, visible and vocal participation in park protection and conservation.

• Parks are neither perfect nor static places. They have internally and externally caused problems, and they are constantly changing. Interpretive programs have not focused on the dynamism of our parks nor on park planning for resource protection or restoration. A building in the process of being restored is an interpretive opportunity to increase public understanding of park operation. NPS should take advantage of this type of opportunity systemwide. Managing controversial issues and cooperating with the public in the future will hinge upon the NPS's ability to provide honest, factual and balanced views to park visitors about resources.

## RECOMMENDATION
**The Department of the Interior should require that its agencies or bureaus develop and distribute environmental education programs and materials dealing with all appropriate natural resource related activities of the Department of the Interior.**

• Implicit within the authority of the Federal government with respect to its natural resource programs is the responsibility to consider the wishes of the public relative to the environmental impacts of the recommendations or actions of government agencies. Citizen involvement can be obtained in a variety of ways including the provision of programs, materials, and technical assistance which give citizens a fundamental understanding of the operation of natural human-altered ecosystems.

## RECOMMENDATION
**The Director of the National Park Service should actively encourage private-sector support of national parks and public participation in park programs and projects by encouraging private-sector support groups of all types for national parks.**

• Successful achievement of the NPS mission requires enhanced public involvement programs reaching into all facets of NPS programs. A good working relationship with local citizens who live near parks is essential. In large part, the continued success of the NPS depends on its ability to build a strong working relationship with the American people. By developing and maintaining communication and cooperation, park personnel could build public understanding of issues and emerging conflicts. The citizens can then effectively contribute their ideas and suggest actions for resolving these concerns.

# Blueprint for the Environment

## PRESERVATION

## DEPARTMENT OF THE INTERIOR
### ASSISTANT SECRETARY for Fish and Wildlife and Parks
### National Park Service
### National Historic Preservation Program

**RECOMMENDATION**
**The Director of the National Park Service should develop new legislation to strengthen federal mechanisms to protect the nation's most significant historic properties and the units of the National Park System.**

• The proposed shopping mall at Manassas Battlefield Park has given national publicity to the current inability of the federal government to protect its parks and historic properties from adverse effects. The existing federal protection legislation (Section 106 of the National Historic Preservation Act) applies only to proposed federal actions, not the actions of private individuals, corporations, or State and local governments. Although private and governmental forces have the ability to adversely affect national parks and nationally significant historic properties, the federal government has limited abilities to protect the national interest.

• The National Park Service (NPS) backlog of additions to the park system has contributed to the development pressures next to National Parks. Legal protections are needed to increase acquisition rates for the park system backlog.

**RECOMMENDATION**
**The Director of the National Park Service should recommend that Congress amend the National Historic Preservation Act to permit a delegation of authority to qualified States to make final decisions, rather than recommendations.**

• Several aspects of the national historic preservation program, notably reviews of certifications for federal tax incentives, currently undergo duplicative reviews at the State and federal levels. This unnecessary duplication causes significant delays in approvals while not adding additional protection to historic properties, since less than five percent of State decisions are overturned.

• Decision-making authority would be delegated to those States with certified professional programs upon request from the State Historic Preservation Officer.

**RECOMMENDATION**
**The Secretary should work with all Interior agencies and with other cabinet offices to strengthen anti-looting efforts to combat the destruction of significant archaeological sites on federal lands.**

## BUDGET RECOMMENDATION
F.Y. 90: **no change**       F.Y. 91: **no change**

## PRINCIPAL AUTHORIZING LEGISLATION
National Historic Preservation Act, as amended (16 USC 470)

## CONGRESSIONAL JURISDICTION
**House Authorizing Committee/Subcommittee**
    Committee on Interior and Insular Affairs
        Subcommittee on National Parks and Public Lands
**Senate Authorizing Committee/Subcommittee**
    Committee on Energy and Natural Resources
        Subcommittee on National Parks, Public Lands and Forests
**House Appropriations Subcommittee**
    Subcommittee on Interior
**Senate Appropriations Subcommittee**
    Subcommittee on Interior and Related Agencies

## RELEVANT STUDIES

## RELATED FEDERAL PROGRAMS
All federal agencies, under Sections 106 and 110 of the National Historic Preservation Act, are charged with developing historic preservation programs to protect agency-owned resources, and resources threatened by agency actions

## PRINCIPAL SOURCES OF EXPERTISE
National Alliance of Preservation Commissions — 301-663-6133
National Alliance of Statewide Preservation Organizations — 617-350-7032
National Conference of State Historic Preservation Officers — 202-624-5465
National Trust for Historic Preservation — 202-673-4000
Preservation Action — 202-659-0915
Society for American Archaeology — 202-833-2322

## IMPLEMENTATION STEPS
Enact legislation to broaden federal authorities to protect nationally significant historic sites.

## BUDGET HISTORY (in millions of dollars by fiscal year) *

|  | 79 | 81 | 83 | 85 | 87 | 88 | 89 |
|---|---|---|---|---|---|---|---|
| Authorized | 100.0 | 150.0 | 150.0 | 150.0 | 150.0 | 150.0 | 150.0 |
| Requested | 45.0 | 55.0 | 0.0 | 0.0 | 0.0 | 0.0 | 0.0 |
| Appropriated | 60.0 | 26.0 | 26.0 | 25.0 | 24.0 | 28.0 | |

**\* Note:** The financial data is for appropriations from the Historic Preservation Fund, which provides matching funds to the States to carry out the national preservation program, and to the National Trust, a private membership organization. It is not possible to separately describe funds and FTEs devoted by the NPS to the program under the National Historic Preservation Act. Most personnel working on the program at NPS have dual responsibilities for cultural resources in the parks (internal programs) and outside the parks (external programs)

## NOTES:

## GREENWAYS

## DEPARTMENT OF THE INTERIOR
### ASSISTANT SECRETARY for Fish and Wildlife and Parks
### National Park Service

**RECOMMENDATION**
**The National Park Service should work to enact a National Scenic and Historic Roadways Protection Act to ensure the wise protection of selected highways and roads that possess significant scenic, historic, or cultural values.**

• The President's Commission on Americans Outdoors called for the creation of a national system of scenic highways and byways. As such, a "National Scenic and Historic Highways Protection Act" would aim to create a national network of highways and secondary roads which pass through important scenic and historic landscapes while protecting and enhancing the scenic qualities of the landscapes through which those routes pass.

**RECOMMENDATION**
**The National Park Service should take the lead in helping to establish a nationwide system of greenline parks to increase the protection of scenic and historic landscapes through the joint effort of local, state and federal governments.**

**RECOMMENDATION**
**The Secretary of the Interior should establish and seek funding for an Office of Greenway Coordination and Assistance within the National Park Service to help establish a network of linear open space (Greenways) to provide outdoor recreation opportunities close to where people live and to help conserve natural and cultural resources.**

**RECOMMENDATION**
**The National Park Service, through its Division of Recreation Resources Assistance, should provide technical and financial assistance to state and local governments and private sector groups for the purpose of encouraging the planning and creation of greenways.**

**RECOMMENDATION**
**The Secretary of Agriculture should link the Forest Service technical expertise and Extension Service delivery capability to develop and implement a major urban forestation grants program. This should be done with cooperation from the Department of the Interior greenways and trails programs and Department of Energy programs for energy conservation and clean air incentives to cities.**

## BUDGET RECOMMENDATION

F.Y. 90: **Increase** of $ 50 million *      F.Y. 91: **Increase** of $ 50 million *
* Initial funding for such an Act should come from existing revenues in the Highway Trust Fund. Development of a national user-fee on off-premise billboards along federal aid highways could raise an additional $100 million per year, of which all or part could be targeted to the Scenic Roadways program.

## PRINCIPAL AUTHORIZING LEGISLATION

## CONGRESSIONAL JURISDICTION

**House Authorizing Committee/Subcommittee**
Committee on the Interior and Insular Affairs
Subcommittee on National Parks and Public Lands
**Senate Authorizing Committee/Subcommittee**
Committee on Energy and Natural Resources
Subcommittee on National Parks, Public Lands and Forests
**House Appropriations Subcommittee**
Subcommittee on Interior
**Senate Appropriations Subcommittee**
Subcommittee on Interior and Related Agencies

## RELEVANT STUDIES

**President's Commission on Americans Outdoors,** 1987, Section III, Part VI
**An Assessment of the Feasibility of Developing a National Scenic Highway System,** report to Congress, USDOT, 1974

## RELATED FEDERAL PROGRAMS

NPS National Historic Landmark Program
NPS National Natural Landmark Program

## PRINCIPAL SOURCES OF EXPERTISE

Coalition for Scenic Beauty — 202-546-1100
National Wildlife Federation — 202-797-6800
American Planning Association — 202-872-0611
Society of Landscape Architects — 202-466-7730

## IMPLEMENTATION STEPS

(1) New legislation — The Administration should propose the "National Scenic and Historic Road-ways Protection Act."
(2) The Secretary of Interior and Secretary of Transportation should sign a memorandum of under-standing and cooperation on scenic highway designations.

## NOTES:

## Blueprint for the Environment

## RIVERS

## DEPARTMENT OF THE INTERIOR
### ASSISTANT SECRETARY for Fish and Wildlife and Parks
### National Park Service

**RECOMMENDATION**
**The National Park Service should update and complete the 1982 Nationwide Rivers Inventory so that it finally achieves its original purpose of representing a thorough list of river segments in the United States that appear to qualify for inclusion in the National Wild and Scenic Rivers Program.**

• Due to a number of time and budgetary constraints, the National Rivers Inventory (NRI) — currently a listing of 1,534 outstanding free-flowing river segments comprising 2 percent of the river miles in the country — was never completed.
• The Inventory could be updated and completed by the Park Service under existing authority of Section 5(d) of the Wild and Scenic Rivers Act without overwhelming cost to the federal government. A thorough and complete NRI would be useful to federal land management agencies in the execution of their Wild and Scenic River planning duties under section 5(d) of the Act and would help states to protect nationally significant rivers under state law.

**RECOMMENDATION**
**The National Park Service, Fish and Wildlife Service, Bureau of Land Management and Forest Service should enter into a joint memorandum of understanding that they will evaluate all potential wild and scenic rivers on their respective lands in a coordinated fashion.**

**RECOMMENDATION**
**The Secretaries of Agriculture and the Interior should, by joint secretarial order, establish a new Joint Interagency Office of River Protection to coordinate and implement a wide range of river planning, technical assistance and management programs for river protection.**

**RECOMMENDATION**
**A Presidential Executive Order should be issued to all federal land management and/or development agencies requiring them to adopt rules and regulations that would permit development activities on rivers listed on the Nationwide Rivers Inventory or a river in a state river system only if there is no prudent and feasible alternative.**

## BUDGET RECOMMENDATION
F.Y. 90: $ 500,000          F.Y. 91: **no change**

## PRINCIPAL AUTHORIZING LEGISLATION
Section 5(d) of the Wild and Scenic Rivers Act (no expiration date)

## CONGRESSIONAL JURISDICTION
**House Authorizing Committee/Subcommittee**
Committee on Interior
Subcommittee on National Parks and Public Lands
**Senate Authorizing Committee/Subcommittee**
Committee on Energy and Natural Resources
Subcommittee on Public Lands, National Parks and Forests
**House Appropriations Subcommittee**
Subcommittee on Interior
**Senate Appropriations Subcommittee**
Subcommittee on Interior and Related Agencies

## RELEVANT STUDIES
Forest Land Resource Management Planning Process
BLM Resource Management planning
American Rivers' Outstanding Rivers List of 1988

## RELATED FEDERAL PROGRAMS
Section 5(a) studies under the Wild and Scenic River Act
Section 11, Wild and Scenic Rivers Technical Assistance
National Forest Management Act
Federal Land Policy Management Act

## PRINCIPAL SOURCES OF EXPERTISE
American Rivers — 202-547-6900

## IMPLEMENTATION STEPS
(1)   Congress should appropriate funds.
(2)   The Agency should establish a geographic information data base.
(3)   The Agency should conduct written surveys of state, local and private groups to identify candidate rivers.

## BUDGET HISTORY (in millions of dollars by fiscal year)
The project was funded from about 1976 through 1980 and funding was stopped.

## MANPOWER HISTORY (in F.T.E.'s by fiscal year)
FY 1977 and 1978 — approximately 8 FTE's.
program ended in 1979.

## Blueprint for the Environment

# Blueprint for the Environment

## DEPARTMENT OF JUSTICE

The Department of Justice is the federal government's primary legal advisor and the federal government's primary litigator. In both roles the Department has a profound effect on environmental implementation and enforcement.

Several of the Justice Department's current legal interpretations have an adverse effect on environmental protection and should be revised. First, Justice should disapprove a Department of the Interior Solicitor's Opinion that the Wilderness Act does not preserve the United States' right to claim future water rights for wilderness areas but instead specifically disclaims any future rights. This interpretation is inconsistent with the purpose and legislative history of the Wilderness Act and may doom some wilderness areas to eventual desiccation.

Second, the Department of Justice should withdraw guidelines issued pursuant to Executive Order 12630 directing federal agencies to conduct a "takings impact analysis" before undertaking any action or implementing any policy that might have takings implications. The guidelines are based on an incorrect interpretation of recent Supreme Court cases, place an onerous burden on regulatory agencies and will unnecessarily chill environmental protection.

Third, the Department of Justice should abandon the now-discredited Unitary Executive Theory; the theory hampers the Environmental Protection Agency ability to enforce administrative orders against other federal agencies and the Agency's ability to regulate individual sources of pollution.

Fourth, the Department of Justice should revise its Freedom of Information Act fee waiver policy guidelines to be consistent with the legislative intent behind the Freedom of Information Act Reform Act. This will ensure openness in government without the loss of efficiency.

The Department of Justice, through the Land and Natural Resources Division, also should set litigation policies that are consistent with the purposes of environmental legislation, emphasize enforcement activity, and advocate stiffer penalties for environmental violations. When representing agencies with conflicting positions on significant environmental issues in the same judicial proceeding, the Department of Justice should consider providing separate or independent counsel for such agencies to ensure adequate representation of agencies charged with protecting the environment.

Moreover, under Superfund, the Department of Justice should seek recovery for cleanup costs from all potentially responsible parties to obtain the maximum deterrent effect. The Department of Justice also should ensure that Superfund monies are used exclusively for costs associated with cleanup. Under the Clean Air Act, the Department should step up its litigation against lagging municipalities and states to enforce their Clean Air Act commitments. And, under the Clean Water Act, the Department should more aggressively enforce industrial pretreatment standards to protect the massive federal investment in sewage treatment plant construction.

Because citizen suits are integral to the enforcement schemes in federal environmental legislation, the Department of Justice should recognize the importance of such suits and offer encouragement and support. Justice also should revise its existing practice of challenging the standing of recognized environmental groups when a prima facie showing of standing has been made. Finally, where citizens have successfully brought suit against a government agency, the Department of Justice should facilitate prompt and fair resolution of attorney fees petitions.

# Blueprint for the Environment

## PROTECTION

# DEPARTMENT OF JUSTICE
## ASSISTANT ATTORNEY GENERAL
### Land and Natural Resources
### Environmental Defense Section

**RECOMMENDATION**

**The Assistant Attorney General should make it the policy of the Department of Justice to emphasize litigating matters consistent with the purposes of federal environmental legislation — i.e. to protect and improve the quality of the natural environment.**

• National environmental legislation seeks to set up rules, standards and goals which will improve the natural environment or protect against its further degradation. The litigation policy of the Department of Justice should reflect this legislative policy. For example, emphasis should be placed on enforcing compliance with Environmental Protection Agency (EPA) rules, defending EPA rules from industry attack and on defending the U.S. Army Corps of Engineers from challenges to denials of permits under Section 404 of the Clean Water Act. Similarly, emphasis should be placed on helping federal facilities comply with environmental statutes and regulations thereby obviating the need to defend federal violators.

**RECOMMENDATION**

**The Department of Justice should continue to initiate and support legislation that adds stricter felony provisions to major environmental statutes.**

• Criminal sanctions are an effective incentive to compliance with environmental laws especially when aggressively prosecuted. Criminal sanctions can be particularly effective in regulating small or under-capitalized companies engaging in environmentally risky activity. Such companies have few corporate resources available for civil damages awards and thus may be little affected by the threat of such awards. A director or officer of such a company, however, will be more careful if he/she must accept personal responsibility for her/his business decisions. Increased sanctions will also be effective with executives of large companies who would be reluctant to incur criminal charges although a civil violation may be economically viable from a business perspective.

• Criminal penalties should be increased across the board, and where appropriate, misdemeanors should be upgraded to felonies for a significantly greater deterrent effect.

## BUDGET RECOMMENDATION
F.Y. 90: **no change**        F.Y. 91: **no change**

## PRINCIPAL AUTHORIZING LEGISLATION

## CONGRESSIONAL JURISDICTION
**House Authorizing Committee/Subcommittee**
Committee on Judiciary
**Senate Authorizing Committee/Subcommittee**
Committee on Judiciary
**House Appropriations Subcommittee**
Subcommittee on Commerce, Justice, State, and Judiciary
**Senate Appropriations Subcommittee**
Subcommittee on Commerce, Justice, State, the Judiciary and Related Agencies

## RELEVANT STUDIES

## RELATED FEDERAL PROGRAMS

## PRINCIPAL SOURCES OF EXPERTISE
Sierra Club Legal Defense Fund, Inc. — 202-667-4500
Natural Resources Defense Council — 202-783-7800

## IMPLEMENTATION STEPS
(1)  Department of Justice and the Environmental Crime Section should continue to initiate and support legislation to increase penalties for environmental crimes.
(2)  Misdemeanors should be reviewed to determine whether they should be upgraded to felonies.

## NOTES:

**Blueprint for the Environment**

# Blueprint for the Environment

## LITIGATION

## DEPARTMENT OF JUSTICE

**RECOMMENDATION**

**The Department of Justice should propose legislation to establish a mechanism for channeling civil and criminal penalties for violations of environmental statutes to support general or site-specific cleanup and mitigation measures and to support further enforcement activity.**

• Channeling such funds into cleanup and mitigation activity ensures the correction of the damage caused by a violation. Channeling funds back to support further enforcement activity (including citizen suits) has the dual effect of enabling a higher level of enforcement activity and creating an incentive to enforcement agencies and personnel to more vigorously prosecute violations — i.e. vigorous prosecution of violators increases funds in the budget.

**RECOMMENDATION**

**The Department of Justice should adopt a more efficient policy with regard to standing for environmental groups to ensure that valid environmental disputes are resolved on their merits.**

• The current Department of Justice practice is to vigorously challenge the standing of well-established environmental groups bringing environmental suits. Because standing usually can be established, this practice often results in the waste of considerable resources that would be better spent reaching the merits.
• Officially recognized and well-established environmental public interest groups should be routinely permitted standing where such an organization makes a prima facie showing that its members reside in an area affected by an actual or threatened environmental injury or can allege violation or deprivation of statutorily granted rights, and that the environmental injury is traceable to the defendant's conduct and could be effectively redressed by a favorable court decision.

**RECOMMENDATION**

**The Assistant Attorney General should investigate the constitutionality, legality and practicality of permitting agencies/subagencies to use separate or independent counsel in judicial proceedings where two or more agencies/subagencies take conflicting positions on significant environmental issues.**

• Two or more independent or executive agencies/subagencies involved in a single proceeding sometimes take conflicting positions on significant environmental issues (e.g., proceedings to determine water rights). In some instances both agencies/subagencies have been represented by a single counsel from either the Justice Department or, in the case of disputing agencies, from the umbrella agency's office of solicitor. This may result in the suppression of important environmental issues and arguments where such concerns are in conflict with other agency concerns.
• To ensure better representation of all disputing agencies, Justice should investigate 1) granting special independent litigation authority

to an agency for a given proceeding, 2) appointing special independent counsel to represent one of the disputing agencies in a given proceeding, or 3) establishing a "Chinese Wall" between Justice attorneys representing agencies with conflicting positions in a given proceeding.

## RECOMMENDATION
### The Attorney General should abolish the present Department of Justice practice of diverting citizen suit settlements to the general fund.

• The Department of Justice is improperly using its settlement review authority under the Clean Water Act (CWA) to extract from citizen suit plaintiffs a portion of the funds awarded in settlement agreements by threatening to challenge environmentally sound citizen suit settlements unless fifty percent of the award is paid directly into the Federal treasury. This deters citizen suits and should cease.

## RECOMMENDATION
### The Attorney General should establish written guidelines to facilitate prompt and efficient resolution of citizens' attorney-fees petitions.

• Resolution of attorney-fees petitions frequently results in litigation that is as lengthy and costly as the underlying case. Guidelines for settling attorney-fees petitions will reduce delay and cost and permit the Land and Natural Resources Division to devote its resources to its primary mission of protecting the environment and public health.

## RECOMMENDATION
### The Assistant Attorney General should implement a litigation policy to ensure that recovery is sought against all potentially responsible parties in order to preserve the maximum deterrent effect of federal hazardous waste cleanup legislation.

• Under federal hazardous waste cleanup legislation (Superfund), the government can seek recovery for cleanup costs of a hazardous waste site from all potentially responsible parties (PRPs). The common practice, however, is to pursue recovery only from those sources which seem the most likely sources for recovery of costs because of a "deep pocket" and/or a high share of liability for the particular site. Certainly, the recovery of costs is of primary importance, but seeking recovery from PRPs with fewer resources or a lesser share of liability has an important deterrent effect. To ignore such PRPs is to encourage companies handling toxic wastes to remain undercapitalized and/or to dispose of their wastes in a decentralized, haphazard manner.

## RECOMMENDATION
### The Assistant Attorney General should implement a policy to ensure that all Superfund monies are used exclusively for costs of litigation related directly to Superfund activities.

• The Department of Justice should use Superfund monies only for costs that are directly and exclusively attributable to cases arising under the imminent hazard (Section 106) and cost recovery (Section 107) provisions of the Superfund legislation. The Assistant Attorney General should develop an accurate and efficient internal accounting system to ensure that Superfund monies are not misspent.

# Blueprint for the Environment

## POLICIES

# DEPARTMENT OF JUSTICE

## RECOMMENDATION

**The Attorney General should reconsider and rescind his concurrence with the Department of Interior Solicitor Opinion M-36914 (Supp. III) July 26, 1988, on Reserved Water Rights for Wilderness Areas.**

• On July 26, 1988, the Secretary of Interior transmitted Opinion M-36914/Supp. III to the Attorney General and requested his concurrence in its conclusion that Congress did not intend to reserve federal water rights for wilderness purposes when it enacted the Wilderness Act .

• The opinion of the Solicitor and the concurrence of the Attorney General create an urgent need for review; as the Attorney General states in his July 28 letter of concurrence, the United States "will not assert reserved wilderness water rights under federal law in any further litigation on behalf of the United States, but will seek water for wilderness purposes where appropriate under state law." There are a number of pending water rights adjudications where water rights for wilderness are at issue. Based on the Solicitor/Attorney General position, the government would be barred from future claims to water for the wilderness areas involved in those adjudications once those claims are abandoned.

• The Opinion concludes that in section 4(d)(7) of the Wilderness Act Congress intended to avoid creating water rights reservation in addition to those already created for the underlying national park, forest or wildlife refuge. The Opinion states that water rights for wilderness areas must be acquired by purchase, pursuant to state law, or Congress can expressly reserve water when it creates a wilderness area.

• The Opinion and relies on ambiguous correspondence from committee files to make categorical conclusions about the meaning of the Wilderness Act, even where better authority indicates that reserved water rights were intended. Careful attention should be given to the Solicitor's Opinion M-36914 of June 25, 1979, 86 I.D. 553-618, which determined that wilderness areas are entitled to the federal reserved water rights necessary to accomplish the purposes for which the areas were established.

## RECOMMENDATION

**The Attorney General should immediately withdraw the Department of Justice Guidelines issued pursuant to Executive Order 12630, "Governmental Actions and Interference with Constitutionally Protected Property Rights," and should urge the President to repeal the order.**

• Executive Order 12630 allegedly was issued in response to several Supreme Court decisions regarding what constitutes a "taking" for which a private landowner must be compensated (usually via an inverse condemnation proceeding). The Order and Guidelines direct federal agencies to produce an extensive "takings impact analysis" before undertaking any action or implementing any policy that might have takings implications. Many such analyses must then be submitted for review by OMB and Department of Justice. See also, OMB Circular No. A-11, June 17, 1988.

• These requirements put an onerous burden on environmental regulatory agencies — a burden that will likely "chill" an agency's willingness to take positive environmental action including issuing regulations, enforcing existing restrictions, or denying permit requests (e.g. Section 404 permits).

187

- The proffered rationale for the Order was to protect the public from unanticipated awards for takings in the wake of the recent Supreme Court rulings, but this logic is flawed. The Order and the Guidelines are overbroad, reaching far beyond the Court's rulings. Furthermore, we are not aware of any significant increase in inverse condemnation awards which would call for such a drastic and sweeping response. Indeed it is not at all clear that the recent Supreme Court cases significantly change existing takings law which has been quite favorable, overall, to government regulation. In sum, the order and guidelines are burdensome, (having a chilling effect on agency action), are overbroad( reaching beyond current Constitutional law) and are simply unnecessary.

## RECOMMENDATION
**The Attorney General and the Department of Justice should cease advocating the theory of the Unitary Executive and recognize the Environmental Protection Agency's administrative order authority.**

- The Department of Justice, as the primary advocate of the Unitary Executive theory, has not recognized the authority of the Environmental Protection Agency to issue administrative orders that are binding on other federal agencies. The Department of Justice should support the Environmental Protection Agency's administrative order authority, recognizing it as an integral part of the environmental enforcement scheme, and essential to their ability to regulate individual sources of pollution, both private and public.
- The expansive vision of Presidential power embodied by the Unitary Executive theory has been substantially rebuffed by the Supreme Court in **Morrisson v. Olson.**

## RECOMMENDATION
**The Environmental Enforcement Section of the Lands and Natural Resources Division should litigate more aggressively against lagging municipalities and States to ensure full compliance with the Clean Air Act.**

- Enforceable commitments have been made by many States and cities to carry out specific emission reduction programs designed to achieve air quality goals. Many of these commitments have not been adopted despite the mandates of the Clean Air Act, with the result that public health continues to suffer. The Division of land and Natural Resources should step up litigation to enforce such commitments.

## RECOMMENDATION
**The Environmental Enforcement Section of the Division of Lands and Natural Resources should aggressively enforce the industrial pre-treatment requirements of the Clean Water Act.**

- States and municipalities have a duty to protect the environment and the huge federal investment in sewage treatment plant construction against the harm from unchecked industrial wastes that are often discharged to those sewage treatment plants. Effective protection will require the Department of Justice to take aggressive action against industries which do not comply with federal pre-treatment standards and against states and municipalities which do not take precautions to enforce pre-treatment standards.

# Blueprint for the Environment

# DEPARTMENT OF STATE

International environmental problems are serious and getting worse, perhaps the greatest single threat to the security and welfare of the United States (rivaled only by the threat of nuclear war). Global warming of the atmosphere threatens the economic stability of the United States and the world. Soil erosion, deforestation, loss of water supplies and pollution threaten the economic welfare, the health and the very survival of hundreds of millions of people. In almost all developing nations, growing populations are exerting unsustainable pressure on the natural resource base and environmental problems are becoming more severe.

Vital U.S. interests are at stake. Global warming threatens loss of the U.S. Midwestern grain belt, 80 percent of U.S. coastal wetlands and most U.S. forests. Massive extinctions of animal and plant species would do irreparable harm to our agriculture, medicine, industry and other endeavors. Even now, one-fourth of all U.S. prescription drugs have their origin in tropical plants and animals. The new science of genetic engineering must begin with genetic materials from the wild — every time a living species becomes extinct we lose not only the species itself but all the possible derivatives that could have been produced from it.

Three-fourths of the earth's people live in developing nations. These nations represent the main hope for expanding markets for U.S. goods and many are of strategic importance. Their cooperation is essential in solving global environmental problems, yet continued environmental degradation and unsustainable population growth continue to undermine the sustainable economic growth and political stability essential to such cooperation.

These problems will be addressed and solutions found only if the United States demonstrates responsible action at home while also exerting international leadership. The Department of State must be the main instrument through which this international leadership is exerted.

Blueprint for the Environment offers the following recommendations, explained in more detail in the individual recommendations contained in this book:

**Set Priorities.** The Secretary of State should announce in an early speech that preventing further harm to the international environment will be a major foreign policy goal of the Department and the Administration, and take steps to ensure that the Department follows through. The Secretary should announce major initiatives to prevent global warming of the atmosphere, ensure that economic development in developing nations is environmentally sustainable, exert leadership aimed at reducing population growth, and conserve the Earth's stock of animal and plant species. He should instruct all Bureaus to report to him on the actions needed to address these issues and on the institutional or other changes that are required, and then direct that the FY 90 budget request for the Department be prepared with special attention to the resources needed in these areas.

**Strengthen the Department's Capabilities.** The Department of State itself must be strengthened if it is to do an adequate job of addressing international environmental issues. The Bureau of Oceans, Environment and Science must be the focal point of the Department's efforts. The Assistant Secretary for the Bureau should take immediate steps to:

1) Ensure that at least two senior, environmentally trained officers are able to remain in the Bureau on a long-term basis to provide badly needed technical expertise and institutional memory.

2) Ensure closer cooperation between the Bureau of Oceans, Environment and Science and the Environmental Protection Agency, which can — through close working relationships and exchange of personnel — give the Bureau the benefit of badly needed technical expertise.

3) Ensure that the Bureau assigns enough properly qualified officers to work on the key issues of global warming, sustainable development in developing nations (including monitoring the performance of the multilateral development banks), reducing the rate of population growth, conserving biological diversity and protecting oceanic resources.

**Strengthen the UNEP.** The United Nations Environment Program — the world's only environmental agency — must play a crucial role if we are to solve these vitally important problems. The United States was contributing $10 million a year to UNEP as long ago as 1974. Since then, UNEP's responsibilities have increased while inflation has reduced the value of our contribution by more than half. We therefore recommend an increase to at least $20 million in FY 90.

**Utilize the Economic Summit.** The seven Economic Summit nations together command half of the world's economic wealth. The Secretary should ensure that the issues of global warming of the atmosphere, conservation of the Earth's biological diversity, reducing the rate of population growth, protection of oceanic resources and environmentally sustainable development in all nations are discussed at the June 1989 Economic Summit, and that the United States makes specific proposals for cooperation among the Summit nations.

**Organize an Environmental Summit.** In order to enable the President to discuss these issues with a wider range of world leaders, the Secretary should take all steps necessary to convene a Global Environmental Summit Meeting, including leaders from all the major industrialized and developing nations and focusing on the world's key environmental problems. This should be a U.S. initiative, in cooperation with other nations and coordinated with the United Nations.

**Focus on Major Worldwide Issues.** The Secretary must work to assure that the attention and resources of the Department of State remain steadfast in their concentration on significant environmental issues that deeply affect the United States and the world. These are:

Minimize global warming;

Promote slower population growth;

Promote sustainable economic development;

Conserve biological diversity;

Protect the ocean environment.

**Departmental Budget.** International agencies have crucially important roles to play if we are to solve the environmental problems described above. The following agencies should receive increased contributions in Fiscal Year 1990, as a matter of the highest priority:

United Nations Environment Program
— increase from $9.5 to $20 million.

United Nations Development Program
— increase from $111 to $116 million.

United Nations Fund for Population Activities
— increase.

Organization of American States (voluntary)
— increase from $7.35 to $15 million.

IUCN — increase from no contribution to $155,000.

# Blueprint for the Environment

## AGENCY FOR INTERNATIONAL DEVELOPMENT

Environmental problems in developing nations are extremely serious and getting worse. Soil erosion, deforestation, loss of water supplies and pollution threaten the economic welfare, the health and the very survival of hundreds of millions of people. Growing populations are exerting unsustainable pressure on the natural resource base, and scientists are warning that we may lose up to one-fourth of all the world's animal and plant species in the next few decades, due mainly to habitat destruction in the tropics. Global warming of the atmosphere is beginning to threaten the resource base of the entire planet and the foundations of almost every economy. While most emissions of greenhouse gases are coming from industrialized nations, projections indicate that developing nations, which are growing more rapidly, will account for most of the future increases in emissions. Global warming of the atmosphere is beginning to threaten the resource base of the entire planet and the foundations of almost every economy. While most emissions of greenhouse gases are coming from industrialized nations, projections indicate that developing nations, which are growing more rapidly, will account for most of the future increases in emissions.

These problems will be addressed and solved only if the United States provides assistance and leadership at home and abroad. The Agency for International Development and the foreign assistance program it administers must play a crucial role.

We offer the following recommendations, which are explained in more detail in the remainder of this book:

FIRST, the Administrator should announce upon taking office that the central theme of the entire foreign assistance program will be sustainable development, and that the Agency for International Development will focus on three priority goals: sustainable economic growth, eliminating poverty and preventing environmental degradation.

The Administrator should declare that:

The Agency for International Development's main way of achieving these goals will be to furnish technical assistance, as opposed to assistance aimed at structural adjustment and development of large physical infrastructures.

The Agency for International Development will maintain its country Missions.

The Agency for International Development will emphasize support for relatively small, local projects that — if successful — are capable of being replicated more widely.

The Agency for International Development will employ sufficient technically competent staff to avoid over-reliance on contractors, and in particular will hire more people with expertise in the environmental priority areas listed above.

The Agency for International Development will act to prevent environmental degradation at the global level due to species loss and global warming, as well as at the national level, and the Agency for International Development will provide environmental assistance to middle-income nations when it is appropriate.

The Agency for International Development's priorities will include expanded efforts to:

Sustain the agricultural resource base and promote environmentally sound food production.

Promote environmentally sound energy development, with an emphasis on energy assistance designed to meet human needs while minimizing global warming.

Meet family planning needs and thereby halt overly rapid population growth.

Conserve tropical forests and biological diversity.

The Agency for International Development will step up its efforts to promote sustainable development in sub-Saharan Africa, the region where degradation of the natural resource base is most severe.

The Agency for International Development will shift its focus in Central America from military-related assistance to development assistance aimed at environmentally sustainable development throughout the region.

The Agency for International Development will cooperate with the Environmental Protection Agency in an expanded effort to help nations prevent misuse of agricultural chemicals and other toxic substances.

We believe the Administrator can adopt these priorities and administer the Agency accordingly under existing law. At the same time, the Agency should propose or support amendments to the Foreign Assistance Act to make these priorities even more clear and add any needed authority the Agency may not now possess.

SECOND, to allow the Agency for International Development to achieve its environmental goals, the Administrator should take immediate steps to recruit additional highly-qualified environmental staff and assign them as Environmental Officers in key Agency Missions and Regional Offices. The Agency cannot execute properly a program focusing on ensuring sustainability of development unless qualified persons are serving in the nations where the key decisions actually are made.

THIRD, strong actions are needed to enable the Agency for International Development to regain its leadership role in the area of population assistance. The budget for population activities must be increased substantially, with an emphasis on family planning services. In addition, the Agency must:

Strengthen the technical focus of the Population Office.

Work to improve population activities of the United Nations Fund for Population Activities and the World Bank.

Build developing-country capacity for population programs and do more to help countries implement population policies.

Recruit and maintain population officers in key countries.

Collect data and do research on rapid population growth.

FOURTH, the Administrator should direct that the Agency for International Development's energy efforts be increased substantially and focused on increased energy efficiency and increased reliance on renewable energy sources, with an emphasis on energy assistance designed to meet human needs while minimizing global warming. U.S. expertise in energy efficiency and renewable energy technologies can be of great assistance to developing nations in reducing their emissions of greenhouse gases. U.S. cooperation with developing nations, spearheaded by the Agency, is essential if we are to minimize global warming.

FIFTH, the Administrator should direct that the Agency for International Development expand greatly its assistance to developing nations to help them conserve animal and plant species and their habitats. The current Agency for International Development Biological Diversity Program is far too small and must be expanded. In order to ensure maximum effectiveness, the Agency should establish clear priorities for allocating assistance. One priority should be that a large part of the funds will be spent to assist countries in protecting habitat areas identified by scientists as having extraordinary importance for the conservation of biological diversity. The Agency also should do more to integrate biological diversity concerns into its other programs, notably agriculture and forestry, and to persuade other donors, multilateral and bilateral, to join in these efforts. The World Bank in particular has much to contribute.

Additional resources will be required to take these essential actions. As detailed in our budget recommendation, we suggest that the FY 90 bilateral aid budget be increased by about 18 percent, and by another 11.5 percent in FY 91. We suggest that most of this amount could be found by cutting other items in the 150 Account.

## Blueprint for the Environment

# Blueprint for the Environment

## GLOBAL WARMING

## DEPARTMENT OF STATE
### OFFICE OF THE SECRETARY

### RECOMMENDATION
**The Secretary of State should announce in an early speech that prevention of harm to the global environment will be a major foreign policy goal of the Administration, and take steps to ensure that the Department follows through.**

• Global environmental problems constitute major threats to the future security and welfare of the United States, and must receive urgent, high-priority attention:

• Global warming of the atmosphere threatens possible loss of the U.S. Midwestern grain belt, 80 percent of U.S. coastal wetlands, and most U.S. forests.

• The Earth is projected to lose up to one-fourth of all its living species within a few decades, if present trends continue. This would cause enormous harm to agriculture, medicine, industry, and other endeavors.

• Many developing nations are using their renewable resources at unsustainable rates and are polluting the local and the global environments that support human life. In many places, human populations are burgeoning to unsustainable levels. This crisis must be addressed now, since three-fourths of the world's people live in these nations.

• The Secretary should announce major initiatives to prevent global warming of the atmosphere, ensure that economic development in developing nations is environmentally sustainable, and conserve the Earth's stock of animal and plant species. He should instruct all Bureaus to report to him on actions they intend to take to address these issues, and on the institutional or other changes that are needed. He should direct that the FY 90 budget request for the Department be prepared with special attention to actions needed to address these issues.

### RECOMMENDATION
**The Secretary of State should request for FY 90 an increase of $22.3 million in the International Organizations and Programs account to ensure adequate resources for the work of key international organizations crucially important to the protection of the world's environment.**

• Many crucially important international environmental problems can be solved only through international cooperation. International organizations must play major roles in promoting and facilitating this cooperation. These agencies have been severely underfunded in recent years, especially when the effects of inflation are taken into account. They must have greater resources if we are to solve international environmental problems of the utmost concern to the United States.

• The following agencies should receive increased contributions in FY 90:

United Nations Environment Program: increase from $9.5 to $20 million.

UNDP — increase from $111 to $116 million.

World Heritage Trust — increase from $220,000

OAS (voluntary) — increase from $7.35 to $15 million.

IUCN — increase from no contribution to $155,000.

# BUDGET RECOMMENDATION
F.Y. 90: **Increase** of $ 35 million    F.Y. 91: **no change**

# PRINCIPAL AUTHORIZING LEGISLATION
None

# CONGRESSIONAL JURISDICTION
**House Authorizing Committee/Subcommittee**
Committee on Foreign Affairs
Subcommittee on Human Rights and International Organizations
**Senate Authorizing Committee/Subcommittee**
Committee on Foreign Relations
Subcommittee on International Economic Policy, Trade, Oceans and Environment
**House Appropriations Subcommittee**
Subcommittee on Foreign Operations, Export Financing and Related Programs
**Senate Appropriations Subcommittee**
Subcommittee on Foreign Operations

# RELEVANT STUDIES

# RELATED FEDERAL PROGRAMS

# PRINCIPAL SOURCES OF EXPERTISE
Natural Resources Defense Council — 202-783-7800
National Audubon Society — 202-547-9009
Sierra Club — 202-547-1141

# BUDGET HISTORY (in millions of dollars by fiscal year)
**For International Organizations and Programs (IO & P)Account**

|  | 88 | 89 |
|---|---|---|
| Requested |  | 200.0 |
| Appropriated | 244.65 | 226.115 |

# MANPOWER HISTORY (in F.T.E.'s by fiscal year)

# NOTES:
1. Agency-by-agency funding trends and our recommendations for FY 90 are as follows:

**IO & P Account (voluntary contributions):**

| Organization | FY88 App. | FY89 Req. | FY89 App. | FY90 Rec. |
|---|---|---|---|---|
| UNEP | 7.84 | 6.8 | 9.5 | 20.0 |
| UNDP | 110.0 | 112.0 | 111.0 | 115.0 |
| CITES | 0.17 | 0.20 | 0.65 | 0.65 |
| World Heritage | 0.22 | 0.20 | 0.22 | 0.50 |
| OAS (voluntary) | 12.0 | 15.0 | 7.349*?? | 15.0 |
| IUCN | 0 | 0 | 0 | 0.155 |

2. **UN Environment Program (UNEP).** Our separate recommendations on global warming and the UNEP Governing Council make it clear that UNEP must play a crucial role on a number of vitally important issues. The United States was contributing $10 million a year to UNEP as long ago as 1974. Since then, UNEP's responsibilities have increased while inflation has reduced the value of our contribution by more than half. We therefore recommend an increase from the FY 89 contribution of $9.5 million to $20 million.

3. **UN Development Program (UNDP).** The $5.0 million increase recommended for the UNDP should be a contribution to UNDP's Energy Fund if that is feasible.

## GLOBAL WARMING

# DEPARTMENT OF STATE

### RECOMMENDATION
**The Secretary of State should ensure that the issues of global warming of the atmosphere, conservation of the Earth's biological diversity, and achieving environmentally sustainable economic development in developing nations, and actions needed to achieve these goals, are discussed at the June 1989 Economic Summit conference.**

• These issues can only be solved through international cooperation. Personal meetings of national leaders are one excellent way of getting these issues firmly on the political agenda and facilitating solutions. The Economic Summit is an especially important forum because the seven summit nations together command at least half of the world's economic wealth.

• The President should urge that the seven summit nations place a high priority on:

1) Identifying and taking actions to minimize global warming on a rapid schedule;

2) Providing sharply increased bilateral and multilateral assistance to conserve threatened habitats and species; and

3) taking steps to ensure sustainable development in developing nations, including actions to reduce population growth, alleviate debt burdens, and build environmental management capacities.

• The President should suggest establishment of a high-level working group of representatives from the summit nations to follow up.

### RECOMMENDATION
**The Secretary of State should take all steps necessary to convene a Global Environmental Summit Meeting, including leaders from all the major industrialized and developing nations, focusing on the world's key environmental problems including global warming of the atmosphere, loss of biological diversity, and how to achieve environmentally sustainable development in developing nations.**

• These issues clearly require top-level attention. It is evident that they can best be solved through international cooperation. Personal meetings of national leaders are one excellent way of getting these issues firmly on the political agenda and facilitating solutions. The proposed Environmental Summit is an especially important forum because no one group of nations can solve these problems: truly global cooperation is needed.

• This should be a U.S. initiative, perhaps in cooperation with selected other nations. It should be coordinated with the United Nations (UN) but not sponsored by the UN.

• The President should urge that the summit nations place a high priority on:

1) Identifying and taking actions to minimize global warming on a rapid schedule;

2) Providing sharply increased bilateral and multilateral assistance to conserve threatened habitats and species; and

3) Taking steps to ensure sustainable development in developing nations, including actions to reduce population growth, alleviate debt burdens, and build environmental management capacities.

195

## RECOMMENDATION

**The Secretary of State should ensure that the question of actions to minimize global warming is on the agenda of the 1989 Governing Council meeting of the United Nations Environment Program and that the United States advocates Governing Council decisions requiring strong actions by the United Nations Environment Program to address the global warming issue.**

• Global warming presents major threats to the world and the United States, including possible loss of the U.S. Midwestern grain belt, 80 percent of U.S. coastal wetlands, and most U.S. forests. The United Nations Environment Program (UNEP) is the international organization best situated to foster international agreement on actions to address the problem.

• The United States should recommend and advocate for Governing Council decisions requiring the following actions by UNEP to address the global warming issue:

1) Development of an international convention to minimize carbon dioxide emissions, and institutional strengthening of UNEP to enable it to serve as the forum for negotiating that agreement.

2) Establishment of a strong UNEP program to identify the needs of developing nations for assistance in energy conservation and renewable energy sources, and catalytic and coordinating actions (in cooperation with national governments and aid agencies, and relevant international bodies) to ensure that those needs are met.

3) Continued preparation by UNEP, in cooperation with WMO and ICSU, of assessments of the scientific evidence concerning global warming and its impacts. The assessment process should be designed to involve scientists from all regions and all the major nations that contribute to the problem.

## RECOMMENDATION

**The Secretary of State should act to ensure that the question of actions to minimize global warming is on the agenda of every United States—Soviet Union summit meeting.**

• Global warming presents major threats to the world and the United States, including possible loss of the U.S. Midwestern grain belt, 80 percent of U.S. coastal wetlands, and most U.S. forests. It is evident that the problem can be solved only through international cooperation.

• Personal meetings of national leaders are one excellent way of getting these issues firmly on the political agenda and facilitating solutions. U.S.—U.S.S.R. summits are especially important forums because the U.S.S.R. has much of the world's coal reserves; uses energy very inefficiently; and has great influence over other Eastern Bloc Nations.

• The President should seek at summit meetings the establishment of ongoing, bilateral working relationships, as well as Soviet cooperation concerning international initiatives such as a global convention and protocols.

• From the time the Administration takes office, the Secretary should seek in other ways to cooperate with the Soviets on the global warming issue. The Bureau of Oceans and International Environmental and Scientific Affairs should promote scientific cooperation through the U.S.—U.S.S.R. bilateral environmental agreement and by other means. At least one specially qualified person (a regular science attaché if possible) should be posted in the Moscow Embassy and instructed to facilitate cooperation on the issue.

## RECOMMENDATION

**The Secretary of State should act to make prevention of global warming a high-priority issue for the Organization for Economic Cooperation and Development and International Energy Agency.**

• Global warming presents major threats to the world and the United States, including possible loss of the U.S. Midwestern grain belt, 80 percent of U.S. coastal wetlands, and most U.S. forests. The

## Blueprint for the Environment

members of the Organization for Economic Cooperation and Development (OECD) and the International Energy Agency (IEA) emit most of the "greenhouse gases" that cause global warming, so these organizations are excellent fora for fostering cooperation on actions to address the problem.

• The United States should encourage OECD and IEA to carry out a study, to be completed within a year, of carbon dioxide emissions and trends in member nations and actions that could be taken by member countries, including the U.S., to reduce emissions at least 20 percent below present levels by the year 2000.

## RECOMMENDATION
**The Secretary of State, after consulting with other relevant departments and agencies, should instruct all relevant embassies and geographic bureaus to foster cooperation aimed at minimizing global warming.**

• Global warming presents major threats to the world and the United States, including possible loss of the U.S. Midwestern grain belt, 80 percent of U.S. coastal wetlands, and most U.S. forests. Strong actions by a relatively few key nations could do a great deal to reduce emissions of the "greenhouse gases" that cause the problem, and to lead other nations to do likewise. U.S. bilateral representations by diplomats and technically qualified staff posted in these nations could do a great deal to bring these actions about.

• Wherever possible, technical representation should be done by regular science attachés; in exceptional cases special attachés should be appointed.

• Embassies where special representation is needed include the European Communities and the major European nations, Japan, the U.S.S.R., China, South Korea, Mexico, Brazil, and India.

## RECOMMENDATION
**The Assistant Secretary for Oceans and International Environmental and Scientific Affairs should make prevention of global warming and ozone depletion top priorities for the Bureau.**

• Global warming presents major threats to the world and the United States, including possible loss of the U.S. Midwestern grain belt, 80 percent of U.S. coastal wetlands, and most U.S. forests. Ozone depletion presents threats of skin cancer and widespread ecological and economic harm. These problems are global and can only be solved through actions by many nations.

• The State Department therefore must play a crucial role. The Bureau of Oceans and International Environmental and Scientific Affairs (OES) has responsibility for these issues and must assign adequate resources to it. At least two full-time officers should be assigned to work on these issues in FY 90 and at least three full-time officers in FY 91.

• The Assistant Secretary also should make sure that fully qualified science attachés or, if necessary, special attachés posted in key embassies are assigned as soon as possible to promote cooperation on global warming (see separate recommendation to Secretary of State).

## RECOMMENDATION
**The Assistant Secretary for International Organization Affairs should act to encourage the United Nations Development Program to re-establish its Energy Office at effective levels and to focus on meeting energy needs in ways that minimize global warming.**

• Global warming presents major threats to the world and the United States, including possible loss of the U.S. Midwestern grain belt, 80 percent of U.S. coastal wetlands, and most U.S. forests. The United Nations Environment Program (UNEP) is the international organization best situated to foster international agreement on actions to address the problem.

## Blueprint for the Environment

# Blueprint for the Environment

## COOPERATION AND CONTINUITY

# DEPARTMENT OF STATE
### Bureau of Oceans and International Environmental and Scientific Affairs

**RECOMMENDATION**
**The Secretary of State, working with the Administrator of the Environmental Protection Agency, should (1) immediately issue regulations phasing out U.S. production and use of chlorofluorocarbons and other ozone-depleting chemicals within 5—7 years, and (2) devise an emergency revision of the international treaty on ozone depletion (the "Montreal Protocol") to achieve a worldwide phase-out in the same time period.**

• The Montreal Protocol, signed in 1987, requires a 10-year 50 percent cut in five ozone-destroying chlorofluorocarbons (CFCs). It freezes, but does not cut, three other ozone-depleting chemicals known as halons. On August 1, 1988, the Environmental Protection Agency (EPA) issued rules under the Clean Air Act for U.S. production and use of these chemicals; the rules precisely mirror the requirements of the Protocol. Because of loopholes in the Protocol and the U.S. rules, emissions of ozone depleters will actually be reduced globally by only about one-third.

• New scientific evidence, however, demonstrates these chemicals must be completely phased out to protect the ozone layer and the climate. CFCs have been conclusively shown to cause the ozone hole over Antarctica, and similar ozone losses have been reported over the Arctic as well. A report by an international panel of more than 100 scientists has also documented the global loss of ozone at 2—3 times the rate previously predicted. More depletion has already been suffered than EPA projected would occur under the Protocol and its rules by the year 2050.

• The import of the new science is not completely lost on industry. Dupont, the world's largest CFC producer, has gone farther than the EPA rules and committed to cease production by the year 2000.

**RECOMMENDATION**
**The Assistant Secretary for Oceans and International Environmental and Scientific Affairs should take immediate steps to ensure closer cooperation between the Bureau and the Environmental Protection Agency.**

**RECOMMENDATION**
**The Assistant Secretary for Oceans and International Environmental and Scientific Affairs should take immediate steps to ensure that at least one senior, environmentally trained officer is able to remain in the Bureau on a long-term basis to provide badly needed technical expertise and "institutional memory."**

# BUDGET RECOMMENDATION
F.Y. 90: **no change**        F.Y. 91: **no change**

## PRINCIPAL AUTHORIZING LEGISLATION
Clean Air Act § 157, 42 U.S.C. § 7457

## CONGRESSIONAL JURISDICTION
**House Authorizing Committee/Subcommittee**
Committee on Energy and Commerce
Subcommittee on Health and Environment
**Senate Authorizing Committee/Subcommittee**
Committee on Environment and Public Works
Subcommittee on Toxic Substances and Hazardous Materials
**House Appropriations Subcommittee**
Subcommittee on HUD — Independent Agencies
**Senate Appropriations Subcommittee**
Subcommittee on HUD — Independent Agencies

## RELEVANT STUDIES
Report of the Ozone Trends Panel (NASA, March 1988)

## RELATED FEDERAL PROGRAMS
Environmental Protection Agency

## PRINCIPAL SOURCES OF EXPERTISE
Natural Resources Defense Council — 202-783-7800
Environmental Defense Fund — 202-387-3500
World Resources Institute — 202-393-4055

## IMPLEMENTATION STEPS
The Administrator should take the following steps as soon as he takes office:
(1) Revise the EPA rules under the Clean Air Act to achieve a virtually complete phase-out of ozone-depleting chemicals in 5—7 years.
(2) Work with the State Department to accelerate the international review of the Montreal Protocol with the goal of adopting a virtually complete phase-out of ozone-depleting chemicals in 5—7 years. The Bureau of Oceans and International Environmental and Scientific Affairs (OES) plays a vitally important role in international environmental protection. However, it suffers from a lack of internal technical expertise. Close cooperation with the Environmental Protection Agency (EPA), which has much of the necessary expertise, can help overcome this handicap, as well as benefit EPA itself.
(3) Recoup the $2—7 billion windfall profit expected to flow to the five CFC producers as prices rise during the phase-out, by establishing a windfall profit fee or auction system under the Clean Air Act or through new legislation.

## NOTES:

**Blueprint for the Environment**

## BIOLOGICAL DIVERSITY

## DEPARTMENT OF STATE
### OFFICE OF THE SECRETARY

**RECOMMENDATION**
**The Secretary of State should announce that conservation of the Earth's biological diversity is a key foreign policy objective, and issue detailed directives to all embassies and geographic bureaus instructing them to highlight the importance of national actions and international cooperation to conserve biological diversity.**

• We face the horrifying prospect of losing, in the next few decades, up to a quarter of all the earth's plant and animal species, due mainly to destruction of tropical forests and other habitats — a wave of extinctions comparable in magnitude to that which destroyed the dinosaurs and many other species some 65 million years ago.
• Conserving the Earth's biological diversity can be accomplished only through strong national actions and international cooperation. Encouragement of such actions and cooperation should be a major U.S. policy goal. One way of furthering this goal should be systematic representations by U.S. diplomatic personnel (in cooperation with Agency for International Development (AID) staff in nations with AID Missions). Issues raised by U.S. Ambassadors and members of the diplomatic corps often have a profound impact on host governments, yet cost relatively little. The existing science advisors within the embassies should be given responsibility for overseeing daily activities involving biological diversity.

**RECOMMENDATION**
**The Assistant Secretary for Oceans and International Environmental and Scientific Affairs should ensure that the Bureau places a high priority on developing and negotiating an international convention to identify and protect plant and animal habitats essential to conservation of biological diversity.**

**RECOMMENDATION**
**The Secretary of State should take the actions necessary for the United States to become a State Member of the International Union for the Conservation of Nature and Natural Resources.**

**RECOMMENDATION**
**The Secretary of State should reassign budget authority for implementation of treaties that promote conservation of biodiversity from the Bureau for International Organization Affairs to the Bureau for Oceans and International Environmental and Scientific Affairs.**

## BUDGET RECOMMENDATION
For membership in International Union for the Conservation of Nature and Natural Resources:

F.Y. 90:   **increase** of $155,000 for State Department
           **decrease** of $ 33,400 each for Interior, Agriculture, NOAA

F.Y. 91:   **increase** of $155,000 for State Department
           **decrease** of $ 33,400 each for Interior, Agriculture, NOAA

## PRINCIPAL AUTHORIZING LEGISLATION
None

## CONGRESSIONAL JURISDICTION
### House Authorizing Committee/Subcommittee
Committee on Foreign Affairs
Subcommittee on Human Rights and International Organizations
### Senate Authorizing Committee/Subcommittee
Committee on Foreign Relations
Subcommittee on International Economic Policy, Trade, Oceans and Environment
### House Appropriations Subcommittee
Subcommittee on Foreign Operations, Export Financing and Related Programs
### Senate Appropriations Subcommittee
Subcommittee on Foreign Operations

## RELEVANT STUDIES
Office of Technology Assessment, **"Technologies to Maintain Biological Diversity"** (1987)
Interagency Task Force Report to Congress, 1985: **"U.S. Strategy on the Conservation of Biological Diversity"** (1985)

## RELATED FEDERAL PROGRAMS
Biological Diversity Program of U.S. AID
International Programs of U.S. Park Service,Fish and Wildlife Service, National Oceanic and Atmospheric Administration and U.S. AID

## PRINCIPAL SOURCES OF EXPERTISE
Natural Resources Defense Council — 202-783-7800
National Audubon Society — 202-547-9009
Sierra Club — 202-547-1141

## NOTES:

## Blueprint for the Environment

# Blueprint for the Environment

## INTERNATIONAL NEGOTIATIONS

## DEPARTMENT OF STATE
Bureau for International Organization Affairs
Bureau of Oceans and International
Environmental and Scientific Affairs

### RECOMMENDATION
**The Secretary of State should direct the Assistant Secretary for International Organization Affairs to establish, in consultation with the Assistant Secretary for Oceans and International Environmental and Scientific Affairs, procedures to ensure that U.S. delegations to important environmental meetings include both technical experts and representatives of U.S. environmental organizations actively involved with the issues to be discussed.**

### RECOMMENDATION
**The Secretary of State should act to ensure that the United States advocates key decisions at the 1989 meeting of the Governing Council of the United Nations Environment Program.**

• The United Nations Environment Program (UNEP) Governing Council meeting is an extremely important forum for international cooperation.

• Before and during the Governing Council, the United States should advocate that UNEP:

1) Develop an international convention to minimize carbon dioxide emissions.

2) Continue to assess the scientific evidence concerning global warming and its impacts.

3) Reconvene the parties to the Montreal protocol on ozone depletion, and complete in the first half of 1989 negotiation of amendments requiring that use of ozone-depleting chemicals cease as soon as possible.

4) stablish a strong program to identify needs of developing nations for assistance in energy conservation and renewable energy sources, and take catalytic and coordinating actions to ensure that those needs are met.

5) Develop and initiate negotiation of an international convention requiring nations to assess the environmental impacts of actions affecting the environments of other countries or the global commons.

6) Implement the Caribbean Regional Seas Program.

7) Systematically identify the needs of developing nations for assistance in improving their ability to safeguard their own environments, and promote international cooperation to meet those needs.

8) Work more closely and systematically with nongovernmental organizations (NGOs). NGOs should be partners in every aspect of UNEP's program, and NGO networks should receive financial support from UNEP.

## BUDGET RECOMMENDATION
F.Y. 90: **Increase** of $ 10 million     F.Y. 91: **no change**

## PRINCIPAL AUTHORIZING LEGISLATION
None

## CONGRESSIONAL JURISDICTION
**House Authorizing Committee/Subcommittee**
Committee on Foreign Affairs
Subcommittee on Human Rights and International Organizations
**Senate Authorizing Committee/Subcommittee**
Committee on Foreign Relations
Subcommittee on International Economic Policy, Trade, Oceans and Environment
**House Appropriations Subcommittee**
Subcommittee on Foreign Operations, Export Financing and Related Programs
**Senate Appropriations Subcommittee**
Subcommittee on Foreign Operations

## RELEVANT STUDIES

## RELATED FEDERAL PROGRAMS

## PRINCIPAL SOURCES OF EXPERTISE
Natural Resources Defense Council — 202-783-7800
National Audubon Society — 202-547-9009
Environmental Policy Institute — 202-544-2600
Sierra Club — 202-547-1141

## IMPLEMENTATION STEPS
UNEP should:
(1) At least triple the size of its Law Unit, which has crucially important responsibilities concerning global warming, ozone depletion, environmental impact assessment, and other matters.
(2) Hire a senior NGO Liaison Officer with extremely high qualifications, including NGO experience.
(3) Expand efforts to help national implement the Cairo Action Plan to protect the African environment.

**Blueprint for the Environment**

# Blueprint for the Environment

## INTERNATIONAL NEGOTIATIONS

## DEPARTMENT OF STATE

### RECOMMENDATION

**The Secretary of State should assign to one Assistant Secretary, or an Ambassador at Large, the responsibility to see that all proposals for Third World debt relief negotiations or settlement contain a strong environment and natural resources quid pro quo for any debt relief.**

• The Third World debt crisis is simultaneously reducing drastically the living standards of the already poor majority in most developing countries; reducing markets for U.S. goods leading to the loss of perhaps one million U.S. jobs; increasing pressure on Third World countries to exploit their natural resources in a vain attempt to earn foreign exchange to pay interest on the debt; and retarding the growth of needed natural resources conservation, education, family planning and health programs. The net result is that the basis for future sustainable economic development is being eroded, and political unrest is increasing in many countries around the world.

• Many experts, including many bankers, believe that significant debt relief will be needed to help developing nations to restart their economies. But special efforts will be needed to ensure that rekindled development will not simply accelerate the recent rapid degradation of natural resources in the Third World.

• Thus, a key component of each debt relief proposal should be an agreement by the debtor to initiate new policies and/or local currency investments, as appropriate, to foster environmentally and socially sustainable development. Recommendations for the needed policy changes and investments can be found in the 1987 U.N. World Commission on Environment and Development Report, "Our Common Future."

• Crucially needed are policies or investments to stem deforestation, loss of biodiversity, water contamination, and soil and wetland loss; to convert to more efficient energy use and sustainable agriculture; to provide health care, sanitation, education and family planning services; and to begin the long process of reforestation.

### RECOMMENDATION

**The Secretary of State should promote diplomatic initiatives necessary for implementation of Multilateral Development Bank environmental reform provision enacted into law as part of FY 86, FY 87, FY 88 and FY 89 foreign aid appropriations bills, and the 1988 Multilateral Development Bank reauthorization bill.**

• The Department of State plays an important role in organizing the diplomatic efforts necessary for the U.S. to express its concerns relative to the activities of the multilateral development banks (MDBs). The Department of State should work to promote environmental reform within the MDBs and the International Monetary Fund (IMF), and the promotion of environmentally beneficial loans. Some of the more important of these reforms are:

1) An increase in environmentally trained staff in all of the MDBs.

2) Increased public consultation during the selection, design and implementation of Bank loans.

3) Increased financing of the Banks' envi-

ronmentally beneficial projects.

4) Increased public access to information on Bank loans.

5) Adequate consultation with environmental and health ministers in the borrowing countries.

6) Adoption of environmental impact assessment procedures that include appropriate elements of the National Environmental Policy Act.

7) Adoption by the U.S. Department of the Treasury of voting guidelines dealing with loans that affect tropical rainforests and wetlands. Further guidelines should be adopted dealing with loans that affect marine ecosystems and large impoundments of rivers, as well as loans to the energy sector.

## RECOMMENDATION

**The Secretary of State should appoint a Coordinator of Population Affairs to work on Population considerations, a topic that should be incorporated into the planning and decision-making of all foreign policy determinations.**

• The role of population within the Department of State has become increasingly confused. The Coordinators for Population have varied as to the degrees of authority they exercised, the scope of their interests and their access to the Secretary of State. The Department of State should not be asked to determine development assistance policy in the area of population; however, it should take population into consideration in making foreign policy decisions.

• The Coordinator for Population should be the moving force for organizing interagency meetings, adhoc National Security Council meetings, and obtaining expert population policy advice for the Secretary and others making decisions on foreign policy. In the past a population analyst was able to provide briefings on the national security issues associated with internal population growth. This position no longer exists and should be re-established.

• The Coordinator for Population Affairs in the State Department should serve as an advisor to the Secretary of State on population policy issues as they affect foreign policy determinations, making sure that population and environment are particularly related. The position of population analyst should be re-established in the Office of Economic Analysis (INC/ER) to analyze the national security issues associated with populations. An international population policy expert should serve as a member of the Advisory Committee of the Department of State's Bureau of Oceans and International Environmental and Scientific Affairs (OES).

# Blueprint for the Environment

## OCEAN PROTECTION

# DEPARTMENT OF STATE
### Bureau of Oceans and International
### Environmental and Scientific Affairs

**RECOMMENDATION**

**The Secretary of State should take immediate steps to meet with key representatives of other nations in order to achieve widespread acceptance and ratification, by the United States and all other nations, for the 1982 Law of the Sea Convention, either as is or amended to address reasonable United States concerns regarding provisions dealing with seabed mining.**

• Broadly stated, the Law of the Sea Convention (LOSC) represents the most ambitious and significant agreement affecting the oceans ever adopted. Regrettably, the U.S. decided against signing the Convention and/or participating as an observer in implementing the seabed mining regime through PrepCom.

• Despite this, U.S. interests, particularly in relation to protection of the marine environment, are well served by the LOSC. When viewed as a whole, the benefits of the LOSC — for all nations — far outweigh any real or theoretical disadvantages. Circumstances have changed drastically since the negotiation of an interna-

tional deep seabed regime under the LOSC. There have been signals from various parties that reasonable U.S. concerns regarding the LOSC's deep seabed mining provisions can be revisited. Opportunities exist, and should be pursued by high-level U.S. officials, to expeditiously find a way for the U.S. and other nations to ratify the LOSC, as is, or amended.

(While the Department of State is the lead on this issue, this same substantive recommendation is being presented to the National Oceanic and Atmospheric Administration and the Environmental Protection Agency.)

## BUDGET RECOMMENDATION
F.Y. 90: **no change**      F.Y. 91: **no change**

## PRINCIPAL AUTHORIZING LEGISLATION

## CONGRESSIONAL JURISDICTION
**House Authorizing Committee/Subcommittee**
Committee on Foreign Affairs
Committee on Merchant Marine and Fisheries
    Subcommittee on Oceanography
**Senate Authorizing Committee/Subcommittee**
Committee on Foreign Relations
Committee on Commerce
Committee on Environment and Public Works
    Subcommittee on Environmental Protection
**House Appropriations Subcommittee**
Subcommittee on Commerce, Justice, State and Judiciary
**Senate Appropriations Subcommittee**
Subcommittee on Commerce, Justice, State, Judiciary and Related Agencies

## RELEVANT STUDIES
Council on Ocean Law policy statements on LOSC **(1986-88)**

## RELATED FEDERAL PROGRAMS
EPA's Office of International Activities
NOAA's International and Intergovernmental Affairs

## PRINCIPAL SOURCES OF EXPERTISE
The Oceanic Society — 202-328-0098
Council on Ocean Law — 202-462-3737

## IMPLEMENTATION STEPS
Convene DOS/OES Advisory Committee on LOSC after initial, preliminary internal/intergovernmental agency review.

## NOTES:

## Blueprint for the Environment

# Blueprint for the Environment

## OCEAN PROTECTION

# DEPARTMENT OF STATE

## RECOMMENDATION

**The Secretary of State should support the United States delegation to London Dumping Convention meetings to resist any efforts to abandon or diminish the use of "black list" and "grey list" emissions control annexes, and treat other criteria for regulating ocean dumping, such as water quality standards, as complementary measures to such annexes.**

• At recent meeting of the London Dumping Convention (LDC) treaty parties, including intersessional gatherings, some individuals, including one or more U.S. officials, have expressed a desire for the LDC parties to consider abandoning, diminishing or relaxing the use of black list/grey list annexes. Those annexes are a foundation of the LDC, and are critical to its success in ensuring effective protection of the marine environment. Under U.S. law, the Ocean Dumping Act and the Clean Water Act appropriately require *both* emissions control-type lists and other environmental quality criteria. Both are needed, and U.S. delegations to LDC meetings should make clear their strong support for continuation and strengthening of both approaches, among others that will ensure protection of the marine environment.

(While the Department of State is the lead on this issue, this same substantive recommendation is being presented to the National Oceanic and Atmospheric Administration and the Environmental Protection Agency.)

## RECOMMENDATION

**The Secretary of State should give full support to the dominant view of treaty parties within the London Dumping Convention to the effect that seabed burial of high-level radioactive wastes is "dumping" under that Convention, and therefore covered by the London Dumping Convention and prohibited.**

• They should require that any efforts to amend the London Dumping Convention (LDC) to permit such activities be grounded in clear and convincing evidence that such high-level radioactive waste (HLW) burial is technically feasible and environmentally acceptable, including a determination that such waste can be effectively isolated from the marine environment.
• In 1984, the treaty parties to the LDC debated the "legality" of seabed burial of HLW. A strong majority of the parties concluded that it was dumping under the LDC, and therefore prohibited since HLW is on the Annex I "black list." The U.S. opposed this view, contending that HLW is not covered by the LDC, and therefore not prohibited.

• The U.S. delegation to future meetings of the LDC should reverse its position and support the majority view on this important issue, and should lend its full support to the application of rigorous criteria along the lines noted in the recommended action before any consideration is given to the possibility of amending the LDC to allow such practices.

(While the Department of State is the lead on this issue, this same substantive recommendation is being presented to the National Oceanic and Atmospheric Administration, the Department of Energy, and the Environmental Protection Agency.)

# RECOMMENDATION

**The United States should lend its full support and active assistance to the ongoing radioactive risk assessment studies that are being carried out under the auspices of the London Dumping Convention, while also continuing to honor and encourage all other nations to abide by the indefinite moratorium on radioactive waste dumping at sea that was agreed to by the London Dumping Convention treaty parties in 1985.**

- The London Dumping Convention (LDC) is the only global agreement concerned solely with the disposal of wastes in the marine environment by dumping. Since 1983, the LDC parties have devoted substantial time to addressing the question of whether low-level radioactive wastes should be dumped at sea. The U.S. dumped such wastes at sea between 1946—1970, and several European countries continued to do so until 1983.
- While the U.S. delegation voted against the 1983 two-year moratorium, and the 1985 indefinite moratorium, both of which were adopted with the support of a strong majority of the treaty parties, the U.S. delegations to the 1986 LDC meeting, and subsequent special intersessional meetings, have exhibited a much more constructive, participatory role in addressing the comprehensive risk-related studies mandated under the indefinite moratorium. That role needs to be continued and strengthened.

# RECOMMENDATION

**The Secretary of State should strive to more effectively protect marine and coastal environments from the inevitable occurrence of oil spills by establishing a comprehensive oil spill liability and compensation regime.**

- Strong support is needed for the establishment of a complementary package of international, national and state laws that will fully compensate victims of oil spill, including damages to natural resources, while also ensuring rapid and effective cleanup responses.
- At present, there exists a fragmented hodge-podge of national and state laws providing inadequate cleanup and damage remedies, taxpayer subsidies to cover cleanup costs, damages that go uncompensated, corporate structures designed to limit exposure of spillers, and other legal barriers to victim recoveries. Substantial time and attention have been devoted to formulating effective statutory remedies to address the continuing problem of oil spill liability and compensation, but Congressional action is still needed.
- The extent to which federal and/or international treaty obligations preserve or preempt coastal state laws is one of the key outstanding issues that still needs to be resolved, and that issue should be addressed in a manner that does not preempt coastal state laws, while also allowing U.S. ratification of the international treaty protocols of 1984 on this subject.

# RECOMMENDATION

**The Secretary of State should seek international agreement on policy regarding removal of offshore oil and gas platforms that encourages removal without adverse environmental effects (i.e., no use of explosives) and resolve legal status of such an agreement vis a vis the 1958 Geneva Convention and the Law of the Sea Convention.**

- The Geneva Convention of 1958 requires that "(any offshore oil or gas) installations which are abandoned or disused must be entirely removed." This provision has always been interpreted to mean that once such an installation has served its useful life, it must be removed from the marine environment. In recent years large numbers of platforms and rigs have reached their useful life, and are slated for removal. In some European countries it is the responsibility of the government to bear the cost of removal. In the U.S. the cost is borne by industry.
- As a result, efforts are underway within the Mari-

time Safety Committee of the International Maritime Organization (IMO) to develop new "Guidelines and Standards" for removal of rigs. As drafter, these guidelines and standards carve out significant exceptions for removal, allowing rigs to remain in place or to be only partially removed under certain conditions. The legal basis for development of these guidelines and standards is a provision of the Law of the Sea Convention that appears to allow for some exceptions. However, the Geneva Convention is in force and the U.S. is a party to that Convention. The Law of the Sea Convention has not yet entered into force and the U.S. is not a party to that Convention.

• Such circumstances require a clear understanding about the legal status of the guidelines and standards being developed at IMO and U.S. obligations regarding such guidelines and standards in light of the legal requirement that the U.S. adhere to the provisions of the Geneva Convention. The guidelines as currently drafted do not provide adequate protection to marine wildlife, because they allow for the use of explosives as a means of removal. The use of explosives has been associated with killings of endangered and threatened sea turtles in the vicinity of the explosion.

## RECOMMENDATION
**The Secretary of State should seek to eliminate vessel source pollution from hazardous materials and sewage and to provide liability and compensation for damage caused by pollution from hazardous materials.**

• The Secretary of State should seek international agreement on measures to implement optional Annexes III and IV of MARPOL and agreement on liability and compensation convention for spills at sea of hazardous and noxious substances, and seek Senate ratification of MARPOL optional Annexes and Hazardous and Noxious Substances (HNS) Convention (if proposed).
• The International Convention for the Prevention of Pollution from Ships (known as MARPOL) regulates discharges from ships in each of its five annexes, with respect to oil, chemicals carried in bulk, chemicals in packages, sewage and garbage. Annexes I, II and V have entered into force. Annexes II and IV, regarding chemicals in packages and sewage, respectively, await ratification from nations representing 50 percent of the world shipping tonnage before they will enter into force. Negotiations

are underway in the Marine Environment Protection Committee (MEPC) of the International Maritime Organization (IMO) to reach agreement on the Annexes to make them more attractive for ratification. Efforts must continue to that end without weakening the effect of the Annexes. The Coast Guard and the State Department share responsibility for conducting these negotiations.
• Efforts are underway internationally to reach agreement on a legal regime for establishing liability and compensation for spills of hazardous and noxious substances from ships (HNS Convention). The Legal Committee of the IMO is conducting these negotiations. The increasing carriage of HNS by shippers worldwide make it imperative that such a convention be concluded to ensure swift and certain compensation of victims of such spills.

## RECOMMENDATION
**The Secretary of State should demonstrate more support for the United Nations Environment Programme-sponsored Regional Seas Programs and more effectively coordinate and centralize the activities which are now scattered among various offices and agencies to effectively restore and conserve important marine environments in the Wider Caribbean Basin and the South Pacific on a regional basis.**

• The U.S. government should recognize that environmental challenges threaten to undermine the Caribbean and South Pacific regions' long-term economic future as well as their present quality of life. Programs to promote conservation of the regions' natural resources are not unnecessary luxuries, but rather are vital components of U.S. foreign

policy in that these programs assist in breaking the connections between poverty, unsustainable exploitation of resources, and political instability.
• The U.S. participation in two regional seas treaties, the Convention for the Protection and Development of the Marine Environment of the Wider Caribbean Region (the Cartagena Convention) and the

Convention for the Protection of the Natural Resources and Environment of the South Pacific Region (SPREP Convention) has been inadequate. The U.S. has never contributed to the Caribbean Trust Fund, leading many counties to question U.S. participation in the regional environmental program. Nor has the U.S. taken the necessary actions to ratify the SPREP Convention. Responsibilities for these programs are dispersed among a number of offices within the State Department.

• Many other U.S. agencies have responsibilities affected by developments in the Regional Seas programs. But the lines of authority and overall responsibility have not been clear. Stronger leadership in demonstrating the U.S. commitment to international cooperation on environmental issues through the United Nations Environment Programme's Regional Seas Program must come through the State Department.

## RECOMMENDATION
**The Secretary of State should encourage regional regulation of fisheries in international meetings and enter into negotiations where lack of constraint on fishing effort on the high seas and/or the use of inappropriate fishing technologies is affecting fish stocks, marine mammals and seabirds.**

• Stocks of fish cannot be adequately managed solely by regulation of the 200 mile Fishery Conservation Zone. In areas off of both the east and west coasts, there are transboundary stocks and species which migrate across the boundary. Unregulated fishing activities in international waters can have an impact on fish stocks within the zone. Certain fishing technologies, e.g. drift gillnets, can have unacceptably high impacts on non-target species.

# Blueprint for the Environment

## SUSTAINABLE DEVELOPMENT

# AGENCY FOR INTERNATIONAL DEVELOPMENT
## OFFICE OF THE ADMINISTRATOR

**RECOMMENDATION**
**The Administrator of the Agency for International Development should announce that the central theme of the Agency's entire foreign assistance program will be sustainable development, and that it will focus on three priority goals: sustainable economic growth, eliminating poverty and preventing environmental degradation.**

• Developing nations face mounting environmental problems that threaten to render economic development unsustainable. Among bilateral aid agencies, the Agency for International Development (AID) is especially well equipped to help nations solve these problems.
• The Administrator should announce that, in addressing the priority problems described above, AID's main method of operation will be to furnish technical assistance, as opposed to assistance aimed at structural adjustment and development of large physical infrastructures. AID should maintain its country Missions. It should emphasize support for relatively small, local projects that — if successful — are capable of being replicated more widely. It should employ sufficient technically-competent staff to avoid over-reliance on contractors, and in particular, hire more people with expertise in the environmental priority areas listed above.
• AID's environment protection priorities should include expanded efforts to:

   1) Sustain the agricultural resource base and promote environmentally sound food production;

   2) Promote environmentally sound energy development with an emphasis on energy assistance designed to meet human needs while minimizing global warming;

   3) Promote family planning policies and meet family planning needs, thereby halting overly rapid population growth that often is a major cause of environmental degradation; and

   4) Conserve tropical forests and biological diversity.
• AID's efforts to prevent environmental degradation should include assistance to middle-income nations whenever appropriate.
• AID should step up its efforts to promote sustainable development in sub-Saharan Africa, the region where degradation of the natural resource base is most severe.

**RECOMMENDATION**
**The Administrator of the Agency for International Development should tale immediate steps to recruit additional highly qualified environmental staff and assign them as Environmental Officers in key Agency Missions and Regional Offices.**

## BUDGET RECOMMENDATION
See separate Recommendation

## PRINCIPAL AUTHORIZING LEGISLATION
Foreign Assistance Act (Expiration Date 1989)

## CONGRESSIONAL JURISDICTION
**House Authorizing Committee/Subcommittee**
Committee on Foreign Affairs
**Senate Authorizing Committee/Subcommittee**
Committee on Foreign Relations
**House Appropriations Subcommittee**
Subcommittee on Foreign Operations, Export Financing and Related Programs
**Senate Appropriations Subcommittee**
Subcommittee on Foreign Operations

## RELEVANT STUDIES
Study by House Foreign Affairs Committee on revision of Foreign Assistance Act, due December 1988

## RELATED FEDERAL PROGRAMS

## PRINCIPAL SOURCES OF EXPERTISE
Natural Resources Defense Council — 202-783-7800
National Audubon Society — 202-547-9009
Environmental Policy Institute — 202-544-2600
Sierra Club — 202-547-1141

## IMPLEMENTATION STEPS
AID should:
(1) Adjust personnel ceilings as necessary to achieve these objectives.
(2) Consider assigning personnel for longer periods within particular countries or regions, to provide continuity.
(3) Explore cheaper methods such as hiring ex-Peace Corps volunteers on contract to oversee specific projects.
(4) Deliver more of its assistance through U.S. PVOs and especially through local NGOs and grass-roots organizations in host countries.
(5) Require that local people be involved in AID projects at all stages of design and implementation.

## NOTES:

## Blueprint for the Environment

# Blueprint for the Environment

## SUSTAINABLE DEVELOPMENT

# AGENCY FOR INTERNATIONAL DEVELOPMENT

**RECOMMENDATION**

**The President and each of the designated Secretaries and Administrators should restructure the priorities of the foreign assistance budget within the 150 Account for foreign assistance to increase the money available to those programs that can contribute to the achievement of an ecologically sustainable development policy.**

• The economic health of other nations is of vital concern to the United State for reasons of national political and economic security as well as on humanitarian grounds. An ecologically sustainable development policy seeks to promote economic growth in other countries by eliminating poverty, protecting the natural resource base, and stabilizing human population growth.

• It is clear that developing countries and donor country governments are in the process of rethinking cooperative relationships. The United States should promote self-sufficiency and economic viability for its developing-country partners. After several decades we have a better concept of what works. But the real emphasis must be on long term ecologically sustainable development with emphasis on the component parts of stabilization of population growth, conservation of natural resources and the environment, and the institution of sustainable development.

• U.S. Foreign Economic assistance has de-clined by 50 percent since 1966, but we have tended to concentrate aid on immediate military or political assistance. For example, of the $15.9 billion appropriated in 1986 for economic and military assistance, $13.3 billion was for bilateral assistance. Roughly half of that amount went to Israel, Egypt and Jordan to maintain a stable Middle East. One-quarter of the amount was used for military base rights agreements in Greece, the Philippines, Spain, and Turkey and for strategic military problems in Pakistan and Central America.

• During that same period of time, the actual levels for assistance to humanitarian concern including food, land and people was $2.5 billion. This small amount of money does not address the critical problem of environmental degradation. For this reason, we are recommending a reprioritization of the 150 account for foreign assistance with increases for bilateral and multilateral aid and stabilization or decreases in military and political assistance.

**RECOMMENDATION**

**The Administrator of the Agency for International Development should reduce the number of bureaus and offices by combining or collapsing them into new or existing structures, with an emphasis on technical assistance.**

• This will focus support for those areas which are components of ecologically sustainable development, and will reduce the size of headquarters staff assigned to other tasks in order to save money.

• This action will also make the organization of the Agency more consistent with the functional emphasis reflected in the Foreign Assistance Act and simplify the structure of the Agency for management purposes.

• Suggested changes:
  1) Bureau for Management becomes an office attached to the Administrator, within which is merged the Office of

215

Equal Opportunity (Personnel and related functions may need to be separated out because of the size of this office).

2) The Bureau for Private Enterprise becomes an Office into which is merged the Office of Small and Disadvantaged Business Utilization.

3) The Bureau for Program and Policy Coordination becomes an Office of the Budget, and the policy function is transferred to the technical bureaus.

4) The Bureau of External Affairs becomes an Office.

5) Three new bureaus will replace the Bureau for Science and Technology: Bureaus for Agriculture and Rural Development; Natural Resources; and Health, Population and Nutrition. These bureaus will consist of the technical offices in the Bureau for Science and Technology, Program and Policy Coordination, Africa, Asia and the Near East, Latin America and the Caribbean, Office of the Science Advisor, Education, Women in Agriculture and Rural Development. All policy guidance, technical backstopping of field missions, and donor coordination will come from these bureaus.

6) The function of the three geographic bureaus will be to maintain country desks to backstop missions, coordinate with the Department of State and bring a geographic perspective to technical decisions.

7) The technical bureaus will be directly involved with Mission staff in the design and creation of Country Development Strategy Statements and sectoral programs. The geographic bureaus will provide relevant information on country-specific issues. Personnel selections will be based on technical needs.

8) The Office of U.S. Foreign Disaster Assistance is moved into the Bureau for Food, Peace, and Voluntary Assistance.

# Blueprint for the Environment

## DEVELOPMENT ASSISTANCE

# AGENCY FOR INTERNATIONAL DEVELOPMENT
## OFFICE OF THE ADMINISTRATOR

**RECOMMENDATION**
**The Administrator of the Agency for International Development should strengthen and expand its forestry assistance, with the objective of meeting needs for fuelwood and other forest products in developing countries, conserving biological diversity, and minimizing global warming of the atmosphere.**

• More than half the world's tropical forests have already disappeared. Much of the rest is under siege. Tropical forests are the homes of perhaps 50 percent of all living species. They help to preserve water supplies and perform other valuable ecological services. Their destruction contributes carbon dioxide to the atmosphere, making more severe the "greenhouse effect" that is warming the atmosphere.
• The Agency for International Development (AID) should step up its forestry activities, with the aim of conserving existing forests and encouraging planting to create new forested areas.

• AID should begin with a country-by-country inventory of forests and the rates at which they are being destroyed. It should estimate the potential for reforestation, and describe the means by which forests can be conserved and reforestation accomplished. It should work with the governments and the public in tropical countries to devise plans for setting and achieving forestry goals (utilizing the mechanisms of the Tropical Forests Action Plan where appropriate). AID also should act vigorously to persuade other donors, multilateral and bilateral, to join in these efforts.

**RECOMMENDATION**
**The Administrator of the Agency for International Development should greatly expand its assistance to developing nations to help them conserve animal and plant species and their habitats.**

• We face the horrifying prospect of losing, in just the next few decades, up to a quarter of all the earth's plant and animal species, due mainly to destruction of tropical forests and other habitats — a wave of extinctions comparable in magnitude to that which destroyed the dinosaurs and many other species some 65 million years ago.
• The Congress has specifically directed the Agency for International Development (AID) to provide assistance to help nations conserve species and their habitats. AID's Biological Diversity Program is currently funded at a level of $4.5 million for FY 89.
• AID's Program currently is funded at far too low a level. The FY 90 budget should provide at

least $10 million for the Program, and the FY 91 budget at least $20 million. In order to ensure effectiveness, AID should develop a strategy and establish criteria for allocating assistance. One criterion should be that a large part of the funds will be spent to assist countries in protecting habitat areas identified by scientists as having extraordinary importance for the conservation of biological diversity.
• AID should do more to integrate biological diversity concerns into its other programs, notably agriculture and forestry.
• AID should also make strong efforts to persuade other donors, multilateral and bilateral, to join in these efforts. The World Bank in particular has much to contribute.

## RECOMMENDATION
**The Administrator of the Agency for International Development should continue and expand its activities to help developing nations address environmental problems caused by industrial pollution and toxic substances, and should request adequate funds for this purpose as part of the FY 90 budget.**

• The environment and health in developing nations increasingly are suffering from industrial pollution and misuse of toxic substances. The United States has more expertise than any other nation concerning ways of solving these problems and could do much to help these nations address and solve these problems at relatively little cost. In cooperation with the U.S. Environmental Protection Agency (EPA), the Agency for International Development (AID) should undertake expanded efforts to assist nations in these areas.
• The first step should consist of country-by-country assessments of these problems and actions necessary to remedy them. In most nations, AID should begin by analyzing problems due to agricultural chemicals, leaving other aspects to EPA.
• AID should then design feasible programs to prevent misuse and overuse of agricultural chemicals. These programs should emphasize improved regulation, information and education, training, increased reliance on low-input agriculture and integrated pest management, and making available relevant U.S. expertise. AID should work with EPA to help solve other problems identified by the assessments.

## BUDGET RECOMMENDATION
For Conservation of Species:
F.Y. 90: **Increase** of $ 5.5 million      F.Y. 91: **Increase** of $ 10 million over FY 90

## PRINCIPAL AUTHORIZING LEGISLATION
Foreign Assistance Act, Sec. 119 (Expiration Date 1989)

## CONGRESSIONAL JURISDICTION
**House Authorizing Committee/Subcommittee**
   Committee on Foreign Affairs
**Senate Authorizing Committee/Subcommittee**
   Committee on Foreign Relations
**House Appropriations Subcommittee**
   Subcommittee on Foreign Operations, Export Financing and Related Programs
**Senate Appropriations Subcommittee**
   Subcommittee on Foreign Operations

## RELEVANT STUDIES
Study by House Foreign Affairs Committee on revision of Foreign Assistance Act, due December 1988
Report to U.S. AID by the Committee on Environment and Health: **"Opportunities to Assist Developing Countries In the Proper Use of Agricultural and Industrial Chemicals,"** (Conservation Foundation, Feb. 1988)

## RELATED FEDERAL PROGRAMS
International programs of U.S. Park Service and Fish and Wildlife Service
Biological diversity efforts of State Department Bureau of Oceans, Environment and Science
International, pollution, and toxics programs of the Environmental Protection Agency

## PRINCIPAL SOURCES OF EXPERTISE
Natural Resources Defense Council — 202-783-7800     Environmental Policy Institute — 202-544-2600
Sierra Club — 202-547-1141

## Blueprint for the Environment

# Blueprint for the Environment

## AGRICULTURE

## AGENCY FOR INTERNATIONAL DEVELOPMENT
### OFFICE OF THE ADMINISTRATOR

**RECOMMENDATION**

**The Administrator of the Agency for International Development should assure that the Agency's agriculture and rural development programs be centered on an ecologically sustainable agriculture development program.**

• This program should concentrate on three primary activities:

1) Developing human resources in the agriculture sector (education, training, technology transfer, institution building, and planning;

2) Designing and implementing small-scale agriculture projects which emphasize the principles and techniques of sustainability and which, if successful, can be replicated by others;

3) Initiating policy dialogue with developing country governments on agricultural and rural policies and macroeconomic policies which affect sustainability;

• Sustainability as described above is best done working as directly as possible with farmers in planning projects so that their own objectives and limitations can be factored in from the outset; working through grassroots organizations, which have proven themselves particularly successful in managing agriculture and rural development projects; and planning the program for a long term — a minimum of 10 and up to 15 years. Infrastructure investment should only be undertaken when it is essential to project sustainability

**RECOMMENDATION**

**The Administrator of the Agency for International Development should work in close cooperation with the World Bank, the International Monetary Fund, and other donors to engage host governments and their Ministries of Agriculture, Planning and Finance in policy dialogue at the macro-economic level and in a joint analysis of agricultural policies to provide developing countries with technical expertise and financial resources to pursue policies of sustainable agriculture for small farmers.**

• The focus of these talks should be the impact of existing policies on sustainability. Subjects should include pricing policies, subsidies, tax systems, exchange rates, the relation of agriculture production to population policies, tariffs, trade policies, land regulation and more general attitudes toward the rural sector.

• The Agency for International Development (AID) should assume a more active role in persuading other donors to adopt sustainability as a focus for planning, implementing and evaluating their agriculture programs. This can be done be establishing regular opportunities for meeting with multilateral donors to plan an ongoing effort for policy change.

# RECOMMENDATION

**The Administrator of the Agency for International Development should continue to provide high-level support for international agricultural research centers, the major regional agricultural research centers, and a few well-established and viable national agricultural research systems, encouraging them to focus more of their resources on the problems of sustainability for small farmers.**

• In so doing the Agency for International Development (AID) will move away from supporting agricultural extension systems where they are not now effective, and will focus on locally-adapted systems of technology transfer which do not overly depend on government support or inputs.

• AID research programs, particularly those carried out through the BIFAD program and the U.S. universities, are truly collaborative and based on a broad interdisciplinary approach to sustainability.

## BUDGET RECOMMENDATION
(Overall Agriculture Budget)
F.Y. 90: $ 655.0 million          F.Y. 91: $ 700.0 million

## PRINCIPAL AUTHORIZING LEGISLATION
Foreign Assistance Act of 1961

## CONGRESSIONAL JURISDICTION
**House Authorizing Committee/Subcommittee**
Committee on Foreign Affairs
Subcommittee
**Senate Authorizing Committee/Subcommittee**
Committee on Foreign Relations
Subcommittee
**House Appropriations Subcommittee**
Subcommittee on Foreign Operations, Export Financing and Related Programs
**Senate Appropriations Subcommittee**
Subcommittee on Foreign Operations

## RELEVANT STUDIES

## RELATED FEDERAL PROGRAMS

## PRINCIPAL SOURCES OF EXPERTISE
National Audubon Society — 202-547-9009    Natural Resources Defense Council — 202-783-7800
Committee on Agricultural Sustainability in Developing Countries — 202-462-0900
Environmental Policy Institute - 202-544-2600

## IMPLEMENTATION STEPS
(1)    Issue an Agency-wide policy directive placing agricultural sustainability unequivocally at the center of the Agency for International Development (AID) goals in agriculture and rural development. AID Washington should provide field missions with a matrix of general principles and criteria — environmental, economic, institutional, political, and social. These principles and criteria should then be adapted in practical terms by field missions to each type of agricultural activity pursued (crops, mixed farming, animal agriculture, forestry, integrated pest management, etc.) and to each major ecological zone in that country.
(2)    field offices should evaluate all ongoing projects for their degree of sustainability and adjust them or add to them to bring them in line with sustainability criteria.

## Blueprint for the Environment

## ENERGY

# AGENCY FOR INTERNATIONAL DEVELOPMENT
## OFFICE OF THE ADMINISTRATOR

### RECOMMENDATION

**The Administrator of the Agency for International Development should direct that the Agency's energy efforts be increased and focused sharply on increased energy efficiency and increased reliance on renewable energy sources, with an emphasis on energy assistance designed to meet human needs while minimizing global warming.**

• Global warming presents major threats to the world and the United States, including possible loss of the U.S. Midwestern grain belt, 80 percent of U.S. coastal wetlands, and most U.S. forests. The problem is a global one. U.S. expertise in energy efficiency and renewable energy technologies can be of great assistance to developing nations in reducing their emissions of greenhouse gases. Hence, U.S. cooperation with developing nations, spearheaded by the Agency, is essential if we are to minimize global warming.

• The Agency for International Development (AID) should take immediate actions, submit FY 90 and 91 budget requests, and support amendments to the Foreign Assistance Act that will make these actions a key part of AID's mission and program. Specifically, the Administrator should:

1) Issue cable guidance to all AID Missions stating that energy efficiency and environmentally sound renewables are to be the centerpiece of AID's energy efforts, with a special emphasis on assistance for least-cost energy planning.

2) Require all AID Missions to discuss AID's role in meeting energy needs, including the potential for increased energy efficiency, in every Country Development Strategy Statement.

3) Announce that AID will not provide any support for large oil- or coal-fired powerplants.

4) Announce that AID, in cooperation with others, will develop by early 1990 a plan for research on how developing nations can meet their energy needs while minimizing global warming.

5) Take all necessary actions to increase the number of AID permanent-hire staff with energy expertise.

6) Strengthen AID's partnership with the Department of Energy, in order to ensure that AID's energy efforts take full advantage of U.S. expertise and technology.

7) Take the Implementation Steps recommended below.

to develop and implement least-cost planning; transportation (including energy-saving methods of mass transit such as light rail, buses and van pools, energy-efficient motor vehicles, human-powered vehicles and railroads), traffic management techniques such as computerization of traffic signals, fuel savings at airports, and transfer of appropriate U.S. technologies; industry; and agriculture.

(5) Encourage host countries to sponsor meetings with officials from the U.S. utility sector that are leaders in energy efficiency and other U.S. experts to discuss the application of least-cost planning techniques.

(6) Encourage host countries to end energy supply subsidies and rationalize energy prices (while noting that subsidies of alternative fuels for the poor may be appropriate for relatively short periods, especially to stem deforestation).

(7) Develop a cadre of U.S. experts from industry, academia, nonprofits, and government agencies capable of providing technical assistance to developing countries concerning energy efficiency and renewables.

(8) Expand efforts to meet the energy needs of the rural poor through improved energy efficiency, as by more efficient stoves.

(9) Expand efforts to meet energy needs, especially those of the rural poor, from environmentally sound renewable energy sources, such as nontraditional biomass (e.g., agricultural residues), village woodlots and other sources of fuelwood and small hydro projects. See separate Recommendation on AID's Forestry Program.

(10) Develop and implement programs of cooperation with newly industrialized countries, middle-income developing nations, and China aimed at meeting energy needs while minimizing global warming.

(11) Systematically work with other bilateral and multilateral development assistance agencies to increase support for energy efficiency.

(12) Initiate a coordinated international effort to ensure that all development aid agencies work together to identify energy needs and meet the associated requirements for financial investments and technical assistance. This effort should feature systematic, country-by-country, end-use analyses, with a designated aid agency taking the lead in each country in cooperation with the host government, and should lead to the development of national programs to meet the energy needs thus identified, with maximum reliance on energy efficiency and environmentally sound renewable energy sources.

## BUDGET HISTORY (in millions of dollars by fiscal year)

for Energy Office, Bureau of S & T:

|  | 87 | 88 | 89 |
|---|---|---|---|
| Requested |  |  | 9.293 |
| Appropriated | 8.028 | 10.0 |  |

The FY 1989 appropriations bill directs AID to step up its efforts to assist developing nations in the areas of energy conservation and renewable energy sources, including some of the specific actions recommended in Section L below. The House Committee Report (House Report No. 100-641) states that this directive was based on the Committee's concern about global warming.

## NOTES:

The FY 1989 appropriations bill directs AID to step up its efforts to assist developing nations in the areas of energy conservation and renewable energy sources, including some of the specific actions recommended in Section L below. The House Committee Report (House Report No. 100-641) states that this directive was based on the Committee's concern about global warming.

# POPULATION

# AGENCY FOR INTERNATIONAL DEVELOPMENT
## Office of Population

**RECOMMENDATION**

**The Agency for International Development should encourage the President of the United States to make a commitment to regain clear leadership for the United States in international population assistance through increased funding for bilateral and multilateral programs and a renunciation of policies set forth at the International Population Conference in Mexico City in 1984.**

• The control of population growth is essential to most developing countries' hopes for economic development and protection of their environments, to the pursuit of broader worldwide benefits such as protecting tropical rainforests, preserving species diversity, and ameliorating the "greenhouse effect"—and perhaps even to future international political stability. A re-ordering of priorities within the Agency for International Development (AID) budget will provide the resources for the United States to begin again to lead worldwide cooperation to address this fundamental issue.

• Throughout most of the past 20 years the U.S. has been the clear leader in the international population assistance effort. However, that position has eroded in recent years for three reasons:

1) a policy enunciated at the International Population Conference in Mexico City in 1984 that is at odds with the views of most of the developing world;

2) inadequate funding levels for population assistance; and

3) the cessation of contributions by the US to the United Nations Population Fund and the International Planned Parenthood Federation.

## BUDGET RECOMMENDATION
F.Y. 90: **Increase** to $ 500 million    F.Y. 91: **Increase** to $ 540 million

## PRINCIPAL AUTHORIZING LEGISLATION
Foreign Assistance Act of 1961

## CONGRESSIONAL JURISDICTION
**House Authorizing Committee/Subcommittee**
Committee on Foreign Affairs
**Senate Authorizing Committee/Subcommittee**
Committee on Foreign Relations
**House Appropriations Subcommittee**
Subcommittee on Foreign Operations, Export Financing and Related Programs
**Senate Appropriations Subcommittee**
Subcommittee on Foreign Operations

## RELEVANT STUDIES

## RELATED FEDERAL PROGRAMS

## PRINCIPAL SOURCES OF EXPERTISE
Population Crisis Committee — 202-659-1833
Alan Guttmacher Institute — 202-296-4012
Planned Parenthood Federation of America — 202-785-3351
Population Institute — 202-544-3300
National Audubon Society — 202-547-9009
Sierra Club — 202-547-1141

## IMPLEMENTATION STEPS
(1)  Make a clear statement of the goals and framework for U.S. population policy and program assistance. Remove all restrictions which currently prevent the provision of the broadest array of contraceptive services.
(2)  Resume the U.S. contribution to the United Nations Population Fund.
(3)  Increase funding levels for international population assistance immediately to $ 450 million, with increments for FY 90 to $ 500 million, FY 91 to $ 540 million, FY 92 to $ 580 million. This will enable the U.S. to pay its fair share of unmet needs for family planning assistance, as estimated by the World Bank. It could be achieved by diverting less than one percent of other aid programs to population assistance now, and seven percent in the year 2000 even without an increase in the aid budget.
(4)  Establish a Presidential Commission on Population Growth and Natural Resource Planning.
(5)  Create an interagency coordinating machinery to connect population policy concerns with the concerns being pursued elsewhere in government such as the study of climate and acid rain, international political stability, world trade and money flows and Third World economic development.

## BUDGET HISTORY (in millions of dollars by fiscal year)

|  | 81 | 83 | 85 | 87 | 88 | 89 |
|---|---|---|---|---|---|---|
| Requested | 238 | 201 | 250 | 250 | 207.5 | 190.9 |
| Appropriated | 190 | 211 | 290 | 234.6 | 197.9 | |

## MANPOWER HISTORY (in F.T.E.'s by fiscal year)

|  | 79 | 81 | 83 | 85 |
|---|---|---|---|---|
| Actual | 97 | 91 | 76 | 111 |

—————— **Blueprint for the Environment** ——————

## POPULATION

# AGENCY FOR INTERNATIONAL DEVELOPMENT

**RECOMMENDATION**
The Director of the Office of Population should recruit a new generation of highly motivated and qualified staff and maintain the system of population officers in key countries.

**RECOMMENDATION**
The Director of the Office of Population should continue support for data collection and research on the consequences and causes of rapid population growth.

**RECOMMENDATION**
The Director of the Office of Population should seek to improve the efficiency of population assistance.

• AID has begun several initiatives in this area recently. The most promising activities are those that act catalytically to stimulate new programs and relieve bottlenecks. Among the new efforts that need to be emphasized are: pilot projects, private sector involvement and long-term sustainability.

**RECOMMENDATION**
The Director of the Office of Population should maintain and strengthen the technical focus provided by the Agency for International Development.

**RECOMMENDATION**
The Director of the Office of Population should make a greater effort to build developing country capacity to conduct their population programs themselves.

• Family planning programs have succeeded most in countries where the policies, resources and commitments have come from the countries themselves. Examples include China, Taiwan, Korea, Colombia, Thailand, Indonesia, and Mexico. Recently a number of new countries have shown the desire to take control of their programs in a similar fashion, including Nigeria, Ecuador, Zaire, Liberia, Sudan and others. It will be important for U.S. population assistance to be structured so that it can make a maximum contribution to the capability of developing countries to implement their own programs.
• New programs should include an increase in long-term, in-country training programs for population-related social scientists, biomedical scientists and health scientists; support for development of population-related research capacity in developing country universities and government organizations; and encouragement for cooperation between developing countries in sharing experiences and information.

**RECOMMENDATION**
The Director of the Office of Population should focus policy activities on operational policies which assist and train developing country governments in policy implementation.

# Blueprint for the Environment

## CONSERVATION LENDING

# AGENCY FOR INTERNATIONAL DEVELOPMENT
## Bureau for Program and Policy Coordination

### RECOMMENDATION
**The Agency for International Development should prepare a detailed study of outstanding loans owed to the United States by Third World countries, and a program under which they can be reduced or totally waived in a way that promotes environmentally sustainable economic development. The renegotiation of debts owed to the United States should include an environmental quid pro quo by which Third World Nations are allowed to trade debt for improved natural resource conservation and management.**

• The Third World debt crisis is simultaneously reducing drastically the living standards of the already poor majority in most developing countries; reducing markets for U.S. goods leading to the loss of perhaps one million U.S. jobs; increasing pressure on Third World countries to exploit their natural resources in a vain attempt to earn foreign exchange to pay interest on the debt; and retarding the growth of needed natural resources conservation, education, family planning and health programs. The net result is that the basis for future sustainable economic development is being eroded, and political unrest is increasing in many countries around the world.

• Many experts, including many bankers, believe that significant debt relief will be needed to help developing nations to restart their economies. But special efforts will be needed to ensure that rekindled development will not simply accelerate the recent rapid degradation of natural resources in the Third World.

• Thus, a key component of each debt relief proposal should be an agreement by the debtor to initiate new policies and/or local currency investments, as appropriate, to foster environmentally and socially sustainable development. Recommendations for the needed policy changes and investments can be found in the 1987 U.N. World Commission on Environment and Development Report, "Our Common Future."

• .Crucially needed are policies or investments to stem deforestation, loss of biodiversity, water contamination, and soil and wetland loss; to convert to more efficient energy use and sustainable agriculture; to provide health care, sanitation, education and family planning services; and to begin the long process of reforestation.

### RECOMMENDATION
**The Administrator of the Agency for International Development should act immediately to improve the AID "Early Warning System" and thereby prevent environmental mistakes by the multilateral development banks.**

• The congressionally mandated Early Warning System is intended to identify proposed multilateral development bank (MDB) loans that may have significant impacts on natural resources and indigenous people and bring these loans to the attention of the Department of the Treasury, MDB staff, and other governments that are members of the MDBs' boards.
• Needed actions include:
    Methods whereby developing-country non-governmental organizations (NGOs) can play a larger role in the operation of the System.
    A cable to all local Agency for International

Development (AID) missions, and to State Department personnel in countries where AID does not operate, reminding them of their responsibilities under the System.

Mechanisms whereby information provided under the System can be shared with other government members of the MDBs.

Increased dialogue with U.S. environmental organizations involved in MDB reform.

Increased on-site investigation, by AID and State Department personnel, of upcoming loans.

Strengthening of the System in non-AID countries through increased coordination with State Department personnel.

Additional AID staff training.

## BUDGET RECOMMENDATION

F.Y. 90: **no change**    F.Y. 91: **no change**

The study required in this recommendation should not be costly (less than $100,000) and should be completed within F.Y. 1989, so no budget cost is included for F.Y. 1990 or 1991.

If debt relief negotiations are satisfactorily implemented, there will be additional costs to the Treasury caused by foregoing expected revenue that is theoretically due for repayment by the borrowers. This cost is attributable to the need for debt relief, not to the environmental component of the negotiations.

## PRINCIPAL AUTHORIZING LEGISLATION

Foreign Assistance Act, 22 U.S.C. 2151(v) and 2399c

Export Import Bank Act of 1945, 12 U.S.C. 635

Agriculture Trade, Development and Assistance Act of 1954, 7 U.S.C. 1727d (P.L. 480)

## CONGRESSIONAL JURISDICTION

**House Authorizing Committee/Subcommittee**

Committee on Banking, Finance and Urban Affairs

Committee on Agriculture

Subcommittee on Department Operations, Research and Foreign Agriculture

Committee on Foreign Affairs

Committee on Ways and Means

**Senate Authorizing Committee/Subcommittee**

Committee on Foreign Relations

Committee on Banking, Housing and Urban Affairs

Committee on Finance

Committee on Agriculture

**House Appropriations Subcommittee**

Subcommittee on Foreign Operations

**Senate Appropriations Subcommittee**

Subcommittee on Foreign Operations

## RELEVANT STUDIES

U.S. Treasury Department Report to Congress on Debt-for-Nature Swaps, April 1988

1987, 1988 Biennial AID Early Warning System Reports

## RELATED FEDERAL PROGRAMS

Title III of Agriculture Trade, Development and Assistance Act of 1954, 7 U.S.C. 1727d (P.L. 480) in which AID and USDA negotiate conversion of food aid loans into local currency funds for development projects in the debtor country.

## PRINCIPAL SOURCES OF EXPERTISE

National Wildlife Federation — 202-797-6600    World Wildlife Fund — 202-293-9800

World Resources Institute — 202-638-6300    The Nature Conservancy — 202-841-5300

Conservation International — 202-429-5660

## Blueprint for the Environment

# DEPARTMENT OF TRANSPORTATION

Federal transportation policy is adrift. The problem was succinctly summarized by one presenter at a recent transportation policy conference:

Many of the major national goals for transportation and other forms of physical infrastructure have been accomplished or have lost favor without being replaced with new ones. The federal government now seems preoccupied with national defense, the social safety net, and interest on the national debt — not with "building the nation." Thus, the strong federal leadership in providing capital for public works, that has come to be expected over recent decades, has become uncertain in the 1980s.

The policy underpinnings for any federal role in the funding and delivery of transportation services must be considerably sharpened. If they are not, the provision of transportation services should be considered a state, local and private function and both funding and allocation decisions should be delegated accordingly.

We do not recommend wholesale federal withdrawal. We do recommend a significant sharpening of focus, and a shift in priorities, based on the following principles:

**Integration.** The federal government has a strong interest in promoting clean air, in providing a secure energy future for the nation, and in protecting the essential aesthetic, cultural and historic attributes of American life. None of these federal interests drive transportation policy, yet transportation policy, or lack thereof, often cripples the promotion of these other objectives. For example, the transportation sector alone consumes more oil than we produce domestically, with obvious adverse consequences to our national energy security objectives. These non-transportation objectives must influence our transportation investment choices. This applies equally to national environmental, historic and cultural objectives as well.

**Least Cost Mobility.** Federal transportation policy must acknowledge the public interest in influencing trip selection so that mobility is provided at the lowest possible public cost. The consumer who chooses to take public transit to work provides direct benefits to the city and the country in terms of improved traffic flow, less pollution, reduced oil consumption, and higher transit revenues. This selection is sometimes made at a marginal sacrifice in individual convenience, privacy and comfort. Subsidies are appropriate to influence consumer selection of transportation mode when the public benefits of the selection exceed the public costs of the subsidy.

**Energy Independence.** The transportation sector now consumes over 62 percent of all petroleum consumed in the United States. In 1987, total transportation oil consumption exceeded total domestic oil production for the first time in history. We recommend that the Department of Transportation adopt the specific goal of keeping transportation oil consumption within the limit of total domestic oil production.

These are the principles on which a sound federal transportation policy should be based. They are consistent with present statements of federal transportation policy yet provide an improved focus for allocating scarce federal funds among competing requests for federal transportation assistance. They are also compatible with — even supportive of — traditional statements of national transportation policy such as promoting safety, contributing to the national economy, and supporting defense and other national security objectives.

Finally, it is time to acknowledge that federal transportation services are significantly underfunded. Our physical transportation infrastructure suffers from deferred maintenance and undercapacity, and needs a significant infusion of new funds. Internalizing previously externalized costs will also cost money. We recommend a significant increase in the federal gas tax to raise funds for reconstruction, efficiency improvements, new capacity, and for reducing external costs. Studies show that a $.30—$.50 increase in the federal gas tax, in addition to raising revenues, would stimulate automobile structure and design improvements providing benefits in fuel economy that more than offset the increased fuel cost. In addition, such a tax would raise the price of gasoline to the point where non-petroleum based fuels become competitive, further reducing the dependence of our transportation structure on oil. A significant gas tax increase is needed now.

The following Blueprint recommendations focus on ground transportation: (1) highways, (2) transit, and (3) railroads. Aviation policy is addressed to the extent aviation subsidies affect the ability of transit (Amtrak) to compete for passenger service and waterway policy is addressed to the extent waterway subsidies affect the ability of railroads to compete for freight service. Non-transportation objectives that require improvements in Coast Guard services are also included in this notebook.

## Highways

The goals of federal highway policy demand re-examination. On one hand, the traditional purposes of major federal-aid highway programs have been met. The Interstate System, designed to interconnect the major metropolitan areas in all regions, is virtually complete. The Secondary System, designed to "get farmers out of the mud" through construction of farm-to-market routes, is also complete. The Primary and Urban Systems, designed to increase road capacity, have lost their federal purpose. The federal-aid highway program has become a form of revenue-sharing: an efficient system for collection and distribution of gas taxes but void of policy.

On the other hand, America faces a severe mobility crunch. Many urban and suburban highway systems have already reached severe overload. Demand is expected to increase anywhere from 30 percent to 50 percent by the year 2000, yet highway capacity will increase no more than six percent. The question is no longer "how much mobility is enough?" Given the fact that we can no longer presume to satisfy all demands for mobility, the more salient questions include "What types of mobility demand will we meet, what types will we ignore or discourage, at what level will we meet it, and who will pay for it?"

The Blueprint recommendations suggest that mobility needs be analyzed in the context of other national goals such as energy efficiency (e.g., a gas tax increase to reduce mobility demand) and clean air (e.g., affirmative consistency determinations affecting project choice). Yet, even assuming these non-transportation goals can be achieved through improved project choice, we still will have more users demanding to use highways than space available. How will we ration this demand?

We propose three improvements in the way the costs and benefits of highway use are allocated:

First, we recommend that new highway investment be allocated based on the principle of cost efficiency: the highest mobility increase possible per dollar spent.

Second, we recommend that highway use be rationed by the principle of willingness to pay: each highway user must be willing to pay the incremental cost of providing the service received by that user. Two industries that simply are not paying the full cost of providing the highway services they use are the trucking and the billboard industries.

Third, we recommend that a small portion of highway investment be allocated in a manner that promotes not just mobility but quality travel through the preservation of scenic and historic landscapes. All other factors being equal, we recommend favoring projects that preserve the scenic and historic aspects of adjacent landscapes over projects that destroy them.

## Transit

Transit policy in the United States—buses as well as rail — has a fundamentally different history than either highway policy or aviation policy.

Although our first national highways were privately owned, since 1916 virtually all new roads in the country have been publicly financed, constructed and owned. Since 1956 highways have had an earmarked source of revenue — the gas tax.

Highway agencies have the right of eminent domain — plenary power to condemn property for highways whenever and wherever needed. Revenues from the highway trust fund are distributed ("apportioned") when authorized — by-passing the annual appropriations process. Until controls were recently placed on highway outlays, state highway agencies could "obligate" (i.e., spend) funds years in advance of their actual apportionment. Since 1970, when Congress created the Aviation Trust Fund, airport authorities have enjoyed many of the same privileges as highway authorities.

Transit, in contrast, was initially private transit; privately owned, operated, and taxed as any other private business. Transit, until 1982, never had a trust fund, and then was funded at a small fraction of the highway trust fund. Capital grants for new construction are largely at the discretion of the Secretary, complicating long-term transit planning. Some transit authorities lack the power of eminent domain. The result is a national transportation construction policy that is irrationally skewed towards those modes with the highest energy and pollution costs per passenger-mile traveled (highway and air) while neglecting the mode that is most energy-efficient and clean — public transit. This is bad public policy.

Transit also loses out in the formulation of national tax policy. The federal tax code encourages commuters to drive alone by allowing employers to provide tax-free parking as an employee benefit, worth $200—$400 per month in major cities such as New York. Fares paid for home-to-work travel on public transit, however, are not tax-deductible. State and local governments can float tax-exempt bonds for highway or airport construction. However, Amtrak and other innovative high-speed rail projects are prohibited from issuing tax-exempt bonds. These inequities must be eliminated.

As a nation, we must greatly increase our investment in clean, energy-efficient alternatives to the private automobile and the airplane. The reason is simple: there is no more room in most urbanized areas to continually expand the land-intensive systems needed to accommodate these modes. A typical U.S. city already devotes almost 40 percent of its land to roads, alleys and parking lots. At the same time, public demand for accessible urban open space for non-motorized travel (bicycling, walking and jogging) is skyrocketing and competes with motorized travel for our public thoroughfares. Commercial establishments want broader sidewalks, tree-lined streets, and other amenities that entice shoppers to downtown locations. Public acceptance of urban air pollution — primarily auto exhaust — is rapidly dwindling as two of every five Americans now live in areas with health-threatening air pollution levels. All these factors converge to resist new highway and airport capacity and encourage energy-efficient, land-efficient and non-polluting transportation modes.

## Railroads

The basic assumption behind a railroad policy that maximizes environmental objectives is that rail freight haulage for the majority of goods transported, especially bulk products such as aggregate, grain, coal and timber is the environmentally preferred alternative. However, since the mid-sixties, the market share of railroads for freight haulage, both in terms of revenue-miles and ton-miles, has declined from 60 percent rail—40 percent trucks to 40 percent rail—60 percent trucks. Truck haulage is more energy-intensive, requires construction and reconstruction of roads with adverse land-use impacts, is more polluting, and results in more accidents with spillage of contaminated materials than rail haulage. In addition, the loss of over 3,000 miles of rail corridor per year to abandonment, and the subsequent destruction of fenced and protected rail rights-of-way to agriculture, development or neglect, represents a serious loss of linear open space suitable for conservation, recreation and historic preservation.

The reversal of ratios in modal split between trucks and railroads would be of no concern to the federal government if it resulted simply from free market choices with all costs (including environmental and energy costs) internalized. However, the delivery of transportation services does not operate in a free market. Railroads do not compete on a "level playing field." Highway construction and maintenance is highly subsidized, and trucks are cross-subsidized by passenger traffic. The Federal Highway Administration calculated in 1982 that trucks pay only 65 percent of the cost to the public of providing the roadways on which they operate. In comparison, railroads pay the entire cost of right-of-way construction and maintenance, and also pay real estate taxes on these corridors. Truck labor agreements are also not regulated but are the result of bargaining agreements while the railroads operate under antiquated labor workrules that cripple industry competitiveness. If these inequities are eliminated, railroads will be able to compete without penalty with the trucking industry.

## NATIONAL POLICY

# DEPARTMENT OF TRANSPORTATION
## OFFICE OF THE SECRETARY

**RECOMMENDATION**

**The Secretary of the Department of Transportation should establish a new office of Assistant Secretary for Environmental and Energy Policy in order to coordinate national transportation policy with national environmental and energy policy objectives.**

• Currently, major environmental and energy policy decisions are made at the modal administration level. These decisions include the review of environmental impact statements, compliance with national air quality laws, decisions pursuant to Section 4(f) of the Department of Transportation Act and historic preservation reviews. This system places final review of agency compliance with environmental laws within the agency that assists in project development. It also precludes the development and implementation of a consistent Department-wide environmental philosophy. Prior to 1981, critical environmental decisions were elevated to the Secretarial level in order to ensure that the Department's policies were, to the maximum extent possible, consistent with national environmental quality goals.

• In addition to overall policy guidance, the Assistant Secretary would be directed to assume final sign-off authority on final Environmental Impact Statements and final Section 4(f) determinations at the request of other federal agencies. This authority will help ensure Department-wide consistency of environmental decision-making.

• In addition to acting as a Department-wide monitor of agency compliance with national environmental and energy goals, the new office would also initiate actions to promote these other important national objectives. Over 65 percent of all oil consumed in the United States is consumed by the transportation sector — more oil than is domestically produced — thus adding to our trade deficit, defeating energy independence objectives, and destabilizing national security. With a specific mandate to increase energy efficiency in the delivery of transportation services this office would place a critical role towards integrating national transportation policy with national energy policy.

## BUDGET RECOMMENDATION
F.Y. 90: **no change ***       F.Y. 91: **no change ***
* No change expected through this reorganization of existing staff

## PRINCIPAL AUTHORIZING LEGISLATION
Section 4(f) of the Department of Transportation Act, 49 U.S.C. 303
The National Environmental Policy Act of 1969, 42 U.S.C. § 4321
The National Historic Preservation Act of 1966 16 U.S.C 470 (f)

## CONGRESSIONAL JURISDICTION
**House Authorizing Committee/Subcommittee**
Committee on Public works and Transportation
Subcommittee on Surface Transportation
**Senate Authorizing Committee/Subcommittee**
Committee on Environment and Public Works
Subcommittee on Water Resources, Transportation and Infrastructure
**House Appropriations Subcommittee**
Subcommittee on Transportation
**Senate Appropriations Subcommittee**
Subcommittee on Transportation and Related Agencies

## RELEVANT STUDIES
**Transportation Energy in the Year 2020**, Imcnutt, Greene and Sperling (TRB, 1988)
**Environmental Considerations in a 2020 Transportation Plan — Constraints or Opportunities?**
(Suhrbier and Denkin, TRB 1988)

## RELATED FEDERAL PROGRAMS
Project Energy Independence (DOE)

## PRINCIPAL SOURCES OF EXPERTISE
Environmental Policy Institute — 202-544-2600
National Trust for Historic Preservation — 202-673-4035

## IMPLEMENTATION STEPS
Secretarial Reorganization Order.

## NOTES:

---

**Blueprint for the Environment**

# Blueprint for the Environment

## NATIONAL POLICY

# DEPARTMENT OF TRANSPORTATION
## ASSISTANT SECRETARY for Governmental Affairs

**RECOMMENDATION**
**The Secretary of Transportation should recommend to Congress an increase in the federal gas tax earmarked for investment in energy-efficient transport modes and for purchase of rail corridors being abandoned.**

• The Secretary of Transportation and Assistant Secretary for Government Affairs should recommend to Congress a $.30-to-$.50/gallon increase in the federal gas tax, phased-in by $.10/gallon annually (phase-in full $.50/gallon increase if oil prices remain below $30/barrel; $.30/gallon increase if oil prices exceed $30/barrel). A portion of the revenues will be earmarked for investment in energy-efficient transport modes and for purchase of rail corridors being abandoned in order to preserve these vital corridors for future transport or trail use. A portion of the gas tax revenues will be used for a rebate program for low-income auto-owning families to offset any adverse impacts on such families.

• U.S. gas prices are half of what they were in 1981 and among the lowest of industrialized nations. In 1987, U.S. gas prices averaged $.82/gallon compared to $3.71 in Italy, $3.58 in Denmark, $2.95 in France, $2.89 in Japan (International Energy Annual, 1987). The key price difference is the level of tax. U.S. gas tax in only $.23/gallon ($.09 federal, $.14 state

average) compared to $1.50 or more in many European nations.

The U.S. oil problem is fundamentally a transportation problem. Transportation uses two-thirds of all U.S. oil, and autos and light trucks account for nearly two-thirds of this. Despite fuel economy improvements made since the oil crises of the 1970s, petroleum use in transportation is growing, up eight percent since 1975. Low gas prices discourage transportation energy-efficiency and fail to reflect the true cost of oil dependency to our economy: the national security cost of dependence estimated at approximately $10/barrel (Energy and Security, 1981), of air pollution, contribution to the "greenhouse effect" and other costs.

• The argument that a gas tax is regressive fails to recognize that high income groups spend more on transport, own more autos and use them more extensively than low or moderate income groups (Dept. of Labor, Consumer Expenditure Survey, 1986). Annual gas expenditures range from $429/year (lowest economic quintile) to $1,892 (highest quintile).

235

## BUDGET RECOMMENDATION

$.10/gallon annual phase-in of gas tax increase (each penny generates approximately $1.1 billion/year)

## PRINCIPAL AUTHORIZING LEGISLATION

None

## CONGRESSIONAL JURISDICTION

**House Authorizing Committee/Subcommittee**
Committee on Ways and Means
Committee on Public Works and Transportation
**Senate Authorizing Committee/Subcommittee**
Committee on Finance
Committee on Environment and Public Works
Committee on Banking and Urban Affairs
**House Appropriations Subcommittee**
Subcommittee on Transportation
**Senate Appropriations Subcommittee**
Subcommittee on Transportation and Related Agencies

## RELEVANT STUDIES

The National Economic Commission, is looking at means to reduce the deficit, including an increase in federal gas tax (chair: Drew Lewis, Robert Strauss)
Alan Greenspan, Chair of Federal Reserve, testified before Congress in support of $.15/gallon gas tax increase (March 7, 1988, Washington Post)
Senator Weicker (CT) and Rep. Beilensen have both introduced legislation to increase gas tax by $.30 ($.10/year) and $.25/gallon, respectively.

## RELATED FEDERAL PROGRAMS

The existing Highway Trust Fund (supported by $.09/gallon federal gas tax) and Mass Transit Account ($.01/gallon gas tax) provide revenues for highways and transit. The federal gas tax was last increased in 1982 by $.05/gallon as part of Surface Transportation Act of 1982.

## PRINCIPAL SOURCES OF EXPERTISE

National Association of Rail Passengers — 202-546-1550
Sierra Club — 202-547-1141
World Resources Institute — 202-638-6300
Rails to Trails Conservancy — 202-797-5400
Environmental Policy Institute — 202-544-2600
Coalition for Scenic Beauty — 202-544-1100

## IMPLEMENTATION STEPS

The Secretary of Transportation and Assistant Secretary for Government Affairs should recommend to and work with Congress to increase the federal gas tax by $.30-to-$.50/gallon, phased-in by $.10/gallon annually. A portion of the revenues (each penny generates $1.1 billion) should be earmarked for energy-efficient transport modes (transit, intercity rail, etc.) for purchase of abandoned rail corridors for future transport or trail use, and for a rebate program for low-income auto-owning families within 125 percent of poverty level) to offset adverse impacts on such families.

## NOTES:

## Blueprint for the Environment

# Blueprint for the Environment

## NATIONAL POLICY

# DEPARTMENT OF TRANSPORTATION

## RECOMMENDATION

**The Secretary of Transportation should assure that all Departmental projects, programs and plans in National Ambient Air Quality Standard non-attainment areas conform with the adopted State Implementation Plan for the area.**

• The Secretary of Transportation, the Federal Highway Administration (FHWA) and the Urban Mass Transit Administration (UMTA) should condition all federal funding of projects that increase transportation capacity in National Ambient Air Quality Standard (NAAQS) non-attainment areas on an affirmative showing that projected growth in vehicle miles traveled (VMT) and projected emissions resulting from such increased VMT are accounted for in the approved State Implementation Plan (SIP) for the area.

• A recent Transportation Research Board Report predicts that by the Year 2005, traffic is expected to increase by 45 percent while new facility construction is expected to increase only six percent. Given this, all new projects must be closely reviewed against the objective of stabilizing or, where possible, reducing traffic growth while maximizing efficiency improvements in existing transportation capacity.

• Section 176(c) of the Clean Air Act prohibits any Metropolitan Planning Organization (MPO) from approving any project plan or program that does not conform to the SIP. The Department of Transportation (DOT) watchdogs this process by 1) certifying the MPO planning process as "continuous, cooperative and comprehensive (3-C)" and 2) reviewing specific projects for conformity with the 3-C process.

• Implementation of Section 176(c) within DOT is presently conducted pursuant to a Memorandum of Understanding (MOU) with Environmental Protection Agency (EPA) entitled "Procedures for Conformance of Transportation Plans, Programs, and Projects with Clean Air Act Implementation Plans (June 12, 1980)." This MOU is fatally flawed in that it has been interpreted by DOT as requiring only that new projects not prohibit implementation of other transportation control measures (TCMs). VMT-generated emissions resulting from new projects are ignored in this analysis. A new MOU, or a change in DOT's interpretation, is needed.

## RECOMMENDATION

**The Secretary of Transportation should make funding eligibility for all High Occupancy Vehicle, bicycle and pedestrian facilities for all categories of federal-aid highway funds covered by Title 23.**

• Since the early 1970s, federal highway authorizing legislation has attempted to encourage various forms of non-motorized and high-occupancy transport. Currently, there are five different provisions of Title 23 under which certain highway funds may be used for carpool/vanpool operations and information, construction of High Occupancy Vehicle (HOV) parking facilities outside the central business district, designation of existing lanes, construction of new HOV lanes and bicycle and pedestrian facilities.

• While most projects are eligible for standard categories of funds (Federal Aid Primary System (FAPS), Federal Aid Urban System (FAUS), Interstate and Interstate 4F), only bicycle facilities are eligible for Interstate substitution and Bridge funds. Further confusing the eligibility question is the fact that carpool/vanpool facilities and pedestrian and bicycle projects are eligible for 100 percent federal funds under Sec. 120 (d), yet, except for bicycles, these projects can not utilize either Bridge or Interstate Substitute funds. Transit-related parking, signalization and information programs are not eligible for 100 percent federal funding.

• The following proposed changes would simplify funding for these programs and eliminate any skewing toward one or another project.

1)  Combine Section 137, parts of 142 and 146 (which cover HOV and transit) into a new Section 146. Any language limiting use of federal funds to certain categories would be revised to include all categories. Section 142(a) (2) which allows use of FAUS funds for rail facilities and bus and rail vehicles should be left as is.

2)  Section 120 (d) should be revised to allow all HOV facilities eligible at 100 percent.

3)  Section 217, which covers bicycle and pedestrian facilities should be revised to make these projects eligible for the broad category of Title 23 funding.

## RECOMMENDATION
**The Secretary of the Department of Transportation should reconsider the Department's present blanket approval of transportation projects that destroy allegedly "minor" segments of parks, recreation areas, historic sites, and wildlife refuges under Section 4(f) of the Department of Transportation Act. In addition, the Department should establish a Section 4(f) advisory board to assist the Secretary in reviewing the Department's procedures for compliance with this law.**

## RECOMMENDATION
**The Secretary of Transportation and the Federal Aviation Administration should actively promote congestion relief measures in order to reduce pressures to build new airports, to preserve the large amounts of land such facilities require and to prevent the exposure of more citizens to noise impacts of new airports.**

• The Associate Administrator for Airports should take the following actions as a means of reducing airport congestion and reducing pressure to build new airports:

1)  Promote construction of short, parallel runways at major airports to absorb general aviation and commuter carriers, thus adding to airport capacity and reducing pressure to expand;

2)  Promote use of sliding scales for landing fees at busy airports to promote distribution of flights to off-peak hours, thereby increasing airport capacity without expansion of facilities;

3)  Promote use of nearby military air facilities to absorb more general aviation and commuter traffic, which adds to airport capacity at nearby commercial airports;

4)  Promote expansion of small reliever airports and mini-hubs to relieve congestion at large, busy airports.

## RECOMMENDATION
**The Administration should oppose enactment of coal slurry pipeline legislation to prevent the degradation and loss of water resources and the undermining of the environmentally sound rail transportation system.**

Blueprint for the Environment

# Blueprint for the Environment

## MASS TRANSPORTATION

## DEPARTMENT OF TRANSPORTATION
### ASSISTANT SECRETARY for Budget and Programs
### Urban Mass Transportation Administration

### RECOMMENDATION
**The Secretary of Transportation should recommend and seek a revitalized federal investment in mass transit.**

• In 1982, the "transit penny" was enacted into law as part of the five-cent increase in the federal gas tax enacted as part of the Surface Transportation Assistance Act of 1982. The penny was to provide "new" money, over and above existing levels of funding (each penny provides approximately $1.1 billion/year). Instead, General Fund support of transit has steadily eroded, amounting to a cut of $1.4 billion since 1981. Thus, the penny has merely served to replace cuts in General Funds and never provided the additional monies promised (unlike the four-cent increase for highways which produced substantial increases in highway spending since 1982). Federal transit funding should rise to at least $5.1 billion/year, the level recommended by the Carter Administration for FY 1982.

• Transit ridership has been growing steadily since 1982, rising from 8.1 billion passenger trips in 1981 to 9.0 billion in 1987. Increased funds are critical to meet capital needs and service expansions/improvements to accommodate ridership growth. Transit capital investment needs are estimated at $31.4 billion from 1988—1992, $6.3 billion/year (American Public Transit Association).

• This needed restoration of transit funding will bring economic benefits and jobs. Every $100 million spent on transit capital projects or transit operations generates $300 million increase in business revenues and supports 8,000—9,000 jobs (American Public Transit Association). Transit funding will also help urban areas to: meet the Clean Air Act standards by providing a clean energy efficient alternative to auto commuting; lessen U.S. dependence on foreign oil; and to slow the loss of open space to roads and sprawling auto-dependent developments by investing in transit rather than highway infrastructure.

### RECOMMENDATION
**The Secretary of Transportation should establish a joint Federal Highway Administration and Urban Mass Transit Administration Office of Program Support to consolidate and centralize common functions.**

# RECOMMENDATION

**The Assistant Secretary for Policy and International Affairs should work with the Federal Highway Administrator and the Urban Mass Transportation Administrator to designate Benefit Assessment Districts (or similar taxing measures on beneficiaries of transport projects) as part of the local match for Federal-Aid Urban, Federal-Aid Primary and Urban Mass Transit Administration Discretionary Grant Projects.**

• The Assistant Secretary for Policy and International Affairs should, as part of this effort, establish a Task Force on Private Sector Financing for Urban Transportation to examine where such Benefit Assessment Districts have been successfully implemented and to serve as a resource center for other cities interested in establishing such mechanisms.

## BUDGET RECOMMENDATION

### PRINCIPAL AUTHORIZING LEGISLATION
Surface Transportation and Uniform Relocation Act of 1987
Executive Reorganization Act. 5 U.S.C. § 901

### CONGRESSIONAL JURISDICTION
**House Authorizing Committee/Subcommittee**
Committee on Public Works and Transportation
Subcommittee on Surface Transportation
**Senate Authorizing Committee/Subcommittee**
Committee on Banking, Housing and Urban Affairs
Subcommittee on Housing and Urban Affairs
**House Appropriations Subcommittee**
Subcommittee on Transportation
**Senate Appropriations Subcommittee**
Subcommittee on Transportation and Related Agencies

### RELEVANT STUDIES
The American Public Transit Association, **"Transit Capital Needs Assessments"**
American Transportation Advisory Committee, ATAC Reports
USDOT, **A Proposal: Surface Transportation Administration** (1978)
July 1986 report by U.S. Dept. of Transportation, **Alternative Financing for Urban Transportation: State of the Practice**

### RELATED FEDERAL PROGRAMS
Federal Aid Highway Program
Health and Human Services (program delivery services)
Federal Aid-Highway Program
Urban Mass Transportation Program

### PRINCIPAL SOURCES OF EXPERTISE
National Association of Railroad Passengers — 202-546-1550    Sierra Club — 202-547-1141
American Public Transit Association — 202-898-4000    U.S. Conference of Mayors — 202-293-7330

### IMPLEMENTATION STEPS
Restore the federal investment in the mass transit program by bringing transit level up to funding levels in 1981, adjusted upwards for inflation. The Secretary of Transportation, supported by the Assistant Secretary for Budget and Programs, would recommend these funding levels to Congress in the President's budget and work for their adoption by the appropriate Congressional committees.

## Blueprint for the Environment

## TRUCKS

# DEPARTMENT OF TRANSPORTATION
## Federal Highway Administration

### RECOMMENDATION
**The Secretary of Transportation should oppose any Congressional efforts to further increase the permitted size and weight of heavy trucks.**

• An increase in the permitted size and weight of heavy trucks would be at the expense of the taxpayer, the railroad industry, and sound environmental policy. Railroads, which compete with trucks for over 60 percent of their cargo, are environmentally preferable modes of transportation because of their advantages in energy consumption, pollution, safety and land use.

• The trucking industry agenda includes an appeal for the increase of permitted sizes and weights on federal interstate and other federal aid highways. Federal and State cost allocation studies show that even at present weights, heavy trucks over 60,000 pounds pay only 65 percent of the costs that they cause to the highway system. Increasing sizes and weights would make that situation far worse, because truck damage to highways increases exponentially with weight. Increasing truck size and weight would grant another subsidy to an already heavily subsidized industry.

• A 1962 American Association of State Highway and Transportation Officials Road Test shows that road damage increases exponentially with increases in axle weight. Thus, a five-axle truck loaded to the 80,000 pound federal weight limit does the equivalent damage of 9,600 automobiles, although it weighs only as much as 20 automobiles.

• Because pavement life-expectancy is highly sensitive to axle loads, any truck weight increase will shorten pavement life. The Director of the Federal Highway Administration Office of Research estimated that the 1975 weight increases could increase traffic-related deterioration by as much as 35 percent. The Administration should oppose any legislative or administrative step which would help to prevent the further deterioration of the nation's highway system, prevent the further shift from rail to truck transportation, and reduce gasoline consumption and dependence on oil imports.

### RECOMMENDATION
**The Federal Highway Administration should support the current right of states to designate and limit access by heavy trucks to the highways capable of handling heavy truck traffic.**

### RECOMMENDATION
**The new Administration, through the Department of Transportation and the Treasury Department, should support the enactment of a federal weight-distance tax on heavy trucks to assess their use and impact on federal highways.**

241

## BUDGET RECOMMENDATION

F.Y. 90: **no change**     F.Y. 91: **no change**

## PRINCIPAL AUTHORIZING LEGISLATION

Surface Transportation Act of 1982
Federal Highway Revenue Act of 1987 (expires 1993 and must be reconsidered by Congress in 1991)

## CONGRESSIONAL JURISDICTION

**House Authorizing Committee/Subcommittee**
Committee on Public Works and Transportation
Subcommittee on Surface Transportation
**Senate Authorizing Committee/Subcommittee**
Committee on Environment and Public Works
Subcommittee on Water Resources, Transportation and Infrastructure
**House Appropriations Subcommittee**
Subcommittee on Transportation
**Senate Appropriations Subcommittee**
Subcommittee on Transportation and Related Agencies

## RELEVANT STUDIES

GAO **"Excessive Truck Weight: A Burden We Can No Longer Support"** 1979
Federal Long Combination Vehicle Study
Western Longer Combination Vehicle Study
TRB Study of Turner Combinations (due in 1990)
Federal Motor Carrier Study (due in 1990)
FHWA Study of Size and Weight Issues (due in 1989)
1982 Highway Cost Allocation Study
513G Alternatives to Heavy Vehicle Use Tax Study, 1988
Feasibility of Federal Weight-Distance Tax Study (from Section 933 of the Deficit Reduction Act of 1984)

## RELATED FEDERAL PROGRAMS

Changes in heavy truck size and weight have direct impacts on federal highway spending requirements, highway safety programs, and on weight-distance tax proposals.

## PRINCIPAL SOURCES OF EXPERTISE

Friends of the Earth — 202-543-4312
Environmental Policy Institute — 202-544-2600
National Association of Railroad Passengers — 202-546-1550
Association of American Railroads — 202-639-2525
Insurance Institute for Highway Safety — 202-333-0770

## NOTES:

——————— **Blueprint for the Environment** ———————

# DEPARTMENT OF TRANSPORTATION
Federal Highway Administration
Office of the Chief Council
Office of Environment and Right-of-Way

## RECOMMENDATION
**The Secretary of Transportation should promote reform of the Highway Beautification Act to help remove visual pollution and blight from America's scenic roadsides.**

• The Highway Beautification Act of 1965 has been amended to the point that the Secretary of Transportation called the current Act "unworkable" in Congressional testimony in 1986. Currently, if a state does not want to risk losing 10 percent of its highway funding, it must ensure that no signs are moved from federal interstate and primary aid highways without paying cash compensation. Yet, because no federal money is available, no removal is taking place. No constitutional requirement for compensation exists: current cash compensation provisions of the Act were included for political reasons, not constitutional.

• According to the General Accounting Office, in FY 1983, 13,522 new billboards went up along federal aid highways. According to the Federal Highway Administration, about 403,000 billboards were located along federal highways in 1986.

• New Legislation should include the following:
Repeal 10 percent penalty provision of current law when states require billboard removal without paying cash compensation;
Repeal legal "vegetation control" provision of current Federal Highway Administration regulations which act as "vegetation destruction" provision;
Add a new section to the Act which prohibits the construction of all new billboards along federal aid highways.

## RECOMMENDATION
**The Secretary of Transportation should work to enact a National Scenic and Historic Roadways Protection Act to ensure that selected highways and roads which, with their immediate environments, possess significant scenic, historic or cultural values are wisely managed and protected.**

## RECOMMENDATION
**The Secretary of Transportation and the Federal Highway Administration should develop and support the legislation creating a new road user fee on off-premise billboards.**

• Road user fees are a well established concept in the United States, with almost $23 billion being collected in federal, state and local governmental units for this purpose in 1979. One major type of road user, however, has escaped road user fees. This is the off-premise highway billboard, a type of advertising that derives its value solely from the public's investment in roads and highways.

## BUDGET RECOMMENDATION
F.Y. 90: **no change**          F.Y. 91: **no change**

## PRINCIPAL AUTHORIZING LEGISLATION
23 U.S.C., Section 131

## CONGRESSIONAL JURISDICTION
**House Authorizing Committee/Subcommittee**
　　Committee on Public Works and Transportation
　　　　Subcommittee on Surface Transportation
**Senate Authorizing Committee/Subcommittee**
　　Committee on Environment and Public Works
　　　　Subcommittee on Water Resources, Transportation and Infrastructure
**House Appropriations Subcommittee**
　　Subcommittee on Transportation
**Senate Appropriations Subcommittee**
　　Subcommittee on Transportation and Related Agencies

## RELEVANT STUDIES
GAO Report, **"The Outdoor Advertising Control Program Needs To Be Reassessed,"** January, 1985
Charles Floyd, **"Should Billboards Be Subject to Road User Fees?"**, Transportation Quarterly, Vol. 36, No. 4
**President's Commission on Americans Outdoors,** 1987, Section III, Part VI
**An Assessment of the Feasibility of Developing A National Scenic Highway System,** report to Congress, USDOT, 1974

## RELATED FEDERAL PROGRAMS
NPS National Historic Landmark Program
NPS National Natural Landmark Program

## PRINCIPAL SOURCES OF EXPERTISE
Coalition for Scenic Beauty — 202-546-1100
American Institute of Architects — 202-626-7300
American Planning Association — 202-872-0611
National League of Cities — 202-626-3000
National Wildlife Federation — 202-797-6800

## IMPLEMENTATION STEPS
(1) Change Existing Law — Amend 23 USC (131).
(2) Change Existing Implementing Regulations and Procedures for 23 USC Section 131.
(3) Create National Advisory Group on Highway Beautification to advise Secretary of Transportation on implementation of Highway Beautification Act.

## BUDGET HISTORY (in millions of dollars by fiscal year)

|              | 88 | 89 |
|--------------|----|----|
| Authorized   | 0  | 0  |
| Requested    | 10 | 10 |
| Appropriated | 0  | 0  |

## MANPOWER HISTORY (in F.T.E.'s by fiscal year)

|            | 88 | 89 |
|------------|----|----|
| Authorized | 10 | 10 |
| Actual     | 2  | 2  |

## Blueprint for the Environment

# Blueprint for the Environment

## OCEAN PROTECTION

# DEPARTMENT OF TRANSPORTATION
### United States Coast Guard
### Office of Marine Safety, Security and Environmental Protection

**RECOMMENDATION**

**The Secretary of Transportation should eliminate plastic pollution in the ocean from vessel sources by rigorous implementation and enforcement of Plastic Pollution Act of 1987 and MARPOL Annex V.**

• Each year, hundreds of thousands of marine mammals, birds, and sea turtles fall victim to plastic pollution in the ocean. The animals become entangled in plastic debris or ingest the plastic, leading to injury and often-times death. One source of plastic garbage in the ocean is ships. In 1987, the United States ratified Annex V of the International Convention for the Prevention of Pollution from Ships, known as MARPOL. Annex V bans the discharge of plastics from all ships, except public vessels, and further restricts discharges of other garbage from ships. The Marine Plastic Pollution Research and Control Act of 1987 (P.L. 100-220, Title II) was enacted to implement Annex V. This new law requires public vessels of the U.S. to comply with the requirements of the Annex within five years. The U.S. Coast Guard has the responsibility to enforce the new law, and is currently developing regulations for its implementation.

**RECOMMENDATION**

**The Secretary of Transportation and the Commandant of the U.S. Coast Guard should request additional funding for enforcement activities under fisheries and environmental laws.**

**RECOMMENDATION**

**The Secretary of Transportation should more effectively protect marine and coastal environments from the inevitable occurrence of oil spills by establishing a comprehensive oil spill liability and compensation regime.**

# RECOMMENDATION
**The Secretary of Transportation and the Commandant of the U.S. Coast Guard should seek international agreement on measures to implement optional Annexes III and IV of MARPOL and agreement on liability and compensation convention for spills at sea of hazardous and noxious substances. They should also seek Senate ratification of MARPOL optional Annexes and HNS Convention (if proposed).**

• The International Convention for the Prevention of Pollution from Ships (known as MARPOL) regulates discharges from ships in each of its five annexes, with respect to oil, chemicals carried in bulk, chemicals in packages, sewage and garbage. Annexes I, II and V have entered into force. Annexes III and IV, regarding chemicals in packages and sewage, respectively, await ratification from nations representing 50 percent of the world shipping tonnage before they will enter into force. Negotiations are underway in the Marine Environment Protection Committee (MEPC) of the International Maritime Organization (IMO) to reach agreement on the Annexes to make them more attractive for ratification. Efforts must continue to that end without weakening the effect of the Annexes. The Coast Guard and the State Department share responsibility for conducting these negotiations.

## BUDGET RECOMMENDATION

### PRINCIPAL AUTHORIZING LEGISLATION
Act to Prevent Pollution From Ships and Plastic Pollution Act of 1987

### CONGRESSIONAL JURISDICTION
**House Authorizing Committee/Subcommittee**
Committee on Merchant Marine and Fisheries
Subcommittee on Coast Guard and Navigation
**Senate Authorizing Committee/Subcommittee**
Committee on Environment and Public Works
Subcommittee on Environmental Protection
**House Appropriations Subcommittee**
Subcommittee on Transportation
**Senate Appropriations Subcommittee**
Subcommittee on Transportation and Related Agencies

### RELEVANT STUDIES
Report of the Interagency Task Force on Persistent Marine Debris, May 1988

### RELATED FEDERAL PROGRAMS
NOAA — Office of General Counsel
NOAA — Fisheries Management
EPA — Ocean Dumping

### PRINCIPAL SOURCES OF EXPERTISE
Oceanic Society — 202-328-0098
Defenders of Wildlife — 202-659-9510
Center for Environmental Education — 202-429-5609
Greenpeace — 202-362-4177

# Blueprint for the Environment

## DEPARTMENT OF THE TREASURY

### Multilateral Development Banks

The multilateral development banks, including the World Bank and the three regional development banks, lend more than $30 billion each year in the Third World. The impact of their lending is enormous, since it often generates far greater amounts of private investment. Unfortunately, the pattern of development promoted by these institutions has had a very serious and negative environmental impact in the Third World.

Projects financed by these institutions, such as large hydroelectric dams and livestock development projects, have often resulted in deforestation, inundation of valuable crop land, and a host of other environmental problems which affect those living in the borrowing countries. More recently, non-project loans, which are often used to pay back foreign creditors, require the borrower to meet certain "conditions" which can have a negative impact on the environment.

Since 1983, close to 20 Congressional hearings have been held to discuss the environmental impact of multilateral development banks lending. As a result, legislation has been enacted each year since 1985 which in some way seeks to improve the environmental performance of the multilateral development banks through activities undertaken by United States Department of the Treasury, United States Agency for International Development, and United States State Department officials. Since these are multilateral institutions, Congressional instructions cannot be made directly to these institutions.

United States conservation organizations, and conservation organizations in other donor and borrower countries of the multilateral development banks, have played an important role in this reform campaign, often through collaboration with United States government officials. Though the multilateral development banks

proposals included in Project Blueprint are by definition directed at United States government agencies, it is understood that private conservation organizations, particularly in this country, will continue to have an important role to play in insuring their success.

The multilateral development banks recommendations addressed to the Department of the Treasury seek to continue and expand the current environmental reform campaign. The first recommendation to the Treasury cites previously enacted legislation and outlines specific reforms that the Treasury should continue to seek within the multilateral development banks.

The second recommendation urges the Treasury to seek reform in the energy lending policies of the multilateral development banks so that they will finance projects that are more economical, more environmentally sensitive, and more likely to address global climactic trends, such as global warming, that are increasingly serious. The third and most far-reaching Treasury recommendation, calls for the Treasury to adopt adequate environmental assessment procedures that must be followed before they can vote on a given multilateral development bank loan.

The multilateral development bank recommendations also include those directed at the United States Department of State, and the United States Agency for International Development. The Department of State is called upon to strengthen support for the United States position within the multilateral development banks through diplomatic means. The Administrator of the Agency for International Development. is urged to strengthen the Early Warning System, a process that should provide more information, at an earlier stage, on loans under consideration by the multilateral development banks.

Together, all of these recommendations

suggests ways in which the United States should continue to pressure the banks to improve the environmental quality of their lending. At the same time, one hopes that adoption of these recommendations will lead to a greater involvement of non-governmental organizations in the lending process, and suggest lending activities that would actually be beneficial to developing country environments, and the global environment that we all share.

## "Debt-For-Nature" Swaps

Sound management of natural resources is essential for sustainable economic development. The basic natural resource systems of air, water, soil and forests which underlie all our economic structures are under attack. The linkage of the debt crisis with natural resources conservation requires some explanation, since it is not clear at first glance, but there is an important connection.

Briefly, in the past eight years or so, developing countries have faced drastically increasing debt service requirements and deteriorating terms of trade for their chief exports. Timber extraction, conversion of mixed farmland to massive unsustainable cash-crop monocultures, and destruction of valuable wetlands are all on the increase. This is leading to deforestation, the extinction of potentially valuable species of plants and animals, erosion of soil, deteriorating downstream water supplies, and to the loss of fisheries potential. Countries are competing with each other for industrial development investments, and some officials have admitted privately they fear that requiring control of highly hazardous pollutants may reduce their attractiveness to investors.

The most obvious example is the tropical rainforest, genetic library for all our future expectations of biotechnology, storehouse of one-half of the species of plants and animals, moderator of regional climate, sponge that holds more than 25 percent of the world's fresh water supply, and disappearing at a rate of 100 acres per minute.

The irony of the debt crisis is that just when the pressure of debt service placed many developing countries in the position of having to increase the rate of exploitation of their natural resources for short-term foreign exchange gains, they are asked at the same time to reduce government budgets, which means to cut or delay the implementation of conservation measures that could reduce the long-term degradation of the resource base.

There may be a way to find the common ground between the creditors and debtors to break the deadlock, to move toward long-term solutions. What is needed is a clear and decisive commitment to what conservationists call "sustainable development," i.e., economic growth based on sound management of the natural resource base.

One beginning step was taken in July 1987, when the government of Bolivia and a conservation group in the United States announced a debt swap of a unique sort — deeply discounted Bolivian debt was purchased on the secondary market, and cancelled in return for protection and management by Bolivia of almost 4 million acres of priceless tropical forest in the watershed of the Amazon.

This is one way to accomplish the dual goals of modest debt relief, and the conservation of significant natural resources, goals that will be crucial for future economic development in Bolivia and elsewhere.

But this is a micro-example which involved only $650,000 of debt. Conservation groups have access to some limited funding to keep this process going, as well as good cooperation with borrowing countries which desire to participate. Unfortunately, their financial resources are nowhere near adequate to the size of the problem.

Debt swaps like that in Bolivia, where debt reduction was traded for improved natural resource conservation, should be strongly considered by all agents of the United States government actively participating in Third World debt negotiations. The Blueprint recommendations call for the United States to provide leadership in promoting environmentally sustainable economic development through an increased number of debt-for-conservation swaps and other mechanisms which will magnify the small but promising efforts made in this direction thus far.

**Blueprint for the Environment**

# Blueprint for the Environment

## DEBT

## DEPARMENT OF THE TREASURY
### OFFICE OF THE SECRETARY

### RECOMMENDATION
**By Executive Order, the President should promote environmentally sustainable economic development by establishing a clear line of responsibility for negotiating agreements to alleviate the Third World debt crisis. The Executive Order should require that all the various debt relief options include the concept of trading debt reduction for improved natural resources conservation and management by the debtors.**

- The Third World debt crisis is simultaneously reducing drastically the living standards of the already poor majority in most developing countries; reducing markets for U.S. goods leading to the loss of perhaps one million U.S. jobs; increasing pressure on Third World countries to exploit their natural resources in a vain attempt to earn foreign exchange to pay interest on the debt; and retarding the growth of needed natural resources conservation, education, family planning and health programs. The net result is that the basis for future sustainable economic development is being eroded, and political unrest is increasing in many countries around the world.
- Many experts, including many bankers, believe that significant debt relief will be needed to help developing nations to restart their economies. But special efforts will be needed to ensure that rekindled development will not simply accelerate the recent rapid degradation of natural resources in the Third World.
- Thus, a key component of each debt relief proposal should be an agreement by the debtor to initiate new policies and/or local currency investments, as appropriate, to foster environmentally and socially sustainable development. Recommendations for the needed policy changes and investments can be found in the 1987 U.N. World Commission on Environment and Development Report, "Our Common Future."
- Crucially needed are policies or investments to stem deforestation, loss of biodiversity, water contamination, and soil and wetland loss; to convert to more efficient energy use and sustainable agriculture; to provide health care, sanitation, education and family planning services; and to begin the long process of reforestation.

### RECOMMENDATION
**The Secretary of the Treasury should assign to the Assistant Secretary for International Affairs the responsibility to see that all proposals for Third World debt relief negotiations or settlement contain a strong environment and natural resources quid pro quo for any debt relief.**

### RECOMMENDATION
**The President and each of the designated Secretaries and Administrators should restructure the priorities of the foreign assistance budget within the 150 Account for foreign assistance to increase the money available to those programs that can contribute to the achievement of an ecologically sustainable development policy.**

## BUDGET RECOMMENDATION
F.Y. 90: **no change**       F.Y. 91: **no change**

## PRINCIPAL AUTHORIZING LEGISLATION
The International Financial Institutions Act, 22 U.S.C. 262 et seq., and 22 U.S.C. 286 b(b) (3), authorizing U.S. participation in the Bretton Woods Agreement
Foreign Assistance Act of 1961

## CONGRESSIONAL JURISDICTION
**House Authorizing Committee/Subcommittee**
Committee on Banking, Finance and Urban Affairs
Committee on Foreign Affairs
Committee on Ways and Means
**Senate Authorizing Committee/Subcommittee**
Committee on Foreign Relations
Committee on Banking, Housing and Urban Affairs
Committee on Finance
**House Appropriations Subcommittee**
Subcommittee on Foreign Operations
**Senate Appropriations Subcommittee**
Subcommittee on Foreign Operations

## RELEVANT STUDIES
U.S. Treasury Department Report to Congress on Debt-for-Nature Swaps, April 1988
The 1987 U.N. World Commission on Environment and Development Report, **Our Common Future**

## RELATED FEDERAL PROGRAMS
Title III of Agriculture Trade, Development and Assistance Act of 1954, 7 U.S.C. 1727d (P.L. 480) in which AID and USDA negotiate conversion of food aid loans into local currency funds for development projects in the debtor country.

## PRINCIPAL SOURCES OF EXPERTISE
National Wildlife Federation — 202-797-6600     World Wildlife Fund — 202-293-9800
World Resources Institute — 202-638-6300     The Nature Conservancy — 202-841-5300
Conservation International — 202-429-5660

## IMPLEMENTATION STEPS
(1)  The Executive Order should establish a clear line of responsibility for making recommendations for solutions to the debt crisis so that any debt relief mechanism must contain the concept of trading debt relief for improved natural resources conservation and management policies and/or investments by the debtors (a "quid pro quo").
(2)  The agreements between borrowers and creditors will have to include promises by industrialized nations to curb their own disproportionate negative impacts on global resources, such as the atmosphere and oceans. A "global bargain" will be required for sustainable development because the debtors are unlikely to accept the implication that policy changes are only needed in the developing countries.
(3)  Some countries, especially in Sub-Saharan Africa, face a financial emergency which requires a quick response from donors and lenders. In such cases, rather than pursuing complex country by country negotiations, it may be appropriate to expedite debt relief for all such countries at once. The required measures to improve natural resources management can be implemented by the borrowers as part of new lending packages, as those countries begin economic recovery.

**Blueprint for the Environment**

# Blueprint for the Environment

## DEBT

# DEPARTMENT OF THE TREASURY

## RECOMMENDATION

**As required by the Fiscal Year 1988 Continuing Resolution, the Department of the Treasury prepared a report on various options for action by the World Bank and other multi-lateral development banks to promote debt-for-nature swaps. Department officials should now proceed to promote the implementation by the multi-lateral development banks of the recommended measures.**

• The Department of the Treasury report recommends the following actions as appropriate for the multi-lateral development banks (MDBs) in the context of debt negotiations:

1) Help developing countries establish conservation priorities.
2) Accommodate debt-for-nature swaps piggybacked onto World Bank and other MDB loans.
3) Serve as information clearinghouses to facilitate debt-for-nature negotiations.
4) Provide incentives for sustainable resource management through structural adjustment and sector loans.
5) Offer technical assistance grants to cover start-up costs of debt-for-nature financing.
6) Make new loans available especially for tropical forest and wetland protection.
7) Establish one or more pilot programs with interested debtor countries to utilize the above listed options in facilitating debt-for-nature swaps.

## RECOMMENDATION

**The Assistant Secretary for International Affairs should require that the Department of the Treasury complete the requirements of the Fiscal Year 1988 Continuing Resolution passed by Congress to analyze the feasibility of establishing a new facility that would purchase discounted debt from private banks and negotiate a settlement with the borrower, to exchange debt reduction or rescheduling for debtor country local currency investment in conservation.**

• The F.Y. 1988 Continuing Resolution requires:

"The Secretary of the Treasury shall undertake an analysis of newly created institutions ... to purchase at market discounts, developing country debt in exchange for domestic currency investments in conservation ..."

• In April 1988, the Department of the Treasury issued a report on several debt-for-nature related ideas, but did not include this particular option. Even though the Continuing Resolution expired at the end of F.Y. 1988, Congress is still interested in this subject.

• The essence of this Congressional directive is that the staff of the Department of the Treasury should take a serious look at hypothetical debt relief options that would involve creation of a new institution to arrange debt settlements.

• This study would provide a crucial part of the analytical basis for the decisions which must be made by the U.S. government in the next few months or years, on how to approach the Third World debt crisis.

251

## RECOMMENDATION

The Department of the Treasury's Office of Developing Nations Finance should take every opportunity to promote debt donations by private commercial banks into local currency debt-for-nature or debt-for-development funds established by non-governmental organizations in the debtor countries, especially in the context of debt restructuring negotiations.

## RECOMMENDATION

The Department of the Treasury should promote debt-for-nature and debt-for-development funds by working with the independent bodies which affect the rules for debt transfer, such as the Financial Accounting Standards Board and the Securities and Exchange Commission. The Treasury should impress upon them the national importance of rulings which favor bank donations of debt into such funds.

• The Financial Accounting Standards Board (FASB) is an independent, private board of accountants which develops the rules used by accountants to perform corporate audits. The Securities and Exchange Commission (SEC) similarly issues rules for public disclosure by corporations. Their rules currently discourage commercial banks from donating debt into debt-for-conservation funds.

• If repayment by the borrower, in the form of local currency placed in a local conservation fund, were to be considered repayment of the debt under FASB and SEC rules, this would greatly encourage participation in such exchanges by commercial banks.

• While the executive branch has authority over neither the SEC (except for appointing the Commissioners) nor the FASB, the influence of the Secretary of the Treasury can be persuasive on both if the argument is fairly presented.

**Blueprint for the Environment**

## MULTILATERAL LENDING

# DEPARTMENT OF THE TREASURY
## ASSISTANT SECRETARY for International Affairs
## Office of Multilateral Development Banks

### RECOMMENDATION
**The Secretary of the Treasury should combat global climate disruption and prevent adverse environmental impacts of energy megaprojects by reorienting current energy lending by the multilateral development banks.**

- The World Bank and the other Multi-Lateral Development banks (MDBs) have emphasized the financing of large energy projects at the expense of investments in energy conservation, end-use efficiency, renewable energy sources, and the dissemination of new energy-efficient technologies. The type of projects financed by these institutions in the past, such as large hydroelectric dams, have caused severe environmental problems in the countries in which they are located. In addition, bank loans to the energy sector have failed to address the growing contribution that developing countries make to global climate disruption.

- The Secretary of the Treasury should direct U.S. Executive Directors to the MDBs to vigorously encourage the banks to reformulate their energy lending policies to emphasize alternatives along the following lines:

  1) U.S. Executive Directors to each of the MDBs should actively seek the promotion by each institution of least-cost energy planning for borrowing countries, emphasizing energy conservation and energy efficiency projects. The planning process should include a comparison of all costs, including environmental, associated with alternative investments in the energy sector, and give priority to conservation, end-use efficiency and renewable energy investments. The U.S. should indicate that it will vote against energy sector loans that do not contain these provisions.

  2) The U.S. Executive Directors should urge the MDBs to use their leverage to encourage macroeconomic reforms in the developing countries, such as electricity pricing, that facilitate energy conservation and increased end-use efficiency.

- The Department of the Treasury, in consultation with the Department of Energy (DOE) should advocate the following reforms:

  Apply integrated least-cost planning principles to energy planning and lending activities.

  Provide substantial financing for improving the efficiency of energy use and conservation where technically and economically feasible.

  Provide technical assistance for establishing and implementing conservation and efficiency programs.

  Provide support for policies within developing countries that encourage conservation and efficiency improvements-pricing and taxation policies which reflect the real costs of energy, standards and labeling policies to help overcome market imperfections, for example.

- U.S. representatives should also try to convince other funders to take the same position.

# BUDGET RECOMMENDATION

## PRINCIPAL AUTHORIZING LEGISLATION

International Financial Institutions Act, 22 U.S.C. 262 and following, and recent amendments codified at 22 U.S.C. 283.290

## CONGRESSIONAL JURISDICTION

### House Authorizing Committee/Subcommittee
Committee on Banking Finance and Urban Affairs
Subcommittee on International Development Institutions and Finance
### Senate Authorizing Committee/Subcommittee
Committee on Foreign Relations
Subcommittee on International Economic Policy, Trade, Oceans and Environment
### House Appropriations Subcommittee
Subcommittee on Foreign Operations, Export Financing and Related Programs
### Senate Appropriations Subcommittee
Subcommittee on Foreign Operations

## RELEVANT STUDIES

Sierra Club publication, "Bankrolling Disasters."
Annual Treasury Department Reports on the environmental performance of the multilateral development banks, dated May 1, 1986; February 17, 1987 and February 5, 1988
U.N. World Commission on Environment and Development Report, **Our Common Future**
World Bank's Annual Report 1987

## RELATED FEDERAL PROGRAMS

U.S. AID Early Warning System
Department of State, Bureau of Oceans and International Environmental and Scientific Affairs

## PRINCIPAL SOURCES OF EXPERTISE

National Wildlife Federation — 202-797-6602
Sierra Club — 202-547-1141
Natural Resources Defense Council — 202-783-7800
Environmental Policy Institute — 202-544-2600
Rainforest Action Network — 415-788-3666
Greenpeace — 202-462-1177
Environmental Defense Fund — 202-387-3500

## IMPLEMENTATION STEPS

(1) Within two years, the U.S. Executive Directors should indicate that they will oppose all loans for large dams and the upgrading or construction of new fossil-fuel fired plants, that do not meet the criteria of least cost planning outlined above.
(2) The Department of the Treasury, and the U.S. Executive Directors to the MDBs, should solicit the support of other donor and borrowing countries for a reorientation of the banks' energy sector lending programs away from costly large-scale projects to the energy alternative investments outlined above.
(3) The U.S. executive Directors should encourage MDB staff to monitor the development of new conservation and energy efficiency technologies, fund research into such technologies and mechanisms for applying them in the developing countries.

## NOTES:

## Blueprint for the Environment

# Blueprint for the Environment

## MULTILATERAL LENDING

# DEPARTMENT OF THE TREASURY

**RECOMMENDATION**
**The Secretary of the Treasury should direct implementation of Multilateral Development Bank environmental reform provisions enacted into law as part of the FY 86, FY 87, FY 88 and FY 89 foreign aid appropriations bills, and the 1988 MDB reauthorization.**

• The Secretary of the Treasury should work to promote environmental reform within the MDBs and the International Monetary Fund (IMF), and the promotion of environmentally beneficial loans. Some of the more important reforms are:
   1) An increase in environmentally trained staff in all of the MDBs.
   2) Increased public consultation during the selection, design and implementation of Bank loans.
   3) Financing of environmentally beneficial projects.
   4) Increased public access to information on Bank loans.
   5) Adequate consultation with environmental and health ministers in the borrowing countries.
   6) Adoption of environmental impact assessment procedures.
   7) Adoption and implementation of voting guidelines dealing with loans that affect tropical rainforests and wetlands, and development of other guidelines relating to marine ecosystems, impoundments of large rivers, and loans for energy production.

**RECOMMENDATION**
**The Secretary of the Treasury should direct implementation of multilateral development bank environmental impact assessment provisions adopted by the Congress in 1987 (and possibly in 1988).**

• Though the Treasury Department is charged with reviewing the environmental aspects of multilateral development banks projects prior to U.S. votes on these projects, they do not usually have adequate information that enables them to make a proper assessment of these projects. The Banks which finance these projects should, ideally, provide this information to the Department of the Treasury, but they do not conduct a systematic environmental assessment of projects. Furthermore, the major elements of the National Environmental Policy Act process that we follow in this country, especially with respect to public participation, are not included in the banks' assessments.

• The U.S. should announce to the banks that after a reasonable time period the U.S. will not vote in favor of development projects which have an impact on the environment unless an environmental assessment is provided by the banks at least 120 days prior to the vote. Further, this information must be available to non-governmental organizations in the United States and in the borrowing country during this time period.
• The U.S. government should provide personnel and technical expertise necessary for the MDBs to both consider, and adopt, systematic environmental assessment procedures.

# RECOMMENDATION

**The Secretary of the Treasury and the Administration should direct the U.S. Executive Directors to the multilateral development banks to vigorously encourage these banks to reject projects that unnecessarily destroy moist tropical forests and to adopt planning procedures that seek to protect tropical rainforests, their rich biological diversity, and the services and functions they provide for developing nations.**

• The activities of the multilateral development banks (MDBs) of which the United States is a member — the World Bank and the Inter-American, Asian and African Development Banks — have major impacts on international tropical moist forests. These banks provide over $25 billion each year for financing development projects. The effects of these massive financial inputs are magnified still further because funds provided by the banks are commonly supplemented by matching or co-financing and often are spent in such high-leverage areas as planning, training, research, institution-building, and technology transfer. In addition, many nations directly modify their development policies to meet the banks' priorities.

• The Department of the Treasury in April of 1988 promulgated special voting instructions directing United States representatives to the MDBs to oppose projects that will destroy tropical moist forests. The standards contain strict criteria that development projects must meet before they will receive the support of the United States Government. The Secretary of the Treasury at the first opportunity should reaffirm these standards. The Department of the Treasury should actively engage MDB staff to give much higher priority to tropical forest conservation and management.

# RECOMMENDATION

**The Secretary of the Treasury and the Administration should direct the U.S. Executive Directors to the multilateral development banks to vigorously encourage these banks to reject projects that unnecessarily destroy wetlands and to adopt planning procedures that seek to protect wetlands and the services and functions they provide for developing nations.**

# RECOMMENDATION

**The Secretary of the Treasury should direct the United States Executive Directors to the Multi-Lateral Development Banks to vote for emphasis of non-motorized transportation projects in transport and urban development lending. In addition, the Secretary should request that the World Bank and other lending agencies prepare a Transportation Impact Assessment for each project with major transportation lending components.**

# RECOMMENDATION

**The Secretary of the Treasury, as a complement to debt relief, should promote environmentally sustainable development by making low-cost funding available through the multi-lateral development banks for developing countries to invest in long-term programs for conservation and management of their natural resources. New legislation and international agreement may be required.**

## TAX POLICY

# DEPARTMENT OF THE TREASURY

**RECOMMENDATION**

**The Secretary of Energy and the Secretary of the Treasury should work together to develop and support legislation to enact a $.10 cent per gallon tax increase on gasoline and diesel fuel in each year of a 10-year period. Ten percent of this revenue should be designated for low-income needs.**

• This tax is intended to reduce the consumption of motor fuels in order to reduce the emission of carbon dioxide and local and regional air pollutants.

• Vehicle fuel economy ranks first in priority for reducing imported oil. Cars and light trucks require one-third of all U.S. oil, a volume equal to imports. It also ranks as a top environmental priority — cars and light trucks produce one-fifth of all U.S. carbon emissions. And though the fuel economy of cars has improved since the 1973 oil crisis, fuel economy can be cost-effectively doubled with existing technology. Unfortunately, fuel economy standards, proposed elsewhere by Project Blueprint, cannot work alone. Price incentives must be used to complement regulatory policy, or else consumers will not be interested in buying fuel-efficient cars.

• The market price for imported oil does not reflect its true cost to the U.S. economy. Some studies estimate that national security costs roughly amount to $10 per barrel. The costs of air pollution and the risks of climate change from using oil make the true cost even higher. Logically, one would assume that these costs should be internalized through a tax on oil regardless of where it is used in the economy. Practically, however, a tax on transportation fuels would be more workable. The potential for increasing the efficiency of oil use in the transportation sector is large. Taxes on transportation fuels would cause fewer problems for competitiveness and employment than taxes in other sectors. Moreover, the collection mechanism is already in place for a road fuels tax.

**RECOMMENDATION**

**The Department of the Treasury should both encourage the production and sale of very highly efficient new cars and light trucks by providing rebates, and discourage inefficient vehicles by imposing an excise tax in order to reduce greenhouse gas and air pollutant emissions.**

• Fuels taxes and fuel economy standards would effectively raise average fuel efficiency, but would not address two important problems. The first is the continued large-scale production of very inefficient cars — gas guzzlers — and

the second is the need to encourage the production of highly efficient cars. A gas-guzzler tax would address the first problem; a rebate mechanism would address the second.

257

# RECOMMENDATION
**The Secretary of the Treasury should recommend amendments to the federal tax code to tax employer-provided parking and exempt employer-provided support for mass-transit and vanpool users.**

• Employer-provided free parking is estimated to be available to 75 percent of the nation's automobile commuters. This fringe benefit is specifically excluded from being taxed (Internal Revenue Code Section 132, 1.132-5T(p). Free parking is considered to be a "working condition fringe benefit." In cities like New York, this is a tax-free fringe benefit worth $200—$400/month. Yet, transit passes worth more than $15/month or employer-provided vanpools are considered to be taxable fringe benefits.

• Free parking is considered to be the most powerful incentive for commuters to drive alone to work. A study in downtown Los Angeles showed that about 78 percent of those whose employers provided free parking drove alone to work. Of those who had to pay $40 or more/month for parking, only 53 percent drove alone. Eliminating this current inequity in the tax code would encourage commuters to seek alternatives to driving alone (carpooling/vanpooling and mass transit) and help alleviate growing congestion. It will also help urban areas achieve federal air quality standards (auto emission being the leading cause of non-attainment) by encouraging greater use of alternatives to single-occupant work trips; to reduce U.S. consumption of non-renewable oil supplies and growing U.S. dependence on foreign oil.

• The Secretary of the Treasury should recommend amendments to the federal tax code to tax employer-provided parking worth more than some dollar level (i.e., $50, $75, $100) per month and increase the tax-exempt portion of employer-provided transit passes to parity with free parking and exempt employer-provided vanpools (typically worth $0-$50/month).

# RECOMMENDATION
**The Assistant Secretary for Tax Policy should eliminate interest deductions on second home mortgages for new structures in environmentally sensitive areas to be consistent with other federal and state programs to conserve wetlands, coastal barriers, riparian and wilderness areas.**

• Many second homes are located in environmentally sensitive areas such as along mountain streams or on coastal barrier islands. The existing Internal Revenue Code which allows deductions for interest paid on mortgages on second homes provides subsidies and incentives for increased development and ownership of vacation homes.

• This prodevelopment provision is inconsistent with other federal programs to conserve wetlands and coastal barriers. For example, the Coastal Barrier Resources Act of 1982 prohibits federal expenditures to promote growth and development within the Coastal Barrier Resources System (CBRS). A Department of the Interior draft report to Congress states, "[M]uch of the intensive construction presently occurring, or that may occur, with the CBRS units appears to be directly subsidized by the existing provisions of the [Internal Revenue] Code."

• Assuming that the average new second home mortgage will be $50,000 with interest at 10 percent or $5,000 per year, that 80,000 new second home mortgages are issued, and that the marginal tax rate is 28 percent, the net revenue for 1990 would be $112 million. Even though the elimination of the second home interest deduction might reduce the issuance of new mortgages and the building of new second homes, the net increase in revenue could amount to $500 million by 1995.

• The elimination of the second home mortgage interest deduction is unlikely to affect low-income taxpayers because they cannot afford to own vacation homes and their marginal tax bracket is only 15 percent.

# Blueprint for the Environment

## PUBLIC PARTICIPATION

## DEPARTMENT OF THE TREASURY
### Internal Revenue Service

### RECOMMENDATION

**The Commissioner of the Internal Revenue Service should increase opportunities for attorneys in private practice to represent plaintiffs in environmental lawsuits by rejecting Revenue Ruling 76-5.**

• Revenue Ruling 76-5, I.R.B. 1976—1,12 also holds that a public interest law firm (PILF) will be denied exemption if it enters into a fee sharing agreement with a private attorney who reserves the right to retain court ordered attorney's fees in excess of the amount the PILF has paid him for services rendered in that case.

• The rationale for this ruling is not clear but the effect has been to limit the number of private practitioners willing to bring environmental lawsuits by prohibiting PILF's agreeing to pay the out-of-pocket and overhead costs of an attorney willing to represent it in a case where , if successful, it would be entitled to recover attorney's fees because it cannot agree to allow an outside attorney to whom pays a minimal hourly rate to retain any of the fees.

• The ruling discourages individual private practitioners and small law firms from representing environmental plaintiffs. Many single practitioners or small law firms simply cannot afford to handle a case without receiving some compensation. On the other hand, many groups cannot afford to pay individual practitioners or small law firms their usual hourly rates.

• A reasonable compromise would be for the environmental group to provide a minimal hourly compensation to the attorney to cover his office expenses as well as out-of-pocket expenses and allow him to apply for and retain any attorney's fees awarded by the court if the action is successful. The rejection of Revenue Ruling 76-5 could substantially increase the number of attorneys willing to represent environmental groups and considerably expand enforcement of environmental laws.

### RECOMMENDATION

**The Commissioner of the Internal Revenue Service should preserve the ability of conservation groups, which are exempt from Federal Income Taxation under Section 501(c) (3) of the Internal Revenue Code, to participate in the confirmation of nonelected government officials.**

• Until recently, a large number of charitable organizations had believed that participation in the confirmation of appointed government officials did not constitute either lobbying for purposes of Section 501(c) (3), Section 501(h) or Section 4911 of the Internal Revenue Code. They also believed that these expenditures were not taxable expenditures under Section 527(f). However, the Internal Revenue Service has recently announced that attempts to influence the confirmation of judges and appointed officials constitutes both lobbying for purposes of Sections 501(c)(3), 501(h) and 4911 and political expenditures under Section 527(f). Since the confirmation of an appointed official belongs to the Senate only, these are not really legislative matters and should not be treated as lobbying. Anyone having relevant information regarding the qualifications of someone to serve in public office should be encouraged, not discouraged, to come forward with that information.

• The application of Section 527(f) not only discourages participation but will produce an anomaly in that a charitable organization with no investment income could participate in the confirmation process without being taxed as the tax is assessed against the lesser of the amount expended by the organization or its investment income, while a charity with investment income would be taxed. This does not make sense. If the problem cannot be resolved administratively, it should be resolved by a change in the law.

## RECOMMENDATION
**The Commissioner of the Internal Revenue Service should preserve the ability of conservation groups, which are exempt from Federal Income Taxation under Section 501(c) (3) of the Internal Revenue Code, to participate in the legislative process.**

• The Internal Revenue Service should reject proposed regulations designed to limit lobbying by 501(c) (3) organizations and instead promulgate regulations which would maximize the ability of charitable organizations to participate fully in the legislative process. In 1976, the Internal Revenue Code was amended by the addition of Sections 501(h) and 4911, which allowed certain charities the right to elect to be treated under new provisions of the Internal Revenue Code which defined and limited their lobbying expenditures. In late 1986, the Internal Revenue Service proposed regulations which would, if implemented, have severely limited the amount of lobbying that 501(c) (3) organizations could do. This is contrary to the spirit and intent of the law which was intended to quantify but also liberalize the extent to which charities can participate in the legislative process. Efforts to constrict participation in the governmental process should be rejected in favor of a new set of regulations designed to provide reasonable guidance to charities on what they can and cannot do while maximizing their opportunity to participate in the governmental process.

**BUDGET RECOMMENDATION**
F.Y. 90: **no change**          F.Y. 91: **no change**

## PRINCIPAL AUTHORIZING LEGISLATION
Internal Revenue Code

## CONGRESSIONAL JURISDICTION
**House Authorizing Committee/Subcommittee**
Committee on Ways and Means
Subcommittee on Oversight
**Senate Authorizing Committee/Subcommittee**
Committee on Finance
Subcommittee on Private Retirement Plans and Oversight of the Internal Revenue Service
**House Appropriations Subcommittee**
Subcommittee on Treasury, Postal Service and General Government
**Senate Appropriations Subcommittee**
Subcommittee on Treasury, Postal Service and General Government

## RELEVANT STUDIES
None

## RELATED FEDERAL PROGRAMS
None

## PRINCIPAL SOURCES OF EXPERTISE
National Wildlife Federation — 202-797-6650     Sierra Club — 202-547-1141

—————— **Blueprint for the Environment** ——————

# Blueprint for the Environment

## ENVIRONMENTAL PROTECTION AGENCY

The next ten years present environmental challenges far greater than any we have faced in the past. The decisions and the policies we formulate will determine the quality of life in this country, and in the rest of the world for hundreds of years. The onerous burden placed by industrial societies on world resources is being duplicated by the less developed countries in their attempt to sustain ever-increasing populations and ever-increasing debt. Scientific consensus continues to form around the notion that the average temperature of our planet is increasing, causing not only uncomfortable summers, but a radically different agricultural future. The depletion of stratospheric ozone has been addressed in an international manner and more severe bans on such chemicals as chlorofluorocarbons are likely in the near future. The burden that we are placing on our fertile lands by the ever increasing use of pesticides could have grave consequences not only for future agricultural production but in the pollution of essential water supplies. Our oceans continue to be a dumping ground for a vast array of industrial refuse threatening to destroy the last reservoir of available protein to an ever-increasing population.

Blueprint For The Environment is an attempt to give direction to the next Administration to come to grips with environmental concerns. What is needed at the Environmental Protection Agency is a leader who can take the many pieces of this Blueprint and create a program for all facets of environmental policy.

New leadership must bring an understanding to the American people of the extent and seriousness of environmental issues. This vital leadership must be supported by resources both human and material to enable the agency to implement its mandate. New leadership must be vigorous in its enforcement of existing environmental law, and should be seeking new Congressional mandates. Under this leadership the Agency must reach out to the people most directly affected by environmental health concerns. More must be spent on education about the consequences of environmental pollution, so that the Environmental Protection Agency is once again viewed by the American people as an agency that is actively protecting their health and their heritage.

We need to recognize the interdependence and integration of environmental issues. The complexity of interrelated effects cannot be ignored. We must seek ways to limit to the greatest extent possible the flow of waste from our industrial processes. We must apply our technological sophistication to reduce our consumption of energy resources. We must apply our scientific research to discover more benign ways of producing adequate food supplies for our ever-increasing world population. The next Administrator of the Environmental Protection Agency, and the Administration in which he or she serves, will have to view environmental issues as international problems. From the concern that our Canadian neighbors share with us over acid rain, to the planet-wide problem of global warming, a more coordinated approach must be taken with other nations.

The two areas in American environmental policy that continue to be of immediate concern are air pollution and the clean up of toxic waste. Although we have made progress in cleaning up our nation's air, the fact remains that over 100 million Americans live in areas that do not meet the health-based standards for ozone or carbon monoxide. Acid rain has already damaged many lakes and streams and has the potential to damage severely our vital forest resources. Hazardous air pollutants have never been dealt with by an effective regulatory program, and the people who live in the vicinity of these facilities continue to be exposed to cancer-causing air pollutants. The next Administration must vigorously push for legislation that addresses the environmental and public health concerns caused by air pollution.

We must also move forward with the current Superfund program. The Congress has given a mandate and funding to the Environmental Protection Agency for the cleanup of toxic waste. However, the program remains bogged down and unable to expedite the removal of these toxic pollutants from our communities. The Agency must have a vigorous enforcement program to assure that the responsible parties at these sites will clean up. The Agency must also explore innovative methodologies that allow for a greater standardization of the clean-up process, thus expediting the vast number of remaining clean-ups.

The new Administration is going to face the herculean task of the clean up of federal facilities. The legacy the Department of Defense and the Department of Energy have left as a result of our nuclear weapons program is a serious threat to our public health. The Environmental Protection Agency must have a greater role in overseeing not only the cleanup of these facilities, but in setting and maintaining standards that will ensure that we do not let this happen in the future.

The new Administration will have to come to grips with the growing concern over the quality of our nation's groundwater. The damage that has been done by pesticides and industrial pollution will be costly to rectify.

In 1970, Earth Day brought into focus for the first time for most Americans the damage that we were doing to ourselves and our environment. Since that time, we have created a web of rules and regulations to protect public health and the health of the environment that supports us. We need to return to the spirit and action released on Earth Day. The problems that we have created we can rectify. We must move away from the attitude that treats environmental concerns as vague, esoteric, legal problems and deal with them as they really are. If we do not cooperate in curbing pollution, energy consumption, and population pressure, then the world will be greatly diminished, and our stewardship will have failed. We must move quickly and deliberately. If we do, we may yet achieve a balance in which we do not merely survive, but grow. Blueprint For The Environment specifies the steps needed at the Environmental Protection Agency to help establish that balance.

# Blueprint for the Environment

## INTERNATIONAL LEADERSHIP

# ENVIRONMENTAL PROTECTION AGENCY
## ASSOCIATE ADMINISTRATOR for International Activities
## Office of International Affairs

### RECOMMENDATION
**The Associate Administrator for International Activities should propose legislation giving the Agency a mandate to engage in international activities, defining its international mission and authorizing funds for this purpose.**

• The Environmental Protection Agency's (EPA) international activities are of great importance as EPA is called on to play a leading role on global issues like ozone depletion and global warming. EPA's Office of International Activities can be a highly effective part of the Agency, providing essential international expertise and contacts.

• At present, however, the Office has no congressional mandate and receives little congressional oversight. It has no line-item budget and is understaffed and underfunded. When past Administrators have shown little personal interest in international matters, the Office has lan-

guished, with unfortunate consequences for important U.S. interests.

• The Administrator should correct this situation by proposing legislation to give the Office a specific congressional mandate and budget authorization. Inter alia, this legislation should provide EPA with authority to work more closely with other federal agencies, including State, Agency for International Development, and Treasury to assure that development projects funded through the multilateral development banks receive effective advance environmental review.

### RECOMMENDATION
**The Administrator of the Environmental Protection Agency should request additional resources for the Office of International Activities as part of the Fiscal Year 90 budget.**

## BUDGET RECOMMENDATION
See separate recommendation on FY 90 budget request for OIA

## PRINCIPAL AUTHORIZING LEGISLATION
None (EPA was created through a reorganization)

## CONGRESSIONAL JURISDICTION
**House Authorizing Committee/Subcommittee**
Committee on Public Works and Transportation
**Senate Authorizing Committee/Subcommittee**
Committee on Environment and Public Works
**House Appropriations Subcommittee**
Subcommittee on HUD — Independent Agencies
**Senate Appropriations Subcommittee**
Subcommittee on HUD — Independent Agencies

## RELEVANT STUDIES
**"Unfinished Business: A Comparative Assessment of Environmental Problems,"** (Washington, D.C.: EPA, Feb. 1987)

## RELATED FEDERAL PROGRAMS
State Department Bureau of Oceans, Environment and Science

## PRINCIPAL SOURCES OF EXPERTISE
Natural Resources Defense Council (T.B. Stoel, Jr.) — 202-783-7800
Environmental Policy Institute — 202-544-2600

## BUDGET HISTORY (in millions of dollars by fiscal year)

|             | 87     | 88     | 89     |
|-------------|--------|--------|--------|
| Requested   |        |        | 1.4406 |
| Appropriated | 1.2749 | 1.3156 |        |

## MANPOWER HISTORY (in F.T.E.'s by fiscal year)

|        | 88   | 89   |
|--------|------|------|
| Actual | 21.5 | 21.5 |

# Blueprint for the Environment

## INTERNATIONAL LEADERSHIP

# ENVIRONMENTAL PROTECTION AGENCY

## RECOMMENDATION

**The United States should lend its full support and active assistance to the ongoing radioactive risk assessment studies that are being carried out under the auspices of the London Dumping Convention, while also continuing to honor and encourage all other nations to abide by the indefinite moratorium on radioactive waste dumping at sea that was agreed to by the London Dumping Convention treaty parties in 1985.**

• The London Dumping Convention (LDC) is the only global agreement concerned solely with the disposal of wastes in the marine environment by dumping. Since 1983, the LDC parties have devoted substantial time to addressing the question of whether low-level radioactive wastes should be dumped at sea. The U.S. dumped such wastes at sea between 1946—1970, and several European countries continued to do so until 1983. While the U.S. delegation voted against the 1983 two-year moratorium, and the 1985 indefinite moratorium, both of which were adopted with the sup-

port of a strong majority of the treaty parties, the U.S. delegations to the 1986 LDC meeting, and subsequent special intersessional meetings, have exhibited a much more constructive, participatory role in addressing the comprehensive risk-related studies mandated under the indefinite moratorium. That role needs to be continued and strengthened.

(While the Environmental Protection Agency is the lead on this issue, the same substantive recommendation is being presented to the Department of State)

## RECOMMENDATION

**The Administrator of the Environmental Protection Agency should encourage the United States delegation to London Dumping Convention meetings to resist any efforts to abandon or diminish the use of "black list" and "grey list" emissions control annexes, and treat other criteria for regulating ocean dumping, such as water quality standards, as complementary measures to such annexes.**

• At recent meetings of the London Dumping Convention (LDC) treaty parties, including intersessional gatherings, some individuals, including one or more U.S. officials, have expressed a desire for the LDC parties to consider abandoning, diminishing or relaxing the use of black list/grey list annexes. Those annexes are a foundation of the LDC, and are critical to its success in ensuring effective protection of the marine environment. Under U.S. law, the Ocean Dumping Act and the Clean Water Act appropriately require *both* emissions control-type lists and other environmental quality criteria. Both are needed, and U.S. delegations to LDC meetings should make clear their strong support for continuation and strengthening of both approaches, among others that will ensure protection of the marine environment.

## RECOMMENDATION

The Administrator of the Environmental Protection Agency should give full support to the dominant view of treaty parties within the London Dumping Convention to the effect that seabed burial of high-level radioactive wastes is "dumping" under that Convention, and therefore covered by the London Dumping Convention and prohibited.

• They should require that any efforts to amend the London Dumping Convention (LDC) to permit such activities be grounded in clear and convincing evidence that such high-level radioactive waste (HLW) burial is technically feasible and environmentally acceptable, including a determination that such waste can be effectively isolated from the marine environment.

## RECOMMENDATION

United States officials should take immediate steps to meet with key representatives of other nations in order to achieve widespread acceptance and ratification, by the United States and all other nations, for the 1982 Law of the Sea Convention.

## RECOMMENDATION

The Associate Administrator for International Activities should take immediate steps to ensure closer cooperation between the Environmental Protection Agency and the State Department's Bureau of Oceans and International Environmental and Scientific Affairs.

## RECOMMENDATION

The Administrator of the Environmental Protection Agency should support the legislative and executive authority required to expand and solidify intergovernmental relationships between the Office of International Activities and other federal agencies and departments, in particular the State Department.

## RECOMMENDATION

The Administrator of the Environmental Protection Agency should expand its activities, in cooperation with the U.S. Agency for International Development, to help developing nations solve environmental problems caused by pollution and toxic substances and request adequate funds for this purpose as part of the FY 90 budget.

## RECOMMENDATION

The Administrator of the Environmental Protection Agency should establish a Global Warming Program under his or her own supervision in order to make sure that the Agency plays a leading role in U.S. efforts to minimize global warming.

## RECOMMENDATION

The Administrator of the Environmental Protection Agency should take all actions necessary to ensure effective enforcement of existing laws regulating exports of hazardous wastes and should propose legislation prohibiting such exports except to nations with which we have bilateral agreements.

—————————— Blueprint for the Environment ——————————

## EXTERNAL AFFAIRS

# ENVIRONMENTAL PROTECTION AGENCY

**RECOMMENDATION**
**The Administrator of the Environmental Protection Agency should create a new, fully-funded Office of Sustainable Agriculture within the Agency, which would work to encourage farmers to use integrated pest management, best fertilizer management practices, and other sustainable agriculture techniques.**

• Each year billions of pounds of chemical pesticides and fertilizers are released into the environment, and each year more are used than before. The application of pesticides in large doses can lead to even more pesticide use, as pests develop resistance to the pesticide. Today, crop losses are about the same as they were decades ago, yet we apply far more pesticides than we did in years past.

• Most of these chemicals never reach the target pest or plant, often seeping into groundwater, running off into surface waters, or spreading through the air as volatilized chemicals, drifting spray, or fog. Many are known carcinogens, teratogens, or immunosuppressive agents. However the full panoply of health and ecological effects of the thousands of registered pesticides generally are not known.

• There is no strong voice for reversing the nation's increasing dependence on these agricultural chemicals. Several management techniques have been shown to allow comparable yields of crops with substantially reduced pesticide and fertilizer use, at a lower final cost to the farmer. Unfortunately, federal programs generally go about their business without seriously considering the many realistic and cost-effective alternatives to heavy chemical use.

• A new, high-visibility Office of Sustainable Agriculture should be created at EPA. It should work within EPA, and with farmers and other groups, to encourage the use of integrated pest management and other sustainable agriculture techniques. The new office should be an integral part of all EPA pesticide program decisions to assure that integrated pest management is always considered in pesticide registration and other decisions. It also should work closely with the USDA low-input agriculture research program, and USDA's Cooperative Extension program.

**RECOMMENDATION**
**The Administrator of the Environmental Protection Agency should seek a new agreement with the Council on Environmental Quality to clarify the National Environmental Policy Act responsibilities within the jurisdiction of the Office of Federal Activities.**

• The Environmental Protection Agency's (EPA) Office of Federal Activities (OFA), located under the Assistant Administrator for External Affairs, is responsible for overseeing all of EPA's responsibilities under the National Environmental Policy Act (NEPA). The EPA Administrator is required by law to comment in writing on all draft and final environmental impact statements (EISs), and is also required to send any environmentally unsatisfactory proposals to the Council on Environmental Quality (CEQ) for resolution.

• OFA's NEPA oversight functions and OFA's close links to EPA regional offices are absolutely essential and must be strengthened. EPA should use the NEPA process aggressively to achieve EPA's own statutory missions, as well as broader statutory environmental policies. OFA must assist federal regional staff in preparing EISs and must also assure that adequate environmental protection is addressed in EISs, and is later actually implemented by federal agencies.

## RECOMMENDATION
**The Environmental Protection Agency should require that its agencies or bureaus develop and distribute environmental education programs and materials dealing with all appropriate natural resource related activities of the Environmental Protection Agency.**

• Implicit within the authority of the Federal government with respect to its natural resource programs is the responsibility to consider the wishes of the public relative to the environmental impacts of the recommendations or actions of government agencies.

Citizen involvement can be obtained in a variety of ways including the provision of programs, materials, and technical assistance which give citizens a fundamental understanding of the operation of natural human-altered ecosystems.

## RECOMMENDATION
**The Administrator should establish, as a priority for the Agency, an active technology transfer program to provide for more rapid dissemination of information on how to reduce the pollution resulting from industrial, commercial and federal activity.**

## RECOMMENDATION
**The Environmental Protection Agency should promptly create a Board of prominent experts to develop an "Environmental Seal of Approval" and a review process by which products and production processes may be submitted for evaluation and designation as environmentally friendly. The planned symbol could be applied to products and processes that conserve energy, that can be recycled, that are biodegradable and that do not contribute to the climate warming trend.**

• Since 1978, West Germany has promoted a program called the Environmental Seal of Approval. An independent "Environmental Jury" was appointed for the purpose of reviewing and awarding the seal to products which are manufactured and operate within pre-established environmental criteria. Once selected, manufacturers may use the symbol in their advertising and packaging as an incentive to consumers. Today, more than 1,500 products in approximately 50 categories have been designated as "environmentally friendly," supplying German citizens with important information to help them in their buying decisions. Japan recently followed suit, instituting a program called "Eco-Mark" and now Canada has announced its own award program. It's time for the world's number one consumer nation to follow suit and implement a similar program for the benefit of American citizens and the world environment.

• America's citizens are increasingly aware of the range of environmental issues that face us, but lack an accessible system by which they can implement wise choices in their daily lives as consumers. Advertisement of an Environmental Seal allows consumers to readily identify environmentally benign products.

## Blueprint for the Environment

## ENFORCEMENT

# ENVIRONMENTAL PROTECTION AGENCY

**RECOMMENDATION**

**The Administrator of the Environmental Protection Agency should make implementation of an effective enforcement program one of the agency's highest priorities. The enforcement program should be reorganized, reinvigorated and funded at a higher level than at present to send a strong signal to polluters that compliance with the law is the ultimate objective of the agency.**

• The Environmental Protection Agency's (EPA) enforcement program has suffered from underfunding, poor organization, lack of support within the agency, a confused mission, and low morale. These problems have undermined the agency's capacity and will to enforce the law, which, in turn, has allowed pollution, which otherwise would have been abated, to continue.

• All enforcement functions should be centralized under an Assistant Secretary for Enforcement with clearly defined lines of responsibility and accountability between field enforcement/inspection personnel and that office. Elevating the position of head of the enforcement program to an Assistant Administrator position will underscore the importance of the function within the agency and enhance the program's visibility in the regulated community.

• The enforcement budget and staff should be increased by 20 percent because of the need for new field inspectors, compliance officers, and for improved data collection and management.

• Compliance information under the various pollution control statutes should be collected and managed under a centralized data system. There should be a complete compliance profile for each permittee.

• EPA should increase its use of criminal sanctions, and toward that end should continue to improve its working relationships with both federal and state law enforcement agencies.

• The job qualifications and pay for inspectors should be increased and appropriate training provided with respect to evidence gathering and witness interrogation.

• EPA should negotiate protocols with the several states providing for lead enforcement authority. EPA should provide technical assistance to the states to enhance the states' enforcement capabilities. If a state does not enforce against a violation that presents a risk of significant harm to the public health or the natural environment within 10 days from date of discovery, or, in the case of a violation that does not create such a risk within 30 days from date of discovery, then EPA should initiate an enforcement action.

**RECOMMENDATION**

**The Environmental Protection Agency should place a high priority on improving the enforcement of the Safe Drinking Water Act, seek full funding to assure federal and state enforcement and initiate an overhaul of the enforcement policies and procedures for the law.**

• Each year, there are tens of thousands of violations of the Safe Drinking Water Act's (SDWA) health-based drinking water standards and the requirements to test for pollutants in drinking water. Over 37 million people are affected by these violations and, according to Environmental Protection Agency (EPA) data, many people have become ill in the last decade from drinking polluted water. The actual number of illnesses may be many times the known number, and many cancer and other chronic disease cases probably will never be linked to the polluted drinking water that has caused them.

• Despite this startling record of noncompliance, EPA and state enforcement of the SDWA has been virtually nonexistent. States have taken the legally required enforcement action against a tiny fraction of the violating water suppliers. EPA, which is required to enforce when the states do not, enforces in very few cases in which the states have failed to do so. Even what the EPA views as the worst violators — the "Significant Non-Compliers" — are enforced against only a third of the time. Moreover, the statutory requirement that the public served water from a violating public water supplier must be notified of the violation, often is ignored.

• This record results from a lack of EPA headquarters and regional office commitment to quickly enforce where states do not, from EPA policies that may violate the law, and from shockingly inadequate EPA resources. In FY 1988, less than one percent of EPA's total enforcement budget went to enforcing EPA's drinking water rules. EPA's SDWA enforcement activities and budget must be substantially increased.

## RECOMMENDATION
**The Assistant Administrator for Air should support an amendment to the Clean Air Act to control over 224 toxic air pollutants utilizing Best Available Control Technology.**

• Controls should be based on impact to public health and environment including long-range transport. Fifty-eight percent of toxic pollution sources into upper Great Lakes is from atmosphere, while twenty-five percent basin-wide.

## RECOMMENDATION
**The Assistant Administrator for Air should support the strengthening of controls over and the transfer of jurisdiction over Outer Continental Shelf air emission to the Environmental Protection Agency.**

• Currently the Department of the Interior (DOI) has jurisdiction to regulate air emission from Outer Continental Shelf (OCS) facilities. DOI's applicable standards for such emissions are less stringent than those applicable to onshore facilities. In areas offshore California this has led to tremendous friction between the state and local communities, on the one hand, and DOI and the oil companies on the other. Other states such as Florida could also be affected by these weak controls in the future. It makes sense for the Environmental Protection Agency, which has jurisdiction over clean air generally, to have jurisdiction over the OCS and to have a consistent regulatory regime for the OCS and onshore areas.

## Blueprint for the Environment

# Blueprint for the Environment

## RESEARCH

# ENVIRONMENTAL PROTECTION AGENCY

**RECOMMENDATION**

**The President, by either executive order or legislation, should establish a National Ecological Research Center at the Environmental Protection Agency.**

• The Environmental Protection Agency (EPA) needs to provide a central organization where government agencies and academic scientists could conduct research on ecology, ecotoxicology, transport of pollutants and related topics. The primary purpose of this Center would be to conduct and coordinate ecological research.

• Currently, at least a dozen federal agencies are performing some type of ecological research and there is no coordination among the projects, and oversight of these scattered programs remains elusive. The consequence is that some research may be being duplicated while other potential research is ignored or bypassed. Funding priorities may also be skewed as a result of this fragmented approach in the federal government.

• The Administrator of the EPA should urge the President to support such reorganization and consolidation of environmental research programs government-wide under a new National Ecological Research Center.

**RECOMMENDATION**

**The Administrator of the Environmental Protection Agency should support a plan for developing and implementing a coherent research program and consider legislation for a single research mandate for the agency.**

• The Environmental Protection Agency's (EPA) current regulatory and enforcement policies are driven by a set of often-conflicting and contradictory legislative mandates. Research efforts needed to support these disparate laws compete for funding and staff. One result is that many of the agency's research efforts are impeded by obstacles that detract from the long-range mission to protect health and environment. A serious effort must be made to improve coordination of the long and short-term research priorities of the air, water, toxics, and other programs.

• A first step that could be taken to integrate the agency's research would be to establish a new research strategy council composed of an EPA Administrator, the deputy administrator, the Assistant Administrator for Research and Development and the deputy assistant administrator for all program offices. This group would oversee the process of defining core research, especially on long-term cross-media problems that are not now the specific responsibility of any office.

• New emphasis must be placed in this area to develop more comprehensive environmental management programs at EPA. This goal would be aided by the appointment of a distinguished scientist to be the assistant administrator.

• There would be no additional budget needed to accomplish these tasks.

## RECOMMENDATION
**The Administrator of the Environmental Protection Agency should order the creation of a new office — within the Office of Research and Development — to develop procedures for evaluating the ecological effects, and work with the program offices in assessing these effects, for proposed regulatory actions.**

• This office would work with other Environmental Protection Agency (EPA) divisions to improve the Agency's understanding and use of ecological effects research for proposed rulemakings. A separate office to conduct or coordinate ecological effects research would help focus more attention on this area and on its relevancy to regulatory actions. The ecological data developed by this office is intended to serve as the agency's early warning system of future environmental problems. The center should have an office which would work with other ecological divisions in other EPA program offices, and the National Ecological Center as well. Activities of this new office should be coordinated with the proposed National Ecological Research Center.

• The budget for this new activity would be $500,000.

## RECOMMENDATION
**The Administrator of the Environmental Protection Agency should establish a Bureau of Environmental Statistics within the Agency.**

• Current reporting of environmental statistics is erratic, inconsistent across programs and seriously incomplete in coverage. Environmental programs are also in the position of reporting on their own programs using statistics largely of their own choosing — a potential conflict of interest.

• The proposed Bureau of Environmental Statistics would be similar in function to the Bureau of Economic Statistics, Labor Statistics or Justice Statistics and would be independent of the program offices to ensure objectivity. Its purpose would be to develop and maintain an authoritative set of statistics to guide the nation's environmental effort. It would track progress toward defined environmental goals and report its finding consistently and regularly — as is currently done, for instance, for national health, employment, inflation, trade balance and other business statistics. This must be carefully coordinated with other agencies.

• This new office would have two functions. First, it would define statistics that adequately describe environmental goals for both human health protection and environmental improvement, as well as measure progress toward those goals. Existing national standards go part way toward this end, but they are incomplete, particularly in regard to environmental/ecological concerns. Second, the office would support its statistics through improved monitoring programs and collection of pertinent administrative measures. This would involve increased funding for various types of monitoring programs, and technical assistance to other federal agencies to improve the quality and consistency of data. The budget of this new bureau would be $50 million annually.

# Blueprint for the Environment
## AIR QUALITY

## ENVIRONMENTAL PROTECTION AGENCY
### ASSISTANT ADMINISTRATOR for Air and Radiation

**RECOMMENDATION**

**The Environmental Protection Agency should undertake a series of important federal actions in support of the states' efforts to attain healthful air quality standards in urban areas.**

• Seventeen years after the Clean Air Act directed the attainment of healthful air quality in our nation's cities, more than 100 million Americans still live in areas that do not meet federal health standards for ozone "smog" and/or carbon monoxide. In many cities, the summer of 1988 was the most polluted in more than a decade. The Environmental Protection Agency (EPA) has predicted that urban air quality will begin to get worse in the early 1990s unless new pollution control measures for motor vehicles and other sources are adopted, but through the '80s the agency has demanded little in the way of new effort from the auto industry, the nation's cities and states, or the other industries that affect urban air quality.

• If Americans are to have healthful air to breathe in the near future, new pollution control requirements must be legislated, particularly for motor vehicles. However, the present Clean Air Act provides authority for a substantially more effective program. The new Administration should seek new legislation; but in the meantime a great deal can be done under existing law to regain the momentum towards better urban air quality that has been lost in the past eight

years.

• Control of industrial and other "stationary" sources of emissions of volatile organic compounds (VOC), precursors of smog, has lagged, for four reasons:

1) Insufficient federal guidance ("control technique guidance" or CTG) in the technologies available to control industrial processes;

2) Federal failure to adopt control requirements for solvents used in cleaning, painting, home products, and elsewhere;

3) Failure to acknowledge and address the regional nature of the ozone smog problem, leaving many of the sources contributing to polluted air unregulated because of being located outside center cities; and

4) Lack of federal leadership in developing programs to provide polluters with incentives to find or develop ways to reduce emissions. Adopting the recommendations listed in the implementation steps would begin to address these problems.

# BUDGET RECOMMENDATION

## PRINCIPAL AUTHORIZING LEGISLATION
Clean Air Act, Title I, Sections 110 & 111, Part D, Title II

## CONGRESSIONAL JURISDICTION
**House Authorizing Committee/Subcommittee**
Committee on Energy and Commerce
Subcommittee on Health and Environment
**Senate Authorizing Committee/Subcommittee**
Committee on Environment and Public Works
Subcommittee on Environmental Pollution
**House Appropriations Subcommittee**
Subcommittee on HUD — Independent Agencies
**Senate Appropriations Subcommittee**
Subcommittee on HUD — Independent Agencies

## RELEVANT STUDIES
Committee on Environment and Public Works, U.S. Senate, Report No. 100-231, **"Clean Air Standards Attainment Act of 1987"** (S. 1894) Nov. 20, 1987
Doniger, D., **"The Dark Side of the Bubble,"** The Environmental Forum, July, 1985
General Accounting Office, **"Air Pollution: Ozone Attainment Requires Long-Term Solutions to Solve Complex Problems,"** GAO/RCED 87-151 (January 1988)
S. Rep. No. 100-231, 100th Congress, 1st Session (1987)
Walsh, M., **"Pollution on Wheels: The Need for More Stringent Controls on Hydrocarbons and Nitrogen Oxides to Attain Healthy Air Quality Levels Across the U.S., A Report to the American Lung Association,"** February, 1988

## RELATED FEDERAL PROGRAMS

## PRINCIPAL SOURCES OF EXPERTISE
Natural Resources Defense Council — 202-783-7800
American Lung Association — 202-682-5864
Sierra Club — 202-547-1141

## IMPLEMENTATION STEPS
(1) Accelerate the federal CTG process to provide guidance for stationary source control actions by the states. CTGs should be based on the best performance attainable by sources in a category, not the control levels routinely reached by existing sources as has often been the case in the past.
(2) Develop federal level rules under Section 111 for control of emissions from solvent uses such as paint coatings, cleaning and degreasing, traffic striping, and household products.
(3) Repeal federal regulations that permit "bubbling" of existing source emissions within non-attainment areas, and reinstate the "dual definition" of the term "source" for use in new source review in non-attainment areas.
(4) Develop federal guidance for emission "auction" programs at the state level, to be used to achieve the five percent annual reduction in areawide emissions from stationary sources called for above. Where states fail to adopt revised State Implementation Plans (SIPs) within six months, impose an auction scheme.
(5) Develop a federal program in support of the states' efforts to achieve five percent annual reduction in the number of vehicle miles traveled each year (VMT), including, as necessary, legislative proposals.
(6) Develop a federal fuels policy for non-attainment areas, based on a comprehensive assessment of the environmental implications of commitments to alternative fuels such as natural gas, methanol, and ethanol, for use in fleets, personal vehicles, and industrial sources. Such an assessment should evaluate the benefits of alternative fuels for reducing urban ozone, carbon monoxide concentrations, and for curtailing emissions of nitrogen oxides. It should also evaluate the environmental effects on global climate, agriculture, and food supply of commitments to methanol or ethanol as major sources of vehicle fuels.

## Blueprint for the Environment

# Blueprint for the Environment

## AIR QUALITY

# ENVIRONMENTAL PROTECTION AGENCY

**RECOMMENDATION**

**The Environmental Protection Agency should support a reauthorized Clean Air Act program to attain health standards in America's urban areas.**

• With the deadlines having passed for attaining health standards under the present Clean Air Act, the Environmental Protection Agency (EPA)/State Non-attainment program is in a state of disarray. A revitalized Clean Air Act is necessary. A revised non-attainment program should establish new action-forcing deadlines; expand the geographical coverage of control programs; increase the number of federally-mandated control measures applicable in continuing non-attainment areas; and include specific federal control measures for pollution sources that are interstate in nature, such as paints and solvents. Auto emission standards must be tightened, and new requirements put in place that will assure better performance in use. Industrial sources of pollution must be given incentives, such as emission fees or auction systems, to adopt better control techniques.

• EPA should use its existing authority to:
1) Impose a construction moratorium for major sources of volatile organic compounds (VOC), nitrogen oxides, or carbon monoxide in areas that do not meet federal health standards for ozone or carbon monoxide health standards.
2) Use discretionary "sanctions" to induce rapid adoption of additional control measures in areas that fail to meet health standards.
3) Enforce the "sanctions" policies of the Clean Air Act.

**RECOMMENDATION**

**The Environmental Protection Agency should revise the current ozone ("smog") air quality health standard ("primary NAAQS") to (1) prevent adverse effects of short term exposures to pollution levels now known to be unsafe; and (2) provide protection against 6—8 hour exposures to unhealthy levels of ozone now common across the country.**

**RECOMMENDATION**

**The Environmental Protection Agency should undertake a comprehensive revision of its policies with respect to State Implementation Plans.**

**RECOMMENDATION**

**The Environmental Protection Agency should take administrative action to improve the progress in controlling motor vehicle emissions.**

## RECOMMENDATION
The Environmental Protection Agency should immediately submit to Congress aggressive toxic air pollutant control amendments — covering both routine and accidental releases — as part of comprehensive amendments to the Clean Air Act.

## RECOMMENDATION
The Environmental Protection Agency should adopt a regulatory program to address the "regional haze" problem, as called for by the Clean Air Act.

## RECOMMENDATION
The Environmental Protection Agency should initiate a comprehensive program to substantially reduce emissions of sulfur oxides.

• The effects of excessive emissions of sulfur and nitrogen oxides on human health and the environment have continued unabated, despite substantial regulatory authority within the present Clean Air Act. While the next Administration should seek enactment of federal acid rain legislation, the EPA can take steps immediately under present authority that will result in substantial emission reductions.

## RECOMMENDATION
The Environmental Protection Agency should implement the Clean Air Act's transboundary pollution control provision by (1) making a finding required by the Clean Air Act that emissions in the United States are causing pollution in another country; and (2) setting in motion the regulatory program called for in the law.

• The Clean Air Act provides for regulation of pollutants emitted in the United States upon a finding by the Environmental Protection Agency (EPA) Administrator that they are contributing to pollution in another country. Last year the United States Court of Appeals for the D.C. Circuit refused to require the agency to act to curtail $SO_2$ emissions under this provision of the Act, on the grounds that the agency had not made such a finding with respect to the acid rain consequences in Canada of American emissions. This fall, the EPA rejected a petition to make such a finding.

## RECOMMENDATION
The Environmental Protection Agency should revise its stack height regulations to eliminate credit for stack height as a means of attaining air quality standards for plants that have not installed available emission control technology.

## RECOMMENDATION
The Environmental Protection Agency should adopt a short-term primary National Ambient Air Quality (health) standard for sulfur dioxide. Environmental Protection Agency analysts have calculated that a standard at the levels recommended would reduce sulfur dioxide emissions by more than eight million tons. The analysis to support such a standard was completed in 1988, though the agency chose not to adopt a standard at the time.

## Blueprint for the Environment

## RECOMMENDATION

**The Environmental Protection Agency should seek comprehensive acid rain control legislation requiring at least a 12 million ton reduction in sulfur oxides over not more than 10 years, and a reduction in nitrogen oxides of not less than 4 million tons.**

• "Acid rain" has become a household term. The effects of excessive sulfur and nitrogen oxides are felt across the country, not just in the Northeast. Sulfate concentrations are highest in the Midwest, where large populations are exposed. Reputable statistical epidemiological analyses have repeatedly concluded that tens of thousands of Americans die prematurely each year as a result of continuing exposure to excessive sulfate concentrations.

## RECOMMENDATION

**The Environmental Protection Agency should act under existing law and within the first year of the new Administration to list as "hazardous air pollutants" at least 50 acutely and chronically toxic air pollutants that the Agency has failed to control.**

• The new Administration should show that it is serious about reducing airborne exposures to toxic chemicals by listing at least 50 hazardous air pollutants within its first year. The pollutants listed should include both chronically toxic pollutants emitted on a "routine" basis, and acutely toxic, flammable, or explosive compounds released during chemical accidents. EPA should establish a binding schedule for issuing emission control standards for the sources of these pollutants within the Administration's first three years.

## RECOMMENDATION

**The Administrator of the Environmental Protection Agency should (1) immediately issue regulations phasing out U.S. production and use of chlorofluorocarbons and other ozone-depleting chemicals within 5—7 years, and (2) work with the Department of State for an emergency revision of the international treaty on ozone depletion (the "Montreal Protocol") to achieve a worldwide phase-out in the same time period.**

• The Montreal Protocol, signed in 1987, requires a 10-year 50 percent cut in five ozone-destroying chlorofluorocarbons (CFCs). It freezes, but does not cut, three other ozone-depleting chemicals known as halons. On August 1, 1988, the Environmental Protection Agency (EPA) issued rules under the Clean Air Act for U.S. production and use of these chemicals; the rules precisely mirror the requirements of the Protocol. Because of loopholes in the Protocol and the U.S. rules, emissions of ozone depleters will actually be reduced globally by only about one-third.

## RECOMMENDATION

**The Administrator of the Environmental Protection Agency should assure that regulations are developed to provide indoor air quality that protect the health and well-being of building occupants in non-industrial settings (e.g., commercial and public access buildings, residences, and "specialized use" buildings such as schools and hospitals).**

## Blueprint for the Environment

## RECOMMENDATION

The Environmental Protection Agency should complete (by the summer of 1989) the precedent-setting rulemaking on benzene (a known cause of leukemia) by establishing that the "safe" level of exposure to a cancer-causing pollutant is no greater than a one-in-one-million lifetime chance of contracting cancer.

## RECOMMENDATION

The Environmental Protection Agency should revive a dormant proposal (under the Toxic Substances Control Act) to ban all asbestos products, with a view to promulgating a five-year phase-out to begin before the close of 1989.

## RECOMMENDATION

The Environmental Protection Agency should complete the rulemaking to ban lead from gasoline by summer 1989. At the same time EPA should begin expedited proceedings to tighten diesel particulate standards and set health-based standards for formaldehyde emission.

• Banning lead from gasoline has been an issue in the Presidential campaign, with both candidates coming down solidly in favor of phasing lead out entirely as soon as possible.
• Diesel particulate is a major source of particles in the respirable range containing hundreds of toxic byproducts of incomplete combustion. Current regulations do not provide for significant pollution controls on new trucks and buses until the mid-1990s and will permit the occurrence of as many as several hundred cancer cases per year. Tightening control requirements will speed commercialization of the "trap oxidizer" technology for removing particulates, and/or the conversion of diesel engines to cleaner fuels.
• Health-based standards for formaldehyde are necessary for areas that commit to conversion of vehicles to methanol as a fuel. Without new standards, such conversions could expose Americans to greatly increased levels of this cancer-causing pollutant.

## RECOMMENDATION

The Environmental Protection Agency should reorient the existing program away from the resource intensive "chemical-by-chemical" approach and toward consolidated action against logical groupings of toxic pollutants and source categories.

• The agency's commitment to holding individual rulemakings for each potentially-regulated chemical is a major cause of the agency's dismal failure to provide protection for public health against airborne toxics. In many cases, toxicologists can identify families of chemicals with similar effects in the human system, or groups of chemicals that can all be controlled by the same control technology or measure. Regulating chemicals that come from common sources — i.e., by source category rather than by pollutant — would provide greater public health benefits while simultaneously being more economical for EPA and more predictable for industry.

# Blueprint for the Environment

## WATER

# ENVIRONMENTAL PROTECTION AGENCY
## ASSISTANT ADMINISTRATOR for Water
### Office of Marine and Estuarine Protection

## RECOMMENDATION

**The Administrator of the Environmental Protection Agency should eliminate all ocean dumping of sewage sludge and industrial waste; minimize ocean dumping of dredge spoil; and prohibit development of ocean incineration.**

• Ocean dumping is regulated internationally by the London Dumping convention, and domestically by the Marine Protection Research and Sanctuaries Act. Under these laws, ocean dumping is only to be permitted when there are no practical land-based alternatives available for managing the waste. Such alternatives include reduction of waste at the source, recycling, treatment and land disposal. Alternatives exist for managing sewage sludge and all industrial waste that is currently dumped. New forms of ocean dumping (e.g., ocean incineration, sub-seabed disposal) should not be pursued until all options for instituting land-based alternatives have been pursued and exhausted. The U.S. (through the Environmental Protection Agency-led delegation to the London Dumping Convention) should support international efforts to phase out ocean dumping (including ocean incineration) on a worldwide basis.

• The basic steps required are:

1) Deny all pending and future permits for ocean dumping of sewage sludge and industrial waste;

2) Rigorously evaluate environmental acceptability of dredge spoil dumping and require active pursuit of land based alternatives prior to issuing any pending or future permits for dredge material dumping;

3) Continue suspension of ocean incineration program, including incineration of municipal solid waste at sea;

4) Support international efforts to phase out ocean dumping, including ocean incineration on a worldwide basis;

5) Rigorously apply the "needs" requirement to all ocean dumping permit applicants so as to apply a hierarchy of waste management options to encourage recycling and recovery over disposal, whether land or ocean based.

## BUDGET RECOMMENDATION
F.Y. 90: **no change**          F.Y. 91: **no change**

## PRINCIPAL AUTHORIZING LEGISLATION
Marine Protection Research and Sanctuaries Act of 1972, 33 U.S.C. 1401 et seq.

## CONGRESSIONAL JURISDICTION
**House Authorizing Committee/Subcommittee**
   Committee on Merchant Marine and Fisheries
      Subcommittee on Oceanography, Fish and Wildlife and the Environment
**Senate Authorizing Committee/Subcommittee**
   Committee on Environment and Public Works
      Subcommittee on Environmental Protection
**House Appropriations Subcommittee**
   Subcommittee on HUD — Independent Agencies
**Senate Appropriations Subcommittee**
   Subcommittee on HUD — Independent Agencies

## RELEVANT STUDIES
OTA **"Wastes in the Marine Environment"**
Science Advisory Board, **"Report on the Incineration of Liquid Hazardous Wastes,"** April 1988

## RELATED FEDERAL PROGRAMS
EPA's Office of water/OMEP Ocean dumping program

## PRINCIPAL SOURCES OF EXPERTISE
   Oceanic Society — 202-328-0098
   Clean Ocean Action — 201-229-6443
   Coastal Alliance — 202-265-5518

## IMPLEMENTATION STEPS
**The Assistant Administrator for Water should expeditiously develop marine water quality criteria for all 126 "priority pollutants," expand that list to include other potentially harmful metals and organic chemicals and require coastal states to develop water quality standards based on those criteria.**

• Under the Clean Water Act, in addition to setting effluent limitations, the Environmental Protection Agency (EPA) is mandated to publish water quality criteria for individual pollutants which set maximum concentration levels for the individual pollutants in the receiving waters. This approach places controls on pollution sources based on an assessment of the concentrations of pollutants in receiving waters below which unacceptable impacts will not occur. The states are then, with EPA oversight, mandated to develop water quality standards for their waters.
• The implementation of this mandate, however, has been inadequate on both the part of the states and the EPA. While implementation has been relatively effective in fresh-water environments, the majority of coastal states have not developed any water quality standards for the "priority pollutants." Further, EPA's FY 89 budget request only allowed for the development of five to ten new criteria.

## Blueprint for the Environment

# Blueprint for the Environment

## WATER

# ENVIRONMENTAL PROTECTION AGENCY

**RECOMMENDATION**

**The Assistant Administrator for Water should support amendments to the Clean Water Act which would strengthen the Ocean Discharge Criteria (Section 403(c)).**

• Section 403(c) of the Clean Water Act requires that all National Pollution Discharge Elimination System-permitted discharges into the marine environment — seaward of the baselines from which the territorial sea is measured — comply with criteria which specify additional factors that must be considered prior to the granting of a permit for discharging into the ocean. The criteria, however, do not apply to marine waters shoreward of the baseline, i.e., estuaries and bays. The criteria also should be strengthened as noted above. The criteria would apply an extra measure of control on discharges into these waters. Legislation has been introduced to require the application of the ocean discharge criteria to estuaries (H.R. 5081).

**RECOMMENDATION**

**The Administrator should finalize Best Available Technology, Best Conventional Technology and New Source Performance Standards controlling discharges from offshore and coastal oil and gas operations within one year.**

• Offshore and coastal oil and gas operations generate huge quantities of drilling and production waste. This waste, usually discharged into the ocean or coastal areas, contains very substantial amounts of oil, grease, BOD and toxic metals and organics, including cadmium, lead, benzene and naphthalene. The Environmental Protection Agency (EPA) has estimated that the annual loading of benzene, a known carcinogen, to the Gulf of Mexico generated by offshore oil and gas operations could exceed 27 tons.

**RECOMMENDATION**

**The Assistant Administrator for Water should promulgate regulations for sediment quality criteria.**

• Heavy metals and organic chemicals tend to concentrate in marine sediments. Currently, no regulations or standards exist for acceptable levels of pollutants in marine sediments. A sediment quality-based approach would place controls on pollution sources, based on an assessment of the concentrations of pollutants in the receiving sediments below which unacceptable impacts will not occur. Such criteria will be useful in determining if shellfish beds should be closed and in determining acceptable dredge material disposal sites.

## RECOMMENDATION

**The Environmental Protection Agency should seek to establish an Aquafund program either as part of Superfund or as a separate program. It should assess the extent of contaminated sediments in our waterways, prioritize sites, undergo pilot demonstration clean-up programs, and fund full scale clean-up activities utilizing destruction and detoxification technologies.**

• Contaminated sediments and toxic "hot spots" exist in many harbors and waterways around the nation. In these areas, pollutants like PCBs congregate in the sediments and work their way up the food chain to people. Given that our waters can only be as clean as their container, it is imperative that equal attention be given to cleaning up the nations' sediment "hot spots" as well as cleaning up the water column.

## RECOMMENDATION

**The Director of Water Enforcement and Permits should achieve full state compliance with the requirement that States identify and control "toxic hotspots"; should interpret State responsibilities to inclu e developing controls for more toxics and more waterbodies; and should substitute federal program action where states do not comply.**

• The 1987 amendments to the Clean Water Act focused renewed attention on the need to control toxics in those waterbodies where, even after full implementation of technology-based controls on discharges, concentrations of toxics would still exceed levels necessary to protect aquatic life and human health. Section 304(1), added in 1987, requires the States, by 2/4/89, to identify these "toxic hotspots" and to develop control strategies for each such "hotspot" that will achieve compliance with water quality requirements no later that 2/4/92. There are two main areas where the Environmental Protection Agency (EPA) policy needs work: the scope of 304(1), and the comprehensiveness of implementation.

## RECOMMENDATION

**The Director of Water Regulations and Standards should achieve full compliance with the requirement that States promulgate numeric water quality standards for toxics and promulgate federal standards where States do not comply.**

• The 1987 amendments to the Clean Water Act established a firm requirement that States adopt numerical water quality standards for toxics which might be present in their rivers, streams and estuaries. These standards are critical to water quality protection because they set benchmarks for limiting discharges from point sources and nonpoint sources (NPS), and they enable planners to calculate whether enough is being done to protect water quality. Yet, many States have no or virtually no standards for toxics other than a simple (difficult-to-enforce) prohibition.
• Section 303(c) (2) (B) of the newly-amended Act requires States to adopt numerics within three years. The Environmental Protection Agency (EPA) has issued a "draft" guidance document saying that States can get around this requirement by adopting procedures for arriving at the numerics.
• This guidance should be revised before being finalized, to conform to the Act. EPA regional officials should then identify all toxics in each State for which numerics are needed (using contractor assistance, as was done before). EPA should step in to adopt numerics for each State that fails to do so itself within the three-year time frame in the statute.

## Blueprint for the Environment

# Blueprint for the Environment

## WETLANDS

# ENVIRONMENTAL PROTECTION AGENCY
### ASSISTANT ADMINISTRATOR for Water
### Office of Marine and Estuarine Protection

## RECOMMENDATION
**The Assistant Administrator of Water should adopt a "no-net-loss of wetlands policy" and propose legislation to Congress to halt the loss of wetlands in the United States and to make protection of this resource a national priority.**

• Currently, there are several federal laws — regulatory and nonregulatory alike — addressing various elements of wetlands protection. These laws, however, are piecemeal, and have been ineffective in deterring the continued alteration and destruction of wetlands, as evidenced by an estimated loss rate of between 350,000 and 450,000 acres of wetlands per year.

• What is needed to halt the loss of wetlands in the United States is a national wetlands protection statute framing a comprehensive, aggressive and effective national program to protect, restore and create wetlands. The overarching goal of such legislation must be to establish a national policy of "no-net-loss" of wetlands and to establish new programs, regulatory as well as nonregulatory, to provide the starting point for a truly meaningful and effective national wetlands protection policy.

• Using concepts, such as the New Jersey Pine Barrens legislation and the 1988 Mississippi River Greenline Park legislation, that enable strong intervention where necessary to protect vital wetland areas, the federal and state governments must undertake aggressive measures if these unacceptable losses are to be stopped and important wetland functions restored to areas where development has gone too far e.g. the Central Valley of California.

## RECOMMENDATION
**The Administrator of the Environmental Protection Agency should urge the President of the United States to issue a Presidential Executive Order establishing a National Wetlands Policy Council to review and implement an entire array of new and innovative recommendations to protect wetlands and to ensure that wetlands protection is made a national priority.**

• The National Wetlands Policy Council would be convened by the Administrator of the Environmental Protection Agency (EPA) in close consultation with the conservation community and others concerned about protection and restoring the Nation's wetlands. The primary purpose of the Council would be to identify those proposals that offer the greatest opportunity to provide lasting protection for the Nation's wetlands and to work to ensure they are timely and fully implemented. Is is envisioned the Council would be a standing body that would continuously monitor and evaluate federal, state and local government efforts to protect wetlands.

## BUDGET RECOMMENDATION
F.Y. 90: **no change** F.Y. 91: **no change**

## PRINCIPAL AUTHORIZING LEGISLATION
None

## CONGRESSIONAL JURISDICTION
**House Authorizing Committee/Subcommittee**
Committee on Public Works and Transportation
Subcommittee on Water Resources
**Senate Authorizing Committee/Subcommittee**
Committee on Environment and Public Works
Subcommittee on Environmental Protection
**House Appropriations Subcommittee**
Subcommittee on Interior
**Senate Appropriations Subcommittee**
Subcommittee on Interior and Related Agencies

## RELEVANT STUDIES
**GAO Report and Corps-EPA Implementation of Section 404 of the Clean Water Act** (1988)
**Wetlands of the United States: Current Status and Recent Trends** (1984)
**Wetlands: Their Use and Regulation** (1984)
**Protection of America's Wetlands: An Action Agenda** The National Wetlands Policy Forum Report (November 1988)

## RELATED FEDERAL PROGRAMS
All federal programs affecting wetlands, including:
Section 404 of the Clean Water Act
U.S. Department of Agriculture farm programs (Swampbuster, Farmers Home Administration Inventory Lands debt restructuring, 1985 Farm Bill provisions)
U.S. Department of the Interior programs (acquisition, National Wildlife Refuge System)
Department of Commerce programs (National Marine Fisheries Service habitat programs, estuarine programs)
Coastal Zone Management Act
Coastal Barrier Resources Act
Endangered Species Act
Marine Mammal Protection Act

## PRINCIPAL SOURCES OF EXPERTISE
National Wildlife Federation — 202-797-6876
Environmental Defense Fund — 202-387-3500
National Audubon Society — 202-547-9009

## NOTES:

## Blueprint for the Environment

# Blueprint for the Environment

## WETLANDS

# ENVIRONMENTAL PROTECTION AGENCY

**RECOMMENDATION**
**The Environmental Protection Agency should strengthen and clarify the Government's wetlands mitigation policy.**

• Considerable confusion exists over the government's policy on mitigating wetland losses. The Army Corps of Engineers (Corps) has implemented a policy which applied mitigation as a means of avoiding regulatory prohibitions against filling of wetlands. In some Corps Districts, abuses in mitigation banking, unwarranted off-site compensation of wetland losses or compensation of losses with different types of wetlands from those converted have resulted in significant loss of certain types of wetlands (e.g. , seasonal wetlands). A clear, consistent statement of regulatory policies on this topic would add uniformity to the program and prevent future wetland losses through application of an unfavorable wetland mitigation policy.

**RECOMMENDATION**
**The Environmental Protection Agency should develop and support the enactment of generic wetlands legislation.**

• There is no coherent national wetlands policy. Some government programs encourage protection of wetlands (Section 404, wetlands acquisition programs), while others contribute to their destruction (farm and road building subsidies, tax incentives, zoning codes). This causes considerable confusion within the government as well as among affected individuals about the importance of wetland protection compared to other uses of wetlands.

**RECOMMENDATION**
**The Assistant Administrator for Water should enhance enforcement against illegal wetland filling activities by line agencies and the Department of Justice.**

• The Environmental Protection Agency (EPA) should reassume its primary enforcement authority over illegal fills, which it has largely delegated to the Army Corps of Engineers, and should dedicate greater resources to their enforcement program. Under current law and regulatory practice EPA and the Corps share authority for enforcement. EPA is to enforce against illegal fill activities where there is no permit, and the Corps against permit violations.

• In Practice, The EPA defers to the Corps for both types of enforcement activities. The result has been little actual enforcement, few fines and the issuance of "after-the-fact" permits retroactively validating the illegal activity. This situation should be rectified, with the EPA reassuming their burden to enforce against unpermitted violations. However, the EPA needs to augment its 404 enforcement program, by assigning additional resources to the program.

# RECOMMENDATION
**The Assistant Administrator for Water should augment use of the Agency's veto authority under section 404(c) of the Clean Water Act, to withdraw important wetlands from commercial development.**

• The Environmental Protection Agency has the authority to withdraw any site from use as a disposal site for dredged and fill material, if the discharge of that material at that site would have an unacceptable adverse effect on municipal water supplies, shellfish beds and fishery areas (including spawning and breeding areas), wildlife, or recreational areas. The EPA has used this authority sparingly, and generally only after a permit has been issued by the Army Corps of Engineers.

# RECOMMENDATION
**The Administrator of the Environmental Protection Agency should request that all Section 404 Program wetlands authorities of the Clean Water Act be transferred to the Environmental Protection Agency.**

• Presently, Section 404 requirements of the Clean Water Act are jointly administered by the Army Corps of Engineers (Corps) and the Environmental Protection Agency (EPA). In addition, several other agencies, such as the Fish and Wildlife Service, have a consultative role in the process. Not only has this joint-jurisdictional arrangement between the Corps and the EPA frustrated the regulated community, but it has been ineffective in deterring the continued loss of wetlands and has been harshly criticized by the environmental community.

# RECOMMENDATION
**The Assistant Administrator for Water should promulgate biological water quality standards protecting wetlands functions.**

• The Environmental Protection Agency (EPA) should use its authority under sections 303 and 304 of the Clean Water Act (CWA) to encourage states to promulgate water quality standards protecting wetlands. State water quality standards play an important role in protecting waters from pollutants that degrade water quality. A state can block the issuance of a federal permit or license that does not comply with its water quality standards (§401 of the CWA).

# RECOMMENDATION
**The Environmental Protection Agency should address cumulative wetlands losses in individual and general permit applications.**

• The tragedy of wetland losses is that they are occurring in small increments around the country. Entire watersheds may be lost through the fills. Small, incremental losses can profoundly affect wetland hydrology or an ecosystem's biological productivity. The 404 program, as it focuses on issuances of individual permits, has no present mechanism for examining cumulative losses, let alone wetland losses that are not generated by issuance of a 404 permit.

# RECOMMENDATION
**The Assistant Administrator for Water should establish clear wetlands mitigation policy requiring sequencing (avoidance first, compensation last) for all Clean Water Act Section 404 permits, and require full compensation in instances of unavoidable impacts to wetlands.**

## Blueprint for the Environment

# Blueprint for the Environment

## GROUNDWATER

## ENVIRONMENTAL PROTECTION AGENCY
### ASSISTANT ADMINISTRATOR for Water

**RECOMMENDATION**
**The Environmental Protection Agency should advocate the adoption of strong and comprehensive federal legislation designed to protect groundwater BEFORE it becomes polluted, rather than merely focusing, as existing programs do, on cleaning up the pollution after the damage is done.**

• A new, comprehensive federal law is critical. Half of the American public, relies on groundwater for drinking water. Many surface waters that support sensitive aquatic and other species are fed by groundwater. Once groundwater is polluted, it is expensive and difficult — sometimes impossible — to clean up. Serious groundwater pollution has now been documented in every state, often by sources of pollution that are completely unregulated, or regulated inadequately.

• The Environmental Protection Agency (EPA) found that over 52,000 people have become acutely ill or poisoned from drinking polluted groundwater from 1971—1985, and that the actual number of people acutely affected may exceed this figure by twenty-five fold. In addition, untold thousands are affected by hidden diseases such as cancer that cannot be linked to their source due to latency periods and other complicating factors.

• New federal legislation should include requirements for controls of all sources of pollution, should use groundwater standards to assure that the direct source controls are working, and should establish ambitious goals for groundwater protection. States should be required to develop groundwater protection programs, to be approved and overseen by EPA.

**RECOMMENDATION**
**The Environmental Protection Agency should rescind the Agency's Ground Water Strategy (1984), and the implementation guidances based on it, and should replace them with a new rule aimed at protecting all groundwater rather than aimed at "differential protection" of groundwater based on its current or currently-expected uses.**

• After substantial internal debate, the Environmental Protection Agency's (EPA) Office of Ground Water Protection issued a "Ground Water Strategy" in 1984 that urges states and other EPA program offices to classify groundwater into several separate categories. Some groundwater would be classified as too polluted or too unlikely to be used to be worthy of careful protection.

• This policy is unwise and short-sighted. It assumes that we know today what groundwater resources we will need in the future. It ignores the important ecological problems that can be caused when polluted groundwater discharges into sensitive surface water ecosystems. It also incorrectly assumes that we are sufficiently knowledgeable to delineate precisely where the "written off" groundwater will go, and that it will not affect other important water supplies.

## BUDGET RECOMMENDATION

The precise current groundwater research and protection budget unknown; it is not currently a budget line item. Our best estimate of the current research and protection budget is $200 million, most of which is going to research — predominantly focused on existing contamination and cleanup. Our recommended government-wide recommended budget for protection and research is approximately $4 billion per year to be phased in over a few years.

## PRINCIPAL AUTHORIZING LEGISLATION

None

## CONGRESSIONAL JURISDICTION

**House Authorizing Committee/Subcommittee**
Committee on Energy and Commerce
Subcommittee on Health and the Environment
**Senate Authorizing Committee/Subcommittee**
Committee on Environment and Public Works
Subcommittee on Environmental Protection
**House Appropriations Subcommittee**
Subcommittee on HUD — Independent Agencies
**Senate Appropriations Subcommittee**
Subcommittee on HUD — Independent Agencies

## RELEVANT STUDIES

U.S. Geological Survey, National Water Summary 1986 — **Hydrologic Events and Groundwater Quality** (1988)
Office of Technology Assessment, **Protecting the Nation's Groundwater From Contamination** (1984)
National Ground Water Policy Forum and the Conservation Foundation, **Groundwater Protection: Groundwater — Saving the Unseen Resource** (1987)
**Protecting the Nation's Groundwater: A Proposal for Federal Legislation** (June 24, 1988) ( available from the National Wildlife Federation)

## RELATED FEDERAL PROGRAMS

The U.S. Geological Survey has an extensive set of ongoing groundwater research, monitoring and mapping programs

## PRINCIPAL SOURCES OF EXPERTISE

National Wildlife Federation — 202-797-6887
Environmental Policy Institute — 202-544-2600
Environmental Defense Fund — 212-505-2100
Natural Resources Defense Council — 212-949-0049

## IMPLEMENTATION STEPS

(1) Develop an administration position in favor of comprehensive federal groundwater legislation.
(2) Work with key members of Congress and coalitions favoring this legislation to obtain enactment of such a law.

## NOTES:

## Blueprint for the Environment

# Blueprint for the Environment

## GROUNDWATER

## ENVIRONMENTAL PROTECTION AGENCY

**RECOMMENDATION**

**The Environmental Protection Agency should establish a vigorous and coordinated agency-wide research and demonstration program effort to develop groundwater pollution source control technologies and methods, as well as waste and source reduction methods, for all major sources of pollution.**

• The Environmental Protection Agency (EPA) now dedicates a small amount of effort to the development of groundwater cleanup technologies, and to the development of better methods for the control of hazardous waste disposal. Few or no resources are dedicated to research into methods and technologies that can be used to control many other major sources of groundwater contamination.

• Better control technologies are needed for numerous sources of contamination, ranging from above ground storage tanks, to nonhazardous waste containing surface impoundments, to agricultural application of pesticides and fertilizers. The recent creation of an Office of Pollution Prevention at EPA is a sign that the Agency intends to encourage more waste and source reduction. This tiny Office needs more resources: waste and source reduction must be the subject of an ambitious research, demonstration and regulatory effort.

• These new research efforts must be coordinated with ongoing groundwater research at EPA and the U.S. Geological Survey. An annual report should be prepared which informs the EPA, Congress and the public of what research is ongoing, what the results are and what it is costing. In addition, a groundwater information clearinghouse should be created, which would make available the results of the research, and which would provide information to the public about groundwater contamination information available from WATSTORE and other information systems.

**RECOMMENDATION**

**The Environmental Protection Agency should revise its land disposal restrictions regulations for underground injection of hazardous wastes to preclude granting variances where migration of hazardous constituents out of the injection zone is likely to occur.**

• The Environmental Protection Agency's (EPA) land disposal ban regulations (implementing Section 3004(d)-(g) of the Resource Conservation and Recovery Act (RCRA)) contain an open-ended variance from the ban on injection of untreated wastes imposed by the 1984 RCRA amendments. The regulations will allow injection of hazardous wastes where migration of some hazardous constituents out of the injection zone is predicted to occur. Since injection is the principal land disposal method and accounts for sixty percent (over 11 billion gallons per year) of waste disposed, this departure from the law could perpetuate land disposal at the expense of environmentally preferable waste management methods including, treatment, recycling and waste reduction.

289

## RECOMMENDATION

**The Environmental Protection Agency should revise the drinking water rules which exempt all groundwater-supplied public water systems from the national requirement to test for certain contaminants, and from the requirement to disinfect the drinking water they supply.**

• Under the 1986 Safe Drinking Water Act Amendments, the Environmental Protection Agency (EPA) is required to issue drinking water regulations to mandate disinfection of water supplied by all public water systems and to issue rules mandating the removal of six specified disease-causing contaminants or microorganisms. In November, 1987, EPA issued proposed rules which would exempt all groundwater-supplied public water systems from these requirements (upon which half of the American Public depends for their drinking water). Thus, only those people who drink water supplied from surface water are assured protection from these disease-carriers. This exemption is illegal and has no rational basis; it should not be embodied in EPA's final rules, which are projected to be issued in late 1988 or early 1989. The Agency's suggestion that it will get around to requiring disinfection by groundwater-supplied public water systems later is not acceptable.

• In a similar action taken many years earlier, EPA decided to exempt all groundwater-supplied public water systems from any national requirements to test for organic pollutants in drinking water (leaving this to state discretion). EPA also decided to allow these groundwater-supplied systems to monitor for most inorganic pollutants only once every three years, rather than annually as surface-water supplied systems must do.

## RECOMMENDATION

**The Environmental Protection Agency should reinvigorate and seek full funding for the Agency's existing groundwater protection programs. These programs include: the Sole Source Aquifer Program, the Critical Aquifer Protection Area demonstration grant program, the Wellhead Protection Area Program.**

• In the Safe Drinking Water Act and its 1986 Amendments, Congress authorized groundwater protection programs, but funding for these programs has been minimal or nonexistent

• Included in these protection programs is the Sole Source Aquifer (SSA) program, which allows the Environmental Protection Agency (EPA) to designate for protection aquifers that are the sole or principal source of drinking water for an area. This program has been severely underfunded; the rules for the program (proposed in 1977) were never issued as final rules. In addition, SSA designation has been largely ignored by other EPA offices. Thus, all EPA programs should establish special protections for SSAs into their regulatory programs.

• The Critical Aquifer Protection Area (CAPA) program has not been funded since enacted in 1986, but has the potential to show states and local governments creative ways to protect groundwater. In addition, the Wellhead Protection Area (WPA) program also has never been funded, but could, if vigorously implemented and fully funded, enhance groundwater protection around public water supply wells.

• Current EPA guidance and its "Interim Final Rule" for the SSA and CAPA programs must be rescinded. These documents state that an aquifer may not be protected under the two programs if, in theory, water could be piped into the area from elsewhere. This requirement is contrary to the Safe Drinking Water Act (SDWA).

# Blueprint for the Environment

## DRINKING WATER

# ENVIRONMENTAL PROTECTION AGENCY
## ASSISTANT ADMINISTRATOR for Water
## Office of Drinking Water

**RECOMMENDATION**
**The Environmental Protection Agency should place a high priority on improving the enforcement of the Safe Drinking Water Act, seek full funding to assure federal and state enforcement and initiate an overhaul of the enforcement policies and procedures for the law.**

• Each year, there are tens of thousands of violations of the Safe Drinking Water Act's (SDWA) health-based drinking water standards and the requirements to test for pollutants in drinking water. Over 37 million people are affected by these violations and, according to Environmental Protection Agency (EPA) data, many people have become ill in the last decade from drinking polluted water. The actual number of illnesses may be many times the known number, and many cancer and other chronic disease cases probably will never be linked to the polluted drinking water that has caused them.

• Despite this startling record of noncompliance, EPA and state enforcement of the SDWA has been virtually nonexistent. States have taken the legally required enforcement action against a tiny fraction of the violating water suppliers. EPA, which is required to enforce when the states do not, enforces in very few cases in which the states have failed to do so. Even what the EPA views as the worst violators — the "Significant Non-Compliers" — are enforced against only a third of the time. Moreover, the statutory requirement that the public served water from a violating public water supplier must be notified of the violation, often is ignored.

• This record results from a lack of EPA headquarters and regional office commitment to quickly enforce where states do not, from EPA policies that may violate the law, and from shockingly inadequate EPA resources. In FY 1988, less than one percent of EPA's total enforcement budget went to enforcing EPA's drinking water rules. EPA's SDWA enforcement activities and budget must be substantially increased.

291

# BUDGET RECOMMENDATION

**Public Water System (PWS) Enforcement**
F.Y. 90: **Increase** of $ 38 million      F.Y. 91: **no change**  plus a first year special appropriation of
$30 million to deal with the backlog of unaddressed past violations
**Underground Injection Control (UIC) Enforcement Budget**
F.Y. 90: **Increase** of $ 20 million      F.Y. 91: **no change**
**Public Water System Grants to States**
F.Y. 90: **Increase** of $ 25 million      F.Y. 91: **no change**
**Underground Injection Control Grants to States**
F.Y. 90: **Increase** of $ 15 million      F.Y. 91: **no change**

# PRINCIPAL AUTHORIZING LEGISLATION

Safe Drinking Water Act (SDWA)

# CONGRESSIONAL JURISDICTION

**House Authorizing Committee/Subcommittee**
  Committee on Energy and Commerce
    Subcommittee on Health and Environment
**Senate Authorizing Committee/Subcommittee**
  Committee on Environment and Public Works
    Subcommittee on Environmental Protection
**House Appropriations Subcommittee**
  Subcommittee on HUD — Independent Agencies
**Senate Appropriations Subcommittee**
  Subcommittee on HUD — Independent Agencies

# RELEVANT STUDIES

GAO, **States' Compliance Lacking In Meeting Safe Drinking Water Regulations,** GAO/CED-82-43
(1982)
National Wildlife Federation, **Danger on Tap** (1988)

# RELATED FEDERAL PROGRAMS

Indian Health Service        Indian Reservation sanitary drinking water program

# PRINCIPAL SOURCES OF EXPERTISE

National Wildlife Federation — 202-797-6887 Natural Resources Defense Council — 212-949-0049

# IMPLEMENTATION STEPS

(1)  Prepare and vigorously seek adoption of substantial increase in EPA SDWA enforcement budget.
(2)  Immediately overhaul the EPA drinking water enforcement guidances to require swift EPA en-
     forcement action if states have not taken formal enforcement action within the 30 day statutory
     period.
(3)  Overhaul as quickly as possible the EPA and state computer violations and enforcement tracking
     systems to assure that all violations and enforcement are immediately reported, that the public is
     notified of all violations, and that EPA notices of violation are immediately issued to public water
     systems that have violated rules.
(4)  Initiate a high priority program to remedy massive backlog of past violations.
(5)  Develop, on fast track, regulations that enable EPA to limit the availability of an administrative
     hearing for administrative orders to situations in which there is a genuine issue of fact as to
     whether a violation occurred.
(6)  Create a task force to conduct a detailed audit each state's reporting of violations to EPA, and to
     conduct a detailed review of whether each primacy state program meets all EPA requirements,
     including adequacy of enforcement.
(7)  Issue formal notices to states with inadequate enforcement or implementation of EPA's intent to
     rescind the state's primacy if improvements are not made.
(8)  Conduct a detailed review of the adequacy of the public notification rules, to ascertain whether
     the PWSs are issuing the notices in a timely fashion, whether the public is actually aware of the
     violations where notice is issued, and what EPA can do to improve the public notification pro-
     gram.
(9)  Produce the statutorily-required annual report to Congress, explaining why the nation's drinking
     water is at risk and why state and EPA enforcement is inadequate.

# Blueprint for the Environment

## DRINKING WATER

# ENVIRONMENTAL PROTECTION AGENCY

### RECOMMENDATION
**The Administrator should revise The Environmental Protection Agency's policies and rules to assure that "noncommunity" water users are protected.**

• The Safe Drinking Water Act establishes "national primary drinking water standards," which set the highest allowable pollution levels for "public water systems" (PWSs). These PWSs are defined as systems supplying piped water for human consumption to at least 15 service connections, or regularly serving at least 25 individuals. Thus, many smaller water systems, and all private residential wells, are not protected by the national drinking water standards.

• However, the Environmental Protection Agency (EPA) also has adopted rules and policies — without any legal basis — that essentially "write off" over 100,000 water systems that do meet the statutory definition of PWS. Under EPA rules, so-called "noncommunity" PWSs are exempted from complying with most (20 of 23) of EPA's currently enforceable drinking water standards. Noncommunity systems are

PWSs — such as those at many schools, hospitals, factories, seasonal resorts, summer camps, and roadside restaurants — that do not serve "year-round residents;" they are used by millions of Americans.

• EPA rules say that these noncommunity systems need not comply with EPA's standards for inorganic contaminants like arsenic and cadmium, nor with the standards for organic contaminants, like several pesticides. Moreover, the handful of standards for pollutants that "noncommunity" PWSs supposedly do have to control — nitrates, coliform bacteria, and turbidity — are virtually never enforced. In FY 1987, for example, there were thousands of violations by noncommunity systems, yet there was virtually no state or federal enforcement against them. These exemptions and enforcement policies should be revoked.

### RECOMMENDATION
**The Administrator of the Environmental Protection Agency should establish a new program at the Office of Drinking Water with a mandate to protect rural water users, and those who use small or "noncommunity" water systems.**

### RECOMMENDATION
**In setting drinking water standards, the Environmental Protection Agency should factor into the standard the exposure to drinking water those contaminants that can come through skin absorption of the compound or inhalation of vapors while showering, cooking and washing.**

## RECOMMENDATION
**The Environmental Protection Agency should revise its reference standards for drinking water intakes in light of new data indicating these reference standards underestimate actual population drinking water consumption rates.**

• In calculating drinking water standards, the Environmental Protection Agency (EPA) has traditionally used reference standards for drinking water intakes of 0.1 liters/kilogram (L/kg) for the child (or 1 liter per day for the 10 kg child) and 0.03 L/kg for the adult (or 2 liters per day for the 70 kg adult). A preliminary report by the National Cancer Institute (NCI) now indicates that EPA's reference standards may underestimate actual consumption rates for almost a quarter of the adult population as well as a significant number of children.

## RECOMMENDATION
**The Environmental Protection Agency should promulgate a generic drinking water standard of 5 parts per billion for any individual synthetic organic chemical for which it has not set a chemical specific standard.**

• The generic synthetic organic chemical (SOC) standard is needed to protect the public from drinking water contaminants for which individual standards have not been promulgated. Currently, drinking water standards cover only 15 SOCs. The Safe Water Drinking Act (SWDA) 1986 amendments establish statutory deadlines for standards to cover 49 SOCs. These standards will cover only a small portion of the SOCs present in drinking water. In Protecting the Nation's Groundwater From Contamination, the Office of Technology Assessment lists hundreds of SOCs that have been known to occur in groundwater, the drinking water source for half the nation's population. The presence of such contaminants presents a health risk which, although difficult to quantify, should be regulated.

## RECOMMENDATION
**The Environmental Protection Agency should promulgate a total synthetic organic chemical (TSOC) standard of 50 micrograms per liter to protect against exposure to multiple contaminants in drinking water.**

• Drinking water is frequently contaminated with more than one chemical. A total standard is necessary to protect against additive effects or synergistic interactions (which yield a total effect greater than the sum of the effects of either chemical measured independently) which are known to occur with chemical mixtures. The Office of Technology Assessment considers the possibility of interactions between multiple contaminants to be potentially one of the most important health issues in groundwater contamination, the source of drinking water for half the country.

## RECOMMENDATION
**The Environmental Protection Agency should regulate contaminants in drinking water if they have been shown to be carcinogenic by either the inhalation or ingestion.**

## RECOMMENDATION
**The Environmental Protection Agency should increase the traditional safety factor to account for intra-individual variability from 10 to 100 when calculating drinking water standards for non-carcinogens.**

## Blueprint for the Environment

## WATER QUALITY

# ENVIRONMENTAL PROTECTION AGENCY
## ASSISTANT ADMINISTRATOR for Water
### Office of Water Regulations and Standards

### RECOMMENDATION
**The Director of Water Regulations and Standards should issue water quality criteria for all remaining priority pollutants and nonconventional pollutants that pose major risks to human health and aquatic life.**

• The Environmental Protection Agency (EPA) has developed a number of water quality criteria (on which States base their water quality standards) for protection of human health and aquatic life. There are a number of pollutants of concern, however, for which such criteria have not yet been developed. EPA should make a quick but comprehensive survey of State needs in this area and identify key pollutants of concern — without regard to whether these pollutants are among the "priority pollutants" listed in Sec. 307(a) of the Act.

• In recent years the pace of criteria development in the Office of Water Regulations and Standards' Criteria and in the Standards Branch has slowed to a crawl. The office produces from one to three "criteria documents" (definitive summaries of the latest science for a particular pollutant) each year. New energy and higher productivity are needed, particularly because the States and Regions have identified a need for new, more creative approaches in criteria development.

• There is a demand for "wildlife protection" and "sediment" criteria as (in some instances) better measure of the chemical, physical and biological integrity of surface waters. Because it has been unable to keep up with the pace of demand for "criteria documents," the Criteria and Standards Division has taken to issuing "water quality advisories" instead, cheaper, less complete versions of criteria documents. A clear policy decision should be made as to whether it is useful and sensible to be taking these halfway measures rather than focusing limited resources on actual criteria development.

### RECOMMENDATION
**The Assistant Administrator for Water and the General Counsel should increase priority and resources for enforcement against National Pollutant Discharge Elimination System and pretreatment violators.**

• The Environmental Protection Agency (EPA) should devote more resources to enforcement of National Pollutant Discharge Elimination System (NPDES) and pretreatment limits.

• The EPA should support citizen suits as a supplement to its enforcement resources. Toward this end, EPA should refrain generally from bringing an additional action when a citizen suit has been begun unless there is a reason why the action is required.

## BUDGET RECOMMENDATION

## PRINCIPAL AUTHORIZING LEGISLATION
Clean Water Act, Section 304

## CONGRESSIONAL JURISDICTION
**House Authorizing Committee/Subcommittee**
Committee on Public Works and Transportation
Subcommittee on Water Resources
**Senate Authorizing Committee/Subcommittee**
Committee on Environment and Public Works
Subcommittee on Environmental Protection
**House Appropriations Subcommittee**
Subcommittee on HUD — Independent Agencies
**Senate Appropriations Subcommittee**
Subcommittee on HUD — Independent Agencies

## RELEVANT STUDIES

## RELATED FEDERAL PROGRAMS

## PRINCIPAL SOURCES OF EXPERTISE
Natural Resources Defense Council — 202-783-7800
Great Lakes Natural Resources Center — 313-769-3351

## IMPLEMENTATION STEPS
(1) Conduct a 60-day survey of State and Regional water quality officials to identify those pollutants which should be priorities for criteria development (or completion, for ones underway).
(2) Establish an internal working schedule for development of these criteria. Where necessary, augment staff and dollar resources.
(3) Stick to criteria development schedule.

## NOTES:

## Blueprint for the Environment

## WATER QUALITY

# ENVIRONMENTAL PROTECTION AGENCY

**RECOMMENDATION**

**The Environmental Protection Agency should reduce or eliminate water quality impacts of municipal and industrial stormwater or runoff by meeting statutory deadlines for all regulations governing stormwater discharges; and ensuring full implementation of, and compliance with, regulations.**

• Stormwater, or runoff from streets, buildings, factories, etc., can be highly contaminated with toxic and other pollutants. When this contaminated stormwater runs into rivers, lakes and coastal waters, it can have a major water quality impact.

**RECOMMENDATION**

**The Environmental Protection Agency should promulgate effluent limitations guidelines for the pesticides industry, identify other major unregulated industries and promulgate effluent limitations guidelines for these toxics sources, by 1991.**

• The Clean Water Act required the Environmental Protection Agency (EPA) to establish nationwide water pollution control regulations by category of industrial dischargers. Under a 1976 Consent Decree between EPA and the Natural Resources Defense Council, EPA agreed to issue regulations for a specific list of industrial categories. Regulations have now been promulgated for all industries except pesticides manufacturers. EPA issued pesticides rules in 1985, but withdrew them after an industry legal challenge.

• In addition, the Clean Water Act, Section 304(m), added by the 1987 Water Quality Act, requires EPA to identify additional industry categories that discharge toxic pollutants, and to issue nationwide regulations for these sources as well, by 1991. According to past EPA studies, major sources of toxics that are not currently subject to nationwide regulations include such industries as hazardous waste treaters, solvent recyclers, paint manufacturers, and industrial laundries. These sources should be identified and regulations should be issued by the 1991 statutory deadline.

**RECOMMENDATION**

**The Assistant Administrator for Water should develop federal and state water quality standards for pollutants that are largely caused by Nonpoint Source pollution (e.g. agricultural chemicals).**

**RECOMMENDATION**

**The Assistant Administrator for Water should seek full funding for state and federal Nonpoint Source programs from Congress.**

## RECOMMENDATION
**The Director of Water Regulations and Standards should develop water quality criteria for sediment and wildlife.**

## RECOMMENDATION
**The Assistant Administrator for Water should promulgate sludge management and technical regulations that protect human health and environment with an ample margin of safety.**

• The Environmental Protection Agency (EPA) is required to develop national, uniform limits on toxics in sludge when it is land-filled or land-spread, sold as fertilizer, ocean dumped (pending phaseout of ocean dumping) or incinerated. The EPA also must write management regulations for state sludge management programs.

• The EPA has missed statutory deadlines for both the technical criteria and the state management regulations. Absent these rules, the public may be exposed to toxics reaching air, water and soil via the many routes of exposure to sludge. Both rules are needed now.

• The EPA has proposed state management rules which are seriously flawed. They do not link sludge management to pretreatment. The final rule should be revised and issued promptly.

## RECOMMENDATION
**The Assistant Administrator for Water should develop sludge analytical methods/techniques (test procedures) to help states and municipalities identify and control toxics in their sewage sludge.**

• The Clean Water Act (CWA) requires the Environmental Protection Agency (EPA) to establish uniform national guidelines for conducting analytical tests for pollutants of concern in surface waters and sludge. States and industries use these standardized protocols to test their effluent for compliance with permit limits and water quality standards.

• The EPA has not, to date, promulgated such procedures for sludge contaminants. While a new "guidance document" has been prepared as part of an EPA interim strategy for addressing sludge contamination, this document does not provide the certainly and legal authority of promulgated guidelines.

• The EPA should propose and promulgate these guidelines so that there are formal guidelines in place by the time the sludge technical regulations are issued.

## Blueprint for the Environment

# Blueprint for the Environment

## PESTICIDE PREVENTION

## ENVIRONMENTAL PROTECTION AGENCY
ASSISTANT ADMINISTRATOR for Pesticides and Toxic Substances
Office of Pesticide Programs

**RECOMMENDATION**
**The Assistant Administrator for Pesticides and Toxic Substances should restructure the risk-benefit analyses (1) to replace yield goals with profit-per-acre goals, (2) to consider crop surpluses when determining the benefits of a high risk product, (3) to factor in a broader range of alternatives, and (4) to not discriminate against significant localized risks.**

• The Environmental Protection Agency's (EPA's) risk-benefit analyses are based on yield goals. Farmers expect yield increases for each commodity every year. As long as this expectation is a goal, EPA's regulatory decisions will be driven by it, and pesticide use will continue to increase in the effort to increase output. If net profit per acre goals replaced yield goals, less pesticides would be applied to optimize production.

• Benefits analyses are biased towards the goal of increased yields year after year. Increased production, however, is not always desirable when markets are not expected to expand, and when the Department of Agriculture needs to reduce crop surpluses. EPA should not justify continued registration on the assumed need to increase production.

• Furthermore, because EPA only considers chemical alternatives, its risk-benefit analyses are severely biased against alternative pest controls. This biased approach perpetuates intensive agricultural practices which are proving to be contrary to the best interests of farmers and the environment.

• Finally, risk-benefit analyses discriminate against localized exposure to high-risk pesticides because low numbers of instances are not generally considered unreasonable (e.g., pesticide contamination of rural drinking water wells). EPA weighs localized risks against the national benefits of the product and can conclude they are "reasonable" according to EPA's standards.

## BUDGET RECOMMENDATION
F.Y. 90: **no change**          F.Y. 91: **no change**

## PRINCIPAL AUTHORIZING LEGISLATION
Federal Insecticide, Fungicide and Rodenticide Act (FIFRA) P.L. 92—516, as amended

## CONGRESSIONAL JURISDICTION
**House Authorizing Committee/Subcommittee**
Committee on Agriculture
Subcommittee on Department Operations, Research and Foreign Agriculture
**Senate Authorizing Committee/Subcommittee**
Committee on Agriculture, Nutrition, and Forestry
Subcommittee on Agricultural Research and General Legislation
**House Appropriations Subcommittee**
Subcommittee on HUD — Independent Agencies
**Senate Appropriations Subcommittee**
Subcommittee on HUD — Independent Agencies

## RELEVANT STUDIES
Environmental concerns and the 1990 Farm Bill by Charles M. Benbrook, Ph.D., presented August 19, 1988 at the Illinois Farm Bureau Annual Meeting, Bloominton, Illinois

## RELATED FEDERAL PROGRAMS

## PRINCIPAL SOURCES OF EXPERTISE
National Audubon Society — 202-547-9009
Institute for Alternative Agriculture — 202-979-8777
Natural Resources Defense Council — 202-783-7800
National Coalition Against the Misuse of Pesticides — 202-543-5450
U.S. Public Interest Research Group — 202-546-9707

## IMPLEMENTATION STEPS
(1)   Replace yield goals with net profit per acre goals.
(2)   Do not discriminate against significant localized risks.
(3)   Consider crop surpluses when determining the benefits of a high risk product.
(4)   Factor a broader range of alternatives.

## BUDGET HISTORY (in millions of dollars by fiscal year)

|              | 83   | 85 | 87   | 88 | 89 |
|--------------|------|----|------|----|----|
| Appropriated | 16.6 |    | 20.6 |    |    |

## MANPOWER HISTORY (in F.T.E.'s by fiscal year)

|        | 81  | 82  | 83  | 84  | 85  | 86  | 87  |       |
|--------|-----|-----|-----|-----|-----|-----|-----|-------|
| Actual | 209 | 175 | 163 | 184 | 224 | 241 | 251 | (FTE)* |

\* FTE = Full Time Equivalents

——————— **Blueprint for the Environment** ———————

# Blueprint for the Environment

## PESTICIDE PREVENTION

# ENVIRONMENTAL PROTECTION AGENCY

**RECOMMENDATION**
**The Assistant Administrator for Pesticides and Toxic Substances should sponsor, develop and promote Integrated Pest Management techniques to help reduce chemical inputs. When undertaking risk-benefits analyses of high-risk chemicals, the Administrator should fully consider Integrated Pest Management alternatives.**

• Under section 28 of the Federal Insecticide, Fungicide, and Rodenticide Act (FIFRA) (7 U.S.C. 136w-3), "The Administrator, in coordination with the Secretary of Agriculture, shall identify those pests that must be brought under control. The Administrator shall also coordinate and cooperate with the Secretary of Agriculture's research and implementation programs to develop and improve the safe use and effectiveness of chemical, biological, and alternative methods to combat and control pests that reduce the quality and economical production and distribution of agricultural products to domestic and foreign consumers." Developing and promoting Integrated Pest Management (IPM) techniques should be an integral part of the Administrator's duties under this section. The Administrator, however, has not sought to implement this provision.

**RECOMMENDATION**
**The Assistant Administrator for Pesticides and Toxic Substances should ensure the establishment of effective procedures to thoroughly screen bioengineered plants and microorganisms for environmental hazards while allowing for their timely and orderly introduction.**

**RECOMMENDATION**
**The Assistant Administrator for Pesticides and Toxic Substances should require registrants to develop Best Management Practices designed to prevent ground water contamination as a condition of the registration or reregistration of pesticides with the potential to leach to ground water.**

• As part of the Environmental Protection Agency's (EPA's) Federal Insecticide Fungicide and Rodenticide Act (FIFRA) mandate, the agency should seek methods to reduce the risks associated with pesticide use. Ground water contamination by pesticides is a major concern linked to normal use of pesticides. Without strong legislative authorities to address this problem, EPA will be unable to fully address the issue. Best Management Practices (BMPs), however, will give farmers a range of methods to reduce the potential problems of leaching chemicals, thus making farmers a part of the solution.

## RECOMMENDATION

The Assistant Administrator for Pesticides and Toxic Substances should require monitoring of ground and surface water at representative geographic locations where pesticides are in high use. Area-wide monitoring should be required where ground or surface water contamination is actually detected.

## RECOMMENDATION

The Assistant Administrator of the Environmental Protection Agency should establish a comprehensive effort to collect, analyze and disseminate data and information on pesticide poisonings and other associated health problems by implementing the recommendatic... design for collection of health problems due to pesticide poisoning.

• Each year there are many incidents of pesticide poisoning, but there is no single source of such information or a cost effective means to collect information of real world risks of pesticides. Over the years the Environmental Protection Agency (EPA) has tried to collect information through various forms of pesticide incident surveillance systems, but funds have been erratic or nonexistent, with the result that the EPA remains ignorant as to how many and what kinds of poisonings are occurring.

• In 1986, the EPA was provided with $200,000 to fund a study by Research Triangle Institute. That study, "Recommended Design for an Annual Survey of Hospital-Treated Pesticide Poisonings," recommended that a cost effective way to collect such information could utilize existing surveys such as the Consumer Product Safety Commission's survey of pesticide-treated injuries due to pesticide exposure in hospitals and emergency rooms; the National Center for Health Statistics' survey of hospital discharges; states' information on reported accidents; and National Institute for Occupational Safety and Health (NIOSH's) Sentinel Event Notification Systems for Occupational Risk (SENSOR) program.

## RECOMMENDATION

The Assistant Administrator for Pesticides and Toxic Substances should implement a pilot project to begin to fulfill the office's obligation under the Endangered Species Act to protect endangered species from the adverse impacts of pesticide exposure.

• The EPA should start implementation of segments of an ESA program with a pilot program in at least six counties covering two uses, such as forest and mosquitoes, or corn and soybeans. As the project is refined and experience with prescriptions for managing pesticides in specified systems is gained, the program should be gradually expanded to the rest of the country and to other uses.

## RECOMMENDATION

The Environmental Protection Agency should ensure that all tolerance levels are supported by full health and safety data and that these tolerances ensure that all consumers, especially children and the elderly, are protected from risk of cancer and other serious adverse health effects.

## RECOMMENDATION

The Environmental Protection Agency should immediately implement the Federal Insecticide, Fungicide and Rodenticide Act statutory mandate to reregister all pesticides. The Agency should ensure that all pesticides have submitted complete and scientifically adequate health and safety data within the next four years and should fully reevaluate all pesticides within the next nine years.

### Blueprint for the Environment

# Blueprint for the Environment

## TOXIC SUBSTANCES

# ENVIRONMENTAL PROTECTION AGENCY
ASSISTANT ADMINISTRATOR for Pesticides and Toxic Substances
Office of Toxic Substances

### RECOMMENDATION
**The Environmental Protection Agency should issue a clarification of its authority under Section 9 of the Toxic Substances Control Act to assure that its regulatory authorities can be exercised at the discretion of the Administrator and that the Agency does not have to defer in the first instance to other agencies which may have overlapping authority.**

• Section 9 of the Toxic Substances Control Act (TSCA) authorizes the Administrator of the Environmental Protection Agency (EPA) to determine whether TSCA or another EPA statute or another agency should address a substance found to pose an unreasonable risk under TSCA. In recent years, EPA has reinterpreted this provision to mean that EPA must defer where another agency has authority to take action against the identified hazard. The result has been the referral of various identified risks to other agencies, primarily Occupational Safety and Health Administration (OSHA), which then fail to act to reduce or eliminate the hazard. EPA should reassert its authority to act at its discretion against substances found to pose unreasonable risks to health or the environment.

### RECOMMENDATION
**The Environmental Protection Agency should seek authority from Congress to require testing of chemicals without the necessity of making an unreasonable risk finding a prerequisite to rulemaking.**

### RECOMMENDATION
**The Environmental Protection Agency should restrict the availability of confidentiality protection for information submitted under Toxic Substances Control Act to legitimate trade secrets, i.e. formula and process information, and should require up-front substantiation of all confidentiality claims.**

### RECOMMENDATION
**The Environmental Protection Agency should foster the development and validation of alternative toxicological tests that do not involve animal subjects in order to meet the urgent need to screen all pesticides and potentially toxic substances prior to their introduction into the environment.**

# BUDGET RECOMMENDATION

## PRINCIPAL AUTHORIZING LEGISLATION
Toxic Substances Control Act

## CONGRESSIONAL JURISDICTION
**House Authorizing Committee/Subcommittee**
Committee on Energy and Commerce
Subcommittee on Transportation, Tourism and Hazardous Materials
**Senate Authorizing Committee/Subcommittee**
Committee on Environment and Public Works
Subcommittee on Hazardous Wastes and Toxic Substances
**House Appropriations Subcommittee**
Subcommittee on HUD — Independent Agencies
**Senate Appropriations Subcommittee**
Subcommittee on HUD — Independent Agencies

## RELEVANT STUDIES
Identifying and Regulating Carcinogens, - Background Paper, Office of Technology Assessment, 1987
U.S. Congress, Office of Technology Assessment, **"Alternatives to Animal Use in Research, Testing, and Education,"** (OTA-BA-273, February, 1986)

## RELATED FEDERAL PROGRAMS

## PRINCIPAL SOURCES OF EXPERTISE
National Resources Defense Council — 212-949-0049
Environmental Defense Fund — 202-387-3500

## IMPLEMENTATION STEPS
(1) Direct the Office of General Counsel to prepare an opinion supporting the Administrator's authority to act on chemical hazards at his/his discretion without having to defer to another agency first under Section 9 of Toxic Substances Control Act (TSCA).
(2) Conclude the asbestos ban rulemaking and issue the final ban and phasedown rule.
(3) Propose and promulgate requirements to reduce exposures to formaldehyde in pressed wood products, home furnishings, and manufactured and conventional housing; and reopen the proceeding to protect apparel workers from the significant risk of cancer posed by their exposures to .2—.3 parts per million of formaldehyde, now that the Occupational Safety and Health Administration (OSHA) proceeding is over and the standard adopted, 1 part per million, will not protect against the risk identified by EPA in 1984.
(4) Seek amendment of Toxic Substances Control Act (TSCA) to clarify the Administrator's discretion to use TSCA to control chemical hazards.
(5) The Environmental Protection Agency should discontinue the practice of specifying in the Toxic Substances Control Act regulations that records of compliance be kept in company files unless requested to be made available in an Environmental Protection Agency inspection. This practice withholds all compliance records from public scrutiny and effectively precludes citizen enforcement actions under Section 20(a)(1) of the statute.

## NOTES:

## WASTE REDUCTION

# ENVIRONMENTAL PROTECTION AGENCY
ASSISTANT ADMINISTRATOR for Solid Waste
and Emergency Response
Office of Solid Waste

### RECOMMENDATION
**The Environmental Protection Agency should strongly encourage maximum recycling of municipal solid waste as a long-term solution to the solid waste disposal crisis.**

• Given that 85 percent of the waste stream is technically recoverable, the Environmental Protection Agency (EPA) should endorse and help states and municipalities to set and achieve goals of greatly accelerated recycling and reuse. Paper and food and yard wastes, as the greatest contributors to the waste stream, should be targeted first. Fifty percent of organics and paper should be composted and recycled respectively, by 1992. Recycling rates for metals and glass should be doubled by that date. And plastics recycling should quintuple at minimum. These goals should be expanded to 75 percent of the municipal solid waste stream by 2000.

• Aluminum, glass, organic waste materials, and ferrous metals are readily recyclable. A variety of technologies and strategies exist to collect, handle, process, and remanufacture these materials.

• Ways to achieve these goals include: banning recyclable and compostable materials from incinerators and landfills; banning put-or-pay contracts whereby communities commit certain tonnages to waste disposal facilities; creating incentives for redesigning the waste stream so materials are recyclable; encouraging states/communities to establish mandatory recycling laws; making recycling as convenient as possible to waste generators; making manufacturers responsible for designing recyclable products; and encouraging the development of end-use manufacturing plants at the local/regional level.

• Along the lines of the Public Utilities Regulatory Policy Act (PURPA), it may make sense to require manufacturing plants to purchase secondary materials if there is a guaranteed supply, they meet specifications, and the secondary materials are cost competitive.

### RECOMMENDATION
**The Environmental Protection Agency Office of Solid Waste and Emergency Response should prioritize and institutionalize the solid waste management hierarchy in the following order: reduce, reuse, recycle, compost, incinerate or landfill.**

• In order to do this the Office of Solid Waste needs to expand and reorient its staff and budget to mirror the emphasis on the first four management options. Additionally, states should be required and provide funding to develop solid waste management plans that incorporate this hierarchy. All federal and state research and development, permitting, and contracting should also reflect the hierarchy. To avoid unnecessary duplication of efforts, the Environmental Protection Agency (EPA) should act as an information and technology clearinghouse to pass on the knowledge and experience gained by local, state, or federal implementation or evaluation of specific projects and/or technologies.

# BUDGET RECOMMENDATION

## PRINCIPAL AUTHORIZING LEGISLATION
Resource Conservation and Recovery Act (RCRA); reauthorization in 1989

## CONGRESSIONAL JURISDICTION
### House Authorizing Committee/Subcommittee
Committee on Energy and Commerce
  Subcommittee on Transportation, Tourism and Hazardous Materials
  Subcommittee on Health and Environment
### Senate Authorizing Committee/Subcommittee
Committee on Environment and Public Works
  Subcommittee on Hazardous Waste and Toxic Substances
### House Appropriations Subcommittee
Subcommittee on HUD — Independent Agencies
### Senate Appropriations Subcommittee
Subcommittee on HUD — Independent Agencies

## RELEVANT STUDIES
**Wrapped in Plastics** (Environmental Action Foundation, 1988)
**Coming Full Circle** (Environmental Defense Fund, 1987)
**Plastics Recycling Action Plan for Massachusetts** (MA Department of Environmental Quality Engineering, 1988)
Draft report of EPA's Municipal Solid Waste Task Force(September 1988)
Report of the Office of Technology Assessment MSW Management (due 1989)

## RELATED FEDERAL PROGRAMS

## PRINCIPAL SOURCES OF EXPERTISE
Environmental Action Foundation — 202-745-4879
Worldwatch Institute) — 403-241-1170
Natural Resources Defense Council — 212-949-0049
Coalition for Recycleable Waste — 301-585-4626

## IMPLEMENTATION STEPS
(1) EPA should encourage source separation and curbside collection of the municipal waste stream.
(2) EPA should establish an information and technology clearinghouse to facilitate knowledge transfer. State plans should be required to include these recycling goals or else explain in detail why they are not feasible in a particular area.
(3) EPA should fund and encourage research and development in recycling and composting.

## NOTES:

# Blueprint for the Environment

## WASTE REDUCTION

# ENVIRONMENTAL PROTECTION AGENCY

### RECOMMENDATION
**The Environmental Protection Agency should encourage the use of products and packaging made from recycled materials that are also either reusable or recycleable. Designing for "disposability" should be discouraged when the primary purpose of the product is not for safety and health.**

• Since packaging comprises 1/3 by weight and in excess of 1/2 by volume of the waste stream, packaging reduction measures are key to reducing the volume of the waste stream. Such actions should not, however, interfere with the ultimate recycleability of the material. Methods of altering packaging priorities and designs should be examined, including the proposed packaging taxes in Massachusetts and New York State. The agency should establish an ongoing dialogue with industry on how to redesign packages and products to produce less waste. Initially conducting a product and package waste audit would alert industry where to start.

• Consumer education regarding the waste implications of product choices would also help to influence manufacturers. An advertising campaign to promote reusable, recycleable, and compostable products could greatly raise awareness as could a label to identify "environmentally friendly" items. The label could be employed only after receiving permission from the Environmental Protection Agency (EPA). Permission would be based on strict standards and include enforcement for unauthorized use. An awards program might also encourage design innovation to minimize weight and volume and maximize recycleability.

• EPA should encourage the use of volume-based disposal rates for items not intended for recycling. Information should be gathered to address the fears that volume based charges will encourage illegal dumping. This and other mechanisms which create direct and clear incentives for recycling and purchasing goods which are recycleable must be researched and promoted.

### RECOMMENDATION
**The Environmental Protection Agency should design and implement a national market development program for recycled materials and products.**

• Currently, 10 percent of the waste stream is recycled, but the volume could increase dramatically with the implementation of aggressive state recycling programs. Markets capable of absorbing the projected volume of materials must be identified and developed. A federal market development strategy should include the following elements:

1) The Environmental Protection Agency (EPA) should issue guidelines for the federal procurement of recycled products and implement a strong federal procurement program. The Resource Conservation and Recovery Act of 1976 (RCRA) directs government purchasers to buy "items composed of the highest percentage of recovered materials practicable, consistent with maintaining a satisfactory level of competition." A uniform federal procurement policy would both increase public-sector use of recycled products and provide an example to the private sector. It would further eliminate the multitude of standards and definitions that now plague state guidelines and serve to make products made with recycled materials standard shelf items instead

of more expensive specialty goods.

2) The federal government should reform the tax code and resource management practices to eliminate subsidies of virgin materials that compete with recycled materials. Many of today's tax codes, pricing mechanisms, quality standards and purchasing practices reflect outdated economic policies based on the underpricing of natural resources. To make up for the bias, the federal government could also provide investment tax credits, low interest loans, or other financial inducements to companies that use recycled products.

## RECOMMENDATION
**The Environmental Protection Agency should advance the use of non-incineration waste management technologies such as recycling and composting which, if done to their maximum capabilities, will accomplish close to the same waste volume reduction as incineration without many of the dangerous side effects.**

• Incineration as a technology for waste disposal is fraught with controversy. It is known to create serious air and land pollution and there is ambiguous information about the realistic ability to control this pollution. In addition to being more expensive than recycling in the long run, the energy recovered from the burning of waste is less than that saved form recycling the materials and is, therefore, an energy-loser in comparison.

• A recent recycling potential assessment done for the city of Seattle demonstrates that it may be possible to achieve recycling rates of over 75 percent with an aggressive program. Incineration will continue to interfere with and displace other more environmentally-benign technologies such as recycling, composting and source reduction. For example, "put or pay" contracts frequently used by incinerator vendors act as disincentives for a community to increase recycling, composting or source reduction. Incineration obligates a community to a specific volume of waste regardless of new developments or advances. And communities must still provide landfills for the frequently toxic ash. Landfilling is more flexible for handling fluctuating amounts of waste. Therefore, incineration should not be accorded a higher value than landfilling in the waste management hierarchy.

• Existing incinerators and any new ones that are approved must nevertheless be required to meet strict pollution control standards. The Environmental Protection Agency (EPA) must strive to maximize the use of environmentally benign and energy conserving processes for solid waste disposal and to minimize processes which create additional pollution and/or destroy natural resources.

## Blueprint for the Environment

# Blueprint for the Environment

## HAZARDOUS WASTE REDUCTION

## ENVIRONMENTAL PROTECTION AGENCY
ASSISTANT ADMINISTRATOR for Solid Waste
and Emergency Response
Office of Solid Waste

**RECOMMENDATION**
**The Environmental Protection Agency Office of Solid Waste and Emergency Response should implement a strong program to reduce the toxicity of municipal solid waste through regulatory action targeting specific toxic components and products in the waste stream.**

• Although household trash is rarely thought of as "toxic," many everyday household products and packaging contain toxic chemicals that harm public health and the environment at the points of manufacture, use, collection and disposal. When disposed of in landfills and incinerators, these toxic components contaminate air, surface water, groundwater, and soil.

• Where alternatives exist, the Environmental Protection Agency (EPA) should ban the use of persistent bioaccumulative chemicals and heavy metals used in the manufacture of household and commercial products, such as pesticides, paints, batteries, inks, dyes, pigments, and wood preservatives. Where no viable alternative currently exists (such as for lead in car batteries), EPA should immediately set standards on the use of toxic chemicals and metals

and develop collections systems to divert these materials from disposal in landfills and incinerators. Taxing mechanisms for toxic materials and products should be implemented where appropriate to reflect the true social cost of their use and to finance collection systems.

• EPA should create an information clearinghouse on research and development of nontoxic products and materials and technologies to detoxify or neutralize hazardous substances. The clearinghouse should be targeted to three groups: manufacturers seeking non-toxic alternatives, schools specializing in product and packaging design, and consumers and businesses needing information on the toxicity of household and commercial products and the availability of non-toxic alternatives.

**RECOMMENDATION**
**The Environmental Protection Agency should establish specific waste reduction goals and a timetable for achieving them so that the effectiveness of the program can be measured.**

• The effectiveness of the Environmental Protection Agency's (EPA) waste minimization program cannot be measured because it has no specific goals or schedule and no way to measure progress. Goals should be established and thereafter factored into the permit process for authorizing new or expanded hazardous waste treatment, storage and disposal facilities.

# BUDGET RECOMMENDATION

## PRINCIPAL AUTHORIZING LEGISLATION

Resource Conservation and Recovery Act (RCRA); reauthorization in 1989

## CONGRESSIONAL JURISDICTION

**House Authorizing Committee/Subcommittee**
Committee on Energy and Commerce
Subcommittee on Transportation, Tourism and Hazardous Materials
**Senate Authorizing Committee/Subcommittee**
Committee on Environment and Public Works
Subcommittee on Hazardous Waste and Toxic Substances
**House Appropriations Subcommittee**
Subcommittee on HUD — Independent Agencies
**Senate Appropriations Subcommittee**
Subcommittee on HUD — Independent Agencies

## RELEVANT STUDIES

GAO, **Hazardous Waste: New Approach Needed to Manage the Resource Conservation and Recovery Act** (1988)
Office of Technology Assessment, **Serious Reduction of Hazardous Waste** (1986)

## RELATED FEDERAL PROGRAMS

## PRINCIPAL SOURCES OF EXPERTISE

Environmental Action Foundation — 202-745-4879
Worldwatch Institute (C. Pollock-Shea) — 403-241-1170
Markets for Recycled Products — 212-566-0990
Natural Resources Defense Council — 212-949-0049

## IMPLEMENTATION STEPS

(1)  Seminars with industry, EPA and toxicologists.
(2)  Establishment of information clearinghouse at EPA.
(3)  EPA survey of toxic components in the waste stream.

## NOTES:

# Blueprint for the Environment

## HAZARDOUS WASTE REDUCTION

# ENVIRONMENTAL PROTECTION AGENCY

**RECOMMENDATION**

**The Environmental Protection Agency should remove many special groups of hazardous waste that are managed under the Resource Conservation and Recovery Act, Subtitle D, State or Regional Solid Waste Plans, or not yet categorized at all, and restore them to the program designed to manage hazardous waste, the Subtitle C Hazardous Waste Management program.**

• Subtitle C of the Resource Conservation and Recovery Act (RCRA) is a federal regulatory scheme that defines and classifies solid waste as hazardous and then provides comprehensive "cradle-to-grave" management for that hazardous waste. Yet a number of waste streams that exhibit the characteristics of hazardous waste have been excluded from management under the Hazardous Waste Management program in Subtitle C.

**RECOMMENDATION**

**The Environmental Protection Agency should extensively revise the federal criteria for state permitting programs of land disposal facilities to reduce the pollution resulting from existing land disposal facilities.**

**RECOMMENDATION**

**The Environmental Protection Agency should review and expand its data collection activities under the Resource Conservation and Recovery Act to produce reliable data on the amounts and types of waste generated, on waste reduction efforts by generators, and on the status of compliance with groundwater monitoring and other Resource Conservation and Recovery Act requirements by treatment, storage and disposal facilities.**

• The Environmental Protection Agency (EPA) lacks accurate data on the amounts and types of hazardous wastes generated, on the nature of waste reduction efforts undertaken by generators, and on compliance by treatment, storage and disposal facilities with groundwater monitoring and other Resource Conservation and Recovery Act (RCRA) requirements. An improved data collection system should be established to produce accurate data on these and other activities to help focus the priorities and shortcomings of the existing RCRA program.

**RECOMMENDATION**

**The Environmental Protection Agency Office of Solid Waste and Emergency Response should develop a plan, timetable and estimate of resources needed for identifying and listing all remaining hazardous wastes.**

• The General Accounting Office recently reported that the Environmental Protection Agency (EPA) has listed only five additional hazardous wastes since 1980, and that the Subtitle C program has suffered greatly from shifts in program implementation approaches.

311

# RECOMMENDATION

**The Environmental Protection Agency should adopt definitions of hazardous waste which can be generally and objectively applied, and which will expand the universe of hazardous wastes covered by the Subtitle C program. To implement a more inclusive hazardous waste management system to protect health and the environment, the Environmental Protection Agency should promulgate additional characteristics for identifying hazardous wastes.**

• For ease of administration, compliance and enforcement, the Environmental Protection Agency should discontinue its current exploration of site-specific, contingency-based standards in favor of more objective and uniform definitions of hazardous wastes. To accomplish this objective, the Office of Solid Waste and Emergency Response (OSWER) should promulgate additional hazardous waste characteristics as mandated by the 1984 Resource Conservation Recovery Act (RCRA) amendments. These new characteristics should at least include carcinogenicity, mutagenecity and teratogenicity, organic toxicity and infectiousness.

# RECOMMENDATION

**The Environmental Protection Agency should revise its land disposal restrictions regulations for underground injection of hazardous wastes to preclude granting variances where migration of hazardous constituents out of the injection zone is likely to occur.**

• The Environmental Protection Agency's (EPA) land disposal ban regulations (implementing Section 3004(d)-(g) of the Resource Conservation and Recovery Act (RCRA)) contain an open-ended variance from the ban on injection of untreated wastes imposed by the 1984 RCRA amendments. The regulations will allow injection of hazardous wastes where migration of some hazardous constituents out of the injection zone is predicted to occur. Since injection is the principal land disposal method and accounts for sixty percent (over 11 billion gallons per year) of waste disposed, this departure from the law could perpetuate land disposal at the expense of environmentally preferable waste management methods including, treatment, recycling and waste reduction.

# RECOMMENDATION

**The Environmental Protection Agency should not weaken its existing standards for hazardous waste incinerators and should set equally stringent standards for industrial boilers and furnaces that burn hazardous waste.**

• The Environmental Protection Agency (EPA) has proposed inadequate protective standards for the many thousands of boilers and furnaces that burn hazardous waste as fuel, and thereby release toxics into the air. EPA intends to downgrade the standards for hazardous waste incineration to make these standards comparable to the inadequate standards to be set for boilers and furnaces.

## Blueprint for the Environment

# Blueprint for the Environment

## HAZARDOUS SITES

# ENVIRONMENTAL PROTECTION AGENCY
### ASSISTANT ADMINISTRATOR For Solid Waste
### and Emergency Response
### Office of Solid Waste

**RECOMMENDATION**
**The Environmental Protection Agency should strongly enforce the Superfund statute, as revised in 1986, which requires the Agency to choose cleanup alternatives that will permanently eliminate toxic threats to human health and the environment. The Environmental Protection Agency needs to eliminate present barriers which prevent it from choosing permanent remedies.**

• Since the Superfund statute was reauthorized in 1986, the Environmental Protection Agency (EPA) has failed to implement one of the most important requirements of the statute as revised: that EPA must select cleanup alternatives for Superfund sites that will permanently eliminate toxic hazards to human health and the environment. That is, Superfund cleanups must significantly reduce the toxicity, mobility and volume of the contaminants present at each Superfund site. Instead of doing this, EPA has largely opted for impermanent and/or unproven remedies.

• To correct this situation, EPA needs to remove the barriers that currently prevent the selection of permanent cleanup technologies. A task force should be created in the Office of Enforcement and Compliance Monitoring to accomplish the following: First, complete and accurate data regarding permanent cleanup technology costs, applicability and vendors must be compiled on a bi-monthly basis, and made available to EPA regional offices. Second, the same must be done for information regarding remedial technologies which have already failed to permanently eliminate toxic hazards at Superfund sites or have produced results in tests which indicate that such failure is likely (e.g., solidification of high organic content contaminants). Third, by June 30, 1989, EPA needs to revise its selection of remedy criteria so that cleanup levels will be considered first and cost-effectiveness will be considered last.

• This information must be publicly available. The bi-monthly reports, the first of which should be distributed by June 30, 1989, should be available for inspection and copying at all EPA Regional Offices as well as EPA Headquarters and should be distributed to a mailing list of all interested parties. The mailing list should be constructed from a list of all parties who have commented upon Superfund guidance documents and /or participated in site-specific public comment opportunities and all those who request their inclusion on the list.

# BUDGET RECOMMENDATION

## PRINCIPAL AUTHORIZING LEGISLATION
Comprehensive Environmental Response, Compensation and Liability Act ("Superfund") Expiration Date: 10/17/91

## CONGRESSIONAL JURISDICTION
**House Authorizing Committee/Subcommittee**
Committee on Energy and Commerce
Subcommittee on Transportation, Tourism and Hazardous Materials
**Senate Authorizing Committee/Subcommittee**
Committee on Environment and Public Works
Subcommittee on Superfund and Environmental Oversight
**House Appropriations Subcommittee**
Subcommittee on HUD — Independent Agencies
**Senate Appropriations Subcommittee**
Subcommittee on HUD — Independent Agencies

## RELEVANT STUDIES
OTA, "Are We Cleaning Up? 10 Superfund Case Studies"
EDF, HWTC, Audubon, NWF, NRDC, Sierra Club, U.S. PIRG, "Right Train, Wrong Track: Failed Leadership in the Superfund Cleanup Program"

## RELATED FEDERAL PROGRAMS

## PRINCIPAL SOURCES OF EXPERTISE
Environmental Defense Fund — 202-387-3500
National Audubon Society — 202-547-9009
National Wildlife Federation — 202-797-6800
Natural Resources Defense Council — 212-949-0049
The Sierra Club — 202-547-1141
U.S. Public Interest Research Group — 202-546-9707

## NOTES:

## Blueprint for the Environment

# Blueprint for the Environment

## HAZARDOUS SITES

# ENVIRONMENTAL PROTECTION AGENCY

**RECOMMENDATION**
**The Environmental Protection Agency's Superfund selection of remedy criteria must be revised so that cleanup alternatives will permanently eliminate toxic threats to human health and the environment.**

• The Environmental Protection Agency's (EPA) current selection of remedy criteria are probably illegal and certainly unsound. Currently nine criteria are used to select Superfund remedial actions; these criteria include non-statutory considerations such as "cost" and "implementability." The priority Congress has given to establishing cleanup levels which protect human health and the environment and which comply with applicable or relevant and appropriate standards of America's environmental law is currently ignored.

**RECOMMENDATION**
**The Administrator of the Environmental Protection Agency should revise the National Contingency Plan and related Agency policies to assure that the toxic poisoning of fish, wildlife and other natural resources as well as "food chain" contamination, are considered and remedied at Superfund sites.**

• Superfund requires the Environmental Protection Agency (EPA) to consider the effects of toxics released at hazardous waste sites on fish, wildlife, and the food chain in deciding whether to schedule sites for cleanup. The law also requires EPA to assure that the environment — as well as human health — is protected from toxics in all Superfund cleanups. Moreover, human health must be protected from "food chain" poisoning — which occurs when people eat fish or game that has accumulated toxics in its tissues. Finally EPA is required by the statute to coordinate all Superfund cleanups with the "trustees" for natural resources at Superfund sites, i.e. those state and federal officials who have the responsibility to manage or protect fish, wildlife, and other natural resources.

**RECOMMENDATION**
**The Environmental Protection Agency should work to assure that cleanups of Superfund sites include restoration of damaged natural resources.**

• The Superfund requires the Environmental Protection Agency (EPA) to protect both human health and the environment. As part of this, the Agency is supposed to coordinate investigations and cleanups of Superfund sites with restoration of damaged natural resources. EPA has, almost entirely, failed to do this; few site cleanups have involved efforts to restore damaged resources.

# RECOMMENDATION

**The Environmental Protection Agency should overhaul its existing Superfund policies and rules to make natural resource trustees full partners in all Superfund decision-making.**

• The Environmental Protection Agency (EPA) Administrator must strive to breathe life into the natural resource damage program under Superfund. This program authorizes state and federal officials to sue responsible parties, acting as "trustees" for the injured natural resources at Superfund sites, to assure that natural resources are fully restored at these sites. However, it has largely remained dead letter because EPA and the trustees have made it a low priority, and have failed to coordinate and take the program seriously in most cases.

# RECOMMENDATION

**The Environmental Protection Agency should adopt final regulations for administering technical assistance grants under Superfund that will enable citizens directly affected by toxic sites to receive grants quickly and easily.**

# RECOMMENDATION

**The Environmental Protection Agency should distribute more technical assistance grants and grant more waivers to the matching fund requirement to citizens' groups, so that they can participate meaningfully in decisionmaking at the site.**

• Currently, only a tiny percentage of Superfund site victims are able to obtain Technical Assistance Grants because so little has been allocated to the program. Thus, at the vast majority of sites, affected citizens remain unable to participate meaningfully in decisions that affect their lives. The public's view is not adequately taken into account in site decisions, contrary to Congressional intent.

# RECOMMENDATION

**The Environmental Protection Agency should adopt an aggressive policy of seeking reimbursement for all Technical Assistance Grants costs from potentially responsible parties.**

• The Environmental Protection Agency (EPA) should be structured in such a way that citizens who have put up matching funds would be reimbursed by potentially responsible parties (PRP). There is no justification for making innocent victims of toxic pollution pay in order to have a say in cleanup actions. Whenever possible EPA should exert pressure on PRP to guarantee the matching funds up front for the citizens' group.

## Blueprint for the Environment

# Blueprint for the Environment

## EXECUTIVE OFFICE OF THE PRESIDENT
## PRESIDENTIAL ACTIONS

# PRESIDENTIAL ACTIONS
# TO PROTECT THE ENVIRONMENT

## Global Warming and Ozone Destruction

**The President should announce in his Inaugural Address or in an Environmental Message that minimizing global warming will be a top priority of his domestic and foreign policy.** He should issue an executive order establishing goals and defining the responsibilities of all relevant agencies. He should work with the Congress to develop and enact appropriate legislation.

**The President should act to ensure that global warming is high on the agendas of both the 1989 Western Economic Summit and the Global Environmental Summit meeting that he has pledged to convene.** These personal meetings of top leaders are an excellent way of building the international consensus and cooperation that are essential for effective global action.

**The President should direct the Secretary of State to make bilateral approaches to key nations, including the Soviet Union and major developing countries like China and India, and to work with other nations to develop, under the auspices of the United Nations Environment Program, a global treaty requiring that $CO_2$ emissions be reduced through increases in energy efficiency and greater reliance on renewable energy sources.** This problem can be solved only through international cooperation, and the

United States can be a leader in bringing about that cooperation. We must set an example by acting to reduce our own $CO_2$ emissions in the ways suggested in the discussion on Energy below.

**The President should propose that other nations join us in a major program to halt tropical deforestation and to plant trees on a massive scale,** in order to reduce the buildup of atmospheric carbon dioxide. As part of that effort, the President should promote a major reforestation program for the United States.

The United States government has recently been an international leader in efforts to halt ozone depletion. U.S. industry seems to be ahead in finding acceptable substitutes for ozone-depleting chemicals. **The President should instruct the Environmental Protection Agency to take all actions necessary to phase out U.S. use of chlorofluorocarbons in five to seven years.** To ensure that CFC emissions from other countries are also stopped, **the President should direct the State Department and the Environmental Protection Agency to work with the United Nations Environment Program and other nations to achieve an equally rapid worldwide phaseout by strengthening the international ozone depletion protocol signed in Montreal in September 1987.**

## Energy

**The President should direct the Secretary of Energy to take immediate steps to develop a National Least-Cost Energy Plan** that allows all energy investments to compete on a fair economic basis, while taking into account the environmental costs associated with fossil

fuel use. The plan would ensure that energy needs are met in the most cost-effective way and allow energy efficiency and renewable energy resources to compete with conventional resources on a level playing field.

**The President should make the slowing of**

the global warming a central goal of U.S. energy policy. Steps should be taken to establish national targets for overall efficiency and the reduction of carbon dioxide emissions.

**The President should take immediate steps to increase federal support of research, development, and commercialization of energy efficiency and renewable energy sources,** each of which has been neglected in recent years.

**The President should propose legislation that will help increase the fuel economy of new automobiles and light trucks to 45 miles per gallon and 35 miles per gallon, respectively, by the year 2000.** Attainment of these targets should be supported by an increased "gas guzzler" tax applied at higher efficiency levels, a "gas sipper" rebate for efficient vehicles, and a gasoline tax to encourage increasing the efficiency of all vehicles.

## Protection of the Oceans

**The President should direct the Environmental Protection Agency, the National Oceanic and Atmospheric Administration, and the Coast Guard to use all existing authorities to prohibit release of toxic and other contaminated wastes into the marine environment.** These actions should include prohibitions on ocean dumping of sewage sludge, industrial wastes and contaminated dredge spoils, pipeline discharges from municipal sewage plants and industrial treatment facilities, and runoff from cities, agriculture, and other sources. The President should also encourage the states to use all their powers to the same ends.

**The President should instruct the Environmental Protection Agency, the Department of the Interior, and the National Oceanic and Atmospheric Administration to increase special protective measures to protect marine resources.** These should include expansion of the marine sanctuaries system, protection of tidal and non-tidal wetlands, and undeveloped barrier islands through elimination of federal subsidies and other

means, ecosystem management of fisheries, and revision of the five-year offshore oil and gas leasing program to exclude environmentally sensitive areas from leasing.

**The President should take initiatives to ensure that the United States will support and promote domestic and international policies that give greater attention to protection and wise use of the marine environment.** As part of this effort, the President should proclaim "Coastweeks" in the fall of 1989 and designate 1990 the "Year of the Coast." The President should strengthen the Coastal Zone Management Program to address issues such as sea level rise and coastal hazards.

**The President should call for U.S. ratification of the 1982 Law of the Sea Convention** and instruct U.S. officials involved in global treaties such as the London Dumping Convention and regional agreements such as those dealing with the Caribbean, South Pacific, and Great Lakes to exercise environmentally sensitive leadership.

## Environmentally Sustainable Development

**The President should announce that solving environmental problems in developing nations will be a central focus of U.S. foreign policy.** He should emphasize that the future of the world depends on the fate of the vast majority who live in developing nations, and that we must work with them to ensure a sound world environment. He should direct the State Department, the National Security Council, and our ambassadors abroad to treat these issues as priorities.

**The President should direct that our bilateral foreign assistance be focused on helping nations achieve sustainable development by:**

- Enhancing their agricultural resource base and promoting environmentally sound food production.
- Meeting their energy needs in ways that are environmentally sustainable, with an emphasis on energy assistance designed to meet human needs while minimizing global warming.
- Conserving tropical forests and biological diversity.
- Stabilizing population.

## Conserving the Earth's Plant and Animal Species

In the next decade, a quarter of all of the earth's plant and animal species may vanish forever due to human actions. We face a wave of extinctions comparable to that which destroyed the dinosaurs and many other species of life 65 million years ago. But it will happen much faster, as a result of the actions of the human species.

**The President should take actions to ensure that conservation of the earth's plant and animal species is a major international and domestic priority of his administration.**

**The President should place species conservation on the agenda of the Global Environmental Summit meeting that he has pledged to convene.**

**The President should direct the Agency for International Development to greatly strengthen its program to assist developing countries in conserving species and habitats.** The President's fiscal 1990 budget should request at least $10 million for this program, rising to $20 million in fiscal 1991. AID should convene a meeting of bilateral and multilateral aid donors to devise methods for increasing their support for species conservation in developing nations. The President should direct the other federal agencies of the executive branch with relevant expertise, such as the Department of the Interior, the National Oceanic and Atmospheric Administration, and the National Science Foundation, to make conservation of biological diversity a high priority.

**The President and the Secretary of State should give strong support to efforts to develop and negotiate an international convention to identify and protect valuable plant and animal habitats on a worldwide basis.** The convention should establish a fund to assist poor nations in conserving habitats. The United States should pledge at least $50 million annually.

In addition, **the President should direct that the United States begin immediately to develop systematic programs of cooperation with nations that possess species-rich, threatened habitats, such as Brazil, Madagascar, Indonesia, and the Andean nations of South America.**

**The President should instruct the Secretary of the Interior to implement vigorously and fully the U.S. Endangered Species Act,** reauthorized in the 100th Congress. He should instruct the Secretary to give special attention to expediting the listing of species, development of recovery plans, and acquisition of habitat.

## Land and Natural Resources

**The President should declare by executive order, and reinforce by other means, that federal lands and resources will be managed under a mandate of conservation stewardship.** These lands and resources should be managed as environmental exemplars for the world.

**The President should take steps to ensure that when public resources are sold or leased, such sale or lease should never occur at less than fair market value.**

**The President should propose increased funding for protection and management of federally-owned lands,** and in particular should support the creation of an American Heritage Trust to more adequately secure and safeguard the natural and historic heritage of the nation.

**The President should affirm his commitment to natural resources protection in U.S. agriculture.** He should, at a minimum, announce his firm commitment to the non-degradation of cropland and soil productivity, the protection of prime farmland from non-agricultural conversion, the protection and restoration of natural wetlands, and expanded research and development of low-input farming systems.

## Pollution

**The President should support and work vigorously for reauthorization of the Clean Air Act,** including acid rain controls that will eliminate at least twelve million tons of sulphur dioxide and four million tons of nitrogen oxides by the year 1998, rigorous standards for toxic air emissions, and deadlines that will bring all areas of the country rapidly into compliance with standards for healthy air. Factions in the Congress and an uncooperative President have delayed reauthorization of this key statute for too many years. Strong Presidential leadership is essential to protect our health and the environment.

**The President should direct the Environmental Protection Agency and the Department of Agriculture to make control of non-point**

## Blueprint for the Environment

sources of water pollution, including storm run-off, a high priority. EPA should require states to control runoff pollution. State non-point source programs must be fully funded. The Department of Agriculture should use its subsidy mechanisms and technical assistance programs to encourage better farming practices, including the planting of buffer strips to prevent erosion and run-off.

The President should make waste reduction and recycling a national priority for both hazardous and solid wastes, through economic incentives to reduce wastes and technical assistance to help state and local governments establish effective waste reduction and recycling programs. EPA should evaluate all regulatory programs for waste reduction opportunities.

The President's fiscal year 1990 budget should request at least a 20 percent increase in EPA's resources.

The President should order the Secretaries of Defense and Energy to develop plans to implement strategies to clean up hazardous waste at federal facilities, especially those facilities that pose the greatest risk to health and the environment.

## Population Growth

The President should establish an official population policy for the United States, and encourage all other nations to do the same. The overall objective should be stopping population growth worldwide.

The President should reassert the federal government's support of population and family planning assistance. This should include restoring financial support for multilateral organizations such as the United Nations Population Fund and the International Planned Parenthood Federation; strengthening the incorporation of population components in economic assistance programs administered by the Agency for International Development; and encouraging the World Bank, the Inter-American Development Bank, Asian Development Bank, and other such funding institutions to incorporate population concerns in their economic assistance programs.

## PREPARING OUR GOVERNMENT FOR ENVIRONMENTAL ACTION

Most of this report discussed the steps that are needed to solve specific problems. But there are overarching actions that must be taken, beginning right now, to show that the new administration is strongly committed to environmental protection and to ensure that our government is capable of acting in the right way.

### Appoint the Best People

The new administration's environmental performance will be determined to a great extent by the character and qualifications of the people appointed to fill key positions. The Administrator of the Environmental Protection Agency (who we suggest should become secretary of a new cabinet department), the Secretary of State, the Secretary of the Interior, the Secretary of Energy, the Secretary of Agriculture, the Administrator of the National Oceanic and Atmospheric Administration — each of these people has the power to do much good or harm to the environment of this nation and the earth. The President must choose these appointees with the greatest care.

### Establish an Effective Presidential Staff

Effective Presidential leadership will depend on the staff that serves the President. We recommend that the President reorganize the Council on Environmental Quality to turn it into a Presidential staff on the environment, headed by a single director who is highly qualified and trusted by the President. The National Security Council, the domestic policy staff in the White House, and the Office of Management and Budget each must include people highly qualified to deal with environmental issues.

### Deliver an Environmental Message Early in 1989

It is essential that the President himself show, by his words and actions, that he truly cares about the environment. President Nixon began, and other Presidents have followed, the tradition of delivering

## Blueprint for the Environment

an annual Environmental Message to the Congress and the nation. This proved to be an effective way of underscoring the importance of environmental problems and focusing attention on Presidential proposals for needed actions. Because of the range and scope of the environmental initiatives that are needed at this time, we recommend that the President resume this tradition and deliver, in the early months of his administration, a message that lays out his environmental program.

## Propose a Fully Adequate Environmental Budget

Many vitally important federal responsibilities are being neglected due to lack of staff and other resources. Some budget increases are essential if we are to prevent environmental degradation and the necessity of much greater expenditures later on. Mindful of the federal budget deficit, we do not recommend vast new expenditures. Many needed actions can be funded by redirecting federal spending. But it is absolutely essential that the budget submitted next February or March — a budget that will prevail until October 1991 — reflect careful analysis of environmental needs and include adequate resources to meet them.

## Provide International Leadership

Global environmental problems cast a shadow over humanity's future. These problems can be solved only through international cooperation. This requires leadership by the President. He should act as rapidly as possible to fulfill his campaign pledge to call for a Global Environmental Summit meeting of world leaders. The President should ensure that environmental issues are discussed at other major international meetings, such as the 1989 Western Economic Summit and any U.S.—Soviet summits. He should stress the importance of these issues in all his meetings with foreign leaders and instruct his ambassadors to do the same.

## Create a New Department of Environmental Protection

The environmental problems we face are of the greatest importance to this nation and the world. Those with principal responsibility for dealing with them must sit in the highest councils of government. Therefore, we recommend that the President propose to the Congress the creation of a new, cabinet-level Department of Environmental Protection to replace the present Environmental Protection Agency.

## Convene a White House Conference on the Environment

Public understanding and the broadest possible consensus are essential if we are to meet the environmental challenges we face. Therefore, we suggest that the President convene, late in 1989, a White House conference on the Environment, resuming a tradition begun by Theodore Roosevelt with the 1908 Governors' Conference on Natural Resources. The participants should include governors, mayors, Members of Congress, scientists, educators, environmentalists, and representatives of business, labor, and religious, women's, minority, and other groups. The purpose should be to foster understanding of the problems we face and to formulate and adopt action plans to address our environmental problems.

## CONCLUSION

We as a nation face an unprecedented environmental crisis. The policies and actions of the new President and his administration will do much to determine whether the earth will remain a habitable place. Adoption of the Blueprint recommendations presented in this report will do much to set the United States on a course that will help sustain life now and in the future.

Blueprint for the Environment and the organizations it represents will do all we can to ensure that these recommendations are implemented. We ask the new President, his appointees, other elected officials and our fellow citizens to join with us in this vital effort.

## Blueprint for the Environment

# Blueprint for the Environment

# EXECUTIVE OFFICE OF THE PRESIDENT
## COUNCIL ON ENVIRONMENTAL QUALITY

Environmental policy should be a major concern of the United States government and of any President. With environmental crises threatening to overwhelm the planet (e.g., global warming), the federal government needs to have a policy unit in the White House which focuses on these issues and can help the President develop policy and initiatives.

That unit has already been established, but it has been allowed to atrophy. It is the Council on Environmental Quality. It needs to be revitalized and re-built as a top priority for the new Administration. In the process, it should also be streamlined so that it can focus on the challenges of leadership and being of real assistance to a President. Prosaic and routine tasks should be shorn away and turned over to regular agencies.

Experience with the Council over 18 years demonstrates that it cannot succeed by trying to be too many things — close Presidential advisors and staff; a standing regulatory body; a think tank; and a lobby in government for the environmental constituency. If it is to be really effective, it needs to recognize that first and foremost it is part of the White House. It should capitalize on that fact by making itself truly a part of the White House staff and see itself as advancing the President's program with respect to the environment. When Presidents sympathetic to the environmental cause are in power, this will allow the most progress to be made. When they are not, the Council on Environmental Quality may not be able to be as independent. But in those cases, the battles over the environment will be fought elsewhere (e.g., in the Congress and the courts).

The Council on Environmental Quality is able to accomplish things only when it is used by a President and is seen by the White House as a part of it, not as an alien appendage. To be able to play a role as part of the President's expert staff, it needs to be able to marshal its resources to focus on the major policy challenges facing a President in the environmental field. It should not be bogged down in routine administrative tasks. It also needs to have a specialized staff so that it can tackle major tasks. And it needs to be able to be efficient and speak with a clear voice.

Those needs give rise to the specific recommendations that the Blueprint Council on Environmental Quality Task Force made.

**One**. Having a Chairman equal to the two other members of the council does not work. The Chairman needs to be in charge and serve as a close Presidential counselor. He should not be hobbled by having to go back to consult with two other Council members. Moreover, he should be able to run the staff and meetings without the confusion over roles with the other two members. Their role has never been clear, and there is no real job for them to do. The analogy to the Council of Economic Advisors never proved to be apt, since the Council on Environmental Quality was not really drawing upon professional judgement to make forecasts. Nor were analogies to multimember regulatory commissions apt since the Council on Environmental Quality has only the most meager regulatory authority.

Accordingly, Blueprint has recommended that the other two members not be appointed. Administrative means should be sought to recast the body along the lines just discussed.

**Two**. In pursuance of the goals enunciated above, the Task Force recommends that the Council on Environmental Quality focus its energies on assisting the President in hammering out his own environmental program and monitoring follow through. In particular, the Council on Environmental Quality should be assigned responsibility for coordinating a federal policy response to global environmental issues such as the issue of greenhouse gases, mass extinction of species, and making development more sustainable both within the U.S. and around the world. If a foresight capability process is established in the White House, the Council on Environmental Quality should bear lead responsibility for the environmental component. The Council on Environmental Quality should also provide a view on whether programs planned for various agencies include elements to advance administration environmental thrusts.

Some routine work must of necessity remain with the Council on Environmental Quality because of its fundamental importance and because it is the only logical place for it to be (having a government-wide vantage point). Among such jobs are overseeing compliance with Council on Environmental Quality National Environmental Policy Act regulations; handling referrals under section 309 of the Clean Air Act and mediating disputes under section 1504 of National Environmental Policy Act regulations; and coordinating efforts by agencies to prepare periodic reports on environmental conditions and trends.

**Three**. The Council on Environmental Quality can and should shed certain tasks which it has historically been asked to undertake. These can be undertaken just as well, if not better, by other entities. These include reports on special problems, research, and public education. Moreover, no real purpose is served anymore by expecting the Council on Environmental Quality to prepare voluminous annual reports collecting data available elsewhere.

Other think tank institutions are publishing annual "state of the environment" reports. The Council on Environmental Quality's annual reports should be concise and focus on identifying deficiencies and proposing remedies.

**Four**. To be able to provide leadership on pressing global problems and advise the President competently in a variety of fields, the Council on Environmental Quality's staff needs to be rebuilt. It only has about a dozen staff now, in contrast to the nearly 60 which it once had. It should have a staff of between 40 and 50, with an annual budget of about $6 million. It needs a staff of about four for eight program units: international affairs, natural resources, agriculture, energy, pollution abatement, economics, law and congressional relations. Moreover, a directorate is needed to manage these units, which would include a staff director, and associate director, and a personnel contracts officer. About $1 million also is needed for contract studies.

With streamlining, funding, and refocusing, the Council on Environmental Quality will be equipped to serve the President well in helping him mold a program to cope with the environmental challenges which are pressing us with renewed intensity on every side. There is no way a President can hope to handle the burdens in a responsible way without such a resource of expert staff advisors.

**Blueprint for the Environment**

## POLICY

# EXECUTIVE OFFICE OF THE PRESIDENT
## Council on Environmental Quality

### RECOMMENDATION
**The Council on Environmental Quality should be headed by a single Presidential appointee. Under re-organization authority or by other administrative action, the President should drop provisions for the other two council members who should not be appointed.**

• The Council on Environmental Quality (CEQ) is indispensable as a body that can look across all agencies to assure that their programs conform to the President's environmental agenda. This function cannot be performed by any one agency outside of the White House. Because CEQ should be an arm of the President in a direct sense, the Chairman should be able to act responsively to a President. It is difficult to do this with a three-member Council. Moreover, meetings of three councilors must operate under the Sunshine Act because of its National Environmental Policy Act authority and since formal votes are taken.

• This model is not suited for an office integrated into the White House structure. In practice, the role of the other two councillors has been unclear. With a rationalized structure, a strong Chairman can hire fully professional staff and direct them to provide the President and others in the White House with competent, confidential and prompt advice on complex subjects after informal consultation with the staff. This role should not be hobbled by disagreements among councillors and confusion over roles.

• Since the Council has little real regulatory authority, it should not be analogized to classic regulatory commissions with a panel of members. The office can be most effective with one high-level Presidential appointee, supported by a substantial staff, that can become an integral part of White House operations.

### RECOMMENDATION
**The Council on Environmental Quality needs to be re-funded to have an adequate staff to perform its mission. A staff of about 40 is needed, which is less than the all-time high of nearly 60, but is a re-building from levels today of about 12 (with only two or three experienced professionals). A budget for Fiscal Year 90 of about $6 million is needed. Early attention should be given to seeking a supplemental appropriation for Fiscal Year 90 of $3.8 million to hire needed staff.**

• At the high point in the mid-1970s, the Council on Environmental Quality (CEQ) had a full-time equivalent staff of nearly 60. By 1981 at the end of the Carter administration, it had 43 on the payroll. A staff of approximately that level is needed once again, plus sufficient funds for contract studies, particularly on complex international issues.

• The following staff are needed: Director, Executive Associate Director, Personnel-contract officer, and professional staff of an average of four each for eight units: international affairs, natural resources, agriculture, energy, pollution abatement, economics, law, and congressional relations. About 10 clerical support staff are also needed for a grand total of

45. When overhead is figured in, that level of staffing would cost about $5 million. Another $1 million is needed for contract studies, producing a grand total of $6 million in needed appropriations. About three-quarters of that amount would be needed in a supplemental appropriation for Fiscal Year 90, less the approximately $870,000 likely to have been appropriated, or $3.8 million.

## RECOMMENDATION
The Council on Environmental Quality should focus its work on the important items of the President's environmental agenda and limit its involvement in routine activities. It should be able to marshall energy to help the President mount major new initiatives on such problems as global environmental crises.

## RECOMMENDATION
The Council on Environmental Quality should de-emphasize certain responsibilities which it has traditionally spent considerable time on, such as preparation of a comprehensive annual report (Environmental Quality Report), across-the-board review of agency programs, reports on issues, research, and public education. Moreover, the Council on Environmental Quality should not be expected to be the principal point of contact of the White House for political purposes with environmental constituencies.

## RECOMMENDATION
The Chairman of the Council on Environmental Quality should promulgate amendments to its National Environmental Policy Act regulations for the consideration of population growth and other socio-economic impacts of federal agency programs and actions.

• Despite the specific mandate of the National Environmental Policy Act (NEPA) to achieve a balance between population and resources, the Council on Environmental Quality (CEQ) has never included population growth and related socio-economic impacts in its regulations governing NEPA analysis. Federal courts have found that NEPA requires consideration of population growth and socio-economic impacts. (See, e.g., McDowell v. Schlesinger, 404 F Supp. 221.) Moreover, litigation regarding whether or not NEPA requires analysis of socio-economic impacts continues, due in part to the failure by CEQ to specifically incorporate this factor into its regulations (see Northern Cheyenne v. Watt, D. Mont.)

• CEQ should incorporate population growth and socio-economic impacts into its specific list of environmental consequences which must be considered in NEPA analysis (40 C.F.R. 1502.16), and develop more detailed guidance to the agencies on conducting this analysis.

# Blueprint for the Environment

## BLUEPRINT BUDGET

# EXECUTIVE OFFICE OF THE PRESIDENT
## OFFICE OF MANAGEMENT AND BUDGET

**RECOMMENDATION**
**The President should ensure that the Fiscal 1990 and Fiscal 1991 budgets provide sufficient resources to address domestic and international environmental problems.**

• This nation and the world face environmental problems unprecedented in scope and magnitude. Environmental issues, like global warming of the atmosphere due to the greenhouse effect, ozone depletion of the stratosphere, ocean pollution, and toxic chemical exposures have aroused widespread public concern.

• Solutions to these and other problems plainly require increased federal actions. Yet many vitally important federal responsibilities are being neglected due to lack of staff and other resources. Some budget increases are essential if we are to prevent environmental degradation and the necessity of greater expenditures later on.

• In a time of fiscal constraint, the Blueprint Project does not recommend vast new expenditures. Many needed actions can be funded by redirecting federal spending. It is absolutely essential that the budget for Fiscal 1990, to be submitted next February or March — a budget that will prevail until October 1991 — reflects careful analysis of environmental needs and includes adequate resources to meet them. This progress must be sustained by the Fiscal 1991 budget.

• The following summarizes the principal budget recommendations of Blueprint for the Environment.

# NEW SAVINGS AND REVENUE FOR FISCAL YEAR 1990: $20.6 Billion

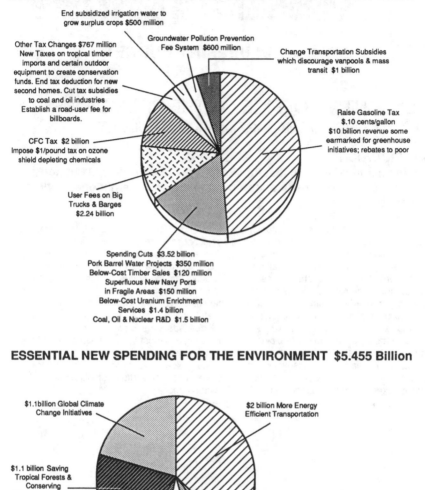

End subsidized irrigation water to grow surplus crops $500 million

Groundwater Pollution Prevention Fee System $600 million

Other Tax Changes $767 million New Taxes on tropical timber imports and certain outdoor equipment to create conservation funds. End tax deduction for new second homes. Cut tax subsidies to coal and oil industries Establish a road-user fee for billboards.

Change Transportation Subsidies which discourage vanpools & mass transit $1 billion

Raise Gasoline Tax $.10 cents/gallon $10 billion revenue some earmarked for greenhouse initiatives; rebates to poor

CFC Tax $2 billion Impose $1/pound tax on ozone shield depleting chemicals

User Fees on Big Trucks & Barges $2.24 billion

Spending Cuts $3.52 billion
Pork Barrel Water Projects $350 million
Below-Cost Timber Sales $120 million
Superfluous New Navy Ports in Fragile Areas $150 million
Below-Cost Uranium Enrichment Services $1.4 billion
Coal, Oil & Nuclear R&D $1.5 billion

## ESSENTIAL NEW SPENDING FOR THE ENVIRONMENT $5.455 Billion

$1.1billion Global Climate Change Initiatives

$2 billion More Energy Efficient Transportation

$1.1 billion Saving Tropical Forests & Conserving Biological Diversity

$130 million Increase U.S. and International Family Planning

$300 million Increased Funding from Land & Water Conservation Fund

$400 million Energy Conservation, Efficiency and

$325 million Increase EPA's Operating Budget

**Bottom Line:** The budget funds essential new programs, cuts environmentally harmful subsidies, and reduces the federal deficit by: $15.2 billion

# ENVIRONMENTAL BUDGET HIGHLIGHTS FOR FY 90

## Spending Increases ..................................................................$5.455 Billion
Environmental Protection Agency ...........................................................................$325 . million
Land & Water Conservation Fund ...........................................................................$300 . million
Fish & Wildlife Service ..............................................................................................$100 . million
Department of Energy's energy efficiency and solar R&D .................................$400 . million
US & International Family Planning .........................................................................$130 . million
Mass Transit ....................................................................................................................$2 . billion
Tropical Forest/Biological Diversity Initiative .......................................................$1.1 . billion
Global Climate Change Initiative .............................................................................$1.1 . billion

## Spending Cuts ...........................................................................$3.52 Billion
Pork Barrel Water Projects ........................................................................................$350 . million
Below-Cost Timber Sales ...........................................................................................$120 . million
Navy homeports in environmentally sensitive areas .........................................$150 . million
Below-Cost uranium enrichment services ............................................................$1.4 . billion
Coal, Oil, and Nuclear R&D .....................................................................................$1.5 . billion

## User Fees, Elimination of Tax Subsidies & Loopholes .......$4.237 Billion
Curb coal and oil tax breaks ....................................................................................$185 . million
End subsidized irrigation water to grow surplus crops .....................................$500 . million
Charge big trucks their fair share for the damage they cause to roads ..............$2 . billion
Increase the inland waterway barge fuel user fee to cover more of the costs of
    maintaining the system........................................................................................$240 . million
Eliminate the current tax on transit passes and vanpools and put them
    on employer provided free parking....................................................................$1 . billion net
Eliminate the interest deductions for new second home mortgages ...............$112 . million
Establish a road user fee for billboards to help preserve scenic corridors & fund trails ...$200 . million

## New Tax Proposals ...................................................................$12.9 Billion
Place 10% excise tax on certain outdoor-use products to go to state watchable
    wildlife programs ...................................................................................................$100 . million
Impose a 2% tax on tropical timber imports and devote revenues to helping
    developing countries save these forests ..........................................................$200 . million
Tax ozone-depleting chemicals at $1 per pound .................................................$2 . billion
Establish a groundwater pollution prevention fee system ................................$600 . million
Impose gas guzzler fee/gas sipper rebate for cars and light trucks............................revenue neutral
Raise gasoline and diesel fuel taxes by 10 cents per gallon with revenues to address
    greenhouse warming & rebates to the poor ....................................................$10 . billion

## Blueprint for the Environment

# I. BUDGET THEMES AND OBJECTIVES

• The neglect of, and in some cases hostility toward, environmental programs during the past eight years has been acknowledged by both presidential candidates. Project Blueprint's budget provides the guidance to put the traditional conservation and pollution control agencies and activities back in a position to meet the challenges ahead. Project Blueprint presents an environmental budget commensurate with the overwhelming sentiment of the American people in favor of environmental protection.

A great many of the environmental objectives can be accomplished by reshaping priorities within cabinet departments without budgetary increases. The ironies of convoluted spending priorities are evident everywhere. We spend more on a Boeing 747 than the whole world devotes to tropical forest research and protection.

• During the past eight years some extraordinarily serious environmental concerns of a global scope have come to the forefront. These include the depletion of the ozone layer, the greenhouse warming of the planet, the destruction of tropical forests, and the elimination of the biological and genetic diversity of the earth. These challenges are so formidable that they require the urgent attention of many agencies and entirely restructured federal spending priorities, both domestically and internationally.

U.S. leadership at the international level is required in order to find and implement solutions to these problems. This means creating new initiatives for cooperative international research, and for carrying out action programs that will save these ecosystems, such as reforestation of degraded tropical forest lands, proper management of natural resources, and payments to tropical forest countries to maintain certain portions of their forests intact.

A major feature of the environmental budget is the increased emphasis on user fees, the elimination of tax subsidies for environmentally damaging programs and the imposition of taxes on gasoline and tropical timber. It is our hope that the American public will support those proposals if the revenues are directed toward environmental problems.

• The proposed environmental budget is much more of a national security budget than ever before, because it focuses on some of the most urgent threats to global stability, namely the potential disruption of the global atmosphere and of the life support systems on which all nations depend.

The Project Blueprint budget provides for a dramatically accelerated governmental initiative to safeguard our atmosphere and to conserve the biological diversity of the planet, particularly through tropical forest initiatives.

# II. SPENDING INCREASES ARE CALLED FOR IN THE FOLLOWING AREAS:

• Boost the Environmental Protection Agency's operating budget by 20 percent to $1.954 billion in FY 90, and at least by 10 percent in FY 91 and FY 92. The Environmental Protection Agency in 1989 is being asked to handle twice 1981's workload with fewer resources than it had in 1975. Net increase for FY 90: $325 million.

• Increase the American Heritage Trust Fund by $300 million for FY 90 and build toward a $1 billion Fund as recommended by the President's Commission on Americans Outdoors. New increase for FY 90: $300 million.

• Boost the Fish and Wildlife Service's budget for endangered species activities from current levels of $367.5 million to $467.5 million for FY 1990 (the level authorized in FY 1988). By fully realizing the FY 1988 authorization levels, the Fish and Wildlife Service will be able to expand

monitoring, research and management programs for "unhunted" wildlife species, seek a stronger legislative mandate and improve ongoing planning for the national wildlife refuge system. Net increase for FY 90: $100 million.

• Step up research and development of energy efficient technologies. Currently, the Department of Energy's Research and Development budget has a heavy emphasis on nuclear and fossil fuel. By cutting the nuclear and fossil fuel Research and Development budget, funding for renewables and efficiency can be boosted without increasing the Department of Energy's overall budget. Net increase for FY 90: $400 million

• Build a billion-dollar federal initiative that addresses the loss of tropical forests and the need to conserve biological diversity. Money would be allocated for expanded research, for

## Blueprint for the Environment

strengthening institutions at home and abroad to deal with these issues, for new international agreements, and for specific conservation actions. Departments and agencies to be involved in these significantly increased efforts include the Agency for International Development, the Department of State, the National Aeronautics and Space Administration, the National Science Foundation, the National Oceanic and Atmospheric Administration, the Smithsonian, the Department of Agriculture, the Forest Service, the Fish and Wildlife Service, and the U.S. Botanical Garden. This would also involve U.S. leadership in persuading other nations to set up international funds that will allow cooperation on major actions to restore degraded Third World lands and protect critical existing forests and other natural resources. The size of the initiative should increase significantly over the next four years. Net increase for FY 90: $1.1 billion.

• Build a billion-dollar federal initiative that addresses global warming and ozone shield depletion. Money would be allocated for expanded global climate research and for implementing solutions to global warming and depletion of the ozone shield. Many of these actions will not only save money over the long run by curtailing the wasteful use of energy, but may very well save our own skins. Departments and agencies which will lead these efforts: The Environmental Protection Agency, the Department of Energy, the National Aeronautics and Space Administration, the National Oceanic and Atmospheric Administration, the National Science Foundation, the Department of State, the Department of the Interior and Multilateral Development Banks. This would also require U.S. leadership in persuading other nations to cooperate on the research programs and action plans. Net increase for FY 90: $1.1 billion.

• Increase the funding for U.S. and international family planning to $531 million in FY 1990. Exploding world population will preclude all attempts to achieve a better quality of life for the developing world unless more is done to promote sound population policies and provide family planning services. Continued population growth in the U.S. aggravates almost every environmental problem our nation faces. Net increase for FY 90: $130 million.

• Increase the mass transit budget authority from $3.15 billion to $5.1 billion. This will help to correct the current serious imbalance in the Department of Transportation's budget of which 73 percent is devoted to highways and aviation. The funds would address the urgent need for energy efficient transportation in cities. Net increase for FY 90: $2 billion.

## III. MAJOR BUDGET CUTS IN FEDERAL SPENDING ARE CALLED FOR IN THE FOLLOWING AREAS:

• Eliminate $300 million of major construction spending on the most environmentally damaging Bureau of Reclamation and Army Corps of Engineers projects. Massive subsidies for economically and environmentally unsound western water projects still prevail even though the Bureau said in 1987 it would get out of the dam building business. Net savings for FY 90: $300 million.

• Rapidly phase-out below-cost timber sales and curtail the Forest Service's road building budget. Throughout this decade, the Forest Service has consistently provided vast subsidies to the timber industry by selling timber at artificially low prices that fail to cover the costs of growing and selling the timber. Halting this practice will result in savings of approximately $300 million by the mid-1990s. Net savings for FY 90: $120 million.

• Cut the Soil Conservation Service's small watershed project funds by $50 million per year to eliminate dam building and stream channelization. The focus of the Soil Conservation Service should be on conserving the soil rather than on behaving like a construction company. Net savings for FY 90: $50 million.

• Eliminate the Navy's "homeport" program on the grounds that it is purely pork barrel with no strategic value and necessitates environmentally damaging harbor dredging and spoil disposal. Former Senator Barry Goldwater called the expansion and establishment of U.S. Navy ports and dredging operations in environmentally-sensitive coastal areas, "one of the biggest political boondoggles I ever heard of." Expected savings for FY 90: $217 million. Expected savings for FY 91: $150 million.

• Stop supplying the nuclear power industry with below cost fuel. The cost of providing uranium enrichment services has escalated from $31.8 million in FY 1981 to $1.2 billion in FY 1989 — a 40-fold increase. By charging $40

Blueprint for the Environment

more per basic unit of enrichment, the U.S. would realize a net savings over the next five years of $7—8 billion. Estimated net savings for FY 90: $1.4 billion.

• Cut spending for nuclear and fossil Research and Development from the combined current levels of $14 billion to $12.5 billion for FY 90. The bulk of nuclear Research and Development should go to improving the safety of existing plants and to developing solutions to the nuclear waste problem. Fossil Research and Development should focus on reducing pollution from existing use of fossil fuels, and on decreasing the total U.S. carbon output. Net savings from the decrease in nuclear and fossil Research and Development for FY 90: $1.5 billion.

## IV. USER FEES, THE ELIMINATION OF ENVIRONMENTALLY HARMFUL SUBSIDIES AND TAX LOOPHOLES AND TAX CHANGES.

• Raise gasoline and diesel fuel taxes by 10 cents per gallon per year for the next ten consecutive years. Under this plan the expected revenues for FY 90 would be $10 billion, $20 billion for FY 91, and more than $100 billion in the year 2000. Ten percent of all revenues should be rebated to the poor. Other revenues should help fund the greenhouse initiative. Net revenues for FY 90: $10 billion.

• Impose a gas-guzzler tax to discourage production of very inefficient cars and trucks and offer a rebate to help assure a market for super high-efficiency cars. The rebate would be paid by the federal government, from the revenue collected through the gas-guzzler tax. This tax and rebate system will be revenue neutral within a period of about five years.

• Cut oil and gas subsidies which allow the industry to write off exploration and development costs. Expensing of drilling and exploration costs allow taxes on the income to be effectively deferred, representing a substantial interest-free loan from the government. These losses to the Treasury are then made up by the taxpayer. In FY 88, $415 million was provided for expensing of oil and gas exploration and development costs, and $35 million for coal. Net revenue for FY 90: $185 million.

• Establish a comprehensive groundwater pollution prevention fee system. Over half of the American public relies on groundwater for drinking water, yet there is no comprehensive program to protect this critical resource from contamination. Currently over 90 percent of funds spent on groundwater are spent on cleanup. A combination plan of user fees and source pollution taxes together would raise an estimated $600 million in FY 90, to be spent on preventative safeguards, which will ultimately save billions of dollars in clean-up costs. These new safeguards would be embodied in a comprehensive federal groundwater pollution prevention statute, which should be promptly enacted. Net revenue for FY 90: $600 million.

• End the availability of subsidized irrigation water for the production of surplus crops. The Department of Agriculture's subsidy to set aside land and the Department of the Interior's subsidization of irrigation water for that same land are inconsistent. In addition, the subsidies damage the environment by encouraging diversion of water from natural systems, construction of water projects, and the additions of salts, other minerals and pesticides to our streams, rivers and wetlands. A Department of the Interior study placed the total costs of these subsidies at $500 million per year. FY 90 savings: $500 million.

• Establish a national billboard tax (road user fee) to promote and enhance the preservation of scenic corridors including roadways, bikeways and trails which will provide an estimated revenue of $200 million annually. Net revenue for FY 90: $200 million.

• Increase the weight-distance tax for trucks over 60,000 pounds from 65 percent of system costs to 100 percent of system costs to produce $2 billion in revenue in FY 90. Heavy trucks are subsidized to the disadvantage of more energy efficient rail transportation. These heavy trucks do not pay for the extensive damage they cause to roads and bridges. A powerful lobby, the trucking industry prevents energy efficient freight transportation by pushing for disproportionately high expenditures for highway construction and maintenance. Net revenue for FY 90: $2 billion.

• Increase the inland waterway barge fuel tax from 10 cents per gallon or 20 percent of operation and maintenance costs for locks, dams and maintenance dredging to 50 cents per gallon in FY 90 for additional revenue of $240 million. Barge canals damage rivers and wetlands and are heavily subsidized. A higher user charge would decrease the pressure for unnecessary barge canal projects. Net revenue gain for FY 90: $240 million.

• To correct the distorted subsidies weighted against energy efficient transportation, the U.S. should tax employer-provided free parking to achieve a revenue gain of $1.5 billion in FY 90 and eliminate the current tax on transit passes and employer-provided vanpools for a loss of $500 million. Net revenue gain for FY 90: $1 billion.

• In addition to the Environmental Protection Agency's phase-back regulations, impose a tax on ozone-depleting chlorofluorocarbons of $1 per pound of chlorofluorocarbon in 1990, rising to $5 per pound in 1993. Net revenue for FY 90: $2 billion.

• Eliminate interest deductions that subsidize the development of new second homes in environmentally sensitive areas. Assuming that the average new second home mortgage will be $50,000 with interest at 10 percent or $5,000 per year, that 80,000 new second home mortgages are issued, and that the marginal tax rate is 28 percent, the net revenue for 1990 would be $112 million. Even with a reduction of the issu-

ance of new mortgages, the net increase in revenue could amount to $500 million by FY 95. Net revenue for FY 90: $112 million.

• Impose a two percent transfer tax on products made in whole or in part from tropical hardwoods and devote the revenues to the $1.1 billion tropical forest initiative. International obligations under the General Agreement on Tariff and Trade and other agreements make it essential to couple any domestic program with initiatives to explain its purpose to and gain the support of the international community. The U.S. should work closely with the International Tropical Timber Organization, the Food and Agriculture Organization, and other appropriate multilateral institutions. Net revenue for FY 90: $200 million.

• Implement a 10 percent excise tax on certain outdoor-use related products and devote the revenue to state programs for management of "watchable" (non-game) wildlife. The program should be structured in a pattern similar to the Wallop-Breaux fishery program and the Pittman-Robertson wildlife program. Annual net revenue: $100 million.

## SUMMARY BUDGET IMPACT*

Total Program Increases: ............................................................$5.45 billion
Total Savings from Program Cuts:................................................$3.52 billion
Total Increased Tax Revenues: ...................................................$17 billion

**\* Note:** These figures reflect rounding and averaging from multi-year savings.

## POTENTIAL BUDGET AREAS FOR RE-PRIORITIZATION

"Few threats to peace and survival of the human community are greater than those posed by the prospects of cumulative and irreversible degradation of the biosphere on which human life depends... Our survival depends not only on military balance, but on global cooperation to ensure a sustainable biological environment."

*Report of the Brandt Commission, 1980*

"Among the dangers facing the environ-

ment, the possibility of nuclear war, or military conflict of a lesser scale involving weapons of mass destruction, is undoubtedly the greatest. The whole notion of security as traditionally understood — in terms of political and military threats to national sovereignty — must be expanded to include the impacts of environmental stress — locally, nationally, and globally. There are no military solutions to 'environmental insecurity'."

*Report of the Bruntland Commission, 1987*

• Several major components of national security are not being addressed in the budget of the Department of Defense; namely, the destruction of the global natural resource base and the disruption of the earth's atmosphere through greenhouse warming and ozone depletion. It is essential to mitigate inter-

national environmental destabilization, which can dramatically affect national security, by earmarking funds for the following: restoration of severely damaged agricultural production zones, setting aside critical natural areas such as watersheds to ensure availability of potable water for major population

**Blueprint for the Environment**

333

centers, and the initiation of reforestation projects in Africa, Latin America and Asia.

The state of the international environment affects American national security and should be considered an integral part of America's defense agenda. The accelerated deterioration of forests and grasslands in Africa, Asia and Latin America has resulted in millions of refugees fleeing one area and intruding into another, producing tremendous strains on existing social, political and environmental systems. The destabilization, skirmishes and political unrest created by these environmental refugees can embroil the United States in international conflicts and necessitate costly emergency relief measures.

The President and the Secretary of Defense should examine the possibility of transferring one percent of the entire yearly Defense budget into programs for restoration of the international environment and for cleaning up toxic and nuclear waste at military weapons facilities. The Department of Energy has estimated the cost of the latter at over $100 billion.

Almost 50 Third World nations have gone from being self-supporting in food to net food importers. Unless this situation is addressed by obtaining sustainable production, the inevitable result will be mounting instability throughout the Third World.

• To fund important environmental initiatives critical to global stability, two other areas merit special attention: the National Aeronautics and Space Administration's budget priorities and the Strategic Defense Initiative. These areas could be especially important if the proposed user fees and tax changes are not enacted into law.

1) A reorientation of the National Aeronautics and Space Administration's budget toward global resources data collection and research should be considered. The first step might be postponing the Space Station (and its focus on manned exploration of space) until the next century and placing the National Aeronautics and Space Administration's priorities on global monitoring activities. If suspended, savings are projected to be about $1 billion in FY 90 and $13.25 billion over the next five years.

2) The Strategic Defense Initiative, also called Star Wars, involves an enormous commitment of resources, and could cause significant environmental damage with radioactive contamination of the earth's surface and atmosphere. In addition, experts have questioned the technical and strategic feasibility of the Strategic Defense Initiative. Potential cuts in this program should be examined. If the program were to be eliminated, savings for FY 90 alone would come to $4.5 — $5 billion.

**Blueprint for the Environment**

# APPENDIX

## The Blueprint Steering Committee

**Defenders of Wildlife**
1244 19th Street, N.W.
Washington, D.C. 20036

**Environmental Action**
1525 New Hampshire Avenue, N.W.
Washington, D.C. 20036

**Environmental Policy Institute**
218 D Street, S.E.,
Washington, D.C. 20003

**Friends of the Earth**
530 7th Street, S.E.
Washington, D.C. 20003

**Global Tomorrow Coalition**
1325 G Street, N.W., Suite 915
Washington, D.C. 20005

**The Izaak Walton League of America**
1401 Wilson Boulevard, Level B
Arlington, VA. 22209

**National Audubon Society**
950 Third Avenue
New York, NY. 10022

**National Audubon Society**
801 Pennsylvania Avenue, S.E.
Washington, D.C. 20003

**National Parks and Conservation Association**
1015 31st Street, N.W.
Washington, D.C. 20007

**National Wildlife Federation**
1400 16th. Street, N.W.
Washington, D.C. 20036

**Natural Resources Council of America**
1015 31st Street, N.W.
Washington, D.C. 20007

**Natural Resources Defense Council**
122 East 42nd Street
New York, NY. 10168

**Natural Resources Defense Council**
1350 New York Avenue, N.W.
Washington, D.C. 20005

**Renew America**
1001 Connecticut Avenue, Suite 719
Washington, D.C. 20036

**Sierra Club**
730 Polk Street
San Francisco, CA. 94109

**Sierra Club**
330 Pennsylvania Avenue, S.E.
Washington, D.C. 20003

**The Oceanic Society**
1536 16th Street, N.W.
Washington, D.C. 20036

**The Wilderness Society**
1400 Eye Street, N.W.
Washington, D.C. 20005

**Trout Unlimited**
501 Church Street, N.E.
Vienna, VA. 22180

**Union of Concerned Scientists**
1616 P Street, N.W., Suite 310
Washington, D.C. 20036

**Zero Population Growth**
1400 16th Street, N.W., Suite 320
Washington, D.C. 20036